Second Edition

Curso segundo

Workbook for a Second Course in Spanish

><]><]><]><]><]><]><]><]><]><]><]><]><]><]><]><]><]><]><]><]><]><

MARVIN WASSERMAN

Former Chairman of the Department of Foreign Languages
Susan E. Wagner High School
Staten Island, New York

CAROL WASSERMAN, Ph.D

Professor of Spanish
Borough of Manhattan Community College of the
City University of New York

AMSCO

AMSCO SCHOOL PUBLICATIONS, INC.
315 Hudson Street, New York, N.Y. 10013

Books by Marvin Wasserman and Carol Wasserman

Curso primero, 2nd Edition
Curso segundo, 2nd Edition
Curso tercero
Prosa moderna del mundo hispánico
Susana y Javier en España, 2nd Edition
Susana y Javier en Sudamérica

Please visit our Web site at: www.amscopub.com

Text and cover design: Merrill Haber

Compositor and Text Illustrations: Monotype Composition Company, Inc.

Text Photo credits: The photographs in this book have been provided through the courtesy of the following organizations:

Corbis Stock Market: pp. 15, 27
Image Bank: pp. 41, 63, 82, 97, 115, 126, 150, 165, 181, 193, 217, 239
Photo Researchers, Inc.: pp. 267, 281
West Stock: p. 138

Cover Photos: *West Stock* - Hand Painted Gourds
Master file - Spain Tile Roofs
Image Bank - San Juan, Puerto Rico

When ordering this book, please specify: either **R 758 W** or
CURSO SEGUNDO / WORKBOOK, SECOND EDITION

ISBN 1-56765-482-7

NYC Item 56765-482-6

Preface

Curso segundo, Second Edition, retains many of the features that made the First Edition so successful. We, the authors, still affirm that effective drill material is the *sine qua non* of foreign-language instruction. We also believe that many of our colleagues want a workbook that contains a variety of exercises that may be adapted to all levels of ability among the students. While a good part of the text reflects the communicative approach to language learning, we have tried not to include any material that might be contrived just for the sake of having it appear to be communicative. There are time-tested approaches to learning a foreign language, and these approaches transcend any methodology that may be in vogue at the time.

Among the newer aspects of this revised workbook, the following should be highlighted to make it even more invaluable.

1. Updated vocabulary which includes words like *computadora, impresora, disco compacto, video,* etc.

2. Shortened exercises to maintain student interest.

3. New verb charts which comprise regular conjugations, irregular verbs, stem-changing verbs and verbs with spelling changes.

4. A shorter section on Hispanic Civilization, but with the additional feature of a cultural quiz to challenge the students.

5. A completely updated section on Reading and Listening, containing selections more relevant to the students' experiences and interests.

6. Exercises that contain illustrations which provide visual association of real-life situations pertaining to the topics being studied.

7. Updated photographs.

Since this is not a basal text, the chapters are not arranged in a cumulative sequence. Therefore, the mastery of a topic does not require mastery of the topics preceding it. This affords the teacher the opportunity to assign chapters in whatever order he or she chooses.

The authors are hopeful that their loyal colleagues who have enjoyed using the First Edition of *Curso segundo* will derive even more satisfaction from this new Second Edition.

The Authors

Contents

PART 4: Nouns, Adjectives, and Adverbs

PART 5: Pronouns

PART 6: Other Grammar Topics

PART 7: Reviewing Vocabulary and Idioms in Context

PART 8: El mundo de habla española

PART 9: Additional Practice in Reading and Listening

Appendixes

Verb Charts   318

     I. Regular Verbs; II. Verbs With Irregular Forms; III. Stem-Changing Verbs;
     IV. Verbs With Spelling Changes

Part 1
Present Tense and Commands

><|><|><|><|><|><|><|><|><|><|><|><|><|><|><|><|><|><|><

1
The Present Tense: Regular Verbs

Helps and Hints

The main difference between English and Spanish verbs is the number of forms. English has fewer verb forms; e.g., in the present tense, we have: *I go, you go, he(she) goes, we go, you go, they go.* Note that the only change is in the third person singular, whereas in Spanish there are six different forms. You will also see that the infinitive form of the verb (*to speak, to eat,* etc.) is one word in Spanish that may end in *-ar, -er,* or *-ir.*

	-AR Verbs	*-ER* Verbs	*-IR* Verbs
	visitar, *to visit*	**correr,** *to run*	**escribir,** *to write*
SINGULAR			
yo	visit*o* *I visit* *I am visiting*	corr*o* *I run* *I am running*	escrib*o* *I write* *I am writing*
tú	visit*as*	corr*es*	escrib*es*
Ud. él ella	visit*a*	corr*e*	escrib*e*
PLURAL			
nosotros nosotras	visit*amos*	corr*emos*	escrib*imos*
vosotros vosotras	visit*áis*	corr*éis*	escrib*ís*
Uds. ellos ellas	visit*an*	corr*en*	escrib*en*

1

1. The six verb forms of the present tense are obtained by dropping the **-ar, -er,** and **-ir** endings of the infinitive and replacing them with the following endings:

	-AR	-ER	-IR
yo	-o	-o	-o
tú	-as	-es	-es
Ud., él, ella	-a	-e	-e
nosotros(-as)	-amos	-emos	-imos
vosotros(-as)	-áis	-éis	-ís
Uds., ellos, ellas	-án	-en	-en

Practice A: Show the following actions by using the form of the verb shown.

EXAMPLE: Ella ___*vive*___ en México.
                              (vivir)

1. Yo _____ a mis padres.
        (ayudar)

2. La chica _____ bien.
              (responder)

3. Tú _____ el dinero.
        (recibir)

4. Vosotras _____ mucho.
                (comer)

5. Ellos _____ agua con la comida.
            (tomar)

6. Mi primo _____ la escalera.
                (subir)

7. Yo _____ la lección.
        (comprender)

8. Uds. _____ en California, ¿verdad?
            (vivir)

9. Nosotros _____ en un banco.
                (trabajar)

10. Ella y yo _____ para Puerto Rico.
                  (partir)

2. A verb in the present tense can be translated in two ways:

Ella **visita** la ciudad dos veces por semana (todos los días).

She *visits* the city twice a week (every day).

Ella **visita** la ciudad hoy.

She *is visiting* the city today.

Visita means *visits* if this happens often or regularly in the present; it means *is visiting* if this is happening now. Similarly:

¿Trabaja el todos los días?

Does he work every day?

¿Trabaja el hoy?

Is he working today?

No estudiamos por la noche; **miramos** la televisión.

We *do not study* at night; we *watch* television.

No estudiamos ahora; **miramos** la televisión.

We *are not studying* now; we are *watching* television.

NEGATIVE QUESTIONS

¿**No escriben** ellos a sus padres todos los días (tres veces por mes)?	*Don't they write* to their parents every day (three times a month)?
¿**No escriben** ellos a sus padres hoy (en este momento)?	*Aren't they writing* to their parents today (at this moment)?

To express the present tense in English, one must choose between two verb forms—a fact that makes it hard for Spanish-speaking students of English to master the English present tense. A typical error of beginners in English is a sentence like "I am going to school every day."

Practice B: Give the English equivalent in two ways if both are possible.

1. ¿Toma ella café con la cena?

   _____

   _____

2. Nosotros no leemos el periódico.

   _____

   _____

3. Yo escribo una carta a mi primo todas las semanas.

   _____

   _____

4. ¿No compras tú una revista hoy?

   _____

   _____

Omission of the Subject Pronoun

3. The subject pronoun in Spanish is often omitted, especially when the verb ending clearly identifies the subject. Therefore, **yo, tú, nosotros,** and **vosotros** do not have to be used except for emphasis:

—¿Escribes una carta?	Are you writing a letter?
—Sí, escribo una carta.	Yes, I am writing a letter.

   But:

—¿Quién escribe la carta?	Who is writing the letter?
—**Yo** escribo la carta.	*I* am writing the letter.

   Practice C: Express in English.

   1. Dividimos la pizza en seis partes.

      _____

   2. Visito muchos lugares de interés cuando voy a España.

      _____

   3. No comes mucho hoy, Juanito.

      _____

   4. ¿A qué hora llegáis esta noche?

      _____

4. When a subject pronoun is omitted, we must infer the subject of the verb from an earlier sentence or trend of the conversation. If the subject is not clear, then the subject pronoun must be used:

SPEAKER 1:	¿Qué lengua habla ese hombre?	What language does that man speak?
SPEAKER 2:	Habla francés.	He speaks French.

But:

SPEAKER 1:	Responde bien.	[He *or* she] is answering well.
SPEAKER 2:	¿Quién responde bien?	Who is answering well?
SPEAKER 1:	**Ella** responde bien.	*She* is answering well.

Practice D: Translate into English.

1. *a.* ¿Dónde vive Felipe? _____

   b. Vive en la Argentina. _____

2. *a.* ¿Cómo hablan ellos español? _____

   b. Hablan muy bien. _____

3. *a.* ¿A qué hora llegan Juan y Elena? _____

   b. Llegan a las seis. _____

Common Regular -AR, -ER, and -IR Verbs

-AR **Verbs**

ayudar, to help
   ayudar a alguien a + *inf.,* to help someone to
bailar, to dance
bajar, to go down
   bajar de, to get off, out of (a vehicle)
cantar, to sing
comprar, to buy
contestar, to answer
desear, to wish, want
enseñar, to teach, show
   enseñar a alguien a + *inf.,* to teach someone to
entrar (en), to enter, go (come) in
escuchar, to listen (to)
estudiar, to study
explicar, to explain
hablar, to speak, talk
llegar, to arrive
   llegar a, to arrive at; **llegar a ser (médico(-a), abogado(-a),** etc.), to become a (doctor, lawyer, etc.)

llevar, to carry, take; to wear
mirar, to look (at)
   mirar la televisión, to watch television
pagar, to pay (for)
pasar, to pass; to spend (time)
preguntar, to ask
prestar, to lend
   prestar atención, to pay attention
sacar, to take out
   sacar buenas (malas) notas, to get good (bad) marks
tomar, to take
   tomar el desayuno (café, etc.), to have breakfast (coffee, etc.)
trabajar, to work
tratar de + *inf.,* to try to
usar, to use
viajar, to travel
visitar, to visit

-ER **Verbs**

aprender, to learn
   aprender a + *inf.,* to learn to
beber, to drink
comer, to eat
comprender, to understand
correr, to run

deber,* to have to, must (see Section 5 below)
leer, to read
prometer, to promise (see Section 5 below)
responder, to answer
vender, to sell

-IR **Verbs**

abrir, to open
asistir a, to attend
cubrir, to cover
decidir, to decide
describir, to describe
dividir, to divide

escribir, to write
partir, to leave, depart
recibir, to receive
subir, to go up
   subir a, to get into or on (a vehicle)
vivir, to live

5. Some verbs are often followed directly by another verb in the infinitive, without a preposition as in English:

Deseo ir al cine.	I wish to go to the movies.
Prometo trabajar mucho.	I promise to work a lot.
Debo estudiar.	I have to study. (I must study.)

Practice E: Complete the Spanish sentences.

1. We wish to receive gifts.

Deseamos _____ regalos.

2. Must I drink the milk?

¿Debo _____ la leche?

3. They promise to visit their grandparents.

Prometen _____ a sus abuelos.

 EJERCICIOS

A. Here are some activities and facts about the Fernández family. Complete each sentence by writing each verb in parentheses in its proper form.

EXAMPLE: Mi madre vende nuestra casa y _____*compra*_____ otra.
                                          (comprar)

---

*Many Hispanics use **deber de** (+ an infinitive) to express obligation or duty, but this is incorrect. **Deber de** is used to express *probability*:

Ella **debe** estar aquí a las ocho.	She must (has to) be here at 8:00.

But:

Ella **debe de** estar aquí ahora.	She must be here now. (= She is probably here now.)

1. José y su hermano Carlos trabajan en un almacén donde _____ ropa.
   (vender)

2. Recibimos dinero de nuestros padres y lo _____ para comprar nuestros libros.
   (usar)

3. Rosa vende su bicicleta y _____ una motocicleta.
   (comprar)

4. En las fiestas bailamos y _____ limonada.
   (beber)

5. En mi cuarto uso la computadora y _____ las revistas.
   (leer)

B. Each sentence on the left is the answer to a question that begins as shown on the right. Write the rest of the question in the blank.

EXAMPLES: Miro la televisión.   ¿Qué _____ *mira Ud. (miras tú)* _____?

Escribimos con lápiz.   ¿Con qué _____ *escriben Uds. (escribís vosotros)* _____?

1. Leemos revistas interesantes.   ¿Qué _____?

2. Vive en Puerto Rico.   ¿Dónde _____?

3. Yo hablo con mi prima.   ¿Con quién _____?

4. El avión para Madrid parte a la una
   de la tarde.   ¿A qué hora _____?

5. Los chicos deben comer la ensalada.   ¿Quiénes _____?

C. Answer the following personal questions with a complete sentence in Spanish:

1. ¿Comprendes todas las lecciones de español?

   _____

2. ¿En qué ciudad viven Uds.?

   _____

3. ¿Sacas buenas notas en tus exámenes de español?

   _____

4. ¿Con quiénes llegan Uds. a la escuela por la mañana?

   _____

5. ¿Asistes a una escuela primaria, intermedia o secundaria?

   _____

D. Express in Spanish.

EXAMPLES: Are they (*m.*) speaking?   *¿Hablan ellos?*
            I do not write.   *Yo no escribo.*

1. Is she listening to the tape?

   _____

2. I am going up to (*para*) sleep now.

   _____

3. Do they (*m. & f.*) drink milk with breakfast?

   _____

4. You (*Uds.*) don't sing very well.

   _____

5. The boys are not dancing at (*en*) the party.

   _____

6. They are writing postcards.

   _____

7. What is he eating now?

   _____

8. Why don't you (*Uds.*) buy a computer (*computadora*)?

   _____

9. Who wants to skate this afternoon?

   _____

10. You (*vosotros*) are not answering well today.

    _____

E. *Idiom Review.* Write the Spanish equivalent as shown by the examples in italics:

1. What school do you attend?   *¿A qué escuela asiste Ud.?*
   What university do they attend?   _____

2. She is getting off the train.   *Ella baja del tren.*
   We're getting out of the car.   _____

3. Are they getting on the bus?   *¿Suben al autobús?*
   Is he getting on the train?   _____

4. You are not paying attention to the
      teacher.   *Tú no prestas atención a la profesora.*
   I'm not paying attention to the speech. _____

5. I'm trying to understand the problem.   *Trato de comprender el problema.*
   They are trying to sell the house.

6. My sister is becoming a doctor.   *Mi hermana llega a ser médica.*

   My uncle is becoming an engineer.   _____

7. She's helping the old lady to cross   *Ella ayuda a la vieja a cruzar la calle.*
   the street.

   I'm helping my friend to use the   _____
   computer.

8. We're learning to swim.   *Aprendemos a nadar.*

   She's learning to skate.   _____

9. I'm teaching my brother to read.   *Enseño a mi hermano a leer.*

   He's teaching Mary to dance.   _____

10. What do you want to have, coffee or milk? *¿Qué deseas tomar, café o leche?*

    What do they (*f.*) want to have, juice   _____
    or soda?

F. *Listening Comprehension.** Your teacher will read to the class ten sentences in Spanish corresponding to the ten groups of sentences listed below. In each group, circle the letter (*a, b,* or *c*) of the correct English equivalent.

1. *a.* I'm taking the train now.
   b. The train is leaving now.
   c. She's taking the train now.

2. *a.* We promise to study tonight.
   b. I promise to study tonight.
   c. They promise to study tonight.

3. *a.* We're describing the programs.
   b. We don't describe the programs.
   c. We're deciding the programs.

4. *a.* Do they speak English?
   b. You speak English.
   c. Do you speak English?

5. *a.* They are not buying the watch.
   b. Is she buying the watch?
   c. She's not buying the watch.

6. *a.* Are they eating now?
   b. Aren't they eating now?
   c. Are you eating now?

7. *a.* He is covering the table.
   b. Are you covering the table?
   c. They are covering the table.

8. *a.* Is she dividing the money?
   b. Who is dividing the money?
   c. Why does he divide the money?

9. *a.* Where do we spend the night?
   b. Where are they spending the night?
   c. Where do you spend the night?

10. *a.* We pay a lot of money.
    b. They are paying a lot of money.
    c. I pay a lot of money.

_____

**To the teacher:* For the exercises in listening comprehension, the parts that are to be read to the class will be found in the Answer Key.

2
The Present Tense: Irregular Verbs*

Helps and Hints

Not all verbs are conjugated regularly. English has very few verbs that are irregular in the present tense; e.g., *to be: I am, she is,* etc. Spanish has many more verbs that are irregular in the present tense. Some are irregular only in the first person singular (*yo*), others have more irregular forms.

I. Verbs Irregular in the First Person Singular

GROUP A: YO Form Ending in -GO

	yo
caer, to fall	*caigo*
hacer, to do, make	*hago*
poner, to put, place	*pongo*
salir, to leave, go out	*salgo*
traer, to bring	*traigo*
valer, to be worth	*valgo*

GROUP B: Other Irregular YO Forms

	yo
caber, to fit	*quepo*
conducir, to lead; to drive	*conduzco*
conocer, to know	*conozco*
dar, to give	*doy*
saber, to know	*sé*
ver, to see	*veo*

1. These verbs are irregular only in the **yo** form. The other forms are regular. The forms **dais** and **veis** do not have accent marks.

Practice A: In each column, write the forms of the verb that are used with the following subjects:

1. el hombre   2. Ud. y yo   3. las chicas   4. yo   5. tú

---

*In the present tense there are certain verbs that undergo spelling changes. These verbs appear in Appendix III and will not appear in the exercises.

	traer	salir	saber	conducir	dar	poner
1.						
2.						
3.						
4.						
5.						

II. Verbs Irregular in All Forms Except Those for NOSOTROS and VOSOTROS

decir to say, tell	*digo*	*dices*	*dice*	decimos	decís	*dicen*
estar to be*	*estoy*	*estás*	*está*	estamos	estáis	*están*
oír to hear	*oigo*	*oyes*	*oye*	oímos	oís	*oyen*
poder to be able, can	*puedo*	*puedes*	*puede*	podemos	podéis	*pueden*
querer to want	*quiero*	*quieres*	*quiere*	queremos	queréis	*quieren*
tener to have	*tengo*	*tienes*	*tiene*	tenemos	tenéis	*tienen*
venir to come	*vengo*	*vienes*	*viene*	venimos	venís	*vienen*

III. Verbs Irregular in All Six Forms

ir, to go	*voy*	*vas*	*va*	*vamos*	*vais*	*van*
ser, to be*	*soy*	*eres*	*es*	*somos*	*sois*	*son*

2. The forms **vais** and **sois** do not have accent marks.

Practice B: Write the verb forms that are used with the given pronouns as subjects.

1. Uds. _____ _____ _____ _____
              (venir)   (tener)   (poder)   (hacer)

---

*Both **estar** and **ser** mean *to be* but cannot be used interchangeably. See Chapter 13.

2. nosotras   _____   _____   _____   _____
                       (querer)   (ser)   (ir)   (dar)

3. yo   _____   _____   _____   _____
                   (decir)   (ver)   (conocer)   (salir)

4. ¿quién?   _____   _____   _____   _____
                   (saber)   (oír)   (decir)   (ser)

5. tú   _____   _____   _____   _____
                   (poder)   (venir)   (estar)   (oír)

 ## Using _PODER, QUERER, IR,_ and _VENIR_ Before an Infinitive

3. **Poder** and **querer** are often followed directly by another verb in the infinitive form; that is, they are not followed by a preposition:

No **puedo ver** la pizarra.   I can't see the chalkboard.

¿**Quiere** (Ud.) **mirar** la televisión?   Do you want to watch television?

4. **Ir** and **venir** are followed by the preposition **a** if they precede an infinitive:

Voy **a** estudiar.   I am going to study.

Hoy mis padres vienen **a** visitar la escuela.   Today my parents are coming to visit the school.

 ## _SABER_ and _CONOCER_

5. **Saber** and **conocer** both mean _to know_ but cannot be used interchangeably.

  a. **Saber** is used for knowing facts, and also means "to know _how_ (to do something)":

    ¿**Saben** Uds. la respuesta?   Do you know the answer?

    No **sé patinar.**   I don't know how to skate.

  b. **Conocer** is used in the sense of _to be acquainted_ (_or familiar_) _with_ people or places:

    ¿**Conoces** a mi amigo José?   Do you know my friend Joseph?

    Mi padre **conoce** muy bien la ciudad.   My father knows the city very well.

CABER and _VALER_

6. **Caber** means _to fit_ in the sense of _there is room_ (_or space_) _for_ someone or something:

No **quepo** en el coche.   There is no room for me in the car.

7. **Valer,** _to be worth,_ is often used in the sense of _to cost:_

Cuánto **vale** la impresora?   How much does the printer cost?

Practice C: Supply the correct form of *saber, conocer, caber,* or *valer,* in accordance with the meaning of the sentence.

1. ¿_____ tú nadar?

2. Yo _____ muy bien mi vecindario.

3. ¿Cuánto _____ estos discos compactos?

4. Quiero _____ a tu amiga Rosa.

5. Estas revistas no _____ en la mesa.

6. Vamos a _____ la lección perfectamente.

◆ EJERCICIOS ◆

A. Write the appropriate forms of the verbs. (In each sentence, the two verbs have the same subject.)

1. Mi hermano _____ ganar más dinero, pero no _____.
   (querer)   (poder)

2. Yo _____ a la escuela a las ocho y media y _____ a las tres.
   (venir)   (salir)

3. ¿_____ tú las ciudades que _____ a visitar?
   (conocer)   (ir)

4. Antes de la comida yo _____ la mesa y _____ los platos de
   (poner)   (traer)
   la cocina.

5. Cuando yo _____ la televisión, _____ buenos programas.
   (mirar)   (ver)

6. Ellos _____ que _____ conducir un coche.
   (decir)   (saber)

7. ¿Dónde _____ Ud. cuando _____?
   (estar)   (comer)

8. Nosotras _____ secretarias y _____ en la misma oficina.
   (ser)   (trabajar)

9. Yo _____ al señor López pero no _____ su dirección.
   (conocer)   (saber)

10. ¿_____ tú traer los discos compactos que _____ en tu casa?
    (poder)   (tener)

B. Answer with a complete sentence in Spanish:

1. ¿Qué ves en el cine?

   _____

2. ¿Qué pueden Uds. leer en la biblioteca?

   _____

3. ¿Cuántos libros trae Ud. por lo general a la escuela?

   _____

4. ¿Dónde está su escuela?

   _____

5. ¿Cuántas cosas hace Ud. durante una hora?

   _____

6. ¿Por qué viene Ud. a la escuela todos los días?

   _____

7. ¿En qué estación del año caen las hojas de los árboles?

   _____

8. ¿Sabes usar una computadora?

   _____

9. ¿Quién tiene más dinero, Ud. o su amigo (amiga)?

   _____

10. ¿Dónde pone Ud. su ropa durante la noche?

   _____

C. Express in Spanish:

1. Can she work today?

   _____

2. We're going to the supermarket soon.

   _____

3. Aren't they coming to the mall (*el centro comercial*) tonight?

   _____

4. I'm not leaving the house yet.

   _____

5. I'm not bringing the tapes next week.

   _____

6. I don't know the answer.

   _____

7. What are they (*f.*) doing here?

   _____

8. Don't you (tú) hear the noise?

_____

9. There is no room for the printer on the table. (The printer does not fit on the table.)

_____

10. We're not neighbors. (Use *ser.*)

_____

D. *Idiom Review.* The following statements tell about a trip you and your family are taking. Your friend tells you about his or her trip. Rewrite each statement making the necessary changes.

1. I'm taking a trip to Spain.
My family is taking a trip to Mexico.

Hago un viaje a España.

_____

2. We are leaving for the airport tomorrow.
I'm leaving for the airport tonight.

Salimos mañana para el aeropuerto.

_____

3. We have to arrive early.
I don't have to arrive before 6:00 P.M.

Tenemos que llegar temprano.

_____

4. My family wants to pay a visit to my
uncle in Madrid.
We want to pay a visit to our relatives
in Mexico City (*La Ciudad de México*).

*Mi familia desea hacer una visita a
mi tío en Madrid.*

_____

_____

5. On the plane I'm always hungry and
thirsty.
And my sister is always sleepy.

*En el avión siempre tengo hambre
y sed.*

_____

E. *Listening Comprehension.* Your teacher will read to the class ten questions in Spanish. After each question is read to you, circle the letter (*a, b,* or *c*) of the most appropriate answer.

1. *a.* Aprendemos español.
b. Aprendo a hablar español.
c. Tenemos una fiesta todos los días.

2. *a.* Sí, es mi amigo Juan.
b. Sí, es mi prima Dorotea.
c. Sí, son mis abuelos.

3. *a.* Está delante de la clase.
b. Estoy en la sala de clase.
c. Es muy popular.

4. *a.* Es su padre.
b. Ella es muy simpática.
c. El profesor da un examen.

5. *a.* Somos mecánicos.
b. Soy estudiante.
c. Son amigos.

6. *a.* Salgo a las tres de la tarde.
b. Salen del teatro a las nueve de la noche.
c. Salen a las tres de la tarde.

7. *a.* Sí, yo sé todos los verbos.
b. No, no sabes cantar.
c. Sí, y también sé cantar en francés.

8. *a.* Decimos «hola».
b. Decimos «adiós, hasta mañana».
c. Digo «hola, ¿cómo están Uds.?»

9. *a.* Veo dos libros.
   b. Vemos un libro.
   c. Vemos dos libros.

10. *a.* Oigo música en la radio.
    b. Oyen música en la discoteca.
    c. Oyes música en el concierto.

La Piramide del Sol, Chichén Itzá, Yucatán, México

3

The Present Tense: Stem-Changing Verbs

Helps and Hints

The verbs in this lesson are often called "shoe verbs" because a list of their irregular forms can be put in the shape of a shoe.

 **O to UE**

-AR Verbs

almorzar, to have lunch

yo	alm*ue*rzo	nosotros(-as) almorzamos
tú	alm*ue*rzas	vosotros(-as) almorzáis
Ud. él } alm*ue*rza ella		Uds. ellos } alm*ue*rzan ellas

-ER Verbs

volver, to return

yo	v*ue*lvo	nosotros(-as) volvemos
tú	v*ue*lves	vosotros(-as) volvéis
Ud. el } v*ue*lve ella		Uds. ellos } v*ue*lven ellas

-IR Verbs

dormir, to sleep

yo	d*ue*rmo	nosotros(-as) dormimos
tú	d*ue*rmes	vosotros(-as) dormís
Ud. él } d*ue*rme ella		Uds. ellos } d*ue*rmen ellas

 *E to IE*

-AR Verbs

cerrar, to close

yo c**i**erro	nosotros(-as) cerramos
tú c**i**erras	vosotros(-as) cerráis

Ud. ⎫		Uds. ⎫	
él ⎬ c**i**erra		ellos ⎬ c**i**erran	
ella ⎭		ellas ⎭	

-ER Verbs

defender, to defend

yo def**i**endo	nosotros(-as) defendemos
tú def**i**endes	vosotros(-as) defendéis

Ud. ⎫		Uds. ⎫	
el ⎬ def**i**ende		ellos ⎬ def**i**enden	
ella ⎭		ellas ⎭	

-IR Verbs

preferir, to prefer

yo pref**i**ero	nosotros(-as) preferimos
tú pref**i**eres	vosotros(-as) preferís

Ud. ⎫		Uds. ⎫	
el ⎬ pref**i**ere		ellos ⎬ pref**i**eren	
ella ⎭		ellas ⎭	

 *E to I (-IR Verbs Only)*

repetir, to repeat

yo rep**i**to	nosotros(-as) repetimos
tú rep**i**tes	vosotros(-as) repetís

Ud. ⎫		Uds. ⎫	
él ⎬ rep**i**te		ellos ⎬ rep**i**ten	
ella ⎭		ellas ⎭	

1. To obtain the stem of *any* verb, drop the infinitive ending (**-ar, -er,** or **-ir**). If the stem of a stem-changing verb has more than one vowel, it is the last vowel that changes: enc**o**ntr-, recom**e**nd-, pref**e**r-, etc. This vowel may be either **o** or **e.** (Not all verbs with stem-vowel **o** or **e** are stem-changing verbs.)

2. Changes in the stem-vowel occur in all the present-tense forms of the verb except those for **nosotros(-as)** and **vosotros(-as).** The stem-vowel **o** changes to **ue;** the stem-vowel **e** changes to **ie** in some verbs, to **i** in others.

Common Stem-Changing Verbs

O **TO** UE

-AR Verbs

acostarse,* to go to bed

almorzar, to have lunch

contar, to tell; to count

costar, to cost (generally third person singular or plural)

encontrar, to find; to meet

jugar (u to **ue),** to play
  jugar al tenis (a las cartas, etc.) to play tennis (cards, etc.)

mostrar, to show

recordar, to remember

sonar, to sound; to ring

soñar (con), to dream (of)

volar, to fly

-ER Verbs

devolver, to return, give back

llover, to rain (third person singular only: **llueve)**

morder, to bite

mover, to move (an object)

moverse,* to move (oneself)

poder,† to be able, can

volver, to return, come (go) back

-IR Verbs

dormir, to sleep
  dormirse,* to fall asleep

morir(se),* to die

E **TO** IE

-AR Verbs

cerrar, to close

comenzar, to begin
  comenzar a + *inf.,* to begin to

confesar, to confess

despertar, to wake (someone)

despertarse,* to wake up

empezar, to begin
  empezar a + *inf.,* to begin to

nevar, to snow (third person singular only: **nieva)**

pensar (en), to think (of)
  pensar + *inf.,* to intend to

sentarse, to sit down

-ER Verbs

defender, to defend

encender, to turn on (the radio, lights, etc.), to light up

entender, to understand

perder, to lose

querer,† to want

-IR Verbs

divertirse,* to enjoy oneself, have a good time

mentir, to (tell a) lie

preferir, to prefer

sentir, to regret, be sorry
  lo siento, I'm sorry

sentirse,* to feel (sick, tired, etc.)

---

*See Chapter 27 for the conjugation of reflexive verbs.
†Although **poder** and **querer** are stem-changing in the present tense, they also undergo other changes in other tenses which the other stem-changing verbs do not undergo.

E to I: -IR **Verbs Only**

pedir, to ask (for), request   **servir,** to serve
reír(se), to laugh   **sonreír,** to smile
repetir, to repeat   **vestir,** to dress (someone)
seguir, to follow; to continue   **vestirse,** * to get dressed

3. The forms of **reír** in the present tense are:

río, ríes, ríe, reímos, reís, ríen

Sonreír is conjugated in the same way as **reír.**

4. The **yo** form of **seguir** is **sigo.** All other forms of **seguir** in the present tense retain the **u:** sig*u*es, sig*u*e, seg*u*imos, etc.

Practice: In each column, write the verb forms that are used with the given pronoun as subject.

1. *yo*	**2.** *nosotros*	**3.** *Uds.*	**4.** *tú*
(encontrar)	(vestir)	(seguir)	(sonreír)
(mover)	(seguir)	(morir)	(encender)
(cerrar)	(defender)	(querer)	(almorzar)
(perder)	(devolver)	(comenzar)	(sentir)
(preferir)	(contar)	(mentir)	(jugar)

▲ EJERCICIOS ▲

A. Repeat the sentence orally, changing the subject and verb as indicated. (Write the new verb forms in the blanks.)

1. No *recordamos* las palabras.

Yo no _____ ....

2. ¿A qué hora *vuelven* ellos del cine?

¿A qué hora _____ nosotras...?

3. ¿Cuántas horas *duermes* tú cada noche?

¿Cuántas horas _____ ella...?

---

*See Chapter 27 for the conjugation of reflexive verbs.

4. Yo siempre *pienso* en las vacaciones.

Nosotros siempre _____....

5. ¿Cuándo *quieren* Uds. ir al cine?

¿Cuándo _____ tú...?

6. Ella *prefiere* ir a la discoteca.

Yo _____....

7. ¿Qué *sirve* tu papá esta noche?

¿Qué _____ tus tías...?

8. Los niños *juegan* al béisbol en el parque.

Mi prima _____....

9. Tú no *entiendes* mi pregunta.

Él no _____....

10. Ese chico *ríe* mucho.

Tú siempre _____....

B. Your friend Lola likes to tease by changing your words slightly. Show how she does this, replacing the given verb with the appropriate form of the verb in parentheses.

EXAMPLE: Yo compro los libros. (perder)
        Yo pierdo los libros.

1. Yo no sé la respuesta. (recordar)

_____

2. ¿A qué hora regresa ella? (volver)

_____

3. Nuestros amigos no dicen la verdad. (confesar)

_____

4. ¿Tienen Uds. mucho dinero? (pedir)

_____

5. La película termina a las diez. (empezar)

_____

6. No comprendo a la profesora. (entender)

_____

7. Mis amigos escuchan el programa. (defender)

_____

8. Yo nunca doy instrucciones. (seguir)

_____

9. Deseamos patinar en el hielo. (preferir)

_____

10. ¿Cuándo apagas las luces hoy? (encender)

_____

C. Your pen pal is curious about your school life. Answer his (her) questions with a complete sentence in Spanish:

1. ¿A qué hora empiezan Uds. la lección de español?

_____

2. ¿Siempre sigues las instrucciones del profesor?

_____

3. ¿Dónde juegan Uds. cuando llueve mucho?

_____

4. ¿A qué universidad piensas ir?

_____

5. ¿A qué hora vuelves a casa todos los días?

_____

D. _Optional Exercise._ Reflexive Verbs (see Chapter 27). Answer with a complete sentence in Spanish.

1. ¿A qué hora te acuestas por lo general?

_____

2. ¿Se duerme Ud. en seguida después de trabajar muchas horas?

_____

3. ¿Dónde se sienta la profesora (el profesor) en la sala de clase?

_____

4. ¿Qué hace una persona cuando se siente enferma?

_____

5. ¿Se viste Ud. rápidamente por la mañana antes de ir a la escuela?

_____

E. Express in Spanish:

1. They have lunch at 1:00. _____

2. Can you come early tonight? _____

3. I'm not repeating the question. _____

4. Why don't they close the window now? ——————————————

5. Isn't she returning the money tomorrow? ——————————————

6. We're losing a lot of money.   ——————————————

7. I'm sorry, sir.   ——————————————

8. She never smiles.   ——————————————

9. It's raining all day (*todo el día*).   ——————————————

10. I'm dreaming of (*con*) the weekend.   ——————————————

F. *Listening Comprehension.* Your teacher will read to the class ten statements in Spanish. After each statement is read, circle the letter (*a, b,* or *c*) of the most logical reply among the three choices.

1. *a.* Pero yo quiero salir.
   b. Las hojas mueren.
   c. Ella lo confiesa.

2. *a.* No, defiendo mi ciudad.
   b. No, yo digo la verdad.
   c. Sí, y también como papas.

3. *a.* Al contrario, es muy barata: cuesta sólo diez dólares.
   b. Sí, cuesta cinco centavos.
   c. Nieva mucho hoy.

4. *a.* Sí, lo sentimos mucho.
   b. Sí, es muy fácil.
   c. No, ella sirve pasteles.

5. *a.* Sí, quiero comer dulces en la escuela.
   b. No, los perros muerden a los niños.
   c. Sí, queremos ir a España y Francia.

6. *a.* Sí, ella almuerza a la una de la tarde.
   b. Sí, almuerzo a medianoche, como siempre.
   c. No, almuerzo a mediodía, como todos los días.

7. *a.* Muy bien; entonces podemos comer a tiempo.
   b. Ella duerme en la cocina.
   c. Ud. repite la pregunta.

8. *a.* Es verdad, ella siempre vuela por el aire.
   b. ¡Claro! Ella es una cocinera excelente.
   c. Sí, él es un buen mecánico.

9. *a.* Tú siempre juegas bien al tenis.
   b. No sé por qué. El profesor enseña muy bien.
   c. Nunca nieva en el verano.

10. *a.* Debemos llevar un paraguas.
    b. Es un buen día para ir a la playa.
    c. El arroz con pollo es delicioso.

4
Formal Commands*

mirar:
   Mir**e** Ud. (Mir**e**n Uds.) el mapa.   Look at the map.

beb**e**r:
   Beb**a** Ud. (Beb**a**n Uds.) el jugo.   Drink the juice.

sub**i**r:
   Sub**a** Ud. (Sub**a**n Uds.) la escalera.   Go up the stairs.
   No sub**a** (no sub**a**n Uds.).   Don't go up(stairs).

venir:
   Veng**a** Ud. (Veng**a**n Uds.) mañana.   Come tomorrow.
   No veng**a** Ud. (No veng**a**n Uds.) mañana.   Don't come tomorrow.

1. To form the command, start with the **yo** form of the present tense. Drop the **-o** ending and replace it as follows:

    -AR verbs: add **-e** or **-en.**
    -ER and *-IR* verbs: add **-a** or **-an.**

2. The command is made negative by placing **no** before the verb.

3. The pronoun **Ud.** or **Uds.** follows the command form but need not be expressed:

               ¡Miren Uds.! }
               ¡Miren!   }   Look!

4. Whether a verb is regular, irregular, or stem-changing, the same rule applies: to form the command, always start with the **yo** form of the present tense:

    yo **traig**o:
       Traiga Ud. (**Traig**an Uds.) la sopa.   Bring the soup.

    yo **veng**o:
       Venga Ud. (**Veng**an Uds.) mañana.   Come tomorrow.

---

*The formal commands of certain verbs undergo spelling changes. These verbs appear in the "Verb Charts" in the Appendix and will not appear in the exercises.

yo **recuerd**o:
> **Recuerd**e Ud. (**Recuerd**en Uds.) el número.   Remember the number.

yo **repit**o:
> **Repit**a Ud. (**Repit**an Uds.) la pregunta.   Repeat the question.

Practice A: Write the **yo** form, then the singular and plural command forms.

EXAMPLES: ver   *yo veo*   *vea Ud.*   *vean Uds.*
              no tomar   *yo no tomo*   *no tome Ud.*   *no tomen Uds.*

1. contestar _____ _____ _____

2. no comer _____ _____ _____

3. vivir _____ _____ _____

4. no salir _____ _____ _____

5. hacer _____ _____ _____

6. traducir _____ _____ _____

7. decir _____ _____ _____

8. tener _____ _____ _____

9. no mostrar _____ _____ _____

10. devolver _____ _____ _____

11. dormir _____ _____ _____

12. no confesar _____ _____ _____

13. defender _____ _____ _____

14. no mentir _____ _____ _____

15. pedir _____ _____ _____

Irregular Command Forms

dar, to give	*dé* Ud.	*den* Uds.
estar, to be	*esté* Ud.	*estén* Uds.
ir, to go	*vaya* Ud.	*vayan* Uds.
saber, to know	*sepa* Ud.	*sepan* Uds.
ser, to be	*sea* Ud.	*sean* Uds.

5. The command form of **dar** has an accent mark in the singular (**dé** Ud.) but not in the plural (**den** Uds.).

> *Practice B:* Complete the Spanish sentences.

1. Go home. _____ Ud. a casa.

2. Be good. _____ Uds. buenos.
   (Use *ser.*)

3. Know the lesson. _____ Ud. la lección.

4. Don't be here late. No _____ Uds. aquí tarde.
   (Use *estar.*)

5. Don't give the hat to Mary. No _____ Ud. el sombrero a María.

Forming Commands With Reflexive Verbs

quedarse, to remain, to stay

Quédese Ud. (**Quédense** Uds.) en casa hoy.	Stay home today.
No se quede Ud. (**No se queden** Uds.) en casa hoy.	Do not stay home today.

sentarse, to sit down

Siéntese (Siéntense) aquí.	Sit down here.
No se siente (No se sienten) allí.	Don't sit down there.

6. To express a command with a reflexive verb, attach **se** to the command form of the verb. Note the accent mark on the stressed vowel.

7. To make the command negative, place **se** between **no** and the verb. (Omit the accent mark in negative commands.)

> *Practice C:* Change each command from the affirmative to the negative or vice versa.

EXAMPLES: Levántese Ud. temprano. *No se levante Ud. temprano.*

No se quiten Uds. los guantes. *Quítense Uds. los guantes.*

1. Lávense las manos. _____

2. No se acueste Ud. ahora. _____

3. Diviértase en España. _____

4. No se despierten Uds. antes de las seis. _____

5. Quédese Ud. aquí. _____

▲ EJERCICIOS ▲

A. As shown in the examples, there are two ways to express "please" in Spanish. Write a sentence in Spanish that has the same meaning as the given sentence, then translate into English.

EXAMPLES: Haga Ud. el favor de venir.
Venga Ud., por favor.   Please come.

Hagan Uds. el favor de no entrar.
No entren Uds., por favor.   Please do not enter.

1. Haga Ud. el favor de volver temprano.

_____

2. Hagan Uds. el favor de traer las cartas.

_____

3. Haga el favor de no decir eso.

_____

4. Hagan el favor de no salir ahora.

_____

5. Haga Ud. el favor de usar la escalera.

_____

B. Show how different people are told to do different things. Items 12–15 require the use of reflexive verbs.

1. Be there at six o'clock, Mrs. Rodríguez. (Use *estar.*)

_____

2. Take the medicine three times a day (*al día.*), Mr. López.

_____

3. Steven and Lola, don't go to the city today.

_____

4. Finish the job now, men.

_____

5. Know the answers tomorrow, students.

_____

6. Have patience, madame.

_____

7. Listen to the music, girls.

_____

8. Read the article tonight, gentlemen.

_____

9. Young man, please put the newspaper on the table. (Use _por favor._)

_____

10. Please close the door, Miss Sánchez. (Use _por favor._)

_____

11. Do not return here before five o'clock, sir.

_____

12. Stay here this afternoon, ladies.

_____

13. Please put on your jacket (_la chaqueta_). (Use _por favor._)

_____

14. Boys, don't get angry.

_____

15. Please sit down here, Mr. González. (Use _por favor._)

_____

Las Cataratas de Iguazú, Argentina

5
Familiar Commands

Helps and Hints
In this lesson, you will learn how to address a command to a friend, member of the family, child, or pet.

canta	**Canta** (tú) ahora.	Sing now.
come	**Come** (tú) la ensalada.	Eat the salad.
escribe	**Escribe** (tú) la carta.	Write the letter.
empieza	**Empieza** a leer.	Begin reading.
vuelve	**Vuelve** pronto.	Come back soon.
da	**Da** el dinero a José.	Give the money to Joseph.
está	**Está** aquí a las dos.	Be here at two o'clock.

1. The familiar command* is identical in form to the third person singular of the present tense. With a few exceptions (see page 29), this is true of *all* verbs.

2. The pronoun **tú** follows the verb but is often omitted.

3. Compare:

¡Oiga Ud.!	**!Oye** (tú)!	Hear! (Listen!)
¡Siga Ud.!	**¡Sigue** (tú)!	Follow! (Continue!)
¡Traduzca Ud.!	**¡Traduce** (tú)!	Translate!
¡Traiga Ud.!	**¡Trae** (tú)!	Bring!

Practice A: Change the form of the command from the formal to the familiar.

1. Almuerce Ud. a mediodía.

   _____ tú

2. Confiese Ud. la verdad.

   _____ tú

3. Tome Ud. café.

   _____ tú

4. Viva Ud. en México.

   _____ tú

5. Traiga Ud. el dinero.

   _____ tú

6. Oiga Ud. la música.

   _____ tú

7. Sepa Ud. la lección.

   _____ tú

8. Conduzca Ud. con cuidado.

   _____ tú

---

*This chapter deals with commands in the familiar *singular,* or **tú** form. For the familiar plural, or **vosotros** form, see Appendix IX.

Irregular Familiar Commands

decir	**Di** (tú) la verdad.	Tell the truth.
hacer	**Haz** el trabajo.	Do the work.
ir	**Ve** a casa.	Go home.
poner	**Pon** el libro aquí.	Put the book here.
salir	**Sal** temprano.	Leave early.
ser	**Sé** bueno.	Be good.
tener	**Ten** paciencia.	Have patience.
venir	**Ven** acá.	Come here.

4. These eight command forms are irregular because they differ from the third-person-singular form of the verb and must be learned individually.

5. Other irregular verbs have *regular* **tú** commands. For example:

traer	**Trae** (tú) los discos.	Bring the records.
oir	**Oye** el ruido.	Hear the noise.
conducir	**Conduce** con cuidado.	Drive carefully.

Practice B: Change the command from the formal to the familiar.

1. Salga Ud. de mi casa.

_____

2. Haga Ud. el favor de escuchar.

_____

3. Ponga Ud. la silla aquí, por favor.

_____

4. Diga Ud. algo.

_____

5. Venga Ud. conmigo en seguida.

_____

Negative Familiar Commands*

Habla bien.	Speak well.
No habl**es** en voz baja.	Don't speak in a low voice.
Vuelve pronto.	Return soon.
No vuelv**as** tarde.	Don't return late.
Divide la pizza.	Divide the pizza.
No divid**as** el dinero.	Don't divide the money.
Haz la tarea.	Do the task.
No hag**as** ese trabajo.	Don't do that work.
Di la respuesta.	Tell the answer.
No dig**as** nada.	Don't say anything.

---

*The negative familiar commands of certain verbs undergo spelling changes. These verbs appear in the Verb Charts in the Appendix and will not appear in the exercises.

6. To form the negative **tú** command, add **-s** to the **Ud.** command form: **diga** Ud.—no diga**s** (tú), etc.:

Mira tú.	**Mire** Ud.	No **mires** tú.
Duerme tú.	**Duerma** Ud.	No **duermas** tú.
Ven tú.	**Venga** Ud.	No **vengas** tú.

Practice C: Change to the negative.

1. Mira la televisión esta noche.

No _____.

2. Aprende esta lección.

No _____.

3. Asiste al concierto.

No _____.

4. Cierra la puerta.

No _____.

5. Envuelve el paquete.

No _____.

6. Pon la impresora allí.

No _____.

7. Ven con nosotros.

No _____.

8. Haz la tarea.

No _____.

9. Ve al museo con Roberto.

No _____.

10. Contesta a mi pregunta.

No _____.

Familiar Commands Used With Object Pronouns*

Háblame, Roberto.	Speak to me, Robert.
No **me** hables, por favor.	Don't speak to me, please.
Siéntate aquí.	Sit here.
No **te** sientes allí.	Don't sit there.
Ponlo en la mesa.	Put it on the table.
No **lo** pongas en la silla.	Don't put it on the chair.
Hazme un favor.	Do me a favor.
No **me** hagas ese favor.	Don't do me that favor.
Tráenoslo ahora.	Bring it to us now.
No nos **lo** traigas hoy.	Don't bring it to us today.
Díselo más tarde.	Tell it to him later.
No **se lo** digas ahora.	Don't tell it to him now.

7. In commands, object pronouns are attached to the verb in the same way as reflexive pronouns (see Chapter 4). When the command is negative, object pronouns are placed between **no** and the verb. Note that the single-syllable command forms take no accent mark when one pronoun

---

*For the forms of object pronouns, see Chapters 24 and 25.

is attached but take an accent mark on the third syllable from the end when two pronouns are added. (Dinos, but Dínos**lo**.)

Practice D: Change to the negative or affirmative.

EXAMPLES: No te levantes tarde.   *Levántate* temprano.
           Hazlo hoy.   *No lo hagas mañana.*

1. No me mires así.   _____ ahora.

2. Hazlos en seguida.   _____ nunca.

3. No la pongas en la cocina. _____ en el comedor.

4. Siéntate junto a mí.   _____ junto a él.

5. No le hables de eso.   _____ de algo mejor.

◢ EJERCICIOS ◣

A. Complete the response with a *tú* command as shown in the example. Do not use object pronouns.

EXAMPLE: Yo quiero comer ensalada.
          Pues, *come ensalada,* si quieres.

1. Yo quiero tomar café.

    Pues, _____, si quieres.

2. Yo quiero volver tarde.

    Pues, _____, si quieres.

3. Yo quiero vender la computadora.

    Pues, _____, si quieres.

4. Yo quiero ser el Presidente de los Estados Unidos.

    Pues, _____, si quieres.

5. Yo quiero hacer las tareas.

    Pues, _____, si quieres.

B. Reply with a *tú* command using object pronouns, as shown in the example.

EXAMPLE: Yo voy a prepararla.
          Pues, *prepárala.*

1. Yo voy a sentarme aquí.

    Pues, _____.

2. Yo voy a ponerlas en la cama.

    Pues, _____.

3. Yo voy a escribirles.

   Pues, _____.

4. Yo voy a hablarte ahora.

   Pues, _____.

5. Yo voy a devolvérselo a ella.

   Pues, _____.

C. Reply with a negative *tú* command as shown in the example.

   EXAMPLE: Yo no quiero hablar.
               Entonces, *no hables.*

   1. Yo no quiero venir hoy.

      Entonces, _____.

   2. Yo no quiero ir al cine.

      Entonces, _____.

   3. Yo no quiero cantar.

      Entonces, _____.

   4. No quiero beber leche.

      Entonces, _____.

   5. No quiero decir eso.

      Entonces, _____.

D. Complete the response with a negative *tú* command as shown in the example.

   EXAMPLE: No voy a decírtelo.
               No me importa; *no me lo digas.*

   1. Yo no voy a vendérsela a nadie.

      No me importa; _____.

   2. No voy a pedirlos.

      No me importa; _____.

   3. No voy a quejarme de ella.

      No me importa; _____.

   4. No voy a darte el dinero.

      No me importa; _____.

   5. No voy a hacerlo.

      No me importa; _____.

E. Juanito's mother will be out for a few hours and is leaving him in the care of a baby-sitter. Tell what his mother tells him to do using familiar commands and using the drawings as guides.

1. (Be good.)

3. (Do your homework.)

2. (Eat your vegetables.)

4. (Drink your milk.)

5. (Go to bed at 9:00.)

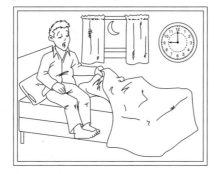

F. Now here is what mom tells Juanito not to do.

1. (Don't be mischievous.)

2. (Don't eat two desserts.)

3. (Don't break the furniture.)

4. (Don't drink soda.)

5. (Don't go to bed late.)

Part 2
Past Tenses

><|><|><|><|><|><|><|><|><|><|><|><|><|><|><|><|><|><|><|><|><|><

6
The Preterit Tense: Regular Verbs*

Helps and Hints

The past tense in English has only one verb form; e.g., *I went, you went, she went,* etc. In Spanish, however, there are six verb forms, as in the present tense. Note the word *did* in the English expressions, "I did not go," "did she eat?"; however, the *did* is not expressed in Spanish.

	-AR Verbs	*-ER* and *-IR* Verbs	
	prestar, *to lend*	**romper,** *to break*	**recibir,** *to receive*
SINGULAR			
yo	prest*é* *I lent*	romp*í* *I broke*	recib*í* *I received*
tú	prest*aste*	romp*iste*	recib*iste*
Ud. él ella	prest*ó*	romp*ió*	recib*ió*
PLURAL			
nosotros nosotras	prest*amos*	romp*imos*	recib*imos*
vosotros vosotras	prest*asteis*	romp*isteis*	recib*isteis*
Uds. ellos ellas	prest*aron*	romp*ieron*	recib*ieron*

---

*Certain regular verbs ending in **-car, -gar** and **-zar** in the preterit undergo changes **only** in the first person singular to preserve the pronunciation: **sacar-saqué, pagar-pagué, comenzar-comencé.** (See Verb Charts in the Appendix.) These verb forms will not appear in the exercises.

1. The preterit tense is equivalent to the past tense in English: *I ate, she went, we talked, did he work?, we did not speak.*

2. To form the preterit, add the following endings to the stem of the infinitive:

	-AR	-ER and -IR
yo	-é	-í
tú	-aste	-iste
Ud., él, ella	-ó	-ió
nosotros(-as)	-amos	-imos
vosotros(-as)	-asteis	-isteis
Uds., ellos, ellas	-aron	-ieron

3. The **nosotros** form of the *-AR* and *-IR* verbs in the preterit is identical to the **nosotros** form in the present tense:

hablamos { we speak (are speaking) / we spoke }   **escribimos** { we write (are writing) / we wrote }

4. *-ER* and *-IR* verbs have the same endings in the preterit.

5. Stem-vowel changes in the present-tense forms of *-AR* and *-ER* verbs do not occur in the preterit:*

	PRESENT	PRETERIT
pensar	yo pienso	yo pensé
defender	Ud. defiende	Ud. defendió
encontrar	ellos encuentran	ellos encontraron
mover	tú mueves	tú moviste

6. The verb **ver** has regular preterit endings but its first and third person singular forms are written without accent marks: **vi,** viste, **vio,** vimos, visteis, vieron.

Practice A: Write the preterit forms of the verbs that are used with the given pronouns as subjects.

EXAMPLE: Uds. _____*contestaron*_____   _____*perdieron*_____   _____*describieron*_____
                        (contestar)   (perder)   (describir)

1. yo   _____   _____   _____
              (abrir)   (comer)   (encontrar)

-IR verbs that have stem changes in the present tense also undergo some stem changes in the preterit: see page 48.

2. tú

    _____   _____   _____
        (recordar)   (responder)   (escribir)

3. nosotros

    _____   _____   _____
        (entender)   (pasar)   (salir)

4. ella

    _____   _____   _____
         (subir)   (prometer)   (entrar)

5. Uds.

    _____   _____   _____
         (cantar)   (partir)   (volver)

7. The following adverbial phrases are typical of the kinds of expressions that are often used with the preterit tense:

> **ayer,** yesterday
>
> **ayer por la mañana,** yesterday morning
>
> **ayer por la tarde,** yesterday afternoon
>
> **anoche,** last night
>
> **la semana pasada,** last week
>
> **el mes pasado,** last month
>
> **el año pasado,** last year
>
> **hace tres días,** three days ago*
>
> **hace diez años,** ten years ago

> _Practice B:_ Complete the English translations.

EXAMPLES: Vivo en Nueva York.   I _live_ in New York.
                 Viví en Madrid hace dos años.   I _lived_ in Madrid two years ago.
                 ¿Dónde vive ella ahora?   Where _does_ she _live_ now?

1. Escriben cartas a sus parientes.

They _____ letters to their relatives.

Escribieron una carta anoche.

They _____ a letter last night.

2. Yo no escucho la cinta ahora.

I _____ not _____ to the tape now.

Yo no escuché el disco compacto antes.

I _____ not _____ to the CD before.

3. ¿A qué hora salen del museo esta tarde?

At what time _____ they _____ the museum this afternoon.

¿A qué hora salieron ayer por la tarde?

At what time _____ they _____ yesterday afternoon?

---

*See page 49.

4. Mi lección de tenis termina a las cinco hoy.

My tennis lesson _____ at five o'clock today.

Mi lección de piano terminó a las ocho ayer.

My piano lesson _____ at eight o'clock yesterday.

5. Ella no devuelve los libros a la biblioteca hoy.

She _____ not _____ the books to the library today.

Ella no devolvió los libros a la biblioteca ayer.

She _____ not _____ the books to the library yesterday.

► EJERCICIOS ►

A. Repeat the sentence, using the new subject.

EXAMPLE: Yo viví en Madrid el verano pasado.
　　　　　　Mis padres *vivieron en Madrid el verano pasado.*

1. Nosotros bailamos toda la noche en la discoteca.

Yo _____.

2. ¿Quién compró la impresora?

¿Quiénes _____?

3. Ellos partieron para Costa Rica la semana pasada.

Él _____.

4. El vestido costó cien dólares.

Los trajes _____.

5. Tú no recordaste mi número de teléfono.

Vosotros _____.

6. La niña subió la escalera muy de prisa.

Los niños _____.

7. ¿Cuántos vasos de agua bebieron Uds.?

¿_____ ella?

8. ¿Viste tú el programa anoche?

¿_____ él _____?

9. ¿A qué hora encendió Ud. la luz de la cocina?

¿_____ tú _____?

10. Nosotras devolvimos los regalos a la tienda.

Yo _____.

B. Change each expression to past time by rewriting each verb in the preterit.

> EXAMPLE: Ud. vuelve tarde hoy.
>
> Ud. _____*volvió*_____ tarde anoche.

1. Hoy visito a mis primos en Los Ángeles.

   El mes pasado _____ a mis parientes en San Diego.

2. Ahora bebemos leche.

   Esta mañana _____ café.

3. En este momento escuchan la música *rock*.

   Anoche _____ la música clásica.

4. ¿Qué venden hoy en el supermercado?

   ¿Qué _____ ayer?

5. ¿A qué hora sales de la escuela generalmente?

   ¿A qué hora _____ ayer?

6. Mi padre compra un coche nuevo hoy.

   La semana pasada _____ una computadora nueva.

7. Siempre vuelve a la misma hora.

   Anoche _____ a las siete y media.

8. Este invierno nieva muy poco.

   El invierno pasado _____ muchísimo.

9. Hoy escribo una carta a mi amigo en San Juan.

   _____ a mis tíos en Miami hace tres días.

10. Ya no llueve.

    _____ mucho hace una hora.

C. Your Spanish class has a visitor from Argentina. Answer his questions about your daily life.

1. ¿Cuánto costó su gorra?

   _____

2. ¿A qué hora de la noche volvió Ud. a casa el sábado pasado?

   _____

3. ¿Qué programa interesante vio Ud. en la televisión anoche?

   _____

4. ¿Compró su familia algo nuevo el mes pasado?

   _____

5. ¿Qué aprendieron Uds. ayer en la clase de español?

_____

6. ¿A qué hora empezó esta clase ayer?

_____

7. ¿Voló Ud. a algún país extranjero el año pasado?

_____

8. ¿Tomó Ud. un buen desayuno ayer por la mañana?

_____

9. ¿A qué escuela asistió Ud. hace cinco años?

_____

10. ¿Dónde vivió su familia hace cuatro años?

_____

D. Write the Spanish equivalent of each sentence.

1. Did she sell her car yesterday?

_____

2. Last night I studied three hours.

_____

3. Didn't you (_tú_) understand the lesson this morning?

_____

4. Where did they (_f._) work yesterday afternoon?

_____

5. Susan attended the same high school last year.

_____

6. Where did you (_tú_) lose your watch?

_____

7. You (_vosotros_) promised to send postcards.

_____

8. Who (_Quiénes_) opened the doors?

_____

9. When did she travel through Europe?

_____

10. I lived in Argentina two years ago.

_____

E. *Listening Comprehension.* Your teacher will read to the class ten questions in Spanish. After each question is read to you, circle the letter (*a,b,* or *c*) of the most appropriate answer.

1. *a.* Cantamos canciones populares.
   b. Vimos a muchas chicas.
   c. Canté una canción puertorriqueña.

2. *a.* Nacimos en 1980.
   b. Nací en Panamá.
   c. Nacimos en Guatemala.

3. *a.* El viento entra.
   b. Siempre cierro las ventanas.
   c. Abro el libro.

4. *a.* No visité México.
   b. Siempre visitamos países hispanos.
   c. Visitamos Chile.

5. *a.* Sí, bajé a la calle.
   b. No bajé del coche.
   c. Sí, bajamos al segundo piso.

6. *a.* Sí, lo vimos a las siete.
   b. No, vi otro más interesante.
   c. Sí, viví en California.

7. *a.* Recibí el paquete ayer.
   b. Recibimos 10 pesos la semana pasada.
   c. Recibí cinco dólares anoche.

8. *a.* Aprendieron la historia de Sudamérica.
   b. Aprendiste muchas cosas.
   c. Aprendí los verbos irregulares.

9. *a.* Sí, nevó mucho.
   b. No, nuestros abuelos volaron por el aire.
   c. Sí, y por eso nos quedamos en casa.

10. *a.* Bebió naranjada.
    b. Bebimos leche.
    c. Bebiste agua.

Monumento a Don Quijote, Personaje de Cervantes, en la Plaza de España de Madrid, España

7
The Preterit Tense: Irregular Verbs

Helps and Hints
This chapter deals with verbs that have irregular forms in the preterit tense. They are divided into *three* main groups.

Group 1: Verbs With Special Preterit Stems

-U-Stems

andar, to walk, go (**anduv-**)	*anduve*	*anduviste*	*anduvo*	*anduvimos*	*anduvisteis*	*anduvieron*
caber, to fit (**cup-**)	*cupe*	*cupiste*	*cupo*	*cupimos*	*cupisteis*	*cupieron*
estar, to be (**estuv-**)	*estuve*	*estuviste*	*estuvo*	*estuvimos*	*estuvisteis*	*estuvieron*
poder, to be able, can (**pud-**)	*pude*	*pudiste*	*pudo*	*pudimos*	*pudisteis*	*pudieron*
poner, to put (**pus-**)	*puse*	*pusiste*	*puso*	*pusimos*	*pusisteis*	*pusieron*
saber, to know (**sup-**)	*supe*	*supiste*	*supo*	*supimos*	*supisteis*	*supieron*
tener, to have (**tuv-**)	*tuve*	*tuviste*	*tuvo*	*tuvimos*	*tuvisteis*	*tuvieron*

-I-Stems

hacer, to do, make (**hic-**)	*hice*	*hiciste*	*hi<u>z</u>o*	*hicimos*	*hicisteis*	*hicieron*
querer, to want (**quis-**)	*quise*	*quisiste*	*quiso*	*quisimos*	*quisisteis*	*quisieron*
venir, to come (**vin-**)	*vine*	*viniste*	*vino*	*vinimos*	*vinisteis*	*vinieron*

-J-Stems

Conducir (to lead, drive), **decir** (to say, tell), and **traer** (to bring) have preterit stems that end in **j.** The ending **-ieron** becomes **-eron:**

conducir (conduj-)	*conduje*	*condujiste*	*condujo*	*condujimos*	*condujisteis*	*condujeron*
decir (dij-)	*dije*	*dijiste*	*dijo*	*dijimos*	*dijisteis*	*dijeron*
traer (traj-)	*traje*	*trajiste*	*trajo*	*trajimos*	*trajisteis*	*trajeron*

1. These preterit forms have no accent marks.

2. The endings that are added to these special preterit stems are:

-e, -iste, -o, -imos, -isteis, -ieron (sometimes **-eron**)

3. The third person singular of **hacer** is **hizo.** In this form, the **c** changes to **z** to represent the same sound before the letter **o.**

4. The preterit of **saber** means *learned* or *found out.* The preterit of **tener** sometimes means *got* or *received:*

Supimos la verdad anoche.   We learned the truth last night.

Tuve una carta ayer.   I got a letter yesterday.

Practice A: Complete each sentence with the preterit form of the verb.

1. ¿Dónde _____ tú la revista?
        (poner)

2. ¿Cuándo _____ Uds. a casa?
        (venir)

3. Nosotras _____ en casa anoche.
        (estar)

4. Él no _____ venir a la fiesta.
        (poder)

5. Ellas _____ la comida a la mesa.
        (traer)

6. Elena no _____ la tarea.
        (hacer)

7. Yo _____ una buena idea en ese momento.
        (tener)

8. Los chicos _____ por las calles.
        (andar)

9. ¿Por qué no _____ Uds. bailar?
        (querer)

10. ¿Qué _____ tú al profesor?
        (decir)

◼◤ Group 2: Verbs With Third-Person Preterit Endings -YO and -YERON*

caer, to fall	**caí**	**caíste**	*cayó*	**caímos**	**caísteis**	*cayeron*
creer, to believe	**creí**	**creíste**	*creyó*	**creímos**	**creísteis**	*creyeron*
leer, to read	**leí**	**leíste**	*leyó*	**leímos**	**leísteis**	*leyeron*
oír, to hear	**oí**	**oíste**	*oyó*	**oímos**	**oísteis**	*oyeron*

5. In this group of verbs, **i** changes to **y** in the endings of the third person singular and plural. All other endings have an accented **i**.

◼◤ Group 3: DAR, IR, SER

dar, to give	*di*	*diste*	*dio*	*dimos*	*disteis*	*dieron*
ir, to go } **ser,** to be }	*fui*	*fuiste*	*fue*	*fuimos*	*fuisteis*	*fueron*

6. The preterit endings of **dar** are the same as those for regular *-ER* and *-IR* verbs.

7. The preterit forms of **ir** and **ser** are identical.

8. The forms **di, dio, fui,** and **fue,** which were once accented, are no longer written with accent marks.

Practice B: Indicate whether the verb is a form of *ser* or *ir* by writing either *ser* or *ir* in parentheses at the beginning of your answer; then give the English equivalent.

1. Fueron a California la semana pasada. _____

2. Fueron buenos presidentes. _____

3. ¿Quién fue esa mujer? _____

4. ¿Quién fue al cine anoche? _____

Practice C: Complete the sentence with the preterit form of the verb.

1. ¿Qué le _____ Ud.?

(dar)

2. Carlos y yo _____ buenos amigos hace diez años.

(ser)

3. ¿Qué _____ del árbol?

(caer)

---

*Verbs that end in **-uir,** like **construir, contribuir,** etc., undergo the same changes, but these verbs will not appear in the exercises. See Verb Charts in the Appendix.

4. Ellos _____ mucho ruido en la calle.
   (oír)

5. Tú no _____ ese libro.
   (leer)

6. ¿Adónde _____ Uds. anoche?
   (ir)

7. Yo no le _____ la cinta.
   (dar)

8. Mi hermana _____ a Inglaterra el verano pasado.
   (ir)

◢ EJERCICIOS ◣

A. Change the verb from the present tense to the preterit. (Write the preterit form in the blank at the right.)

EXAMPLE: Mi padre *es* profesor. _____*fue*_____

1. ¿Qué *traen* ellos a la tertulia? _____
2. Yo no *quiero* oír esa música. _____
3. Él no *hace* bien el trabajo. _____
4. ¿Adónde *vas*? _____
5. Los alumnos de la clase de inglés *leen* tres novelas. _____
6. Nosotros *venimos* a casa muy tarde. _____
7. ¿Dónde *está* ella? _____
8. Por fin ellas *saben* la verdad. _____
9. Yo le *digo* la respuesta. _____
10. Él me *da* todo el dinero. _____
11. ¿Quiénes *son* esos señores? _____
12. ¿No *oyes* la televisión? _____
13. ¿Quién no *puede* ver la película? _____
14. ¿*Andáis* vosotros con ella? _____
15. El profesor no *cree* la excusa. _____
16. ¿Qué *dicen* Uds.? _____
17. Estos libros no *caben* en el estante. _____
18. No *sabemos* la respuesta. _____
19. Ella *conduce* su coche rápidamente. _____
20. ¿Dónde *pongo* las revistas? _____

B. Answer with a complete sentence in Spanish:

1. ¿Dónde $\begin{cases} \text{estuvo Ud.} \\ \text{estuviste tú} \end{cases}$ ayer por la mañana?

   _____

2. ¿Fueron Uds. a España el verano pasado?

   _____

3. ¿Cuántos libros $\begin{cases} \text{leíste tú} \\ \text{leyó Ud.} \end{cases}$ la semana pasada?

   _____

4. $\begin{cases} \text{¿Tuvo Ud.} \\ \text{¿Tuviste tú} \end{cases}$ una carta ayer de Puerto Rico?

   _____

5. ¿A qué hora $\begin{cases} \text{vino Ud.} \\ \text{viniste tú} \end{cases}$ a la escuela hoy?

   _____

6. ¿Quién fue el último alcalde de $\begin{cases} \text{su} \\ \text{tu} \end{cases}$ ciudad?

   _____

7. $\begin{cases} \text{¿Trajo Ud.} \\ \text{¿Trajiste tú} \end{cases}$ $\begin{cases} \text{su} \\ \text{tu} \end{cases}$ radio a la escuela hoy?

   _____

8. $\begin{cases} \text{¿Dijo Ud.} \\ \text{¿Dijiste tú} \end{cases}$ una mentira a $\begin{cases} \text{su} \\ \text{tu} \end{cases}$ profesor ayer?

   _____

9. ¿Qué $\begin{cases} \text{quiso Ud.} \\ \text{quisiste tú} \end{cases}$ hacer el domingo pasado?

   _____

10. ¿Oyeron Uds. música *rock* ayer en la clase de matemáticas?

    _____

C. Each statement is the answer to a question that begins as shown. Write the rest of the question.

EXAMPLES: Puse la carta en la mesa.   Yo vine a las ocho.
            ¿Dónde *pusiste la carta*?   ¿Quién *vino a las ocho*?

1. Ellos no dijeron nada.

   ¿Qué _____?

2. Estuvimos en el supermercado.

   ¿Dónde _____?

3. Yo lo hice hace cuatro días.

   ¿Cuándo _____?

4. Fue a Inglaterra.

   ¿Adónde _____?

5. Fue mi sobrino José.

   ¿Quién _____?

D. Give the Spanish equivalent of the following.

1. They (*f.*) brought the CD's yesterday.

   _____

2. Did he go to the concert last Saturday?

   _____

3. When did you (*Ud.*) come home?

   _____

4. They (*m.*) didn't say very much.

   _____

5. To whom did they (*f.*) give the money?

   _____

6. Last night we didn't walk very far. (Use *andar.*)

   _____

7. What did you (*Uds.*) do last summer?

   _____

8. A lot of snow fell last winter.

   _____

9. They were friends twenty years ago.

   _____

10. Did John get the tennis racket? (Use *tener.*)

   _____

11. Robert did not believe his brother.

   _____

12. How many books did they read last month?

   _____

13. I could not (= was not able to) arrive on time.

   _____

14. Susan and Arthur wanted to buy the tape recorder.

   _____

15. Where was he two days ago?

   _____

E. *Listening Comprehension.* Your teacher will read to the class ten questions in Spanish. After each question is read to you, circle the letter (*a, b,* or *c*) of the most appropriate answer.

1. *a.* No leí nada.
   b. Leímos tres libros.
   c. Leyeron una buena novela.

2. *a.* Hice mi tarea.
   b. Aprendimos los verbos irregulares.
   c. Hicieron cosas interesantes.

3. *a.* Visitó a mis abuelos.
   b. Fui a California.
   c. Tomó el tren para Europa.

4. *a.* Sí, los trajimos ayer.
   b. No, los comieron en casa.
   c. Sí, los trajeron esta mañana.

5. *a.* Lo pusiste en la mesa.
   b. Lo puse en la silla.
   c. Lo pusieron en la cama.

6. *a.* Vino a las siete.
   b. Vine a casa.
   c. Vine a las cuatro y media.

7. *a.* Anduvimos por la plaza principal.
   b. Anduvimos por la comida.
   c. Anduve por el centro comercial.

8. *a.* Le dijimos la verdad.
   b. Le dijo una mentira.
   c. Le dije algo interesante.

9. *a.* La supimos ayer por la tarde.
   b. La supo anoche.
   c. La supe esta mañana.

10. *a.* Pudiste terminar la tarea.
    b. Pude traer los discos compactos.
    c. Pudimos comer una ensalada.

SUPPLEMENT 1

-IR Verbs With Stem Changes in the Preterit

-IR verbs that have stem changes in the present tense will also undergo stem changes in the third-person forms of the preterit. In these forms, the stem vowel of the infinitive changes as follows:

1. **e** becomes **i.**

preferir:	preferí	preferimos
	preferiste	preferisteis
	pref*i*rió	pref*i*rieron

Other verbs in this group: **corregir, divertirse, herir, mentir, pedir, reír (sonreír), repetir, seguir, sentir, servir, vestir.** Note the conjugation of **reír** and **sonreír:**

(son)reír:	(son)reí	(son)reímos
	(son)reíste	(son)reísteis
	(son)r*i*ó	(son)r*i*eron

2. **o** becomes **u.**

dormir:	dormí	dormimos
	dormiste	dormisteis
	d*u*rmió	d*u*rmieron

Also in this group: **morir.**

▲ EJERCICIOS ▲

F. Complete each sentence with the appropriate preterit form of the verb:

1. Anoche mis amigos _____ mucho en la fiesta.
(divertirse)

2. ¿Cuántos discos compactos _____ José?
(pedir)

3. Ayer en un accidente de coches _____ seis personas.
(morir)

4. ¿Qué _____ su tía anoche?
(servir)

5. ¿A qué hora _____ Ud. esta mañana?
(vestirse)

6. Ayer mi abuela _____ enferma.
(sentirse)

7. ¿Dónde _____ tu primo anoche?
(dormir)

8. El profesor _____ al oír mi respuesta.
(sonreír)

9. Yo _____ las faltas de mi amigo y él _____ las mías.
(corregir) (corregir)

10. ¿_____ tu padre cuando oyó el chiste?
(reír)

▰▰ SUPPLEMENT 2

Expressing "Ago" in Spanish

Ago = **hace,** which is used with the preterit tense. *Ago* can be expressed in Spanish in two ways:

I saw her two hours ago. { La vi **hace dos horas.** / **Hace dos horas que** la vi.

They arrived a week ago. { Llegaron **hace una semana.** / **Hace una semana que** llegaron.

▲ EJERCICIOS ▲

G. Write the alternate construction, then give the English equivalent.

EXAMPLE: Partieron hace dos días.
Hace dos días que partieron. *They left two days ago.*

1. Hace tres años que vinieron a Nueva York.

_____

2. Fuimos al concierto hace un mes.

_____

3. Hace seis meses que nació.

_____

4. Trajeron las cintas hace una hora.

_____

5. Hace cinco minutos que la profesora explicó el concepto.

_____

6. Me dio el dinero hace cuatro días.

_____

H. Express in Spanish in _two_ ways:

1. We ate in a restaurant three days ago.

_____

2. I arrived at school twenty minutes ago.

_____

3. They went home an hour ago.

_____

4. She was here six weeks ago.

_____

5. We had (use _tomar_) breakfast a half hour ago.

_____

8
The Imperfect Tense

		-AR Verbs	*-ER* and *-IR* Verbs	
		contestar, *to answer*	**vender,** *to sell*	**dormir,** *to sleep*
		I was answering	*I was selling*	*I was sleeping*
		I used to answer	*I used to sell*	*I used to sleep*
		I answered	*I sold*	*I slept*
	yo	contest*aba*	vend*ía*	dorm*ía*
	tú	contest*abas*	vend*ías*	dorm*ías*
	Ud., él, ella	contest*aba*	vend*ía*	dorm*ía*
	nosotros, nosotras	contest*ábamos*	vend*íamos*	dorm*íamos*
	vosotros, vosotras	contest*abais*	vend*íais*	dorm*íais*
	Uds., ellos, ellas	contest*aban*	vend*ían*	dorm*ían*

1. To form the imperfect tense of all verbs except **ir, ser,** and **ver,** add the following endings to the stem of the infinitive:

	-AR Verbs	-ER and -IR Verbs
yo	**-aba**	**-ía**
tú	**-abas**	**-ías**
Ud., él, ella	**-aba**	**-ía**
nosotros(-as)	**-ábamos**	**-íamos**
vosotros(-as)	**-abais**	**-íais**
Uds., ellos, ellas	**-aban**	**-ían**

2. Note the accent mark on the first **a** of the ending **-ábamos.**

3. The imperfect tense is often equivalent to English *used to . . .* or *was (were) . . . -ing:**

$$\text{ella } \textbf{escribía} \left\{ \begin{array}{l} \text{she was writing} \\ \text{she used to write} \end{array} \right.$$

$$\textbf{hablábamos} \left\{ \begin{array}{l} \text{we were speaking} \\ \text{we used to speak} \end{array} \right.$$

4. The imperfect tense expresses an action in the past that (1) occurred regularly or repeatedly *or* (2) was in progress:

(1) **Jugábamos** al béisbol todos los sábados.　　We played (used to play) baseball every Saturday.

(2) María **estudiaba** y Raúl **escribía** cartas.　　María was studying and Raúl was writing letters.

Practice A: For each verb, write the form of the imperfect tense that is used with the given pronoun as subject.

1. ella 　　_____　　_____　　_____
　　　　　　　(comprender)　　　　(estar)　　　　　(venir)

2. nosotros 　_____　　_____　　_____
　　　　　　　　(ayudar)　　　　(escribir)　　　　(comer)

3. Uds. 　　_____　　_____　　_____
　　　　　　　(sentir)　　　　(defender)　　　　(andar)

4. tú 　　_____　　_____　　_____
　　　　　　　(poner)　　　　　(salir)　　　　(pensar)

Irregular Verbs in the Imperfect Tense

There are only three verbs that are irregular in the imperfect tense: **ser, ir,** and **ver.**

	ser, *to be*	**ir,** *to go*	**ver,** *to see*
	I was *I used to be*	*I was going* *I used to go* *I went*	*I was seeing* *I used to see* *I saw*
yo	*era*	*iba*	*veía*
tú	*eras*	*ibas*	*veías*
Ud., él, ella	era	iba	veía
nosotros(-as)	*éramos*	*íbamos*	*veíamos*
vosotros(-as)	*erais*	*ibais*	*veíais*
Uds., ellos, ellas	*eran*	*iban*	*veían*

---

*The imperfect tense of **hacer** has a special meaning when used idiomatically in expressions such as **hacía dos años que vivíamos allí.** See Chapter 32.

5. Note the accent marks on the **e** of **éramos** and the **i** of **íbamos.**

6. The imperfect tense of **ver** is irregular in that it retains the **e** of the infinitive ending **-er.**

Practice B: For each verb, write the form of the imperfect tense that is used with the indicated subject.

1. ella y yo   _____   _____   _____
                          (ser)   (ir)   (ver)

2. usted no   _____   _____   _____
                          (ir)   (ser)   (ver)

3. los chicos _____   _____   _____
                          (ver)   (ir)   (ser)

■■ **Expressions Often Used With the Imperfect Tense**

7. The following adverbial phrases are typical of the kinds of expressions that often occur with verbs in the imperfect tense:

> **algunas veces,** sometimes   **generalmente, normalmente,** generally
>
> **a menudo**   } often   **siempre,** always
> **muchas veces**   **todos los días,** every day

Note that such phrases indicate a repeated or recurrent action. Thus, they may serve as a clue to the proper tense if you have to choose between the preterit and the imperfect.

Practice C: Complete the English translations.

EXAMPLES: Vivíamos en Chicago cuando éramos jóvenes.

We _*lived (were living, used to live)*_ in Chicago when we ____*were*____ young.

Me visitaban a menudo en el campo.

They ____*visited (used to visit)*____ me often in the country.

1. Yo estudiaba mis lecciones todos los días.

I _____ my lessons every day.

2. Ellos comían en la cafetería.

They _____ in the cafeteria.

3. ¿Que hacían Uds. mientras ellos dormían?

What _____ while they _____?

4. ¿Qué leías cuando yo miraba la televisión?

What _____ when I _____ television?

5. Íbamos al cine los sábados.

   We _____ to the movies on Saturdays.

6. Siempre salíamos de casa temprano.

   We always _____ the house early.

   Practice D: Complete the Spanish sentence with the appropriate form of the verb.

1. (ser) They used to be good students

   _____ buenos estudiantes.

2. (ir) My parents went to the country every summer.

   Mis padres _____ al campo cada verano.

3. (ver) Which program were you watching?

   ¿Qué programa _____ Uds.?

4. (ver) We often saw her at school.

   La _____ muchas veces en la escuela.

5. (irse) Sometimes I left early.

   Algunas veces me _____ temprano.

6. (ser) Anita and I were close friends.

   Anita y yo _____ amigas íntimas.

7. (ser, ir) When you (*tú*) were young, did you often go to the movies?

   Cuando _____ joven, ¿_____ a menudo al cine?

▲ EJERCICIOS ▲

A. Write the appropriate form of the verb in the imperfect tense.

   EXAMPLE: (decir) Los niños nunca ____*decían*____ la verdad.

   1. (ir) ¿Adónde _____ Uds. cuando encontraron a Juan?

   2. (hacer) ¿Qué _____ Ud. en el museo?

   3. (llegar) A menudo nosotros _____ tarde a la escuela.

   4. (pensar) ¿Qué _____ tú de ese hombre?

   5. (ser) _____ las siete cuando llegaron a casa.

   6. (partir) El tren siempre _____ a las ocho en punto.

   7. (beber) En el verano yo generalmente _____ té helado (iced tea).

8. (leer/mirar) Mientras mis padres _____ las revistas, mi hermano y yo

    _____ la televisión.

9. (ir) Nosotras _____ al cine cuando vimos a Carlos.

10. (viajar) Nuestra familia siempre _____ durante el verano.

11. (volver) ¿A qué hora _____ ellos los domingos?

12. (ver) Mi hermana y yo siempre _____ buenas películas en ese cine.

13. (acostarse) ¿A qué hora te _____ tú los viernes?

14. (levantarse) Yo me _____ a las siete todos los días.

15. (dormirse/estar) Mi abuelo siempre se _____ cuando _____
sentado en el sillón.

B. Change each verb to past time using the imperfect tense. (Write the new verb form in the blank at
the right.)

EXAMPLE: Ella *es* mi amiga.   _____ *era* _____

1. ¿Dónde *estás,* Roberto?   _____

2. Siempre *repiten* la misma pregunta.   _____

3. Mi padre *trabaja* en una oficina grande.   _____

4. ¿Adónde *vamos* todas las semanas?   _____

5. A menudo *llueve* en las montañas.   _____

6. ¿A qué hora *cierran* las puertas por la noche?   _____

7. Generalmente *ven* buenos partidos de béisbol en el estadio.   _____

8. Jorge y yo no *somos* buenos jugadores de tenis.   _____

9. Ella no *sabe* cocinar bien.   _____

10. ¿Qué *tienes* en la mano?   _____

C. Your Spanish teacher has invited his/her friend from Colombia to your class. She would like to
know about the past experiences of some students. Answer her questions with a complete sentence in Spanish.

1. ¿A qué escuela iba Ud. cuando tenía diez años?

_____

2. ¿Siempre sabía Ud. hablar español?

_____

3. ¿Qué hora era cuando Ud. salió de casa esta mañana?

_____

4. ¿Qué hacía Ud. esta mañana mientras tomaba el desayuno?

_____

5. Cuando Ud. estaba en el quinto grado, ¿cómo se llamaba su mejor amiga (amigo)?

_____

D. Express in Spanish:

   1. We were coming to school.

_____

   2. Where (*Adónde*) were they going?

_____

   3. My uncle used to live in Mexico.

_____

   4. I always used to see that program on television.

_____

   5. My grandparents always traveled through Costa Rica.

_____

   6. We were not using the computers in class.

_____

   7. The cats used to sleep all afternoon.

_____

   8. It was raining a lot yesterday.

_____

   9. My cousin used to get up late on Saturdays. (reflexive verb)

_____

 10. Were you (*tú*) eating hamburgers?

_____

 11. We used to be good friends.

_____

 12. Were you (*tú*) writing to your grandmother?

_____

 13. He used to go to bed at eleven o'clock. (reflexive verb)

_____

 14. Was John drinking coffee or tea?

_____

 15. Where were William and Frank before?

_____

E. *Listening Comprehension.* Your teacher will read to the class ten sentences in Spanish. After each sentence is read to you, circle the letter (*a, b,* or *c*) of the correct English translation.

1. *a.* Where were you going?
   b. Where were they going?
   c. Where was he going?

2. *a.* It snowed every day.
   b. It was snowing all day.
   c. It was raining all day.

3. *a.* We could not arrive on time.
   b. They couldn't arrive on time.
   c. Could she arrive on time?

4. *a.* She always got up at 6:00.
   b. We always get up at 6:00.
   c. We always used to get up at 6:00.

5. *a.* We used to see interesting programs.
   b. We see interesting programs.
   c. They used to see interesting programs.

6. *a.* What did she want to do?
   b. What did you wish to do?
   c. Where did you want to go?

7. *a.* While we were reading, the telephone rang.
   b. While they read, the telephone rang.
   c. While she read, the telephone rang.

8. *a.* What was the teacher saying?
   b. What were you saying to the teacher?
   c. What did the teachers say?

9. *a.* They used to be rich lawyers.
   b. He was a rich lawyer.
   c. He is a rich lawyer.

10. *a.* Did they live in San Juan?
    b. I lived in San Juan.
    c. We used to live in San Juan.

9

The Preterit and Imperfect Tenses Compared

Helps and Hints

The difference in usage between the preterit and the imperfect tenses can sometimes be difficult to see. In this chapter, by means of examples, we will try to show the differences.

1. Verbs in a sentence are in the same tense if their actions occur at the same time:

¿Qué **hicieron** Uds. cuando ellos **entraron**?

What did you do when they came in?

¿Qué **hacían** Uds. mientras yo **estudiaba**?

What were you doing while I studied (was studying)?

2. The preterit interrupts the imperfect:

La profesora **explicaba** la regla cuando **sonó** el timbre.

The teacher was explaining the rule when the bell rang.

3. Verbs in a narration are in the preterit if their actions occurred at one time in the past. They are in the imperfect if their actions occurred regularly or repeatedly in the past.

a. **Esa mañana** José **fue** el primero en levantarse. Se **vistió** de prisa, se **lavó, bajó** a la cocina, **tomó** una taza de café y **salió** de casa sin despertar a nadie.

b. **Todas las mañanas** José **era** el primero en levantarse. Se **vestía** de prisa, se **lavaba, bajaba** a la cocina, **tomaba** una taza de café y **salía** de casa sin despertar a nadie.

... José was the first to arise. He dressed quickly, washed up, went downstairs to the kitchen, drank a cup of coffee, and left the house without waking anyone.

Passage **a** describes what José did on a particular morning; a phrase such as **Esa mañana** is either expressed or implied. Passage **b** describes what José did regularly or repeatedly or often; a phrase such as **Todas las mañanas** is either expressed or implied. Aside from such clues, note that the two passages can have the same English translation.

Practice A: Underline the more appropriate verb form.

1. While I was studying, she listened to the tapes.

Mientras yo (estudié/estudiaba), ella (escuchó/escuchaba) las cintas.

2. This morning I got up early, dressed, and had a cup of coffee.

Esta mañana me (levanté/levantaba) temprano, me (vestí/vestía) y (tomé/tomaba) una taza de café.

3. Yesterday afternoon she wrote a letter.

Ayer por la tarde (escribió/escribía) una carta.

4. While she wrote, it started to snow.

Mientras (escribió/escribía), (empezó/empezaba) a nevar.

4. The time of day in the past is expressed by the imperfect:

Eran las siete cuando llegaron.

It was seven o'clock when they arrived.

5. The imperfect is used to describe people, places, or events in the past:

a. **Había** una vez dos atletas que **eran** muy fuertes. **Se llamaban** Lola y Felipe. Los dos **tenían** los ojos azules. Cuando **andaban** por los pasillos de la escuela, todos los estudiantes los **admiraban.**

There were once two athletes who were very strong. Their names were Lola and Felipe. Both had blue eyes. When they walked along the school's corridors, all the students admired them.

b. Las montañas de ese país **eran** altas y hermosas.

The mountains of that country were high and beautiful.

c. Cuando mi tío **vivía** en Puerto Rico, a menudo **iba** a Ponce.

When my uncle lived in Puerto Rico, he often went to Ponce.

In **c,** the verb **vivía** is in the imperfect because it expresses a continuous action in the past ("lived" = "was living").

6. The preterit is used if the action ended in the past:

Cuando mi tío vivía en Puerto Rico, **fue** a Ponce para visitar a un amigo, y **se quedó** por dos días.

When my uncle lived in Puerto Rico, he went to Ponce to visit a friend, and he stayed for two days.

Practice B: Underline the more appropriate verb.

1. What time was it when they came in?

¿Qué hora (fue/era) cuando (entraron/entraban)?

2. My friend's computer was old.

La computadora de mi amiga (fue/era) vieja.

3. When we were in Spain we went to Seville, where we stayed for five days.

Cuando (estuvimos/estábamos) en España (fuimos/íbamos) a Sevilla, donde nos (quedamos/quedábamos) cinco días.

4. It was nine o'clock in the evening and the streets were empty.

(Fueron/Eran) las nueve de la noche y las calles (estuvieron/estaban) vacías.

Verbs With Special Meanings in the Preterit or the Imperfect

Preterit   Imperfect

conocer

Conocí a Pepe en Panamá.   **Conocía** a la mayoría de los invitados.
I *met* (= because acquainted with) Pepe in Panama.   I *knew* most of the guests.

saber

Supe la verdad ayer.   **Sabía** que el cuento era verdadero.
I *learned* (*found out*) the truth yesterday.   I *knew* that the story was true.

tener

Tuve un regalo de mi abuelo.   **Tenía** un regalo para mi prima.
I *got* (*received*) a gift from my grandfather.   I *had* a gift for my cousin.

Note: Care is also needed in choosing between the preterit and the imperfect of **ser, estar, poder,** and **querer.** In some cases, using one tense rather than the other may result in a slight shift in meaning:

Pude llegar a tiempo.   **Podía** llegar a tiempo.
I *managed* to arrive on time.   I *was able* to arrive on time.

When in doubt, it is best to use the imperfect since that tense is most likely to convey the "ordinary" past-tense meanings of these four verbs.

 EJERCICIOS

A. Change the verb from the imperfect to the preterit or vice versa.

EXAMPLE: Yo siempre *comía* a las siete.

Ayer ____*comí*____ a las ocho.

1. Todos los días *estudiábamos* por la tarde.

   Ayer _____ por la noche.

2. ¿Qué *hicieron* Uds. anoche?

   ¿Qué _____ Uds. cuando empezó a llover?

3. Mis parientes de Nevada *vinieron* a visitarnos la semana pasada.

   Mis parientes de Colorado _____ todos los veranos.

4. Mientras yo *andaba* por el parque, encontré a Lola.

   Primero _____ por el parque; luego encontré a Lola.

5. Todos los años *viajábamos* por Europa.

   El año pasado _____ por Sudamérica.

6. Yo *dormí* siete horas anoche.

   Yo _____ ocho horas cuando tenía once años.

7. Esta tarde vi a mi primo y *fui* al cine con él.

   Mientras yo _____ al cine, vi a mi primo.

8. Cuando estaban en Madrid, *visitaban* muchos sitios de interés.

   Cuando estaban en Madrid, _____ el Museo del Prado un domingo por la tarde.

9. Todas las noches *veíamos* los mismos programas en la televisión.

   Anoche _____ un programa excelente.

10. ¿Dónde *viviste* hace cuatro años?

    ¿_____ en Argentina mientras tu padre trabajaba en Buenos Aires?

B. *Instructions:* Here is an account of a teenager's morning from the time he/she got up to the time he/she left the house. For each verb, choose the preterit or the imperfect.

Esta mañana yo _____ a las seis. De repente mi madre me _____
                                    1. (levantarse)   *2. (llamar)*

y me _____ que _____ que pasar al comedor para tomar el
      3. (decir)   *4. (tener)*

desayuno, porque _____ las seis y cuarto ya. Yo _____ en seguida
                 5. (ser)   *6. (bajar)*

y _____ a desayunar. Mientras _____ al comedor, _____
  7. (ir)   *8. (pasar)*   *9. (ver)*

a mi hermano y le _____. Yo _____ que _____
                     10. (saludar)   *11. (saber)*   *12. (ser)*

tarde; por eso _____ muy rápido después del desayuno. _____ de
          13. (vestirse)   *14. (salir)*

casa a las siete y _____ con mi amiga Juana en la esquina.
         15. (encontrarse)

C. *Instructions:* Play the game of "Prosecuting Attorney" with a classmate. You are the prosecuting attorney trying to reconstruct a crime committed near your school. Your classmate must answer each question.

1. ¿Qué tiempo hacía cuando Ud. entró en la escuela esta mañana?

   _____

2. ¿Qué hora era cuando Ud. y sus amigos vinieron a la escuela hoy?

   _____

3. ¿Dónde estaba Ud. ayer por la tarde?

   _____

4. ¿De qué hablaban hoy Ud. y sus amigos mientras venían a la clase de español?

   _____

5. ¿Mientras Ud. llegaba a la escuela esta mañana, vio a algunas personas extrañas?

   _____

D. Express in Spanish:

1. While we were in school, the weather was nice ("good").

    _____

2. What were you (*tú*) doing when we came home?

    _____

3. This morning I left my house, waited for the bus, and went downtown. (to wait for = *esperar*)

    _____

4. While we were going to school, we saw our friends.

    _____

5. It was ten o'clock when they finally arrived.

    _____

6. Yesterday morning we listened to CD's for an hour. (to listen to = *escuchar*)

    _____

7. Then we had ("took") lunch and went downtown.

    _____

8. While they traveled, it snowed a lot.

    _____

9. Did you know that she was my aunt?

    _____

10. She used to dance very well, but one night she fell. (to fall = *caerse*)

    _____

E. *Listening Comprehension.* Your teacher will read to the class ten sentences in Spanish. After each sentence is read to you, circle the letter (*a, b,* or *c*) of the correct English translation.

1. *a.* Where were you when I called?
   b. Where were they when I called?
   c. Where was he when they called?

2. *a.* They used to stay there four hours.
   b. He stayed there four hours.
   c. They stayed there four hours.

3. *a.* It was one o'clock when she came in.
   b. It was one o'clock when they came in.
   c. It was one o'clock when I came in.

4. *a.* He got up, got dressed, and had coffee.
   b. I got up, got dressed, and had coffee.
   c. I was getting up, getting dressed, and having coffee.

5. *a.* While we were walking through the street, Charles saw us.
   b. While we walked through the street, we saw Charles.
   c. While they walked through the street, they saw Charles.

6. *a.* When he studied at the University of California, he took a trip to Mexico.
   b. When they studied at the University of California, they took trips to Mexico.
   c. When I studied at the University of California, I used to take trips to Mexico.

7. *a.* What time was it when they arrived?
   b. What time was it when she arrived?
   c. What time was it when they were arriving?

8. *a.* We always wear gloves when it is cold.
   b. We always wore gloves when it was cold.
   c. She always wore gloves when she was cold.

9. *a.* I did not know the answer to that question.
   b. Didn't you know the answer to that question?
   c. Did you know the answer to that question?

10. *a.* We used to sleep all night.
    b. We slept all night.
    c. They slept all night.

la Costa del Sol, España

10

The Present Perfect and Pluperfect Tenses

A. The Present Perfect (*el Perfecto*)

Hemos caminado cinco kilómetros hoy.	We have walked five kilometers today.
¿**Has comprendido** la lección?	Have you understood the lesson?
Yo no **he dormido** en toda la noche.	I haven't slept all night.

1. The Spanish *perfecto* corresponds to the English present perfect tense.

2. The *perfecto* is translated as shown in the three model sentences above. Other examples:

¿**Han ido?**	Have they gone?
Ella no **ha estudiado.**	She has not studied.
Yo no lo **he visto.**	I have not seen it.

3. The *perfecto* is made up of two elements, the present-tense form of the verb **haber** followed by a past participle:

	caminar, *to walk*	**comer,** *to eat*	**recibir,** *to receive*
	I have walked	*I have eaten*	*I have received*
yo	*he caminado*	*he comido*	*he recibido*
tú	*has caminado*	*has comido*	*has recibido*
Ud. él ella	*ha caminado*	*ha comido*	*ha recibido*
nosotros nosotras	*hemos caminado*	*hemos comido*	*hemos recibido*
vosotros vosotras	*habéis caminado*	*habéis comido*	*habéis recibido*
Uds. ellos ellas	*han caminado*	*han comido*	*han recibido*

4. The present tense of **haber** is conjugated as follows: **he, has, ha, hemos, habéis, han.** These forms cannot stand alone. They must be followed by a past participle.

THE PAST PARTICIPLE

5. Past participles of Spanish verbs are formed by adding the following endings to the stem of the infinitive:

$$-AR \text{ verbs add } \textbf{-ado:} \qquad \textbf{habl}ar \longrightarrow \textbf{habl}\textbf{ado,} \textit{ spoken}$$

$$-ER \text{ and } -IR \text{ verbs add } \textbf{-ido:} \qquad \begin{cases} \textbf{com}er \longrightarrow \textbf{com}\textbf{ido,} \text{ eaten} \\ \textbf{viv}ir \longrightarrow \textbf{viv}\textbf{ido,} \textit{ lived} \end{cases}$$

6. The **-o** ending of the past participle does not change for number or gender when it follows a form of the verb **haber.***

   Practice A: Write the past participle of the verb and give the English equivalent.

   EXAMPLE: Yo he _____*tomado*_____ .   _____*I have taken*_____ .
                              (tomar)

   1. Tú has _____ .   _____
                  (aprender)

   2. Hemos _____ .   _____
               (jugar)

   3. Uds. han _____ .   _____
                  (pedir)

   4. ¿Quién ha _____ ?   _____
                  (salir)

   5. Yo he _____ .   _____
               (comprender)

   6. Habéis _____ .   _____
               (cantar)

USING THE *PERFECTO* IN NEGATIVE STATEMENTS AND QUESTIONS

Roberto ha tomado café.   Roberto has had coffee.
Roberto **no** ha tomado café.   Roberto has not had coffee.
Ellos **han comido** mucho.   They have eaten a lot.
¿Han comido ellos mucho?   Have they eaten a lot?
¿Han comido mucho los muchachos?[†]   Have the boys eaten a lot?

7. To change a statement in the *perfecto* to the negative, place **no** directly before the form of **haber.**

---

*A past participle may function as an adjective often used with the verb **estar,** and therefore must change for gender and number: e.g.,

   La puerta está cerrada.   The door is closed.
   Los libros están vendidos.   The books are sold.

[†]If a question is short and its complete subject is "long," that is, has almost as many syllables as the rest of the sentence, the subject is often placed at the end of the question.

8. To change a statement in the *perfecto* to a question, place the subject after the past participle.

   Note: If no subject noun or pronoun is expressed, the statement is changed to a question by a rising intonation in the voice:

Ha llegado tarde.   He has arrived late.
¿Ha llegado tarde?   Has he arrived late?

   Practice B: Change to (*a*) the negative and (*b*) a question.

EXAMPLE: Ella ha recibido un paquete.
                  a. Ella no ha recibido un paquete.
                  b. ¿Ha recibido ella un paquete?

1. Ellas han usado la computadora.

   a. _____

   b. _____

2. Hemos respondido bien.

   a. _____

   b. _____

3. Mis padres han salido de la casa.

   a. _____

   b. _____

4. Tú has jugado mucho hoy.

   a. _____

   b. _____

5. Los estudiantes han estudiado poco.

   a. _____

   b. _____

IRREGULAR PAST PARTICIPLES

A. Past participles ending in **-ído:**

Infinitive	Past Participle
caer, to fall	*caído,* fallen
creer, to believe	*creído,* believed
leer, to read	*leído,* read
oír, to hear	*oído,* heard
traer, to bring	*traído,* brought

B. Other irregular past participles:

Infinitive	Past Participle
abrir, to open	**abierto,** opened
cubrir, to cover	**cubierto,** covered
decir, to say, tell	**dicho,** said, told
descubrir, to discover	**descubierto,** discovered
escribir, to write	**escrito,** written
hacer, to make, do	**hecho,** made, done
morir, to die	**muerto,** died
poner, to put, place	**puesto,** put, placed
romper, to break	**roto,** broken
ver, to see	**visto,** seen
volver, to return	**vuelto,** returned

Practice C: Complete each sentence with the appropriate form of the verb in the present perfect.

EXAMPLE: Nosotros _____*hemos escrito*_____ las cartas.
                                            (escribir)

1. Ellos no _____ la ciudad.
                          (ver)

2. ¿Qué _____ Ud.?
                (decir)

3. Yo _____ las ventanas.
              (abrir)

4. ¿ _____ tú las cintas?
            (traer)

5. Un actor famoso _____ esta mañana.
                              (morir)

6. Los alumnos _____ a las preguntas del profesor.
                          (contestar)

7. Mi primo y yo _____ temprano.
                            (volver)

8. ¿Qué _____ los chicos?
                (perder)

9. ¿No _____ Ud. esa novela?
                (leer)

10. La clase ya _____.
                          (empezar)

B. The Pluperfect (*el Pluscuamperfecto*)

¿A qué hora **habían salido** ellos?   At what time had they left?
Alberto dijo que **había visto** la película.   Alberto said that he had seen the film.

9. The *pluscuamperfecto* consists of the imperfect tense of **haber** + a past participle: **habían salido, había visto,** etc. This corresponds to the English pluperfect tense: *they had left, I had seen,* etc.

Practice D: Complete the English translations.

1. Hemos hablado con los profesores.

   _____ with the teachers.

2. Creo que han ido al concierto.

   I believe that _____ to the concert.

3. Creíamos que ella había dicho una mentira.

   We believed that she _____ a lie.

4. Era evidente que ellos habían muerto en seguida.

   It was evident that they _____ immediately.

5. ¿Dónde has puesto las revistas?

   Where _____ the magazines?

6. ¿Cuánto tiempo habías pasado en el campo?

   How long _____ in the country?

Practice E: Write the verb in the appropriate form of the *pluscuamperfecto.*

1. Los abuelos _____ la semana pasada.
   (llegar)

2. Yo no _____ el programa esa noche.
   (ver)

3. ¿Quién _____ bien a las preguntas?
   (responder)

4. Juan y yo _____ temprano.
   (volver)

5. Tú no _____ nada en la escuela.
   (hacer)

▲ EJERCICIOS ▲

A. Supply the missing verb, which is the *perfecto* form of the verb used at the beginning of the sentence. (The subjects are the same.)

EXAMPLE: María no habla con Ricardo ahora, pero creo que ____*ha hablado*____ con él esta
        mañana.

1. Los jóvenes no comen mucho en este momento, pero creo que _____
   mucho antes.

2. Esta noche no vemos buenos programas en la televisión, pero es verdad que _____
   buenos programas en otras noches.

3. «¿A qué hora vuelve Juana del baile?» «Yo creo que ella _____ ya.»

4. «¿Qué hace el niño en casa ahora?» «No lo sé, pero dicen que _____
   mucho ruido esta mañana.»

5. Ahora abre las puertas; ya _____ las ventanas.

B. Proceed as in exercise **A,** but this time the missing verb is in the *pluscuamperfecto.*

EXAMPLE: Yo escribí una novela. Ellos dijeron que yo ____*había escrito*____ una buena novela.

1. ¿Qué comió ella en la cena? Dijeron que _____ demasiado.

2. Ellos fueron a Inglaterra. Escribieron que _____ a Inglaterra y a España también.

3. José leyó una revista vieja. Él me dijo que _____ un periódico también.

4. Los chicos rompieron la ventana de la sala. Los padres dijeron que ellos _____ la ventana de la cocina también.

5. Yo no volví a casa temprano. Mi madre le dijo a mi padre que yo no _____ antes de la medianoche.

C. With a classmate, practice asking and answering the following questions.

1. ¿Has descubierto algo interesante en la clase de español?

_____

2. ¿Qué has oído recientemente en la radio?

_____

3. ¿Qué habías hecho antes de venir a la escuela hoy?

_____

4. ¿Ha comprendido la clase todos los verbos?

_____

5. ¿Qué has traído hoy a la escuela?

_____

6. ¿Habías escrito novelas cuando eras muy joven?

_____

7. ¿Qué ha dicho a la clase hoy la profesora (el profesor) de español?

_____

8. ¿Ha roto tu papá todos los platos del desayuno?

_____

9. ¿Habían muerto muchos soldados americanos en la Segunda Guerra Mundial?

_____

10. ¿Dijeron en la radio que había nevado anoche?

_____

D. Give the Spanish equivalent.

1. *a.* We have not gone to the movies. _____

   b. They had not gone to the fair. _____

2. *a.* Have you (*tú*) seen my CD's today? _____

   b. Had you (*Uds.*) seen the game (*el partido*) the other day? _____

   _____

3. *a.* He hasn't read the magazine yet. _____

   b. Lola hadn't read the article yet. _____

4. *a.* Had the authors written more books? _____

   _____

   b. Has the author written another novel? _____

   _____

5. *a.* My father had not sold the car. _____

   b. I haven't sold my bicycle. _____

6. *a.* Where had your cousins worked? _____

   b. Where has your uncle worked? _____

7. *a.* What had the girl seen? _____

   b. What have the men seen? _____

8. *a.* He thinks I have bought the tickets. _____

   _____

   b. I thought he had bought the printer. _____

   _____

9. *a.* She says that the child has spent all the money. _____

   _____

   b. She said that the children had spent ten dollars. _____

   _____

10. *a.* Do you (*tú*) know that we've brought the skates? _____

   _____

   b. Did you (*tú*) know that we had brought the tape recorder? _____

   _____

E. *Listening Comprehension.* Your teacher will read to the class ten sentences in Spanish. After each sentence is read to you, circle the letter (*a, b,* or *c*) of the correct English translation.

1. *a.* What have you done?
   b. What has she done?
   c. What had you done?

2. *a.* I hadn't returned yet.
   b. They hadn't returned yet.
   c. They haven't returned yet.

3. *a.* When had you arrived?
   b. When had they arrived?
   c. When has he arrived?

4. *a.* I have not had good luck.
   b. You have not had good luck.
   c. Hasn't she had good luck?

5. *a.* They had already died.
   b. Have they already died?
   c. Had they already died?

6. *a.* What has fallen?
   b. What had fallen?
   c. What fell?

7. *a.* I had come to see you.
   b. I've come to see you.
   c. We have come to see you.

8. *a.* I had not covered the table.
   b. I have not covered the table.
   c. You haven't covered the table.

9. *a.* We've received the packages.
   b. He had received the packages.
   c. I had received the packages.

10. *a.* They have worked all day.
    b. Had they worked all day?
    c. They had worked all day.

Part 3
Other Verb Forms

><|><|><|><|><|><|><|><|><|><|><|><|><|><|><|><|><|><|><|><|><

11
The Future Tense
and
the Conditional

Helps and Hints
The Spanish future and conditional differ from the English in that they are made up of a single word, rather than the English which uses a helping word: *will* for future, *would* for conditional.

The Future Tense

Mañana yo **iré** al cine.	Tomorrow I will go to the movies.
¿Dónde **estarás** tú más tarde?	Where will you be later?
El verano próximo **viajaremos** por España.	Next summer we will travel through Spain.

1. The future tense is formed with the Spanish infinitive, and is expressed in English by two words: I *will go,* they *will take,* etc.

2. The following phrases are typical of the kinds of expressions often used with the future tense:

más tarde, later
mañana, tomorrow
mañana por la mañana, tomorrow morning
mañana por la tarde, tomorrow afternoon
mañana por la noche {tomorrow evening / tomorrow night

la semana próxima / **la semana que viene** } next week

el mes próximo / **el mes que viene** } next month

el año próximo / **el año que viene** } next year

72

Regular Verbs in the Future Tense

	tomar, *to take*	**prometer,** *to promise*	**escribir,** *to write*
	I will take, etc.	*I will promise,* etc.	*I will write,* etc.
yo	tomar**é**	prometer**é**	escribir**é**
tú	tomar**ás**	prometer**ás**	escribir**ás**
Ud., él, ella	tomar**á**	prometer**á**	escribir**á**
nosotros, nosotras	tomar**emos**	prometer**emos**	escribir**emos**
vosotros, vosotras	tomar**éis**	prometer**éis**	escribir**éis**
Uds., ellos, ellas	tomar**án**	prometer**án**	escribir**án**

3. For all three conjugations, the future tense of regular verbs is formed by adding the following endings to the infinitive: **-é, -ás, -á, -emos, -éis, -án.**

Practice A: Write the indicated form of the verb in the future tense.

EXAMPLE: ellos ___*practicarán*___   ___*volverán*___   ___*permitirán*___
              (practicar)   (volver)   (permitir)

1. yo   _____   _____   _____
              (aprender)   (bailar)   (recibir)

2. tú   _____   _____   _____
              (partir)   (mirar)   (responder)

3. los chicos _____   _____   _____
              (jugar)   (perder)   (subir)

4. Ana y yo no _____   _____   _____
              (comer)   (trabajar)   (vivir)

5. ¿quién . . . ? _____   _____   _____
              (dormir)   (beber)   (cantar)

Practice B: Translate the words in italics into English.

EXAMPLE: ¿A qué hora *llegarán* mañana?   ___*will they arrive*___

1. ¿Cuándo *venderás* tu casa?   _____

2. Yo creo que *ellos recibirán* mucho dinero.   _____

3. *No hablaré* con ese chico.   _____

4. Ellos dicen que *irán* mañana si hace buen tiempo.   _____

5. *Comeremos* en un restaurante esta noche.   _____

Irregular Verbs in the Future Tense

Verbs that are irregular in the future tense are divided into three groups:

GROUP A: The **e** in the infinitive ending **-er** is dropped.

caber to fit	**cabré**	**cabrás**	**cabrá**	**cabremos**	**cabréis**	**cabrán**
haber* to have (helping verb)	**habré**	**habrás**	**habrá**	**habremos**	**habréis**	**habrán**
poder to be able	**podré**	**podrás**	**podrá**	**podremos**	**podréis**	**podrán**
querer to want	**querré**	**querrás**	**querrá**	**querremos**	**querréis**	**querrán**
saber to know	**sabré**	**sabrás**	**sabrá**	**sabremos**	**sabréis**	**sabrán**

GROUP B: The **e** or **i** in the infinitive endings **-er** and **-ir** is changed to **d.**

poner to put	**pondré**	**pondrás**	**pondrá**	**pondremos**	**pondréis**	**pondrán**
salir to leave, go out	**saldré**	**saldrás**	**saldrá**	**saldremos**	**saldréis**	**saldrán**
tener to have	**tendré**	**tendrás**	**tendrá**	**tendremos**	**tendréis**	**tendrán**
valer to be worth, cost	**valdré**	**valdrás**	**valdrá**	**valdremos**	**valdréis**	**valdrán**
venir to come	**vendré**	**vendrás**	**vendrá**	**vendremos**	**vendréis**	**vendrán**

GROUP C: The verbs **decir** (future stem **dir-**) and **hacer** (future stem **har-**).

decir to say, tell	**diré**	**dirás**	**dirá**	**diremos**	**diréis**	**dirán**
hacer to do, make	**haré**	**harás**	**hará**	**haremos**	**haréis**	**harán**

Note: All verbs in the future, whether regular or irregular, take the same endings: **-é, -ás, -á, -emos, -éis, -án.**

---

*These forms of **haber** are used in the future perfect (**habré hablado,** *I will have spoken*), which is not taught in this book. The third person singular, **habrá,** is used as the future tense of **hay.** See Appendix VII.

Practice C: Write the indicated forms of the future tense.

1. nosotros no _____ _____ _____ _____
                            (venir)   (decir)   (saber)   (tener)

2. ellos _____ _____ _____ _____
                       (poner)   (hacer)   (poder)   (querer)

3. yo _____ _____ _____ _____
                      (decir)   (salir)   (caber)   (hacer)

4. ¿quién...? _____ _____ _____ _____
                       (poner)   (saber)   (decir)   (tener)

5. tú _____ _____ _____ _____
                      (querer)   (hacer)   (valer)   (saber)

Practice D: Complete the Spanish translations with the appropriate form of the verb in parentheses.

1. They won't tell the truth. (*decir*)

   No _____ la verdad.

2. I'll put the packages in the car. (*poner*)

   _____ los paquetes en el coche.

3. Some day these paintings will be worth a lot of money. (*valer*)

   Algún día estas pinturas _____ mucho dinero.

4. We will not be able to attend the meeting. (*poder*)

   No _____ asistir a la reunión.

5. Will you (*tú*) come with us? (*venir*)

   ¿_____ con nosotras?

SUPPLEMENT

Using the Present Tense With Future Meaning

In spoken Spanish, the near future is often expressed in the present tense, which is used:

a. Instead of the future tense.

    Te **veo** mañana.   I'll see you tomorrow.
    Dentro de poco **vienen.**   They will come shortly.

b. In the expression **ir a** + *infinitive.*

    Voy a hacerlo más tarde.   I'm going to do it later.
    Van a ver una película esta noche.   They're going to see a movie tonight.

Practice E: You are having a conversation with a friend. Each time you say what you or someone else will do, your friend makes a similar statement in a different way and also changes the italicized words as shown in the example.

EXAMPLE: YOU: Mañana yo compraré _____*una camisa nueva*_____.

               FRIEND: (una gorra nueva) _*y yo voy a comprar una gorra nueva*_

1.   YOU: Esta noche mi familia y yo comeremos en _____*un restaurante mexicano*_____.

      FRIEND: (un café francés)

      _____

2.   YOU: Mi profesor dará _____*un examen*_____ mañana.

      FRIEND: (una fiesta)

      _____

3.   YOU: La semana próxima mis padres saldrán para _____*Costa Rica*_____.

      FRIEND: (Ecuador)

      _____

4.   YOU: Mañana por la noche estudiaré para un examen de _____*historia*_____.

      FRIEND: (inglés)

      _____

5.   YOU: Tú harás algo _____*fantástico*_____ esta tarde.

      FRIEND: (maravilloso)

      _____

The Conditional

Yo **iría** al cine, pero no tengo dinero.	I would go to the movies, but I don't have any money.
¿Dónde **estarías** sin mí?	Where would you be without me?
No **podrían** usar la computadora.	They would not be able to use the computer.

4.   The conditional is formed in the same way as the future tense: by adding the following endings to the infinitive: *-ía, -ías, -ía, -íamos, -íais, -ían.*

5.   The conditional is translated into English by using the helping verb *would:* "I *would go,*" "*would* you speak?," "they *would* not *run,*" etc.

Regular Verbs in the Conditional

	tomar, *to take*	**prometer,** *to promise*	**escribir,** *to write*
	I would take, etc.	*I would promise,* etc.	*I would write,* etc.
yo	tomar*ía*	prometer*ía*	escribir*ía*
tú	tomar*ías*	prometer*ías*	escribir*ías*
Ud., él, ella	tomar*ía*	prometer*ía*	escribir*ía*
nosotros, nosotras	tomar*íamos*	prometer*íamos*	escribir*íamos*
vosotros, vosotras	tomar*íais*	prometer*íais*	escribir*íais*
Uds., ellos, ellas	tomar*ían*	prometer*ían*	escribir*ían*

▰▰ Irregular Verbs in the Conditional

Verbs that have irregular stems in the future tense have the same irregular stems in the conditional.

GROUP A: The **e** in the infinitive ending **-er** is dropped.

caber:	cabría	cabrías	cabría	cabríamos	cabríais	cabrían
haber:	habría	habrías	habría	habríamos	habríais	habrían
poder:	podría	podrías	podría	podríamos	podríais	podrían
querer:	querría	querrías	querría	querríamos	querríais	querrían
saber:	sabría	sabrías	sabría	sabríamos	sabrías	sabrían

GROUP B: The **e** or **i** in the infinitive endings **-er** and **-ir** is changed to **d**.

poner:	pondría	pondrías	pondría	pondríamos	pondríais	pondrían
salir:	saldría	saldrías	saldría	saldríamos	saldríais	saldrían
tener:	tendría	tendrías	tendría	tendríamos	tendríais	tendrían
valer:	valdría	valdrías	valdría	valdríamos	valdríais	valdrían
venir:	vendría	vendrías	vendría	vendríamos	vendríais	vendrían

GROUP C: The verbs **decir** (conditional stem **dir-**) and **hacer** (conditional stem **har-**).

decir:	diría	dirías	diría	diríamos	diríais	dirían
hacer:	haría	harías	haría	haríamos	haríais	harían

Practice F: Write the indicated form of the conditional.

1. la niña   _____   _____   _____   _____
                  (comer)   (venir)   (decir)   (hablar)

2. ¿quiénes . . . ? _____   _____   _____   _____
                       (hacer)   (tener)   (saber)   (dividir)

3. tú y yo   _____   _____   _____   _____
                 (contestar)   (poner)   (poder)   (decir)

4. yo   _____   _____   _____   _____
                  (querer)   (comprar)   (salir)   (hacer)

5. tú   _____   _____   _____   _____
                  (dormir)   (decir)   (saber)   (venir)

Practice G: Translate the italicized words into English.

1. El profesor dijo que *daría* un examen.   _____

2. ¿Qué *usaríamos* para arreglar los patines?   _____

3. *Yo no tomaría* el autobús para llegar allí.   _____

4. ¿Qué *sabrías* de ese juego?   _____

5. *Ella no diría* una mentira.   _____

6. *No haríamos* eso.   _____

7. ¿Qué *podríamos* hacer sin dinero?

▲ EJERCICIOS ▲

A. In each sentence, the verb in italics is used again with a change of subject. Supply the missing verb form in the future.

EXAMPLE: Yo no *haré* el trabajo pero él lo _____*hará*_____.

1. Nosotros *tomaremos* el tren, pero ellos _____ el autobús.

2. Ellos no *podrán* ir a la tienda, pero yo _____ ir.

3. Mi amiga no *aprenderá* los verbos irregulares, pero Uds. los _____.

4. Ud. no *tendrá* el dinero, pero mis padres lo _____.

5. Ella *saldrá* temprano y yo _____ tarde.

6. Yo *venderé* mi bicicleta y mi tío _____ su coche.

7. Yo te *diré* un secreto. ¿Qué me _____ tú?

8. Esta noche *veremos* un buen programa en la televisión. ¿Qué _____ vosotros?

9. María *llegará* a la fiesta a las seis. ¿A qué hora _____ sus amigas?

10. ¿Quién *querrá* acompañarnos al concierto? Nuestros padres _____ acompañarnos.

B. Proceed as in Exercise **A,** but this time supply the *conditional* form of the missing verb.

EXAMPLE: Tú *dirías* la verdad, pero él _____*diría*_____ una mentira.

1. Ella *iría* al centro, pero nosotros no _____.

2. ¿*Escribirían* Uds. las tarjetas, o las _____ José?

3. Ud. no *tendría* el dinero necesario, pero mis padres lo _____.

4. ¿Quiénes *harían* las tareas? Mis tíos las _____.

5. ¿*Trabajarían* los chicos? No, pero yo _____.

6. ¿Dónde *pondrías* los paquetes? Yo los _____ en la mesa.

7. Mi padre *iría* a España, pero mis hermanos _____ a Portugal.

8. Una revista *valdría* tres dólares. ¿Cuánto _____ dos?

9. «¿Qué *serías* sin mí?» «Yo _____ muy feliz.»

10. Nosotros *vendríamos* con Pepe y Lola. ¿Con quiénes _____ Uds.?

C. Without changing the subject, write the appropriate form of the verb in the future tense.

EXAMPLE: Ella dice que _____*hará*_____ el trabajo.
                                    (hacer)

1. Yo digo que _____ el dinero mañana.
                      (tener)

2. ¿Dice él que _____ los discos esta noche?
(traer)

3. Decimos que _____ mañana a las dos de la tarde.
(salir)

4. Los niños dicen que _____ buenos.
(ser)

5. ¿Dices tú que _____ la verdad?
(decir)

6. Yo sé que _____ comprar la cinta.
(querer)

7. Escriben que _____ el viaje el mes próximo.
(hacer)

8. ¿Decís que _____ el dinero en el banco?
(poner)

9. ¿Dice ella que _____ en casa antes de las siete?
(estar)

10. ¿Dice Ud. que no _____ tarde esta noche?
(volver)

D. Without changing the subject, write the appropriate form of the verb in the conditional.

EXAMPLE: Ellos dijeron que _____*vendrían*_____ temprano.
(venir)

1. Julio dijo que _____ con nosotros.
(ir)

2. Pensábamos que _____ el programa.
(ver)

3. ¿Dijiste que _____ para el examen?
(estudiar)

4. Yo le dije que le _____ con su trabajo.
(ayudar)

5. Ellos declararon que _____ ganar el premio.
(querer)

6. Sabíamos que _____ el domingo.
(venir)

7. Escribieron que _____ en Bolivia el mes próximo.
(estar)

8. Ud. dijo que me _____ la verdad.
(decir)

9. Ella le dijo a la profesora que _____ la lección.
(saber)

10. ¿Dijeron ellas que _____ esas cosas?
(hacer)

E. Answer with a complete sentence in Spanish:

1. ¿Qué dirá Ud. mañana a su profesora (profesor) de español?

_____

2. ¿Qué haría Ud. con un millón de dólares?

_____

3. ¿Cuánto valdría una buena bicicleta?

_____

4. ¿Viajará su familia por un país extranjero el año que viene?

_____

5. ¿Cuánto pagarían Uds. por una buena computadora?

_____

6. ¿Cómo llegarán Uds. mañana a la escuela?

_____

7. ¿Quién servirá la comida en su casa esta noche?

_____

8. ¿En qué clase de restaurante le gustaría comer?

_____

9. ¿A qué hora se acostará Ud. el sábado próximo?

_____

10. ¿Se divertirían Uds. en una discoteca?

_____

F. Give the Spanish equivalent.

1. *a.* Where will you go next week? (you = *tú*)

_____

b. Where would you go afterwards? (you = *Uds.*)

_____

2. *a.* She says that she will have the tickets tonight.

_____

b. He said that he would have the money tomorrow afternoon.

_____

3. *a.* I say that I will come to school on time.

_____

b. I said that I would come home early.

_____

4. *a.* What will they do next month?

_____

b. What would you do with all the money? (you = *vosotras*)

_____

5. *a.* Will you be able to go the party? (you = *Uds.*)

_____

b. Would you be able to come to dinner (*a comer*)? (you = *Ud.*)

_____

6. *a.* What will your father say?

_____

b. What would your parents say?

_____

7. *a.* Where will she be tomorrow?

_____

b. Would he be there later?

_____

8. *a.* In five minutes it will be one o'clock.

_____

b. It is five o'clock in New York; what time would it be in Spain?

_____

9. *a.* Where will we stay in Mexico City?

_____

b. Where would I stay in Madrid?

_____

10. *a.* I'll put on a coat if it's cold.

_____

b. He would put on a cap, but he doesn't have it (*no la tiene*).

_____

G. Your friend would like to do what you will do but is unable to. Each time you say what you will do, your friend says that he/she would like to do it too.

EXAMPLE: YOU: Esta noche iré al cine.
            FRIEND: Yo iría también, pero no puedo.

1.   YOU: Más tarde saldré para el centro.

FRIEND: _____

2.   YOU: Esta noche tendré los discos compactos.

FRIEND: _____

3.   YOU: El sábado me quedaré en casa.

FRIEND: _____

4. YOU: La semana próxima venderé mi bicicleta.

FRIEND: _____

5. YOU: Esta tarde escribiré unas cartas.

FRIEND: _____

H. *Listening Comprehension.* Your teacher will read to the class ten statements or questions in Spanish. In each case, circle the letter of the correct translation.

1. *a.* I will not tell the answer.
   b. He will not tell the answer.
   c. I would not tell the answer.

2. *a.* Who will bring the tapes?
   b. Who would bring the tapes?
   c. Who brought the tapes?

3. *a.* Would they like to ski this winter?
   b. Do you like skiing this winter?
   c. Would you like to ski this winter?

4. *a.* I know they will be good friends.
   b. I knew they would be good friends.
   c. I know they were good friends.

5. *a.* How many hours will they work?
   b. How many hours would they work?
   c. How many hours will you work?

6. *a.* I wouldn't play tennis with her.
   b. He won't play tennis with her.
   c. He will not play tennis with her.

7. *a.* Joseph would drive his father's car.
   b. Joseph will drive his father's car.
   c. Will Joseph drive his father's car?

8. *a.* How much would the tickets cost?
   b. How much will the ticket cost?
   c. How much will the tickets cost?

9. *a.* He won't stay home this afternoon.
   b. Would they stay home this afternoon?
   c. Will he stay home this afternoon?

10. *a.* He would wash with cold water.
    b. I'll wash with cold water.
    c. Would you wash with cold water?

Vendedora en Guatemala

12
The Progressive Tenses

Helps and Hints

The Spanish progressive tenses (*to be + ing*) may also be expressed by the simple one-word tense; e.g.,

I am speaking. { *Yo hablo.*
{ *Yo estoy hablando.*

They were eating. { *Ellos comían.*
{ *Ellos estaban comiendo.*

The decision whether to use a simple or progressive tense goes beyond the scope of this book. For your purposes, you may use either one.

Ramón **está hablando.**　　　　Ramón is speaking.
Ramón **estaba hablando.**　　　Ramón *was* speaking.
¿Están comiendo ellos?　　　　Are they eating?
¿Estaban escribiendo las muchachas?　Were the girls writing?

1. The progressive tenses consist of a form of **estar** + *a present participle.*

The Present Participle

hab**lar**　　　　　com**er**　　　　　viv**ir**
habl***ando,*** speaking　　com***iendo,*** eating　　viv***iendo,*** living

2. To form the Spanish present participle, or *gerundio,* drop the infinitive endings and add as follows:

　　　　　　　-AR VERBS　　　　-ER AND -IR VERBS
　　　　　　　Add **-ando.**　　　Add **-iendo.**

3. The Spanish *gerundio* usually has the same meaning as the English present participle, which ends in *-ing.**

---

*The *gerundio* can be used as an adverb meaning *by . . . -ing:*

　Gana su dinero **trabajando** mucho.　　　He earns his money *by working* hard.

　Partiendo temprano llegarás allí antes del anochecer.　*By leaving* early you will get there before nightfall.

　This use of the *gerundio* should not be confused with the use of the English gerund as a verbal noun:

　　　Smoking is bad for the health = **El fumar** es malo para la salud.
　　　Swimming is a good sport = **El nadar** es un buen deporte.

4. In questions, the subject of the verb follows the *gerundio,* except for **Ud.** and **Uds.:**

¿Estaban corriendo **ellos**?	Were they running?
¿Qué está mirando **él**?	What is he looking at?
¿Está estudiando **María**?	Is María studying?

But:

¿Estaba **Ud.** corriendo?	Were you running?
¿Qué están **Uds.** mirando?	What are you looking at?

Practice A: Write the *gerundio* of each verb and translate it into English.

EXAMPLE: beber: *bebiendo, drinking*

1. volver: _____   **4.** hacer: _____

2. recibir: _____   **5.** pensar: _____

3. viajar: _____   **6.** subir: _____

Practice B: Change each sentence to a question.

EXAMPLE: Alberto está cantando.   *¿Está cantando Alberto?*

1. Ellos no estaban trabajando.

_____

3. El chico está jugando.

_____

2. Uds. están comiendo.

_____

4. Ud. estaba escribiendo.

_____

Gerundios With Short Stems

dar	**ser**	**ver**
dando, giving	*siendo,* being	*viendo,* seeing

Irregular Gerundios

A. Ending in **-yendo:**

caer	*cayendo,* falling
construir	*construyendo,* constructing
creer	*creyendo,* believing
ir	*yendo,* going
leer	*leyendo,* reading
oír	*oyendo,* hearing
traer	*trayendo,* bringing

Chapter 12 **85**

B. Others:*

decir	*diciendo,* saying, telling
dormir	*durmiendo,* sleeping
poder	*pudiendo,* being able
venir	*viniendo,* coming

Practice C: Complete each Spanish sentence and its English translation with the appropriate present participles.

EXAMPLE: Están ___*trabajando*___ en la ciudad.   They are ___*working*___ in the city.
                          (trabajar)

1. Estamos _____ la casa.   We are _____ the house.
             (vender)

2. Tú estabas _____ mucho ruido.   You were _____ a lot of
             (hacer)   noise.

3. Estoy _____ una buena novela.   I am _____ a good novel.
          (leer)

4. ¿Qué estaban _____ ellas?   What were they _____?
               (decir)

5. Él está _____ en la sala.   He is _____ in the living
           (dormir)   room.

Note: The present participles of the verb **ir** and **venir** are generally not used with **estar** to form the progressive tenses. The simple (one-word) tenses are used instead.

| ¿Adónde **ibas**? | Where were you going? |
| Mañana **vienen** a casa. | Tomorrow they are coming home. |

Practice D: Translate into Spanish.

1. I am going home.   _____ a casa.
2. I was going to school.   _____ a la escuela.
3. She was coming to the city. _____ a la ciudad.
4. She is coming to our house. _____ a nuestra casa.

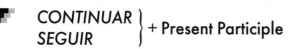

CONTINUAR
SEGUIR } + Present Participle

Siguen durmiendo.   They continue (keep on) sleeping.
¿Continuaba bailando?   Did she continue to dance? (Did she keep on dancing?)

_____

*See page 89.

5. **Continuar** or **seguir** followed by the *gerundio* means *to continue (keep on) doing something.*

   Practice E: Translate the italicized words into English.

   1. *Sigo trabajando* en la fábrica.   _____ in the factory.

   2. ¿Por qué *sigues leyendo* ese libro aburrido?   Why _____ that boring book?

   3. *Continuamos viendo* los mismos programas.   _____ the same programs.

   ## The Relation Between the Simple and Progressive Tenses in English and Spanish

   I buy = yo **compro**   I am buying = $\begin{cases} \text{yo } \textbf{compro} \\ \textbf{estoy comprando} \end{cases}$

   What was she writing? = $\begin{cases} \text{¿Qué } \textbf{escribía} \text{ ella?} \\ \text{¿Qué } \textbf{estaba escribiendo} \text{ ella?} \end{cases}$

6. The English present progressive tense (*I am buying,* etc.) can be expressed in Spanish in two ways:

   a. by using the present tense (yo **compro**).

   b. by using the present progressive (yo **estoy comprando**). This tense consists of the present tense of **estar** + a present participle.

7. The English past progressive tense (*she was writing,* etc.) can be expressed in Spanish in two ways:

   a. by using the imperfect tense (ella **escribía**).

   b. by using the imperfect progressive (ella **estaba escribiendo**). This tense consists of the imperfect tense of **estar** + a present participle.

   Practice F: Express the same thought by using **estar** + a present participle.

   EXAMPLES: Ellas bailan ahora.   *Ellas están bailando ahora.*
              ¿Dormías tranquilamente?   *¿Estabas durmiendo tranquilamente?*

   1. No escriben a sus padres   _____

   2. Tú leías muy bien.   _____

   3. ¿Quién toma agua?   _____

   4. ¿Almuerzan Uds. temprano?   _____

   5. Dábamos un paseo por la playa. _____

◢ EJERCICIOS ◣

A. Each statement is the answer to a question that begins as shown. Write the rest of the question. (Pronouns in parentheses indicate to whom the question is addressed.)

EXAMPLE: Ella estaba patinando sobre el lago.

¿Quién _____*estaba patinando sobre el lago*_____ ?

¿Dónde _____*estaba patinando ella*_____ ?

1. Estamos trayendo las cintas y los discos compactos.

¿Qué _____? (Uds.)

2. Estoy trabajando en casa.

¿Dónde _____ hoy? (tú)

3. Ricardo y María estaban bailando.

¿Quiénes _____?

4. Roberto está durmiendo ahora.

¿Quién _____ ahora?

5. Yo no estaba haciendo nada.

¿Qué _____? (tú)

B. Answer in the corresponding form of the progressive tense. You may use the hints or your own words.

EXAMPLES: ¿Comen Uds. ahora?   ¿Qué decían ellos?
           Sí, estamos comiendo ahora.   *Ellos estaban diciendo una mentira.*

1. ¿Qué escriben ellos a sus padres? (unas cartas)

_____

2. ¿Qué pones en el estante? (tres libros)

_____

3. ¿Qué leía la madre a sus hijos? (cuentos de niños)

_____

4. ¿Cómo cantaban los niños? (horriblemente)

_____

5. ¿Dónde pasa Ud. este verano? (aquí en la ciudad)

_____

C. Express in Spanish in two ways, as shown in the examples.

EXAMPLES: What is he doing now?   *¿Qué hace él ahora?*   *¿Qué está haciendo él ahora?*
They were writing letters.   *Escribían cartas.*   *Estaban escribiendo cartas.*

1. Where were the children sleeping that night?

_____

2. The boys are playing in the pool.

_____

3. What are you bringing to the party?   (you = *Uds.*)

_____

4. Is she using that computer?

_____

5. We're eating at this moment.

_____

6. What was he telling his parents?

¿Qué les ——————————— a sus padres? ¿Qué les ——————————— a sus padres?

7. Were you doing that (*eso*)?   (you = *vosotros*)

_____

8. We were going up the stairs.

_____

9. They're constructing an apartment house.

_____

(Translate the following as shown on page 85.)

10. I continue going to that school.

_____

D. *Listening Comprehension.* Your teacher will read to the class ten questions in Spanish. After each question is read to you, circle the letter of the most appropriate reply.

1. *a.* Estoy mirando las nubes.
   b. Estamos mirando la casa.
   c. Estaba mirando el edificio.

2. *a.* Está comiendo.
   b. Estábamos practicando el español.
   c. Estaba jugando al béisbol.

3. *a.* Vivo en Guatemala.
   b. Estaba viviendo en Chile.
   c. Ud. está viviendo en Segovia.

4. *a.* Estás diciendo eso al profesor.
   b. Estoy diciendo eso a mi tío.
   c. Estaba diciendo eso a mis abuelos.

5. *a.* Sí, sigo estudiando.
   b. No, estamos estudiando francés.
   c. No, siguen trabajando.

6. *a.* Estaba leyendo una novela clásica.
   b. Leen una revista importante.
   c. Está leyendo un artículo interesante.

7. *a.* No, estamos dando una fiesta.
   b. Sí, estoy dando una fiesta grande.
   c. Sí, damos la fiesta en casa de Ramón.

8. *a.* Estoy durmiendo ahora.
   b. No puedo dormir esta noche.
   c. Estamos durmiendo en este momento.

9. *a.* Sí, y pronto podemos ir a esquiar.
   b. Sí, estaba nevando mucho ayer.
   c. No es posible, porque estamos en invierno.

10. *a.* Sí, está lloviendo mucho.
   b. No, la lluvia estaba cayendo.
   c. No, hacía buen tiempo.

 SUPPLEMENT

-IR Verbs That Have a Stem Change in the Present Participle

If an *-IR* verb has a stem change in the third-person forms of the preterit (see page 48), the same change occurs in the present participle. The stem vowel of the infinitive changes as follows:

		Present Participle
1.	**e** becomes **i:**	sentir s*i*ntiendo
		pedir p*i*diendo
2.	**o** becomes **u:**	dormir d*u*rmiendo

Practice G: Complete each sentence with the *gerundio* of the indicated verb.

1. La clase está _____ las frases.
                  (repetir)

2. ¿Estaban _____ los chicos?
              (mentir)

3. Estamos _____ la misma ruta.
             (seguir)

4. ¿Quiénes estaban _____ en esa habitación?
                (dormir)

5. Todo el mundo está _____.
              (reír)

6. Dijeron que el viejo estaba _____.
               (morir)

13
Expressing "To Be" in Spanish: SER and ESTAR; Some Idioms With HACER and TENER

Helps and Hints

To be is expressed in more than one way in Spanish, as will be shown in this chapter.

Some Spanish Equivalents of "To Be"

Mi madre **es** abogada.	My mother *is* a lawyer.
Estoy en casa.	I *am* at home.
Hoy **hace** frío.	Today it *is* cold.
Ella **tiene** hambre.	She *is* hungry.
Trabajan en una fábrica.	They *are* working in a factory.
Hay treinta alumnos en la clase.	There *are* thirty pupils in the class.

1. *To be* is expressed in Spanish by using (1) **ser** or **estar,** (2) the third-person-singular forms of **hacer** in weather expressions, and (3) the verb **tener** in certain idioms. The forms of *to be* used as helping verbs in the English present progressive "disappear" when the tense is expressed by the Spanish simple present (*they are working* = **trabajan**). They also vanish when the English idiom *there is, there are* is expressed as **hay.***

Uses of SER

A. *To Express Identity*

¿Qué **es** eso?	What is that?
Es una casa.	It is a house.
¿Qué **son** ellos?	What are they?
Son mecánicos.	They are mechanics.
¿Quién **es** esa mujer?	Who is that woman?
Es mi madre.	She is my mother.

---

*When *there* means "in that place," *there is* (*are*) is expressed by **allí está(n):**

    There are the books you are looking for.   **Allí están** los libros que buscas.

B. *To Describe a Personal Trait or Physical Characteristic*

¿Cómo **es** su profesora?	How is your teacher? (= What sort of person is she?)
Es muy inteligente.	She is very smart.
Juan **es** alto y fuerte.	Juan is tall and strong.
La ciudad **es** grande y hermosa.	The city is large and beautiful.

C. *To Express Nationality, Religious Affiliation, Place of Origin, Material of Which Something is Made*

¿**Es** Ud. cubano?	Are you Cuban?
No, **soy** puertorriqueño.	No, I am Puerto Rican.
¿**Es** Ud. católica?	Are you (a) Catholic?
No, **soy** protestante.	No, I am (a) Protestant.
¿De dónde **son** Uds.?	Where are you from?
Somos de España.	We are from Spain.
¿De qué **es** su reloj?	What is your watch made of?
Es de oro. No **es** de plata.	It is (made of) gold. It is not silver.

D. *To tell the Time, Date, or Day of the Week (see Appendices III, IV, V, VI)*

¿Qué hora **es**?	What time is it?
Son las siete.	It is seven o'clock.
¿Cuál **es** la fecha?	What is the date?
Es el tres de enero.	It is January 3rd.
¿Qué día **es**?	What day is it?
Es lunes.	It is Monday.

Uses of *ESTAR*

A. *To Express Location or Position*

¿Dónde **están** sus amigos?	Where are your friends?
Están en el banco.	They are in the bank.
¿Dónde **está** San Juan?	Where is San Juan?
Está en Puerto Rico.	It is in Puerto Rico.

B. *To Express a Reversible State That Often Alternates With Its Opposite: Well and Sick, Sad and Happy, Hot and Cold, Seated and Standing, etc.**

¿Cómo **estás**, Juan?	How are you, Juan? (= How do you feel?)
Estoy bien. No **estoy** enfermo.	I am well. I am not sick.
¿**Está** abierta o cerrada la puerta?	Is the door open or closed?
Está cerrada. No **está** abierta.	It is closed. It is not open.
¿**Estás** triste o contenta, Elena?	Are you sad or happy, Elena?
Estoy contenta. No **estoy** triste.	I am happy. I am not sad.

---

*But not such opposites as *rich and poor* or *young and old,* which are not alternating states. Such adjectives are used with **ser.**

C. *As a Helping Verb in the Progressive Tenses* (*see Chapter 12*)

¿Qué **estás** haciendo?	What are you doing?
Estoy comiendo ahora.	I am eating now.
¿**Están** Uds. leyendo una novela?	Are you reading a novel?
No, **estamos** mirando la televisión.	No, we are watching television.

◼◤ Some Comments Concerning *SER* and *ESTAR*

2. Both **ser** and **estar** may be followed by an adjective:*

Ella **es alta.**
Los hombres **están tristes.**

3. Only **ser** may be followed by a noun:

Somos profesoras.
Soy médico.

4. Although they have similar meanings, **feliz** is used with **ser** but **alegre** and **contento** are used with **estar:**

¿**Eres feliz?**
¿**Estás contento?** } Are you happy?

Practice A: Underline the correct verb.

1. Mi tía (es / está) enferma hoy.

2. El señor González (es / está) de Nicaragua.

3. Camarero, la sopa (es / está) fría.

4. Felipe y yo (somos / estamos) buenos amigos.

5. ¿(Son / Están) contentas ellas?

6. Nuestra casa (es / está) de madera.

7. Esas mujeres (son / están) portuguesas.

8. ¿Qué (son / están) Uds. haciendo ahora?

9. ¿Quién (es / está) esa persona?

10. Mi madre (es / está) muy cansada esta noche.

11. ¿Qué (es / está) eso?

12. Hoy (es / está) sábado.

13. ¿Dónde (es / está) él?

14. ¿De dónde (son / están) ellas?

15. Nuestro pueblo (es / está) pequeño.

16. ¿(Es / Está) abierta la ventana?

17. Yo (soy / estoy) el tesorero del club.

18. ¿Quiénes (son / están) esos hombres?

19. Uds. (son / están) hermanos, ¿verdad?

20. ¿Por qué (eres / estás) triste?

◼◤ Idioms With *HACER* and *TENER*

A. Hacer + noun = *to be* + adjective

¿Qué tiempo **hace**?	How is the weather?
Hoy **hace calor.** No **hace frío.**	Today it is warm. It is not cold.

---

*The adjective must agree in gender and number with the noun or pronoun that it modifies. See Chapter 19.

5. The verb **hacer** is used in the third person singular to talk about the weather. (See Appendix VII–B.)

    B. Tener + noun = *to be* + adjective

Tengo frío.	I am cold.
¿Tienes sed?	Are you thirsty?
¿Cuántos años **tiene** ella?	How old is she?
Tiene veinte años.	She is twenty years old.

6. In certain idioms, **tener** is translated as *to be*. (See Appendix VII–A.)

◼◤ The Relation Between the Spanish Present Tense and "To Be" as Helping Verb

Leo una novela.	I *am reading* a novel.
Ellas **van** al cine esta noche.	They *are going* to the movies tonight.
¿**Viene** Ud. a nuestra casa?	*Are* you *coming* to our house?

7. The progressive tenses in English, which take the form *to be . . . -ing,* can be expressed in Spanish in two ways; see page 86. When the English present progressive (for example, I *am reading*) is expressed in Spanish by the present tense, the helping verb *to be* is not translated.

◼◤ The Idiom HAY

Hay algo interesante aquí.	*There is* something interesting here.
¿**Hay** muchas personas allí?	*Are there* many people there?

8. **Hay** means *there is, there are, is there?* and *are there?* (See Appendix VII–C.)

    Practice B: Underline the verb that completes the sentence correctly, that is, the verb corresponding to *am, are, is,* or *there are* in the equivalent English sentence.

  1. Vamos a la playa si (es / está / hace) calor.

  2. ¿(Es / Está / Tiene) interesante su libro?

  3. ¿Dónde (hacen / están / son) los niños?

  4. Esta noche yo (tengo / soy / estoy) sueño.

  5. Luisa no (tiene / es / está) bien esta mañana.

  6. En mi ciudad (hay / son / están) edificios grandes.

  7. El vestido de Isabel (está / tiene / es) de lana.

  8. Los señores López (están / son / tienen) de Venezuela.

  9. Nosotros (somos / estamos / tenemos) alegres porque hoy no hay clases.

  10. ¿Qué hora (es / está / hace) ahora?

▲ EJERCICIOS ▲

A. Supply the missing words in accordance with the change of subject. Be sure to change the agreement of the adjective where necessary.

EXAMPLE: Mi hermana está enferma hoy.

Nosotros ___*estamos enfermos*___ hoy.

1. Mi familia es de Bolivia. Mis tíos _____ de Colombia.

2. ¿Están cerradas las puertas? ¿_____ el edificio?

3. Yo no soy rico. Nuestra familia no _____ tampoco.

4. Su primo es argentino. Mis amigas _____ también.

5. Nuestras clases son grandes. Mi clase de inglés _____ también.

6. ¿Dónde están Uds.? ¿Dónde _____ tú?

7. Tenemos mucho frío. Yo _____ también.

8. Mis primos son jóvenes. Tú _____ también.

9. El reloj es de plata. Los platos _____ de plata también.

10. Las habitaciones son pequeñas. El cuarto no _____.

B. In each pair of sentences, one sentence requires a form of **ser,** the other, a form of **estar.** Complete the sentences with the correct verb forms.

EXAMPLES: Ella ___*es*___ mi amiga.   Hoy no ___*está*___ bien.

Ellos ___*están*___ allí.   ___*Son*___ mis primos.

1. Juan _____ en casa ahora.   Él _____ un buen chico.

2. Mi camisa _____ de algodón.   _____ en la cama.

3. Nosotros _____ enfermos hoy.   _____ amigos.

4. ¿Quién _____ tú?   ¿Dónde _____ tú?

5. ¿_____ Uds. bomberos?   ¿_____ Uds. cansados?

6. Mis padres _____ jóvenes.   _____ en California.

7. Yo _____ triste ahora.   _____ profesor de español.

8. Ellos _____ bien.   _____ de Alemania.

9. Yo _____ feliz.   _____ alegre.

10. ¿Cómo _____ ellas?   ¿_____ ellas bonitas?

C. The editor's word processor has gone haywire due to a computer crash. Rearrange the words to form logical sentences.

1. ¿   está   no   María   escuela   hoy   la   en   por   qué   ?

2. interesantes   de   estos   son   televisión   programas   muy

3. y   son   mis   simpáticos   jóvenes   tíos

4. de   nuestra   es   delgada   profesora   español   y   alta

5. de   sala   las   de   clase   abiertas   están   puertas   la

D. Make each expression a complete sentence by adding a form of *ser* or *estar.*

EXAMPLE: las chicas pobres: *Las chicas son pobres.*

1. la mujer simpática: _____

2. los alumnos mexicanos: _____

3. nuestro vecino inglés: _____

4. mis hermanas altas: _____

5. la comida fría: _____

6. el arquitecto famoso: _____

7. la señora de Cuba: _____

8. los hombres en la calle: _____

9. la gorra de nilón: _____

10. el abuelo enfermo: _____

E. Describe each picture using **ser, estar, tener,** or **hacer.**

EXAMPLE:

La bicicleta está en el sótano.

1.

_____

2.

_____

3.

7.

4.

8.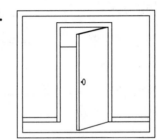

5.

9.

6.

10.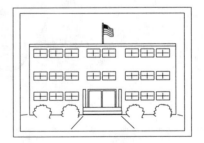

F. *Listening Comprehension.* Your teacher will read to the class ten questions in Spanish. After each question is read, circle the letter of the most appropriate answer.

1. *a.* Está enferma.
   b. Está enfermo.
   c. Es bonita.

2. *a.* Estoy en Chicago.
   b. Son de Los Ángeles.
   c. Soy de Nueva York.

3. *a.* Está en la cama.
   b. Es de nilón.
   c. Somos de Panamá.

4. *a.* Está allí.
   b. Está enfermo.
   c. Es inteligente.

5. *a.* Están muy bien.
   b. Somos felices.
   c. Son muy simpáticos.

6. *a.* No, es abogado.
   b. Sí, está en casa.
   c. No, son arquitectos.

7. *a.* Sí, es un buen hombre.
   b. No, está enfermo hoy.
   c. Sí, estoy en casa.

8. *a.* Tengo un dólar.
   b. Tenemos doce años.
   c. Tengo catorce años.

9. *a.* No, somos jóvenes.
   b. No, son muy jóvenes.
   c. Sí, es muy vieja.

10. *a.* Hace calor.
    b. Son las ocho.
    c. Es jueves.

Cancún, México

14
Uses of the Infinitive

Quiero hablar contigo.	I want to speak with you.
Voy a ver una película.	I'm going to see a film.
Trato de aprender.	I'm trying to learn.
Antes de salir, tomo el desayuno.	Before going out, I have breakfast.

1. In Spanish, an infinitive may follow a conjugated verb directly, a conjugated verb + a preposition, or a preposition by itself.

Some Verbs That Are Followed Directly by an Infinitive

deber, should, ought to, have to, to be supposed to
    Debemos asistir a la reunión.   We have to (are supposed to) attend the meeting.

desear, to wish, want
    Deseamos partir en seguida.   We wish to leave at once.

esperar, to hope
    Esperan llegar a tiempo.   They hope to arrive on time.

pensar, to intend
    Ella **piensa quedarse** en casa.   She intends to stay home.

poder, to be able, can
    No **puedo oír** la música.   I can't (am not able to) hear the music.

preferir, to prefer
    Preferimos comer en casa.   We prefer to eat at home.

querer, to want
    ¿**Quiere** (Ud.) **ver** el menú?   Do you want to see the menu?

saber, to know how
    Él no **sabe manejar.**   He doesn't know how to drive.

Practice A: Answer each question as indicated.

1. ¿Esperas llegar temprano?   Sí, _____.

2. ¿Piensa Ud. viajar este verano?   No, no _____.

3. ¿Quiere José jugar?   No, no _____.

4. ¿Sabes nadar?   Sí, _____.

5. ¿Deben Uds. beber mucha agua?   Sí, _____.

Some Verbs That Require the Preposition A Before an Infinitive

aprender a, to learn to
    ¿**Aprendes a** patinar?   Are you learning to skate?

ayudar a, to help to
    ¿Quién la **ayudó a** levantarse?   Who helped her to get up?

enseñar a, to teach to
    El maestro nos **enseñó a** escribir.   The teacher taught us to write.

comenzar a ⎫
empezar a ⎭ to begin to
    Comienzan a comprender.   They are beginning to understand.
    Empezó a llover.   It began to rain.

invitar a, to invite to
    Invítelos **a** comer con nosotros.   Invite them to eat with us.

ir a, to be going to
    Voy a hablar con ella.   I'm going to speak with her.

venir a, to be coming to
    Venimos a verlo.   We're coming to see it.

salir a, to go (come) out to
    ¿**Sales a** jugar?   Are you coming out to play?

volver a, (to do something) again
    El alumno **volvió a** hacer la tarea.   The student did the homework again.

Practice B: Complete each sentence in Spanish.

1. My brother is learning to skate.   Mi hermano _____ patinar.

2. Are you going to have breakfast now?   ¿_____ desayunar ahora?

3. It is beginning to snow.   _____ nevar.

4. I'm inviting her to go with us.   La _____ ir con nosotros.

5. He is sleeping again.   _____ dormir.

Some Verbs That Require the Preposition *DE* Before an Infinitive

acabar de, to have just
    Acaban de llegar.   They have just arrived.
    Acababan de llegar.   They had just arrived.

acordarse de, to remember
    Se acordaron de ir a la tienda.   They remembered to go the store.

alegrarse de, to be glad
    Me alegro de verte.   I'm glad to see you.

cesar de   to stop (doing something)
dejar de
    Cesaron de comer.   They stopped eating.
    Él nunca **deja de** hablar.   He never stops talking.

olvidarse de, to forget
    Me olvidé de traer el paquete.   I forgot to bring the package.

tratar de, to try
    Trata de acabar sus tareas.   He is trying to finish his homework.

Practice C: Complete each sentence in Spanish.

1. They have just come in.   _____ (entrar)

2. She is glad to do it.   _____ (hacerlo)

3. Stop shouting.   _____ (gritar)

4. We're trying to study.   _____ (estudiar)

5. Is she forgetting to bring the CDs?   _____ (traer los discos compactos)

Infinitives as Objects of Prepositions

Antes de salir, apagamos las luces.   Before going out, we put out the lights.

Al ver el accidente, llamé a la policía.   On seeing the accident, I called the police.

Sin estudiar no se puede aprender.   Without studying you can't learn.

Trabajo **para ganar** dinero.   I work (in order) to earn money.

2. Any verb that follows a preposition must be in the infinitive form. In phrases such as **antes de salir** and **sin estudiar,** the meaning of the infinitive is generally expressed in English by a form that ends in -*ing.* This should not be confused with the Spanish present participle (**hablando, comiendo,** etc.)* when translating the equivalent English phrases into Spanish.

3. Compare the following sentences:

    Buscando su anillo, encontró el reloj que había perdido.   (While) looking for her ring, she found the watch she had lost.

    Al salir del edificio, vimos a nuestros amigos.   (On) leaving the building, we saw our friends.

---

*See page 83.

Practice D: Express in Spanish.

1. Running down the street, he bumped into his friend Carlitos.

_____ por la calle, dio con su amigo Carlitos.

2. Instead of going to the movies, I stayed home.

_____ al cine, me quedé en casa.

3. On arriving home, they turned on the television.

_____ a casa, pusieron la televisión.

4. After closing the door, I turned on my computer.

_____ la puerta, encendí mi computadora.

5. Without eating well, one can't be in good health.

_____ no se puede estar en buena salud.

6. Before skating, put on your helmet.

_____ ponte el casco.

◢ EJERCICIOS ◢

A. Complete the sentences with the correct preposition (**a** or **de**). If the sentence does not require a preposition, do not write one.

1. ¿Qué piensan Uds. _____ hacer hoy?

2. ¿Quién te invitó _____ ir al cine?

3. Volvieron _____ ver el film.

4. Ud. se ha olvidado _____ traer el libro.

5. ¿Prefieren Uds. _____ ver el menú?

6. Ella no sabe _____ hablar inglés.

7. Después _____ llegar, se sentaron a comer.

8. ¿Quieres _____ tomar algo en este café?

9. ¿Cuándo empezaron _____ ganar dinero?

10. Los invitados acaban _____ entrar.

B. Underline the expression in parentheses that could *not* be used to complete the sentence.

1. Mi madre nos (ayuda a, trata de, alegra de) preparar la comida.

2. (Aprendemos a, Esperamos, Venimos a) verlos a Uds. mañana.

3. La clase (empieza a, trata de, enseña a) comprender el concepto.

4. Los niños (invitan a, vuelven a, van a) jugar al béisbol.

5. (Acaban de, Aprenden a, Salen a) salir de la escuela.

C. Write the questions that are answered by the given statements.

    EXAMPLE: Sí, vamos a verla.
                ¿Van Uds. a ver la película?

  1. Sí, me alegro de tener el coche esta noche.

    _____

  2. Lo hacemos antes de salir.

    ¿Cuándo _____ ?

  3. No, no voy a visitar esa ciudad.

    _____

  4. Queremos ir a México.

    ¿Adónde _____ ?

  5. No pensamos viajar porque no tenemos suficiente dinero.

    ¿Por qué _____ ?

D. Express in Spanish:

    1. Are you (tú) going to bring the tapes tonight?

        _____

    2. She has just paid for the dinner. (omit *for*.)

        _____

    3. Is she coming to play in our band?

        _____

    4. Our students are learning to speak Spanish.

        _____

    5. He left without saying good-bye.

        _____

    6. I don't want to hear the news.

        _____

    7. Are you (*Uds.*) glad to be here?

        _____

    8. Stop talking so much. (tú)

        _____

    9. I tried to listen to the program.

        _____

    10. Were they able to go to the concert?

        _____

E. *Listening Comprehension.* Your teacher will read aloud ten questions in Spanish. After each question is read, circle the letter of the most appropriate answer.

1. *a.* No, pero espero aprender algún día.
   b. Sí, me alegro de verte.
   c. No, pero sabemos ir en bicicleta.

2. *a.* Van a ver una película.
   b. Puedo hacerlo muy bien.
   c. Voy a visitar a mi tío.

3. *a.* Sí, pero nos olvidamos de apagar las luces.
   b. Sí, y también volvimos a ver a Rosa.
   c. No, porque debemos llegar temprano.

4. *a.* Acabo de recibir un telegrama.
   b. Llamaré por teléfono a José.
   c. Después de salir, tomaré el autobús.

5. *a.* Dejamos de correr a las siete.
   b. Debo correr rápidamente.
   c. Comenzamos dentro de cinco minutos.

6. *a.* Debo llegar temprano.
   b. Debes pagar el dinero.
   c. Piensas quedarte en casa.

7. *a.* Prefiero tomar el tren.
   b. Van a andar.
   c. Me acordé de tomar el tren.

8. *a.* María cesa de cantar.
   b. Francisco va a venir.
   c. Yo te invito a venir.

9. *a.* Sí, prefiero salir.
   b. No, voy a quedarme aquí.
   c. No, quiero volver a casa.

10. *a.* Quiero ver una película vieja.
    b. Espero tener el disco compacto.
    c. Te invito a mirarla conmigo.

15
The Present Subjunctive

The Subjunctive After Impersonal Expressions and Certain Verbs

Es necesario salir temprano.	It is necessary to leave early.
Es necesario que yo **salga** temprano.	It is necessary for me to leave (that I leave) early.
Ella quiere aprender español.	She wants to learn Spanish.
Ella quiere que tú **aprendas** español.	She wants you to learn Spanish.
Prefiero hablar despacio.	I prefer to speak slowly.
Prefiero que ellos **hablen** despacio.	I prefer that they speak slowly.
Esperamos ir al concierto.	We hope to go to the concert.
Esperamos que Ud. **vaya** al concierto.	We hope that you will go the concert.

1. The subjunctive form of the verb is generally used after:

   a. *impersonal expressions:* **es necesario que, es posible que, es importante que,** etc.

   b. *verbs of wishing, asking, or telling (someone to do something):* **querer, pedir, decir,** etc.

   c. *verbs that express feeling (hoping, fearing, being sorry, etc.):* **esperar*, temer, sentir, alegrarse,** etc.

2. In such cases, the subjunctive can be used only if there is a change of subject:

   Ella quiere que **yo** aprenda.   *She* wants *me* to learn.

   If no change of subject occurs, the infinitive is used: **Ella** quiere **aprender.**

***Esperar** may also be followed by a verb in the indicative: "Esperamos que tú irás al partido de fútbol." "We hope that you will go to the soccer game."

3. A clause that contains a verb in the subjunctive is generally introduced by **que.**

4. A verb in the present subjunctive may have either a present or a future meaning:

Espero que ella tenga el dinero. $\begin{cases} \text{I hope she has the money.*} \\ \text{I hope she will have the money.*} \end{cases}$

Formation of the Present Subjunctive

5. To conjugate a verb in the present subjunctive, use the singular and plural forms of the formal command (see Chapter 4). The **Ud.** form is the same as the first and third person singular; the **Uds.** form is the same as the third person plural. The other three forms of the subjunctive are obtained by adding the endings **-s, -mos,** and **-is** to the **yo** form of the subjunctive. (For stem-changing verbs, see §7, below.) For example:

Formal Command		Present Subjunctive	
poner	**ponga** (Ud.)	**ponga**	**pongamos**
		pongas	**pongáis**
		ponga	**pongan**
tomar	**tome** (Ud.)	**tome**	**tomemos**
		tomes	**toméis**
		tome	**tomen**
pensar	**piense** (Ud.)	**piense**	**pensemos**
		pienses	**penséis**
		piense	**piensen**
volver	**vuelva** (Ud.)	**vuelva**	**volvamos**
		vuelvas	**volváis**
		vuelva	**vuelvan**

6. Note that the present subjunctive forms of verbs with spelling changes are obtained in the same way. (See the Verb Charts in the Appendix.)

EXAMPLES: buscar-busque, etc.; pagar-pague, etc.; rezar-rece, etc.; coger-coja, etc.; erigir-erija, etc.; seguir-siga, etc.; conocer-conozca, etc.; conducir-conduzca, etc.; vencer-venza, etc.; contribuir-contribuya, etc.; enviar-envíe, etc.; continuar-continúe

7. The **nosotros** and **vosotros** subjunctive forms of *stem-changing* verbs are obtained as follows:

---

*Note that the English conjunction *that* is often omitted, but the Spanish equivalent **que** must be used.

(1) *-AR* AND *-ER* VERBS

If the command form has **ie** or **ue** in its stem, the **nosotros** and **vosotros** forms retain the stem vowel of the infinitive:

piense—pensemos, penséis
vuelva—volvamos, volváis

(2) *-IR* VERBS

    a. If the command form has **ie** in its stem, this changes to **i** in the **nosotros** and **vosotros** forms:

(sentir) sienta Ud.   sienta, sientas, sienta, | sintamos, sintáis, | sientan

    b. If the command form has **ue** in its stem, this changes to **u** in the **nosotros** and **vosotros** forms:

(dormir) duerma Ud.   duerma, duermas, duerma, | durmamos, durmáis, | duerman

    c. If **i** is the stem vowel in the command form, it is the stem vowel in all six forms (including those for **nosotros** and **vosotros**):

(pedir) pida (Ud.)   pida, pidas, pida, pidamos, pidáis, pidan
(seguir) siga (Ud.)   siga, sigas, siga, sigamos, sigáis, sigan

8. Verbs that have irregular command forms will have the same irregular forms in the present subjunctive:

dar:	*dé, des, dé, demos, deis, den*
estar:	*esté, estés, esté, estemos, estéis, estén*
ir:	*vaya, vayas, vaya, vayamos, vayáis, vayan*
saber:	*sepa, sepas, sepa, sepamos, sepáis, sepan*
ser:	*sea, seas, sea, seamos, seáis, sean*

Practice A: Write the six forms of the present subjunctive.

EXAMPLE: recibir: *reciba, recibas, reciba, recibamos, recibáis, reciban*

1. necesitar: _____

2. beber: _____

3. escribir: _____

4. hacer: _____

5. ver: _____

6. almorzar: _____

7. perder: _____

8. ser: _____

9. estar: _____

10. decir: _____

11. tocar: _____

12. morir: _____

13. jugar: _____

14. traducir: _____

15. preferir: _____

Practice B: Change the infinitive to the present subjunctive.

EXAMPLE: Queremos bailar esta noche.

Queremos que tú ___*bailes*___ también.

1. Es necesario escribir cartas.

Es necesario que yo _____ una carta.

2. Prefiero comer carne.

Prefiero que Ud. _____ ensalada.

3. Esperan venir esta tarde.

Esperan que nosotras _____ mañana.

4. Temo entrar en esa casa.

Temo que ellos _____ en ese edificio.

5. Es importante empezar ahora.

Es importante que ella _____ en seguida.

Some Impersonal Expressions That Require the Subjunctive in the QUE Clause

es dudoso, it is doubtful
es importante, it is important
es lástima, it is a pity
es posible, it is possible
es imposible, it is impossible
es necesario, it is necessary
es probable, it is probable

Practice C: Supply the subjunctive forms as shown in the example.

EXAMPLE: Es posible que ellos ___*vengan*___ ___*lean*___ ___*hablen*___
(venir)   (leer)   (hablar)

1. Es lástima que tú no _____ _____ _____
(ir)   (escribir)   (volver)

2. Es dudoso que él _____ _____ _____
(contestar)   (almorzar)   (decir)

3. Es probable que nosotros _____ _____ _____
(ser)   (estar)   (saber)

▰▰ Impersonal Expressions That Are Not Used With the Subjunctive*

Es seguro que ellos **vendrán** mañana.   It is certain that they will come tomorrow.
Es verdad que él **tiene** el dinero.   It is true that he has the money.

9.   Impersonal expressions that express certainty are not followed by the subjunctive in the **que** clause.

Practice D: Complete the sentences as shown by the examples in italics.

1.   It's important for you to study (that you study).   *Es importante que tú estudies.*

a.   It's important for you to be here (that you be here).

Es importante que tú _____ aquí.

b.   It's important for you to have (that you have) money.

Es importante que tú _____ dinero.

c.   It's important for you to come on time (that you come on time).

Es importante que tú _____ a tiempo.

2.   It is necessary for me to go.   *Es necesario que yo vaya.*

a.   It is necessary for me to leave.   Es necesario que _____.

b.   It is necessary for me to eat.   Es necesario que _____.

c.   It is necessary for me to run.   Es necesario que _____.

3.   It is certain that they will leave.   *Es seguro que ellos saldrán.*

a.   It is certain that they will take the medicine.

Es seguro que _____ la medicina.

b.   It is certain that they will be doctors.

Es seguro que _____ médicos.

c.   It is certain that they will win.

Es seguro que _____.

4.   It is possible for me to learn that.   *Es posible que yo aprenda eso.*

a.   It is possible for me to be there early.

Es posible que _____ allí temprano.

b.   It is possible for me to buy the books.

Es posible que _____ los libros.

c.   It is possible for me to know the subjunctive.

Es posible que _____ el subjuntivo.

_____

*If these expressions are negative, they require the subjunctive, e.g.,
   No es verdad que él tenga el dinero.

Verbs That Require the Subjunctive in the QUE Clause

A. WISHING

querer, to want   **desear,** to wish   **preferir,** to prefer

Ella **quiere** que yo **vaya** a la fiesta.*   She wants me to go (that I go) to the party.

¿**Prefieres** que ella **se quede** en casa?   Do you prefer that she remain at home?

Practice E: Complete the sentences as shown by the examples in italics.

1. He wants us to leave.   *Quiere que salgamos.*

   a. He wants us to go.   Quiere que _____.

   b. He wants us to come early.   Quiere que _____ temprano.

   c. He wants us to work.   Quiere que _____.

2. He wants me to travel.   *Quiere que yo viaje.*

   a. He wants me to use the computer. Quiere que yo _____.

   b. He wants me to eat.   Quiere que yo _____.

   c. He wants me to get up.   Quiere que yo _____.

3. Do they prefer that we eat less?   *¿Prefieren que comamos menos?*

   a. Do they prefer that we drink more?   ¿Prefieren que _____ más?

   b. Do they prefer that we be there?   ¿Prefieren que _____ allí?

   c. Do they prefer that we stay?   ¿Prefieren que _____?

B. TELLING, ASKING, ORDERING, FORBIDDING, PERMITTING

decir, to tell   **mandar,** to order   **prohibir,** to forbid

pedir, to ask   **permitir,** to permit

Él dice que **yo venga.** } †
Él **me** dice que **venga.** }   He tells me to come.

Pedimos que **ella venga** temprano. }
Le pedimos que **venga** temprano. }   We ask her to come early.

¿Permite Ud. que **ellos fumen?** }
¿**Les** permite Ud. que **fumen?** }   Do you permit them to smoke?

---

*A direct translation from English may produce an erroneous equivalent in Spanish. For example, the equivalent of *she wants me to call* is not **ella me quiere llamar,** which means *she wants to call me,* but **ella quiere que yo llame.**

† The two sentences do not always have the same meaning. In some cases, omitting the object pronoun may require a different translation. **Él dice que yo venga** may mean "He says that I should come," which does not necessarily imply that he says that *to me.* Similarly, the first sentence of the second pair (**Pedimos que. . .**) may mean "We ask that she come early," which leaves it unclear whether we are asking *her* or someone else (perhaps her parents).

10. The verbs **decir, mandar, pedir, permitir,** and **prohibir** may be used with or without object pronouns.* If they are used with object pronouns, the subject pronoun is omitted before the verb in the **que** clause. (The subject pronoun in the **que** clause may be omitted in either case.)

Practice F: Complete the sentences as shown by the examples in italics.

1. They tell us to work.
{ *Dicen que nosotros trabajemos.*
Nos dicen que trabajemos. }

    a. They tell us to study.   Dicen que _____.

                                          _____ dicen que _____.

    b. They tell us to rest.   Dicen que _____.

                                          _____ dicen que _____.

2. She asks them to get up.
{ *Ella pide que ellos se levanten.*
Ella les pide que se levanten. }

    a. She asks them to sit down.   Ella pide que _____.

                                     Ella _____ pide que _____.

    b. She asks them to remain.   Ella pide que _____.

                                     Ella _____ pide que _____.

3. My parents don't permit me to smoke.
{ *Mis padres no permiten que yo fume.*
Mis padres no me permiten que fume. }

    a. My parents do not permit me to eat
        hamburgers.   Mis padres no permiten que _____
                                        hamburguesas.

                                        Mis padres no _____ permiten que
                                        _____ hamburguesas.

    b. My parents do not permit me to go
        out late.   Mis padres no permiten que _____
                                          tarde.

                                        Mis padres no _____ permiten que
                                        _____ tarde.

C. EXPRESSING FEELINGS

    alegrarse de, to be glad   **sentir,** to be sorry   **temer,** to fear

    esperar, to hope   **tener miedo de,** to be afraid of

Practice G: Complete the sentences as shown in the example.

EXAMPLE: I'm sorry to be here.   Siento estar aquí.
         a. I'm sorry that he is here.   *Siento que él esté aquí.*
         b. I'm sorry that he does not have the money. *Siento que él no tenga el dinero.*
         c. I'm sorry that he doesn't know the address. *Siento que él no sepa la dirección.*

1. Are you afraid to cross the street?   ¿Tienes miedo de cruzar la calle?

    a. Are you afraid that I will cross the street?   ¿Tienes miedo de que _____
                                                 la calle?

---

*The verbs **mandar, permitir,** and **prohibir** may also be used with the infinitive, but this usage is beyond the scope of this book; e.g.,
  My parents do not permit me to smoke.   Mis padres no me permiten fumar

b. Are you afraid that I will go home?   ¿Tienes miedo de que _____
   a casa?

c. Are you afraid that I will leave?   ¿Tienes miedo de que _____?

2. We hope to see the film.   Esperamos ver la película.

   a. We hope that you will see the film.   Esperamos que _____ la
      película.

   b. We hope that you will take the money.   Esperamos que _____ el
      dinero.

   c. We hope that you will do the work.   Esperamos que _____ el
      trabajo.

3. I'm glad to be here.   Me alegro de estar aquí.

   a. I'm glad that they are here.   Me alegro de que _____ aquí.

   b. I'm glad that they are speaking.   Me alegro de que _____.

   c. I'm glad that they are returning.   Me alegro de que _____.

D. To Doubt, Deny, Be Uncertain

   dudar, to doubt   **negar (ie),** to deny   **no estar seguro, -a,** not to be sure

   Practice H: Complete the sentences as shown in the example.

EXAMPLE: I doubt that he will listen.   Dudo que él escuche.
           a. I doubt that he will go.   Dudo que él *vaya.*
           b. I doubt that he will come.   Dudo que él *venga*
           c. I doubt that he will arrive on time.   Dudo que él *llegue* a tiempo.

1. She denies that you are smart.   Ella niega que tú seas inteligente.

   a. She denies that you know the truth.   Ella niega que tú _____ la
      verdad.

   b. She denies that you work here.   Ella niega que tú _____ aquí.

   c. She denies that you want money.   Ella niega que tú _____ dinero.

2. We are not sure that they are coming.   No estamos seguros de que vengan.

   a. We are not sure that they are going.   No estamos seguros de que _____.

   b. We are not sure that they speak Spanish. No estamos seguros de que _____
      español.

   c. We are not sure that they hear the music. No estamos seguros de que _____
      la música.

11. Dudar, negar, no estar seguro, -a, and other expressions of doubt or denial require the subjunctive in the **que** clause. When **dudar** and **negar** are used *negatively,* however, they are followed by the indicative since they express certainty. For the same reason, **estar seguro, -a** is also followed by the indicative.

Practice I: Complete the sentences as shown in the examples.

EXAMPLES: I doubt that he will run.   Dudo que él corra.
           I do not doubt that he will run.   No dudo que él *correrá*.
           He does not deny that you have money.   No niega que tú tienes dinero.
           He denies that you have money.   Niega que tú *tengas* dinero.

1. She is not sure that we will eat there.   Ella no está segura de que comamos allí.

    She is sure that we will eat there.   Ella está segura de que _____
                                                  allí.

2. We doubt that the teacher will give the exam.   Dudamos que la profesora dé el examen.

    We do not doubt that the teacher will give the   No dudamos que la profesora
    exam.   _____ el examen.

3. The teacher does not deny that Spanish is   El profesor no niega que el español es
    easy.   fácil.

    The teacher denies that Spanish is easy.   El profesor niega que el español
                                                   _____ fácil.

◤ EJERCICIOS ◢

A. Repeat the sentence orally, replacing the verb in italics with the appropriate form of the verb in
parentheses. (Write the new verb form in the blank at the right.)

EXAMPLE: Quiero que *bailes.* (aprender)
          Quiero que aprendas.   *aprendas*
                                                       _____

1. Dudan que *volvamos* temprano. (regresar)   _____
2. Prefiere que *vengas* a casa. (ir)   _____
3. La profesora nos dice que *leamos* mucho. (estudiar) _____
4. Me alegro de que *sepan* la verdad. (decir)   _____
5. Queremos que ellos *vayan* al cine con nosotras. (andar) _____
6. Es lástima que no *comprendan* a ese hombre. (conocer) _____
7. No están seguros de que *necesitemos* el mapa. (vender) _____
8. Me piden que *entre en* el cuarto. (salir de)   _____
9. El general quiere que los soldados *luchen.* (ser valientes) _____
10. Niego que Pablo *compre* los artículos. (querer) _____

B. You are being interviewed and asked questions about your preferences and opinions. Answer with
a complete sentence in Spanish.

1. ¿Prefiere Ud. que su profesor haga un largo viaje a un país lejano?

_____

2. ¿Quiere Ud. que el día escolar (school) empiece más tarde?

   _____

3. ¿Es necesario que todo el mundo use la computadora?

   _____

4. ¿Es lástima que Uds. tengan que asistir a la escuela?

   _____

5. ¿Teme Ud. que el profesor (la profesora) dé un examen mañana?

   _____

6. Le pide a Ud. su padre que trabaje los sábados y domingos?

   _____

7. ¿Quiere su madre que Ud. vuelva a casa temprano los sábados por la noche?

   _____

8. ¿Niega Ud. que su profesora (profesor) de español sea la mejor profesora (el mejor profesor) de la escuela?

   _____

9. ¿Esperan sus padres que Ud. llegue a ser médico (médica)?

   _____

10. ¿Es importante que nosotros conservemos energía?

    _____

C. Pepe is a very recalcitrant little boy, but his mother wants him to do certain things. Follow the example.

EXAMPLE: PEPE: No quiero bañarme.
             MADRE: Pero yo quiero que tú te bañes.

1. PEPE: No quiero comer mi cereal.
   MADRE: _____.

2. PEPE: No quiero beber leche.
   MADRE: _____.

3. PEPE: No quiero levantarme temprano.
   MADRE: _____.

4. PEPE: No quiero hacer mis tareas.
   MADRE: _____.

5. PEPE: No quiero dormir.
   MADRE: _____.

D. Express in Spanish:

   1. *a.* It is a pity that he does not have a good printer.

_____

      b. It is important for him to have the money.

_____

   2. *a.* Do you (*Ud.*) want to see the program?

_____

      b. Do you want her to see the program?

_____

   3. *a.* He does not doubt that you (*tú*) can do it.

_____

      b. He doubts that they will be able to play soccer tomorrow.

_____

   4. *a.* They are asking him to tape the concert tonight.

_____

      b. They are telling me to serve the salad.

_____

   5. *a.* Is it possible to go to the movies tonight?

_____

      b. It is impossible for them to go to the theater.

_____

   6. *a.* I'm sorry to hear that (*eso*).

_____

      b. I'm sorry that they will not hear the music.

_____

   7. *a.* We hope that you (*Uds.*) will be able to attend the party.

_____

      b. We hope to attend the meeting tomorrow evening.

_____

   8. *a.* I want you (*tú*) to be here this afternoon.

_____

      b. I want to be there later.

_____

   9. *a.* They are afraid that he will tell a lie.

_____

      b. Are they afraid to tell the truth?

_____

10. *a.* It is necessary for me to pay the bill.

_____

    b. It is necessary to pay the bills every month.

_____

E. *Listening Comprehension.* Your teacher will read aloud ten questions in Spanish. After each question is read, circle the letter of the most appropriate answer.

1. *a.* Quiero que digas la verdad.
    b. Quiero que digan algo interesante.
    c. No quieres que diga nada.

2. *a.* Sí, vamos a la playa muy temprano.
    b. No, no es posible, porque me gusta el cine.
    c. No es posible porque tengo que quedarme en casa.

3. *a.* No, dudo que haga buen tiempo.
    b. Sí, creo que hará mal tiempo.
    c. No, quiero que haga mal tiempo.

4. *a.* No, preferimos que te sientes allí.
    b. No, preferimos que se sienten allí.
    c. Sí, prefiero que se siente aquí.

5. *a.* Mando que traiga el mensaje.
    b. Manda que traigamos los billetes.
    c. Manda que traigas los discos compactos.

6. *a.* No, no es necesario visitarla.
    b. No, no es necesario que la visite.
    c. Sí, es necesario que la visites.

7. *a.* No quiero que venga nunca.
    b. Quiero que vengan a las ocho.
    c. Quieres que venga muy temprano.

8. *a.* Sí, pido que contesten.
    b. No, no pedimos que conteste.
    c. No, no pedimos que contesten.

9. *a.* Sí, temo que toquen música clásica.
    b. Sí, temo que toques música popular.
    c. No, no temo que toque música *rock.*

10. *a.* No, no quiero conducir.
    b. No, hay mucho tráfico ahora.
    c. Sí, quiero que conduzcan ahora mismo.

Avenida Nueve de Julio, Buenos Aires, Argentina

16
The Imperfect Subjunctive

Helps and Hints

In this chapter, we will show how the subjunctive is used in past time.

Es posible que **vengan** más tarde.	It is possible that they will come later.
Era posible que **vinieran** (**viniesen**) más tarde.	It was possible that they would come later.
Esperan que **vayas** a casa.	They hope that you will go home.
Esperaron que **fueras** (**fueses**) a casa.	They hoped that you would go home.
Queremos que Uds. **estén** allí temprano.	We want you to be there early.
Queríamos que Uds. **estuvieran** (**estuviesen**) allí temprano.	We wanted you to be there early.

1. The *present* subjunctive is generally used in the **que** clause when the verb in the main clause is in the present or the future tense. The present subjunctive is often translated by the English future tense (*will*).

2. When the verb in the main clause is in a past tense (that is, in the imperfect or the preterit), the *imperfect* subjunctive is used in the **que** clause. The imperfect subjunctive is often translated with the word *would*.

Formation of the Imperfect Subjunctive

3. The imperfect subjunctive is formed from the *third person plural* of the *preterit* tense (see Chapters 6 and 7). Remove the **-ron** ending, add **-ra** or **-se** to the preterit stem, and conjugate as follows:

	Preterit, 3rd Person Plural	Imperfect Subjunctive	
		-ra FORM	**-se** FORM
tomar	**toma**ron	toma*ra*	toma*se*
		toma*ras*	toma*ses*
		toma*ra*	toma*se*
		tomá*ramos*	tomá*semos*
		toma*rais*	toma*seis*
		toma*ran*	toma*sen*

decir	**dij**eron	dije***ra***	dije***se***
		dije***ras***	dije***ses***
		dije***ra***	dije***se***
		dijé***ramos***	dijé***semos***
		dije***rais***	dije***seis***
		dije***ran***	dije***sen***
poner	**pusi**eron	pusie***ra***	pusie***se***
		pusie***ras***	pusie***ses***
		pusie***ra***	pusie***se***
		pusié***ramos***	pusié***semos***
		pusie***rais***	pusie***seis***
		pusie***ran***	pusie***sen***

4. The **-ra** and **-se** forms are usually interchangeable; that is, either form may be used in most cases. (The exceptions are not treated in this book.) However, since the **-ra** form is more commonly used today, we shall use this form for the rest of the chapter.

Practice A: Write the forms of the imperfect subjunctive.

EXAMPLE: hablar: *hablara, hablaras, hablara, habláramos, hablarais, hablaran*

1. escribir: _____

2. andar: _____

3. tener: _____

4. conducir: _____

5. ser: _____

6. querer: _____

7. oír: _____

8. pedir: _____

9. poder: _____

10. estar: _____

Practice B: Using the verb in parentheses, complete the sentence with the form of the imperfect subjunctive.

EXAMPLE: (ir)   Ella quiso que nosotros _____*fuéramos*_____ al cine.

1. (vender)   Era necesario que nosotros _____ la casa.

2. (ser)   Yo dudaba que ella _____ inteligente.

3. (volver)   Pidieron que ellos _____ temprano.

4. (cantar)   Yo no quería que tú _____ solo.

5. (saber)   Era imposible que Uds. _____ la verdad.

6. (dar)   Yo sentí que el profesor _____ el examen.

7. (hacer)   Se alegraron de que yo _____ eso.

8. (tener)   Yo esperaba que vosotras _____ los discos compactos.

9. (poder)   Fue dudoso que ella _____ ir con nosotros.

10. (comer) Era imposible que él _____ tanto.

▲ EJERCICIOS ▲

A. Complete the change in tense by replacing the present subjunctive with the imperfect subjunctive.

EXAMPLE: Quiero que Ud. *conteste.*

Quería que Ud. ___*contestara*___.

1. Siento mucho que no *tengas* el tiempo.

   Sentí mucho que no _____ los documentos.

2. Prefieren que *vayamos* con ellos.

   Preferían que _____ con Uds.

3. Ella pide que tú la *acompañes* a la fiesta.

   Ella pidió que tú la _____ al restaurante.

4. Espero que Uds. no *sufran* mucho.

   Esperaba que Uds. no _____ demasiado.

5. Nos alegramos de que ellos *ganen* el concurso.

   Nos alegrábamos de que ellos _____ la competición.

B. Complete the change in tense by replacing the imperfect subjunctive with the present subjunctive.

EXAMPLE: Prefería que ellos *vinieran* temprano.

Prefiero que ellos ___*vengan*___ antes de las seis.

1. ¿Querías que yo *viera* ese programa?

   ¿Quieres que yo _____ esa película?

2. Dudábamos que *pudieran* jugar al tenis por cuatro horas.

   Dudamos que _____ llegar antes de las siete.

3. Nos dijeron que trajéramos los discos.

   Nos dicen que _____ las cintas.

4. Era dudoso que *robaran* las joyas.

   Es dudoso que _____ los diamantes.

5. Esperábamos que Uds. no lo *hicieran* tan pronto.

   Esperamos que Uds. lo _____ lo más pronto posible.

C. Carlitos and Sarita are arguing over what each other wants or wanted the other one to do. Follow the example and complete the blank spaces.

EXAMPLE: CARLITOS: Yo quiero que tú leas *este libro.*   (otro libro)
              SARITA: Y yo quería que tú leyeras otro libro.

1. CARLITOS: Yo quiero que tú vengas conmigo *al cine.*   (a la fiesta)

   SARITA: _____

2. CARLITOS: Yo quiero que tú traigas *las cintas.*   (los discos compactos)

   SARITA: _____

3. CARLITOS: Yo quiero que tú vayas *a la tienda.*   (al centro comercial)

   SARITA: _____

4. CARLITOS: Yo quiero que tú estés *en mi casa.*   (en casa de Pedro)

   SARITA: _____

5. CARLITOS: Yo quiero que tú comas *una hamburguesa.*   (papas fritas)

   SARITA: _____

D. Express in Spanish.

   1. *a.* It is necessary for them to arrive on time.

   _____

   b. It was necessary for them to arrive early.

   _____

   2. *a.* I doubt that they will go to the shopping center (**centro comercial**).

   _____

   b. I doubted that they would go downtown.

   _____

   3. *a.* I'm afraid he won't have the tickets.

   _____

   b. I was afraid he wouldn't have the videocassette.

   _____

   4. *a.* It is a pity that we won't see that film.

   _____

   b. It was a pity that we did not see that program last night.

   _____

5. *a.* They asked me to write them a letter.

_____

   b. They ask me to write it (*f.*) now.

_____

6. *a.* He doesn't want you (*tú*) to come to the movies.

_____

   b. He wanted you (*Uds.*) to come home.

_____

7. *a.* We were sorry that she wasn't there.

_____

   b. We are sorry that she isn't here.

_____

8. *a.* I told them to bring the CDs.

_____

   b. I will tell them to bring the tapes.

_____

9. *a.* I hope he listens to the rock concert (**concierto de rock**).

_____

   b. I hoped he would listen to the music.

_____

10. *a.* It was doubtful that they heard the news yesterday.

_____

   b. It is doubtful that they will hear the program.

_____

E. *Listening Comprehension.* Your teacher will read aloud ten statements in Spanish. After each statement is read, circle the letter of the most appropriate response.

   1. *a.* Era necesario que yo me quedara en tu casa.
       b. Me gustaban esos programas de televisión.
       c. Pero tenía que volver a casa temprano.

   2. *a.* Es verdad, porque la profesora insistía.
       b. Sí, todos iban a la fiesta.
       c. No, porque ellos vendieron el coche allí.

   3. *a.* Mamá preparaba un plato delicioso.
       b. Íbamos a ver un film interesante.
       c. Me alegraba también, porque ella da muchas tareas.

4. *a.* Buena idea, porque queríamos comer temprano.
   b. Estaba lloviendo toda la noche.
   c. Los partidos siempre son interesantes.

5. *a.* Lo siento mucho; es muy simpático.
   b. Me alegro mucho, porque es muy amable.
   c. Bien, tengo que ir con ella al centro.

6. *a.* Muy bien, papá; tengo que hacer muchas cosas.
   b. Pero yo prefiero salir porque está lloviendo mucho.
   c. Me gusta mucho este teatro.

7. *a.* De acuerdo. Nos encontraremos a las siete.
   b. Gracias, ella se siente mejor ahora.
   c. Gracias, pero no tengo suficiente dinero.

8. *a.* Yo me alegro mucho, porque así cometerá más crímenes.
   b. Todos los profesores de español son criminales.
   c. Es dudoso que lo encuentren, porque nadie puede identificarlo.

9. *a.* Hay que bajar la temperatura en casa durante el invierno.
   b. Bien, vamos a visitarle mañana en la Casa Blanca.
   c. Usaremos los acondicionadores de aire todo el día.

10. *a.* Nos gustaba mucho esa música.
    b. No me interesan esas películas.
    c. El tema era muy interesante.

17
The Imperfect Subjunctive in "If" Clauses

Helps and Hints
Have you ever wished for something you knew was almost impossible to obtain. For example, "If I won the lottery," If I were taller," If the summer lasted the whole year." In this chapter, you will learn how to express these thoughts.

A	B
Si estudias, aprenderás.	Si **estudiaras, aprenderías.**
If you study, you will learn.	If you studied, you would learn.
Viajaremos si tenemos el dinero.	**Viajaríamos** si **tuviéramos** el dinero.
We will travel if we have the money.	We would travel if we had the money.
¿Si Uds. van a España, cuándo partirán?	¿Si Uds. **fueran** a España, cuándo **partirían**?
If you go to Spain, when will you leave?	If you went to Spain, when would you leave?

1. In the sentences of column *A,* we indicate what *will* happen if something else occurs. In the sentences of column *B,* we indicate what *would* happen if something occurred or were to occur (now or in the future).

2. In the sentences of column *A,* the "if" clauses state a condition in the present tense. The verb in the main clause is in the future tense.

3. In the sentences of column *B,* the "if" clauses are of two types:

   a. They state a condition that is contrary to fact or reality. "We would travel if we had the money" implies that *we don't have the money.*

   b. They express a degree of uncertainty. Note the tone of the last sentence ("If you went to Spain, ..."), which sounds as if the speaker were only "supposing."

   In either **3a** or **3b,** the verb in the "if" clause is in the imperfect subjunctive. The verb in the main clause is in the conditional.

   Practice: Complete the Spanish sentences with a verb in the present indicative or the imperfect subjunctive (whichever is appropriate).

1. If I didn't leave now, I would see him.

   Si yo no _____ ahora, lo vería.

2. If he can go, I'll accompany him.

   Si él _____ ir, lo acompañaré.

3. If you went to the party, you would have a good time.

   Si tú _____ a la fiesta, pasarías un buen rato.

4. If I learn the subjunctive, I will be very smart.

   Si _____ el subjuntivo, seré muy inteligente.

5. What would they do if they lost their money?

   ¿Qué harían si _____ su dinero?

◢ EJERCICIOS ◣

A. Answer the following personal questions with a complete sentence in Spanish.

1. ¿Qué harías si ganaras un millón de dólares en la lotería?

   _____

2. ¿Si fueras el profesor (la profesora) de español, darías muchos exámenes?

   _____

3. ¿Si tú pudieras viajar a algún país extranjero, qué país escogerías?

   _____

4. ¿Si fueras la directora (el director) de la escuela, qué cambios efectuarías (bring about)?

   _____

5. ¿Si fueras astronauta, adónde te gustaría ir?

   _____

6. ¿Si vieras a uno de tus profesores en la calle, qué le dirías?

   _____

7. ¿Si la televisión no existiera, qué haría tu familia para divertirse después de la cena?

   _____

8. ¿Si nevara en julio, qué pensarías?

   _____

9. ¿Si tu padre comprara un yate, adónde irían Uds.?

   _____

10. ¿Si tú telefonearas a tu profesora (profesor) de español, qué pensaría ella (él)?

    _____

B. Change the sentence so that the "if" clause expresses a condition requiring the use of the imperfect subjunctive.

EXAMPLE: Si vienes mañana, hablaré contigo.
Si vinieras mañana, hablaría contigo.

1. Si aprenden español, podrán conversar con los españoles.

   _____

2. Si tengo el coche, daré un paseo por la tarde.

   _____

3. ¿Si nieva mañana, iremos a esquiar?

   _____

4. ¿Si leo un buen libro en vez de mirar la televisión, seré más inteligente?

   _____

5. ¿Si no escuchas música *rock,* morirás de aburrimiento?

   _____

C. Exercise in originality. Complete each sentence with an original phrase.

EXAMPLE: Si yo tuviera hambre, ___*comería mucho*___.

1. Si tú estudiaras más, _____.

2. Si _____, ella estaría más contenta.

3. Si fuéramos al concierto, _____.

4. Si _____, mis padres estarían enfadados.

5. Si mi profesor nos diera un examen hoy, _____.

D. Express in Spanish each of the following.

1. If we invited them to the theater, would they come?

   _____

2. If you drove, I would not go with you.

   _____

3. If the teacher gave you a test tomorrow, when would you study?

   _____

4. If I got up late, would I be able to go with them?

   _____

5. If you earned two hundred dollars, would you buy the printer?

_____

6. If we went to the shopping center, what would we buy there?

_____

7. If they brought the CD, would you (*Uds.*) listen to it?

_____

8. If she were to go out now, would you (*Uds.*) follow her?

_____

9. If I bought a computer, would you use it?

_____

10. If they went to a concert, where would they sit ("seat themselves")?

_____

E. *Listening Comprehension.* Your teacher will read aloud ten statements in Spanish. Each statement is a reply to a question. After the statement is read, circle the letter of the question that is being answered.

1. *a.* ¿Cómo se sentirían Uds. si ganaran mucho dinero en la lotería?
   b. ¿Adónde irían Uds. si pudieran viajar?
   c. ¿Qué harían Uds. si tuvieran mucho dinero?

2. *a.* ¿Qué haría Ud. si fuera al cine?
   b. ¿Qué haría Ud. si su profesor (profesora) anunciara que iba a dar un examen difícil?
   c. ¿Cuándo se acostaría Ud. si tuviera sueño?

3. *a.* ¿Si Ud. pudiera aprender una lengua extranjera, cuál preferiría?
   b. ¿Si Ud. pudiera hacer un viaje, qué país visitaría?
   c. ¿Si tú pudieras conducir el coche, adónde irías?

4. *a.* ¿Si Ud. me encontrara en la calle a las tres de la tarde, qué diría?
   b. ¿Si Ud. me llamara por teléfono por la mañana, qué diría?
   c. ¿Si Ud. escribiera al Presidente de los Estados Unidos, cómo empezaría la carta?

5. *a.* ¿Qué estudiarían Uds. si tuvieran un examen difícil?
   b. ¿Qué harían Uds. si no tuvieran dinero?
   c. ¿Qué harían Uds. si sacaran malas notas en todas sus clases?

6. *a.* ¿Saldrían Uds. de casa si su mamá preparara una buena comida?
   b. ¿Qué harían Uds. si alguien gritara «¡Fuego?» en su casa?
   c. ¿Qué dirían Uds. si un buen amigo visitara su casa?

7. *a.* ¿Qué haría Ud. si no tuviera nada de comer en casa?
   b. ¿Adónde iría Ud. para comprar ropa?
   c. ¿A qué hora iría Ud. a la escuela todos los días?

8. *a.* ¿Qué comería Ud. si tuviera hambre?
   b. ¿Qué ocurriría si Ud. saliera para la escuela a las cinco de la mañana?
   c. ¿Por qué iría Ud. a un concierto?

9. *a.* ¿Qué harían Uds. el verano próximo?
   b. ¿Cuándo irán Uds. al campo?
   c. ¿Qué haría el profesor (la profesora) si Uds. no estudiaran?

10. *a.* ¿Adónde irías para nadar?
    b. ¿Cuándo irías a nadar?
    c. ¿Por qué irías a la playa?

La Fortaleza del Viejo San Juan, Puerto Rico.

Part 4
Nouns, Adjectives, and Adverbs

⋊⋉⋊⋉⋊⋉⋊⋉⋊⋉⋊⋉⋊⋉⋊⋉⋊⋉⋊⋉⋊⋉⋊⋉⋊⋉⋊⋉⋊⋉⋊⋉⋊⋉⋊⋉⋊⋉

18
Gender; Nouns and Articles in the Singular and Plural; the Contractions AL and DEL; Using DE to Express Possession

---

Helps and Hints

One of the big differences between English and Spanish is the gender of nouns. In English, if a noun does not refer to a human being or animal, its gender is neuter, e.g., hat, food, happiness, etc. Spanish has no neuter gender. Therefore, a noun, even if it refers to a thing or idea, is either masculine or feminine.

 Gender

Singular	*Plural*

MASCULINE NOUNS DENOTING MALES

el muchacho, the boy	**los muchachos,** the boys
el profesor, the teacher	**los profesores,** the teachers
el hombre, the man	**los hombres,** the men

MASCULINE NOUNS DENOTING CONCEPTS OR INANIMATE OBJECTS

el plato, the dish	**los platos,** the dishes
el baile, the dance	**los bailes,** the dances
el placer, the pleasure	**los placeres,** the pleasures
el derecho, the right (to do something)	**los derechos,** the rights

FEMININE NOUNS DENOTING FEMALES

la **muchacha,** the girl   las **muchachas,** the girls
la **profesora,** the teacher   las **profesoras,** the teachers
la **abuela,** the grandmother   las **abuelas,** the grandmothers
la **madre,** the mother   las **madres,** the mothers

FEMININE NOUNS DENOTING CONCEPTS OR INANIMATE OBJECTS

la **idea,** the idea   las **ideas,** the ideas
la **explicación,** the explanation   las **explicaciones,** the explanations
la **computadora,** the computer   las **computadoras,** the computers
la **frase,** the sentence   las **frases,** the sentences
la **pared,** the wall   las **paredes,** the walls

1. All Spanish nouns are either masculine or feminine.

2. A noun that denotes a male is masculine.

3. A noun that denotes a female is feminine.

4. A noun that denotes an idea, a concept, or an inanimate object may be masculine or feminine.

5. All masculine nouns take the definite articles **el** (*sing.*) and **los** (*pl.*).

6. Most feminine nouns take the definite articles **la** (*sing.*) and **las** (*pl.*).

7. Many masculine nouns end in **-o.**

8. Many feminine nouns end in **-a, -d,** and **-ión.**

MASCULINE PLURAL NOUNS THAT REFER TO A "MIXED" GROUP OF MALES AND FEMALES

los **hermanos,** the brothers, the brother(s) and sister(s)
los **tíos,** the uncles, the aunt(s) and uncle(s)
los **padres,** the fathers, the father and mother, the parents
los **señores Rivera,** Mr. and Mrs. Rivera

Practice A: Express in Spanish:

1. The grandmother and grandfather _____

2. The king and queen _____

3. Her girlfriends and boyfriends _____

4. His father and mother _____

5. The sons and daughters _____

Making Nouns Plural

9. Nouns that end in a vowel add **-s** to form the plural:

el cuaderno, the notebook   **los cuadernos,** the notebooks
el hombre, the man   **los hombres,** the men
la tía, the aunt   **las tías,** the aunts

10. Nouns that end in a consonant add **-es** to form the plural:

la flor, the flower   **las flores,** the flowers
el animal, the animal   **los animales,** the animals
la pared, the wall   **las paredes,** the walls

11. Nouns that end in **-z** change the **-z** to **c** before adding **-es**:

la luz, the light   **las luces,** the lights
el lápiz, the pencil   **los lápices,** the pencils

12. Nouns ending in **-n** or **-s** that have an accent mark on the last syllable drop the accent in the plural:

la lección, the lesson   **las lecciones,** the lessons
el francés, the Frenchman   **los franceses,** the Frenchmen

Exception:

el país, the country   **los países,** the countries

13. If a noun of more than one syllable ends in **-n** and has no accent mark, it takes an accent mark over the stressed vowel in the plural:

la orden, the order   **las órdenes,** the orders
el joven, the young man   **los jóvenes,** the young men, the young people

14. Nouns ending in **-s** in the singular that are stressed on the next-to-last syllable remain the same in the plural:

el **paraguas,** the umbrella   los **paraguas,** the umbrellas
el **lunes,** (on) Monday   los **lunes,** (on) Mondays

Special Cases

MASCULINE NOUNS THAT END IN -a

el* **artista,** the artist   los **artistas,** the artists
el* **atleta,** the athlete   los **atletas,** the athletes
el **clima,** the climate   los **climas,** the climates
el **día,** the day   los **días,** the days
el **drama,** the drama   los **dramas,** the dramas
el **mapa,** the map   los **mapas,** the maps
el **problema,** the problem   los **problemas,** the problems
el **programa,** the program   los **programas,** the programs

FEMININE NOUNS THAT END IN -o

la **foto,** the photograph   las **fotos,** the photographs
la **mano,** the hand   las **manos,** the hands
la **radio,** the radio   (*radio sets* = **los** radios)
(el **radio,** the radio set)

FEMININE NOUNS THAT TAKE el IN THE SINGULAR BECAUSE OF A STRESSED FIRST SYLLABLE BEGINNING WITH a- OR ha-

el **agua,** the water   las **aguas,** the waters
el **alma,** the soul   las **almas,** the souls
el **hacha,** the axe   las **hachas,** the axes
el **hambre,** the hunger   (generally not in the plural)

Practice B: Write the plural forms. (Include the articles.)

1. el primo _____
2. la mujer _____
3. la ciudad _____
4. el cinturón _____
5. la catedral _____
6. el título _____
7. la nación _____
8. la hermana _____
9. la carne _____
10. el examen _____

11. el águila _____
12. el crucigrama _____
13. la amistad _____
14. el jueves _____
15. el interés _____
16. el pez _____
17. el jardín _____
18. la costumbre _____
19. la piel _____
20. el dolor _____

 The Indefinite Articles: *Un, Una, Unos, Unas*

un artículo, an (one) article   **unos** artículos, some articles
una cinta a tape   **unas** cintas, some tapes

---

*When referring to women, these nouns have the feminine forms **la** artista (*pl.,* **las** artistas) and **la** atleta (*pl.,* **las** atletas).

15. The indefinite article (**un, una**) means *a, an, one.* The plural forms (**unos, unas**) mean *some, a few.*

Practice C: Express in Spanish:

1. *a.* an idea _____ **4.** *a.* one park _____

    b. some ideas _____   *b.* some parks _____

2. *a.* a bank _____ **5.** *a.* one page _____

    b. some banks _____   *b.* some pages _____

3. *a.* a favor _____

    b. some favors _____

The Contraction AL

Voy *al* banco.   I'm going to the bank.
Quiero ir *a la* ciudad.   I want to go to the city.
Viajamos *a los* países de Centroamérica.   We're traveling to the countries of Central America.
Me gusta ir *a las* tiendas.   I like to go to the stores.

16. When the preposition **a** precedes **el,** the two words combine to form the word **al.** There are no other contractions with **a.**

Practice D: Write the correct form of the definite article with **a.**

1. ¿Cuándo vas _____ cine?   **4.** ¿Qué traen Uds. _____ clases?

2. Hoy no vamos _____ escuela.   **5.** Quiero ir _____ partido de tenis.

3. Siempre voy _____ conciertos.

The Contraction DEL

Hablo **del** hombre   I am speaking of the man.
    de los chicos.   of the boys.
    de la película.   of the movie.
    de las clases.   of the classes.

17. When the preposition **de** precedes **el,** the two words combine to form the word **del.** There are no other contractions with **de.**

Practice E: Write the correct form of **de** plus the definite article.

1. Mi madre sale _____ cocina.   **4.** ¿Quiénes salen _____ edificios?

2. Mi hermano viene _____ mercado.   **5.** Es el libro _____ profesor.

3. Hablamos _____ chicas.

■■ Using *DE* to Express Possession

¿**De** quién es la casa?	Whose house is it?
Es la casa **de** Juan.	It is Juan's house.
La casa es **de** Juan.	The house is Juan's.
el cuarto **de** María	María's room
la pluma **del** chico	the boy's pen
el maestro **de** los chicos	the boys' teacher
el amigo **de la** tía	the aunt's friend
el amigo **de las** tías	the aunts' friend

18. Possession is expressed in Spanish by **de** or **de** + the definite article. **De** is used before a person's name.

19. In English, the position of the apostrophe—'s or s'—indicates whether the possessor is singular or plural. Note this when translating into Spanish. There is no apostrophe in Spanish.

Practice F: Answer the question in two ways as shown in the example, using the clue in parentheses. Then write the English equivalents.

EXAMPLE: ¿De quién es el libro? (Ana)   *Whose book is it?*
               a. *El libro es de Ana.*   *The book is Ana's.*
               b. *Es el libro de Ana.*   *It is Ana's book.*

1. ¿De quién es el periódico? (la maestra)   _____

     a. _____   _____

     b. _____   _____

2. ¿De quién son los lápices? (el director)   _____

     a. _____   _____

     b. _____   _____

3. ¿De quiénes son las raquetas de tenis? (los jugadores)   _____

     a. _____   _____

     b. _____   _____

4. ¿De quiénes es la casa? (las muchachas)   _____

     a. _____   _____

     b. _____   _____

5. ¿De quién es la pulsera? (María)   _____

   a. _____   _____

   b. _____   _____

Using *DE* to Say What Something Is Made Of

¿**De** qué es el reloj?	What is the watch made of?
El reloj es **de** oro.	The watch is made of gold.
Es un reloj **de** oro.	It is a gold watch.
una gorra **de** lana	a woolen cap
un pastel **de** manzana	an apple pie
la ensalada **de** atún	the tuna fish salad

20. De precedes the noun denoting the material or ingredients of which something is made.

   Practice G: Continue the pattern shown in the first two items.

1. ¿De qué es la camisa? (seda)   *What is the shirt made of?*
   a. La camisa es de seda.   *The shirt is made of silk.*
   b. Es una camisa de seda.   *It is a silk shirt.*

2. ¿De qué es el sandwich? (pollo)   *What is the sandwich made with?*
   a. El sandwich es de pollo.   *The sandwich is (made with) chicken.*
   b. Es un sandwich de pollo.   *It is a chicken sandwich.*

3. ¿De qué es la silla? (madera)   _____

   a. _____   _____

   b. _____   _____

4. De qué es el helado? (vainilla)   _____

   a. _____   _____

   b. _____   _____

5. De qué son los pantalones? (lana)   _____

   a. _____   _____

   b. _____   _____

6. De qué son los zapatos (cuero)   _____

   a. _____   _____

   b. _____   _____

▲ EJERCICIOS ▲

A. Repeat each sentence orally, using the plural forms of the expressions in italics. (Write the plural forms in the blanks.)

1. ¿Qué hacen Uds. *el viernes*? _____

2. Para subir, tenemos que pasar *al ascensor.* _____

3. Voy a cantar *la canción.* _____

4. ¿De qué *país* son ellos? _____

5. Tengo *una pregunta* para ti. _____

6. Hay *un árbol* en *el jardín.* _____

7. En *la exposición* hablamos *al artista.* _____

8. Roberto tiene *un problema.* _____

9. ¿Qué tienen en *la mano*? _____

10. En *el techo* hay *una luz.* _____

11. Hay *un hospital* cerca de *la estación.* _____

12. Hay *un hotel* al lado *del puerto.* _____

13. Después *de la clase* vamos *al cine,* y luego
    a la estación. _____

14. Quiero comprar *un reloj* y *una pulsera.* _____

15. El precio *del diamante* es muy alto. _____

B. Write the opposite gender.

1. una madre _____
2. el hijo _____
3. unos abuelos _____
4. la profesora _____
5. las reinas _____

6. una directora _____
7. los señores _____
8. un nieto _____
9. la hermana _____
10. los artistas _____

C. Form sentences in Spanish according to the pictures.

EXAMPLES:

Son los guantes del niño.

Es la gorra de la mujer.

1. _____

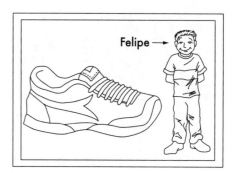

5. _____

2. _____

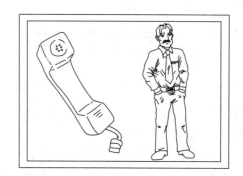

6. _____

3. _____

7 _____

4. _____

8. _____

9. _____   10. _____

D. Form a sentence with each group of words, as shown in the example.

EXAMPLE: mi hermano   dar   los billetes   el cajero
Mi hermano da los billetes al cajero.

1. nosotros   dar   la comida   el perro

_____

2. ellos   escribir   las cartas   las primas

_____

3. mi madre   mandar   el dinero   el banco

_____

4. el chico   prometer   un regalo   la madre

_____

5. yo   prestar   diez dólares   Juan

_____

E. Give the Spanish equivalent.

1. *a.* Henry's school   _____

   b. Mary's class   _____

2. *a.* the boys' team   _____

   b. the girls' club   _____

3. *a.* the woolen socks   _____

   b. the nylon blouse   _____

4. *a.* a fish dinner   _____

   b. the hamburger lunch   _____

5. *a.* the king and queen

_____

   b. the husband and wife

_____

6. *a.* Mr. and Mrs. Rodríguez

_____

   b. the sister and brothers

_____

7. *a.* the general's orders

_____

   b. the young men's rights

_____

8. *a.* some countries of the north

_____

   b. some cities of the south

_____

9. *a.* a tennis racket

_____

   b. the baseball gloves

_____

10. *a.* the leather shoes

_____

    b. the woolen clothing

_____

11. *a.* some motorcycles

_____

    b. a photograph

_____

12. *a.* the iron axes

_____

    b. the steel bridge

_____

13. *a.* some days

_____

    b. some dramas

_____

14. *a.* the ladies' voices

_____

    b. the men's umbrellas

_____

15. *a.* the chocolate ice cream

_____

    b. the strawberry pie

_____

16. *a.* a pearl necklace

_____

    b. a diamond bracelet

_____

17. *a.* the problem of the examinations

_____

    b. the climate of the country

_____

18. *a.* the solutions to the crossword
       puzzles

_____

    b. the route to the sea

_____

19. *a.* the road from the port to the building

    _____

    b. the street from the house to the school

    _____

20. *a.* the map of the cities

    _____

    b. the taste of the water

    _____

La Ciudad de Quito, Ecuador

19

Adjectives: Agreement and Position; Adverbs

Helps and Hints

Spanish and English differ in the number of forms of the adjective. In English, the adjective has only *one* form: big, green, Spanish, intelligent, thin, etc. In Spanish, the adjective has several forms, depending on the gender and number of the noun to which it refers. You will also note the difference in position of the adjective.

Agreement of Adjectives

ADJECTIVES WITH FOUR FORMS

rico:	El comerciante es **rico.**	The merchant is rich.
rica:	La mujer es **rica.**	The woman is rich.
ricos:	Los comerciantes son **ricos.**	The merchants are rich.
ricas:	Las mujeres son **ricas.**	The women are rich.

1. An adjective that ends in **-o** in the masculine singular has four possible endings, depending on the gender and number of the noun it modifies:*

masculine singular . . . . . .**-o**   masculine plural . . . . . .**-os**
feminine singular . . . .**-a**   feminine plural . . . .**-as**

Note: If an adjective modifies two or more nouns of different genders, the masculine plural form is used.

El comerciante y **la mujer** son **ricos.**   The merchant and the woman are rich.
El chico y **la chica** son **buenos.**   The boy and the girl are good.

Practice A: Write the correct form of the adjective.

1. (pequeño)   Las chicas son _____.

2. (alto)   Los edificios son _____.

3. (delgado)   La mujer es muy _____.

4. (rojo)   El sombrero es _____.

5. (amarillo)   Las faldas y los vestidos son _____.

---

*An adjective is said to modify a noun if it describes the person or thing that the noun refers to: the *smart* girl, a *good* idea, the men are *tall,* etc.

ADJECTIVES WITH TWO FORMS

pobre:	El viejo es **pobre.**	The old man is poor.
	La vieja es **pobre.**	The old woman is poor.
pobres:	Los viejos son **pobres.**	The old men are poor.
	Las viejas son **pobres.**	The old women are poor.

2. An adjective that does not end in **-o** in the masculine singular generally has only two forms: singular and plural. The masculine and feminine forms are the same.

   Practice B: Write the correct form of the adjective.

   1. fácil: Los ejercicios no son _____.

   2. grande: Mi casa es muy _____.

   3. inteligente: Las gatas son _____.

   4. popular: José y su hermano son _____.

   5. difícil: El crucigrama no es muy _____.

   6. feliz:*   Los señores Pereda son _____.

Adjectives of Nationality

Juan es mexican**o** pero **María** es cuban**a.**   Juan is Mexican but María is Cuban.

3. Adjectives of nationality that end in **-o** in the masculine singular have the usual four forms: mexican**o, -a, -os, -as,** chilen**o, -a, -os, -as,** etc.

   español—español**a**
   francés—frances**a**

Mi tío es **español;** no es **francés.**	My uncle is Spanish; he is not French.
Mi tía es **española;** no es **francesa.**	My aunt is Spanish; she is not French.

4. If an adjective of nationality ends in a consonant in the masculine singular, add **-a** for the feminine singular. If the masculine singular form has an accent mark on the last vowel, the accent mark is omitted in all other forms.

   español**es**—español**as**
   frances**es**—frances**as**

Mis tíos son español**es;** no son frances**es.**	My uncles (*or* uncle and aunt) are Spanish; they are not French.
Mis tías son español**as;** no son frances**as.**	My aunts are Spanish; they are not French.

---

*As with nouns that end in **-z,** change the **-z** to **-c** before adding **-es.**

5. If an adjective of nationality ends in a consonant in the masculine singular, add **-es** for the masculine plural and **-as** for the feminine plural.* (Remember to omit the accent mark.)

Practice C: Write the correct form of the adjective.

1. (alemán)   La señora Schmidt es _____.

2. (argentino) Mis amigos son _____.

3. (portugués) Mi primo es _____.

4. (inglés)   Las mujeres son _____.

5. (francés)   Los señores Beaumont son _____.

6. (español)   ¿Es _____ su prima?

Position of Adjectives

ADJECTIVES THAT FOLLOW THEIR NOUNS

Leo una **novela interesante.**	I'm reading an interesting novel.
Mi amigo José es un **hombre rico.**	My friend José is a rich man.
Los **libros extranjeros** son caros.	Foreign books are expensive.
Las **comidas españolas** son deliciosas.	Spanish meals are delicious.

6. In Spanish, descriptive adjectives and adjectives of nationality generally follow the nouns they modify. Compare this with English word order: "the *white house*" = la **casa blanca.**

ADJECTIVES THAT PRECEDE THEIR NOUNS

Tengo **tantos libros** interesantes en mi casa.	I have so many interesting books in my house.
Hay **muchas casas** bonitas en mi calle.	There are many pretty houses on my street.
Mi amiga favorita tiene **poco dinero.**	My favorite friend has little money.

7. Adjectives of *quantity, number,* and *amount* generally precede their nouns, as in English.

Practice D: Place the adjective in the correct blank—before or after the noun. Remember to change the form of the adjective when necessary.

EXAMPLE: Aquí hay ___*muchas*___ personas _____.

1. inteligente: Los _____ chicos _____ son mis primos.

2. italiano: Mi _____ amigo _____ se llama Roberto.

****Cortés,** *courteous,* is not an adjective of nationality and therefore does not follow this rule:

Felipe es **cortés.**	Felipe is courteous.
María es **cortés** también.	María is courteous too.

3. cuánto: ¿_____ muchachos _____ hay en la clase?

4. poco: _____ hombres _____ saben la verdad.

5. verde: Quiero comprar las _____ camisas _____.

Adverbs Ending in -*MENTE*

Los niños están alegres y juegan **alegremente.**	The children are happy and play happily.
La lección es fácil y la aprendemos **fácilmente.**	The lesson is easy and we learn it easily.
El alumno atento escucha **atentamente.**	The attentive pupil listens attentively.

8. English can change some adjectives to adverbs by adding the ending -*ly;* soft—soft*ly*, quick—quick*ly,* etc. The Spanish equivalent of -*ly* is **-mente:** alegre—alegre**mente,** correcto—correcta**mente,** etc. The ending is added to the feminine form of the adjective. If the adjective has an accent mark, the accent mark is retained when **-mente** is added.*

Practice E: Complete each sentence by writing the adverbial form of the adjective as shown in the example.

EXAMPLE: Juan es muy rápido y corre *rápidamente.*

1. La gramática no es muy clara, pero la profesora la explica muy _____.

2. Los padres son cariñosos y tratan a sus hijos _____.

3. El alumno es cortés y habla muy _____.

4. Las chicas son inteligentes y hablan muy _____.

5. Las reglas son difíciles y las aprendemos _____.

Note: Some adverbs in Spanish do not end in **-mente:**

bien, well	**despacio,** slowly (synonym of **lentamente**)
mal, badly	**de prisa,** quickly (synonym of **rápidamente**)

▲ EJERCICIOS ▲

A. For each statement the first speaker makes, the second speaker makes a similar statement. Change the form of the adjective (where necessary) to agree with the new subject.

EXAMPLE: Los hombres son ingleses.

   Las mujeres son ____*inglesas*____.

---

*When there is a series of adverbs ending in **-mente,** only the last adverb adds **-mente;** e.g., los alumnos escuchan atenta y alegremente.

1. María es muy *inteligente.*

   Alberto es muy _____.

2. Los edificios no son *altos.*

   La casa no es _____.

3. ¿Es *alemana* su amiga?

   ¿Es _____ su tío?

4. ¿*Cuántos* dólares tienes?

   ¿_____ monedas tienes?

5. Esta lección es muy *difícil.*

   Esos verbos son muy _____.

6. Damos al gato muy *poca* comida.

   Damos a los perros muy _____ huesos.

7. Esa iglesia es muy *antigua.*

   Las casas de Salamanca son muy _____.

8. Estas expresiones son *útiles.*

   Este libro es muy _____.

9. *Todos los* veranos vamos al campo.

   _____ semanas visitamos a nuestros abuelos.

10. Tomás y Elena son *ingleses.*

    Francisca es _____.

B. Rewrite each sentence using an antonym (opposite) of the italicized adjective.

EXAMPLE: Mis amigos son *ricos.*   Mis amigos son pobres.

1. La casa del profesor es *vieja.* _____

2. La biblioteca contiene *muchas* novelas. _____

3. Vivimos en una calle *estrecha.* _____

4. Mi madre siempre lleva vestidos *negros.* _____

5. Tenemos un coche muy *grande.* _____

6. Mis abuelos parecen ser muy *jóvenes.* _____

7. Esas tiendas son muy *feas.* _____

8. Los alumnos de mi clase son *malos.* _____

9. ¿Son *débiles* los chicos? _____

10. Dicen que los elefantes son muy *estúpidos.* _____

C. The authors' word processor has gone haywire. Rearrange the words to form correct sentences.

EXAMPLE: pobres   tienen   las   dinero   poco   personas
Las personas pobres tienen poco dinero.

1. célebres   casas   en   grandes   actores   los   viven

_____

2. españoles   visitan   norteamericanas   niños   ciudades   varias   algunos

_____

3. hermoso   felices   las   alegremente   en   parque   el   chicas   juegan

_____

4. inteligente   la   difíciles   explica   conceptos   claramente   muy   profesora   los

_____

5. muy   programa   miembros   club   presentan   varios   interesante   del   un

_____

D. Answer each of the following personal questions with a complete sentence in Spanish:

1. ¿En su opinión, son inteligentes o estúpidos los gatos?

_____

2. ¿Cuando Ud. saca una nota mala en un examen, están alegres o tristes sus padres?

_____

3. ¿En su opinión, es fácil o difícil el español?

_____

4. ¿Siempre escucha Ud. atentamente a sus profesores, o habla incesantemente con sus compañeros(-as) de clase?

_____

5. ¿De qué color tiene Ud. los ojos?

Tengo _____

E. Express in Spanish:

1. *a.* The sky is blue.   _____

    b. The blue sky is beautiful.   _____

2. *a.* The bicycles are new.   _____

    b. The new bicycles are not cheap. _____

3. *a.* The store is old.   _____

   b. The old store is large.   _____

4. *a.* The soldiers are English.   _____

   b. The English soldiers are not weak.   _____

5. *a.* How many children are there (*hay*)   _____
       in the school?

   b. There are many young students   _____
       (*estudiantes*).

6. *a.* They are very patient.   _____

   b. They wait very patiently.   _____

7. *a.* They listen to popular music.   _____

   b. They listen attentively.   _____

8. *a.* My brother drives very fast.   _____

   b. My mother drives very slowly.   _____

9. *a.* She is a magnificent singer.   _____

   b. She sings magnificently.   _____

10. *a.* The teachers are very good.   _____

   b. They teach very well.   _____

F. *Listening Comprehension.* Your teacher will read aloud a short sentence in Spanish followed by the first two or three words of a second sentence. Underline the pair of words that can be used to complete the second sentence.

EXAMPLE: (Your teacher reads: "María es muy rica. José también...")

   a. <u>es rico</u>   *b.* son ricos   *c.* es rica

1. *a.* es alto   *b.* son altas   *c.* es alta

2. *a.* son estúpidos   *b.* es inteligente   *c.* son inteligentes

3. *a.* está enferma   *b.* está bien   *c.* están enfermas

4. *a.* soy alemana   *b.* somos alemanes   *c.* soy portugués

5. *a.* son jóvenes   *b.* es popular   *c.* son populares

G. *Listening Comprehension.* Your teacher will read aloud a question in Spanish. Underline the most appropriate reply.

EXAMPLE: (Your teacher reads: "¿Cómo es su amiga Juana?")

        a. Es alto y hermoso.
        b. <u>Es rica y bonita.</u>
        c. Son altas y bonitas.

1. *a.* Es viejo y generoso.
    b. Son viejos y generosos.
    c. Es pobre y vieja.

2. *a.* películas interesantes
    b. lecciones fáciles
    c. programas cortos

3. *a.* Es francesa.
    b. Son portugueses.
    c. Soy española.

4. *a.* bueno
    b. perfección
    c. perfectamente

5. *a.* mala
    b. horribles
    c. terrible

20
Adjectives With Shortened Forms

uno, a, an, one	*un* hombre, a man, one man
alguno, some	*algún* hombre, some man
ninguno, no	*ningún* hombre, no man
bueno, good	un *buen* hombre, a good man
malo, bad	un *mal* hombre, a bad man
primero, first	el *primer* hombre, the first man
tercero, third	el *tercer* hombre, the third man

1. The shortened forms of these adjectives are used only before a masculine singular noun. Otherwise they have the same endings as other adjectives whose masculine singular forms end in **-o.** Note that the forms **algún** and **ningún** have an accent mark over the **u.**

Bueno, malo, primero, tercero

un **buen** libro
un libro **bueno** } a good book

el **primer** edificio
el edificio **primero** } the first building

un **mal** chico
un chico **malo** } a bad boy

el **tercer** estudiante
el estudiante **tercero** } the third student

2. These four adjectives may precede or follow their nouns. Note all the forms and positions of **bueno:**

el **buen** profesor   el profesor **bueno**
los **buenos** profesores   los profesores **buenos**
la **buena** profesora   la profesora **buena**
las **buenas** profesoras   las profesoras **buenas**

3. These adjectives are usually placed *after* the noun if they are emphasized:

El **mal** perro nunca obedece a su amo.   The bad dog never obeys his master.

But:

Es un perro **malo;** nunca obedece a su amo.   He is a *bad* dog; he never obeys his master.

Lean Uds. la **tercera lección.**   Read the third lesson.

   But:

Lean Uds. la **lección tercera,** no la primera.   Read the *third* lesson, not the first (one).

   Practice A: Write the correct form of the adjective.

  1. (malo)   Roberto es un _____ jugador de tenis.

  2. (ninguno) No tenemos _____ problema.

  3. (tercero) Mi _____ clase no es interesante.

  4. (primero) Es el _____ concierto del año.

  5. (bueno)   Mi madre prepara _____ comidas.

  6. (uno)   El perro es _____ animal doméstico.

  7. (alguno) _____ juegos son muy interesantes.

  8. (malo)   Son _____ programas.

  9. (tercero) Vamos a ver el _____ partido de tenis.

10. (bueno)   Tú eres un _____ amigo.

11. (alguno) ¿Puede Ud. recomendar _____ plato?

12. (primero) Escriban Uds. el ejercicio _____.

13. (uno)   Ella es _____ persona importante.

14. (bueno)   Hoy hace _____ tiempo.

15. (ninguno) No me gusta _____ revista.

▅◣ Gran, grande

Albert Einstein fue un **gran** científico.   Albert Einstein was a great scientist.

La reina Isabel fue una **gran** mujer.   Queen Elizabeth was a great woman.

Don Quijote y *Oliver Twist* son **grandes** novelas.   *Don Quijote* and *Oliver Twist* are great novels.

Barcelona es una ciudad **grande.**   Barcelona is a big (large) city.

Esos atletas tienen los brazos **grandes.**   Those athletes have large arms.

4. The Spanish word for *great* is **gran** before a noun in the singular, **grandes** before a noun in the plural. These forms are the same for both genders.

5. When **grande** follows its noun, it means *big* or *large*.

   Practice B: Write the appropriate form of the adjective: *gran, grande,* or *grandes.*

1. Los chicos viven en una casa _____.

2. Pablo es un _____ amigo mío.

3. Paca es también mi _____ amiga.

4. Mis hermanos son _____ personas.

5. Ellos tienen coches _____.

San, Santo, Santa

San Felipe, Saint Philip	**Santa** María, Saint Mary
San José, Saint Joseph	**Santa** Ana, Saint Anne

Santo Domingo, Saint Dominick
Santo Tomás, Saint Thomas

6. The title *Saint* is **San** before the names of male saints. The two exceptions are **Santo Domingo** and **Santo Tomás.** The form **Santa** is used before the names of female saints.

Practice C: Write the Spanish word for *Saint* before each name.

1. _____ Juan   4. _____ Domingo

2. _____ Marta   5. _____ Pedro

3. _____ Bárbara

▲ EJERCICIOS ▲

A. Express the italicized words in Spanish. In sentences 1, 2, 3, and 8 express the italicized words in *two* ways.

1. Mr. Smith is a *good teacher.*

   El señor Smith es _____.

2. Pedro and Felipe are *bad players.*

   Pedro y Felipe son _____.

3. Do you have *the first CD?*

   ¿Tienes _____?

4. *a. Some lessons* are very interesting.

   _____ son muy interesantes.

   b. No lesson is interesting.

   _____ es interesante.

5. *a Saint Francis* was very religious.

   _____ era muy religioso.

   b. St. Joseph's Day is March 19.

   El día de _____ es el 19 de marzo.

6. *a.* He is *a great president.*

   Es _____.

   b. Do you live in *a big building?*

   ¿Viven Uds. en _____?

7. *a.* *Some day* they'll arrive early.

   _____ llegarán temprano.

   b. *Some week* we'll go to Puerto Rico.

   _____ iremos a Puerto Rico.

8. *The third building* on the right is my house.

   _____ a la derecha es mi casa.

9. *a.* *No man* is perfect.

   _____ es perfecto.

   b. *No person* can enter.

   _____ puede entrar.

10. *a.* I am spending *one day* in Madrid.

    Paso _____ en Madrid.

    b. They are spending *an afternoon* in Barcelona.

    Pasan _____ en Barcelona.

Guanaco en el Parque Nacional Torres del Paine, Chile

21
Comparison of Adjectives

Helps and Hints

We often compare one item or person with another. For example: "I am tall, my sister is taller than I am, and my father is the tallest in the family." In this chapter, you will learn how to express these and other comparisons.

 Expressing Equality

tan. . .como

Los chicos son altos.	The boys are tall.
Las chicas son altas también.	The girls are tall too.
Los chicos son **tan** altos **como** las chicas.	The boys are as tall as the girls.
Las chicas son **tan** altas **como** los chicos.	The girls are as tall as the boys.

1. **Tan** + *adjective* + **como** means *as. . . as,* and is used like its English equivalent to express equality between persons or things.

   Practice A: Change the two sentences to one sentence expressing an equality.

   EXAMPLE: La profesora es inteligente. Los estudiantes son inteligentes también.

   La profesora es tan inteligente como los estudiantes.

   or

   Los estudiantes son tan inteligentes como la profesora.

   1. Mi tío es viejo. Mi padre es viejo también.

   _____

   2. Esta lección es fácil. La otra lección es fácil también.

   _____

   3. Gilberto es simpático. Rosa es simpática también.

   _____

   Practice B: Express a new equality by reversing the order of comparison. (Watch the adjective agreement)

   EXAMPLE: María es tan rica como Felipe.
   Felipe es tan rico como María.

1. Mi papá es tan inteligente como mi mamá.

   _____

2. Los edificios rojos son tan modernos como las casas nuevas.

   _____

3. Su abuela es tan generosa como su abuelo.

   _____

tanto(-a). . .como*

Tengo **tanto** dinero **como** tú.	I have as much money as you.
Ella recibe **tantas** cartas **como** María.	She receives as many letters as María.

2. To express *as much. . .as* in Spanish, use **tanto(-a)** + *noun* + **como;** to express *as many. . .as,* use **tantos(-as)** + *noun* + **como.**

   Practice C: Write the correct form—*tanto, tanta, tantos,* or *tantas.*

   1. Yo leo _____ libros como Ud.

   2. José no hace _____ trabajo como Enrique.

   3. Pedro bebe _____ leche como su hermana.

   4. Vemos _____ películas como tú.

   5. Tenemos _____ discos compactos como ella.

◼️ Expressing Inequality

THE COMPARATIVE DEGREE

Juan y Ana son altos, pero Juan es **más** alto **que** Ana.	Juan and Ana are tall, but Juan is taller than Ana.
Algunos dicen que los perros son **más** inteligentes **que** los gatos (. . .que los gatos son **menos** inteligentes **que** los perros).	Some say that dogs are more intelligent than cats (. . .that cats are less intelligent than dogs).

3. To express comparison between persons or things, we use **más** + *adjective* + **que** (*more. . . than*) or **menos** + *adjective* + **que** (*less. . .than*).

4. In English, many inequalities are expressed by attaching the suffix *-er* to an adjective: small—smaller, tall—taller, warm—warmer, etc. In Spanish, *smaller* becomes "more small," *taller* becomes "more tall," etc.

   Practice D: Change each sentence as shown in the example.

---

*Although this expression is used in comparing *nouns,* it is included in this chapter because of its similarity to **tan. . .como.**

EXAMPLE: Los niños y las niñas son altos.
           Los niños son más altos que las niñas.

1. Paco y Carlos son bajos.   _____

2. Mi casa y su casa son grandes.   _____

3. Ramón y yo estamos tristes.   _____

4. Mi madre y mi tía son bonitas.   _____

5. Mi padre y mi hermano están   _____
    cansados.

COMPARISON OF NUMBER OR QUANTITY

Tengo **más** libros **que** tú.	I have more books than you.
Tengo **más de** seis libros.	I have more than six books.
Hay **menos** alumnos en esta clase **que** en esa clase.	There are fewer pupils in this class than in that class.
Hay **menos de** veinte alumnos en esta clase.	There are fewer than twenty pupils in this class.

5. The words **más** and **menos** may precede *nouns* as well as adjectives. Before a number, Spanish uses **de** rather than **que** for English *than*.

Practice E: Complete the sentence with *que* or *de*.

1. Enrique tiene más _____ cuatro televisores en su casa.

2. Yo tengo más dinero _____ mi amiga Elena.

3. Hay menos _____ diez miembros en este club.

4. Mi prima me manda más cartas _____ mi primo.

5. Tú eres menos fuerte _____ yo.

THE SUPERLATIVE DEGREE

¿Quién es **el alumno más alto de** la clase?	Who is the tallest pupil in the class?
Dolores es **la más alta de** la clase.	Dolores is the tallest in the class.
¿Cuál es la cinta **mas popular de** la colección?	Which is the most popular tape in the collection?
Esta cinta es **la más popular de** la colección.	This tape is the most popular in the collection.

6. The superlative degree (English *the...-est* or *the most...*) is expressed in Spanish by **el (la, los, las) más. . . .** The definite article agrees with its noun in gender and number even if the noun is not expressed: "es **la** más al**ta** de la clase," *she is the tallest in the class* (the noun **alumna** or **chica** is understood).

7. Note how the superlative degree is expressed when a noun is used: *the richest man* becomes "the man most rich" (**el hombre más rico**); *the smartest woman* becomes "the woman most smart" (**la mujer más inteligente**).

8. After a superlative, the word *in* is expressed by **de** in Spanish:

el cuarto más pequeño **de** la casa   the smallest room *in* the house

Practice F: Complete the Spanish expressions.

EXAMPLE: the largest book in the library

el libro _____*más grande de la*_____ biblioteca

1. the smallest computer in the office

la computadora _____ oficina

2. the most difficult lessons in the book

las lecciones _____ libro

3. the most interesting story in the magazine.

el cuento _____ la revista

4. the strongest athlete in the school

el atleta _____ escuela

5. the least tall boy in the group (least = *menos*)

el muchacho _____ grupo

Special Adjectives of Comparison

Paco, Ana y Felipe son tres jugadores de béisbol.	Paco, Ana, and Felipe are three baseball players.
Paco es muy bueno.	Paco is very good
Ana es **mejor que** Paco.	Ana is better than Paco.
Felipe es **el mejor del** grupo.	Felipe is the best in the group.

9. **Mejor** (*pl.,* **mejores**), *better, best,* is one of four adjectives that do not use **más.** (Compare English *good, better, best.*) The following adjectives have irregular comparative forms:

bueno, -a buenos, -as } good	mejor mejores } better	el (la) mejor los (las) mejores } the best
malo, -a malos, -as } bad	peor peores } worse	el (la) peor los (las) peores } the worst

joven **jóvenes** } young	**menor** **menores** } younger*	**el (la) menor** **los (las) menores** } the youngest*

viejo, -a **viejos, -as** } old	**mayor** **mayores** } older*	**el (la) mayor)** **los (las) mayores** } the oldest*

Practice G: Supply the correct form of the comparative or superlative.

EXAMPLE: Yo soy malo, pero ellos son ____*peores*____ que yo.

1. María es muy buena, pero Luis es _____ que ella.

2. Juanita y Roberto son malos, pero Rosa y Alberto son _____ _____ de la clase.

3. Mi hermana tiene quince años. Yo tengo trece años. Yo soy _____ que mi hermana.

4. Mi padre tiene cuarenta y seis años. Mi madre tiene cuarenta y cuatro años. Mi abuelo tiene setenta y mi abuela tiene sesenta siete. Mis abuelos son _____ _____ de la familia.

Summary

A. EXPRESSING EQUALITY: **tan. . .como; tanto(-a). . .como**

María y Juana son **tan** ricas **como** Antonio.   María and Juana are as rich as Antonio.
Tengo **tantas** revistas **como** ellos.   I have as many magazines as they (do).

B. EXPRESSING INEQUALITY

(1) *Comparative Degree:* **más. . .que** or **menos. . .que**

Ellos son **más** pobres **que** nosotros.   They are poorer than we (are).
Esta botella contiene **menos** leche **que** ésa.   This bottle contains less milk than that one.

(2) *Superlative Degree:* $\left.\begin{array}{l}\textbf{el}\\\textbf{la}\\\textbf{los}\\\textbf{las}\end{array}\right\}$ **más (menos). . .de**

la muchacha **más** inteligente **de** la clase   the smartest girl in the class

C. IRREGULAR FORMS

The adjectives **bueno(-a), malo(-a),** and **joven** have irregular comparative forms: **mejor (peor) que,** *better (worse) than;* **mayor (menor) que,** *older (younger) than.* These have the superlative forms **el (la) mejor,** *the best,* **el (la) mayor,** *the oldest,* etc.

---

*These may also be expressed by the regular forms:

younger	{ **más joven** { **más jóvenes**	youngest	{ **el (la) más joven** { **los (las) más jóvenes**
older	{ **más viejo, -a** { **más viejos, -as**	oldest	{ **el (la) más viejo(-a)** { **los (las) más viejos(-as)**

EJERCICIOS

A. Express the same idea by starting the sentence with the words in italics.

EXAMPLES: Mi padre es mayor que *mi madre.*
Mi madre es menor que mi padre.

Los leones son más feroces que *los tigres.*
Los tigres son menos feroces que los leones.

1. Yo tengo menos dinero que *mis amigos.*

_____

2. El calor es peor que *el frío.*

_____

3. ¿Es Juana más inteligente que *Dorotea?*

¿Es _____

4. Los diamantes son más caros que *las perlas.*

_____

5. Estos discos compactos son mejores que *esa cinta.*

_____

B. Begin the sentence with the words in italics, using an adjective of opposite meaning.

EXAMPLE: El perro es más débil que *el lobo.*
El lobo es más fuerte que el perro.

1. Mi casa es más pequeña que *su casa.*

_____

2. El señor López es más rico que *la señora González.*

_____

3. Ella tiene más amigos que *nosotros.*

_____

4. Tu escuela es más antigua que *mi casa.*

_____

5. Marta está más triste que *Guillermo.*

C. Answer the following personal questions with a complete sentence in Spanish:

1. En su opinión, ¿es el español tan importante como el inglés?

_____

2. ¿Quién es el (la) estudiante más alto (alta) de la clase?

_____

3. ¿Es Ud. mayor que su padre?

_____

4. ¿Quién es su mejor amigo (amiga)?

_____

5. ¿Es su clase de español la más interesante de la escuela?

_____

6. ¿Quién es el menor (la menor) de su familia?

_____

7. ¿Es su abuela más alta que Ud.?

_____

8. ¿Es su profesor (profesora) más inteligente que Ud.?

_____

9. ¿Ve Ud. tantos programas de televisión como su hermano (hermana)?

_____

10. ¿En su opinión, quién fue el peor presidente de los Estados Unidos? ¿Y quién fue el mejor?

_____

D. Describe each picture as in the example.

EXAMPLE:

La chica es ____*es más alta que*____ el chico.

1. Juanito es _____ Sarita.   2. El mendigo es _____ el rico.

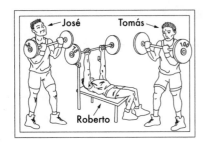

3. Tomás _____ los tres.

4. Una casa _____ la otra casa.

5. Pedro es _____ Pablo.

E. Express in Spanish as shown by the examples in italics:

1. I am as tall as you. *Yo soy tan alto como Ud.*

   a. I am as intelligent as you.   _____

   b. She is as lazy as he.   _____

   c. They are as bad as she.   _____

2. Is he lazier than his brother? *¿Es él más perezoso que su hermano?*

   a. Is he smarter than his sister?   _____

   b. Are you younger than your cousin?   _____
      (two ways)

   c. Are we better than the teacher?   _____

3. Juana is the prettiest girl in the class. *Juana es la muchacha más bonita de la clase.*

   a. It is the largest school in the
      neighborhood.   _____

   b. They are the tallest boys in the club.   _____

   c. He is the richest man in the city.   _____

4. Ana is the smartest in the class. *Ana es la más inteligente de la clase.*

   a. Louise is the tallest in the family.   _____

   b. I am the oldest in the group.   _____

   c. They are the most studious in
      the class.   _____

5. *a.* Mary is richer than Louis.   _____

    b. Charles is the richest in the group.   _____

    c. She has more than ten dollars.   _____

F. *Listening Comprehension.* Your teacher will read to the class ten statements in Spanish. In each case, circle the letter of the statement that is logically consistent or has the same meaning.

1. *a.* Yo tengo veinte años y Ud. tiene dieciocho años.
    b. Yo tengo dieciocho años y Ud. tiene veinte años.
    c. Tengo más años que Ud.

2. *a.* Él tiene ocho libros y ella tiene nueve.
    b. Ella tiene diez libros y él tiene diez también.
    c. Ella tiene más de ocho libros y él tiene menos de ocho.

3. *a.* Hay veinte chicas y diecisiete chicos.
    b. Hay veintidós chicas y veinte chicos.
    c. Hay cincuenta y cinco alumnos.

4. *a.* Los jóvenes saben tanto como los viejos.
    b. Los jóvenes no saben tanto como los viejos.
    c. Los jóvenes saben más cosas que los viejos.

5. *a.* Jorge tiene más dinero que Pablo.
    b. Pablo tiene menos dinero que Jorge.
    c. Pablo tiene más dinero que Jorge.

6. *a.* Yo tengo más dinero que tú.
    b. Tú tienes más dinero que yo.
    c. Yo tengo menos dinero que tú.

7. *a.* Ella es peor que él.
    b. Él es peor que ella.
    c. Él es mejor que ella.

8. *a.* Paco tiene tantos años como Paula.
    b. Paula es menor que Paco.
    c. Paula es mayor que Paco.

9. *a.* David es el más fuerte de los tres.
    b. David es menos fuerte que Roberto.
    c. Roberto es más fuerte que Tomás.

10. *a.* Roberta es menos gorda que Juanita.
    b. Gilda es la menos gorda de las tres.
    c. Juanita es la más gorda de las tres.

SUPPLEMENT:

The Absolute Superlative (*-ísimo*)

una casa **grandísima**   a very large house
unos gatitos **pequeñísimos**   some very small kittens

10. The absolute superlative is a special form of the adjective that ends in **-ísimo(-s)** or **-ísima(-s).** The suffix means *very, extremely, unusually.* It can also mean *very much* or *very many:*

> Te quiero **muchísimo.** (adverb)* I love you very much.
>
> Ella tiene **muchísimas** amigas.* She has very many friends (*f.*).

11. Some adjectives undergo a spelling change before the **-ísimo** suffix is added:

> La vieja tenía el pelo **blanquísimo.**   The old woman had very white hair.
> (The **c** in **blanco** changes to **qu** to retain the hard *k* sound before **i.**)
>
> Los discursos fueron **larguísimos.**   The speeches were very long.
> (The **g** in **largo** changes to **gu** to retain the hard *g* sound before **i.**)
>
> Eran ocasiones **felicísimas.**   They were very happy occasions.
> (The **z** in **feliz** changes to **c** before **i.**)

Practice H: Complete the Spanish expressions with the *-ísimo* form of the adjective.

1. the very wide avenue

   la avenida _____

2. a very happy marriage

   un matrimonio _____

3. the extremely dry climate

   el clima _____

4. a very bitter taste (bitter = *amargo, -a*)

   un sabor _____

5. some very beautiful churches (Use *bello, -a.*)

   unas iglesias _____

6. The news pleased them very much.

   La noticia les gustó _____.

7. They worked very hard ("much") and earned very little.

   Trabajaron _____

   y ganaron ._____

Muchísimo as an adverb and **muchísimo, -a, -os, -as as an adjective are the only forms to express very much (many). Muy cannot be used here.*

22
Demonstrative Adjectives and Pronouns

Demonstrative Adjectives

THIS	THESE
este lápiz, this pencil	**estos** lápices, these pencils
esta revista, this magazine	**estas** revistas, these magazines

THAT	THOSE
ese hombre, that man	**esos** hombres, those men
esa mujer, that woman	**esas** mujeres, those women

THAT (OVER THERE)	THOSE (OVER THERE)
aquel edificio, that building	**aquellos** edificios, those buildings
aquella casa, that house	**aquellas** casas, those houses

1. *This* and *these* are expressed in Spanish as follows:

> **este** + masculine singular noun
>
> **esta** + feminine singular noun
>
> **estos** + masculine plural noun
>
> **estas** + feminine plural noun

2. *That* and *those* are expressed in Spanish as follows:

> **ese** + masculine singular noun
>
> **esa** + feminine singular noun
>
> **esos** + masculine plural noun
>
> **esas** + feminine plural noun

3. *That* and *those* are also expressed by the forms **aquel, aquella, aquellos, aquellas,** but these forms are used to point out persons or objects that are at some distance from both the speaker and the person spoken to.

Practice A: Write the Spanish word for *this* or *these.*

1. _____ cinta   3. _____ mesas

2. _____ hombres   4. _____ mes

Practice B: Write the Spanish word for *that* or *those,* using the forms **ese, esa,** etc.

1. _____ ciudades   3. _____ caja

2. _____ sombrero   4. _____ lápices

Practice C: Write the Spanish word for *that* or *those,* using the forms **aquel, aquella,** etc.

1. _____ muchachos   3. _____ monumento

2. _____ computadoras   4. _____ casa

Practice D: Write the appropriate form of the Spanish demonstrative adjective.

1. _____ casas   6. _____ relojes
      (these)   (those, over there)

2. _____ chico   7. _____ edificio
      (that)   (this)

3. _____ universidad   8. _____ pueblos
      (this)   (these)

4. _____ escuela   9. _____ profesores
   (that, over there)   (those)

5. _____ chicas   10. _____ ciudad
      (those)   (that)

◼◼ Demonstrative Pronouns

Me gusta **este** periódico pero no me gusta **ése.**   I like *this* newspaper but I don't like *that one.*

Esa impresora es mejor que **ésta.**   *That* printer is better than *this one.*

Estos niños son más gandes que **aquéllos.**   *These* children are bigger than *those* (at a distance).

4. The demonstrative adjective must be followed by a noun. The adjective and its noun can be replaced by a demonstrative pronoun, which is used to avoid repetition:

   estos niños y **aquéllos** = estos niños y **aquellos niños**
   esa casa y **ésta** = esa casa y **esta casa**

5. Unlike the adjective forms, the demonstrative pronouns have an accent mark on the stressed vowel: **éste, ése, aquél, aquélla,** etc.

   Practice E: Write the pronoun that can be used in place of the given expression.

EXAMPLE: esta casa   ___*ésta*___

1. esas cintas   _____
2. este cuarto   _____
3. aquella vista   _____
4. ese coche   _____

5. estas ideas   _____
6. aquel edificio   _____
7. estos billetes   _____

Practice F: Write a phrase consisting of a demonstrative adjective and a noun that could be replaced by the given pronoun.

EXAMPLE: aquél   *aquel hombre* (*aquel chico, aquel libro,* etc.)

1. ésos   _____
2. ésta   _____
3. ésa   _____

4. aquéllas   _____
5. éstos   _____

◢ Neuter Demonstrative Forms

Esto es horrible.	This is horrible.
Eso no me gusta.	I do not like that.
¿Qué es **aquello**?	What is that?

6. **Esto, eso,** and **aquello** are neuter forms and refer to an idea or a preceding statement.

7. The neuter forms are also used to refer to an object that cannot be immediately identified. Once the identification is made, the neuter form can be replaced by a demonstrative pronoun that indicates gender and number:

—¿Qué son **esto** y **eso**?	What are this and that?
—Son plantas.	They are plants.
—No me gusta esta planta, pero me gusta **ésa.**	I don't like this plant, but I like that one.
—**Eso** es feo. ¿Qué es?	That is ugly. What is it?
—Es un edificio.	It's a building.
—No me gusta ese edificio, pero me gusta **éste.**	I don't like that building, but I like this one.

◢ EJERCICIOS ◢

A. In the following exercise, you make a statement and your friend agrees but adds his/her own preference, as shown in the example.

EXAMPLE: Quiero comprar esa *blusa*. (traje)   Y yo quiero comprar ese traje también.

1. Vamos a aquella *tienda.* (supermercado)   Y nosotros _____.

2. Estos *coches* son grandes. (motocicletas)   Es verdad, pero _____.

3. Mi madre quiere comprar ese *escritorio.*   Y mi tía _____
   (sillas)   _____.

4. Mañana vamos a visitar esos *museos*   Y nosotros _____
   (ciudad)   _____.

5. Ellos caminan por esa *calle.* (paseos)   Y ellas _____.

6. Aquel *teatro* está en la esquina. (casa)   Y _____ en la otra esquina.

7. Necesito esta *gorra.* (sombrero)   Y yo _____.

8. Tú debes tomar este *refresco.* (bebidas)   Y tú _____.

9. Vamos a pedir esos *postres.* (limonada)   Y nosotros _____.

10. Aquellos *hombres* son inteligentes. (mujeres) Y _____.

B. Pedro and Marta are in a department store. Marta asks Pedro different questions about his preferences in various departments. Show how Pedro responds, as in the example.

EXAMPLE: ¿Quieres comprar este libro?
           (*that one*) No, pero quiero comprar ése.

1. ¿Quieres comer estas frutas?

   (*those*) _____.

2. ¿Quieres mirar esos guantes?

   (*these*) _____.

3. ¿Quieres comprar este disco compacto?

   (*that one* [over there]) _____.

4. ¿Quieres escuchar esa cinta?

   (*this one*) _____.

5. ¿Quieres ver esta raqueta?

   (*that one*) _____.

C. Express in Spanish.*

1. *a.* This bicycle and that one are expensive.   _____

   b. That bicycle and this one are cheap.   _____

2. *a.* These CD's and those are old.   _____

   b. Those CD's and these are popular.   _____

Keep in mind: Adjectives must agree in gender and number with the nouns they modify.

3. *a.* I want to buy those shoes and these.   _____

    b. These shoes and those are comfortable.   _____

4. *a.* That drink and this one are delicious.   _____

    b. This drink and that one are sweet.   _____

5. *a.* We go to that supermarket and this one.   _____

    b. Those supermarkets and these are new.   _____

6. *a.* I'm buying these films and those (over there). _____

    b. That film (over there) and this one are good. _____

7. *a.* That magazine and this one are interesting. _____

    b. Let's buy these magazines and those.   _____

8. *a.* I want to read this article and that one.   _____

    b. These articles and those are bad.   _____

9. *a.* I believe this.   _____

    b. I do not believe that.   _____

10. *a.* What is that (over there)?   _____

    b. What is this?   _____

El Centro de Santiago, Chile

23
Possessive Adjectives and Pronouns

The following list illustrates the difference between a possessive adjective and a possessive pronoun.

Adjective	Pronoun
my house	mine
your book	yours
his school	his (in this case, they are identical)
her computer	hers
our family	ours
your city	yours
their car	theirs

Possessive Adjectives

MY

mi amigo, my friend   **mis** amigos, my friends
mi revista, my magazine   **mis** revistas, my magazines

YOUR (familiar singular)

tu abrigo, your coat   **tus** abrigos, your coats
tu clase, your class   **tus** clases, your classes

YOUR, HIS, HER, THEIR

su coche $\begin{Bmatrix} \text{your} \\ \text{his} \\ \text{her} \\ \text{their} \end{Bmatrix}$ car   **sus** coches $\begin{Bmatrix} \text{your} \\ \text{his} \\ \text{her} \\ \text{their} \end{Bmatrix}$ cars

(su casa)   (house)   **(sus** casas)   (houses)

1. The forms **mi, tu,** and **su** are the same for masculine and feminine nouns. The plural forms **mis, tus,** and **sus** are used when the thing possessed is in the plural.

Practice A: Write the possessive adjective.

1. _____ profesor   4. _____ libros
        (their)   (my)

2. _____ escuela   5. _____ raquetas
        (my)   (his)

3. _____ padre   6. _____ discos compactos
        (her)   (your, fam. sing.)

SU(-S) AND ITS SUBSTITUTES

2. **Su(-s)** has several meanings: _your, his, her, its, their._ For greater clarity, **su(-s)** may be replaced by expressions like the following:

his book: **el libro de él**   your book: **el libro de Ud. (Uds.)**
his books: **los libros de él**   your books: **los libros de Ud. (Uds.)**

her book: **el libro de ella**   their book: **el libro de ellos (ellas)**
her books: **los libros de ella**   their books: **los libros de ellos (ellas)**

Practice B: Replace the given expression with a phrase that clarifies the intended meaning of **su(-s),** as indicated in parentheses.

EXAMPLE: (your) sus libros   _los libros de Ud._

1. (her)   sus amigos   _____

2. (their)   sus cuadernos   _____

3. (his)   su hermana   _____

4. (your, _pl._) su problema   _____

5. (their)   su tía   _____

OUR

nuestro tío, our uncle   **nuestros** tíos, our uncles
nuestra tía, our aunt   **nuestras** tías, our aunts

YOUR (FAMILIAR PLURAL)

vuestro pueblo, your town   **vuestros** pueblos, your towns
vuestra ciudad, your city   **vuestras** ciudades, your cities

3. **Nuestro** and **vuestro** have four possible endings (**-o, -a, -os, -as**) depending on whether the person or thing possessed is masculine or feminine, singular or plural.

Practice C: Write the possessive adjective. ("your" = _fam. pl._)

1. _____ cocina   4. _____ casa
        (our)   (your)

2. _____ equipo   5. _____ automóvil
        (your)   (our)

3. _____ cuartos
        (our)

Practice D: Write the possessive adjective in the form required by the noun at the right.

1. su hermano   _____ hermana

2. mis zapatos   _____ chaqueta

3. tu radio   _____ televisores

4. nuestro teatro   _____ discos compactos

5. vuestras amigas   _____ sobrino

Possessive Pronouns

Yo tengo **mi** periódico y ella tiene **el suyo.**   I have *my* newspaper and she has *hers.*
Él tiene **su** cartera y yo tengo **la mía.**   He has *his* wallet and I have *mine.*

4. The possessive adjective is always followed by a noun. The adjective and its noun can be replaced by a possessive pronoun, which is used to avoid repetition:

mi periódico y **el suyo** = mi periódico y **su periódico**

Possessive Adjective	*Possessive Pronoun*
mi abuelo, my grandfather	**el mío**
mi abuela, my grandmother	**la mía**
mis hermanos, my brothers	**los míos** } mine
mis plantas, my plants	**las mías**
tu sombrero, your hat	**el tuyo**
tu corbata, your tie	**la tuya**
tus sobrinos, your nephews	**los tuyos** } yours
tus lámparas, your lamps	**las tuyas**
nuestro sofá, our sofa	**el nuestro**
nuestra computadora, our computer	**la nuestra**
nuestros perros, our dogs	**los nuestros** } ours
nuestras clases, our classes	**las nuestras**
vuestro sillón, your armchair	**el vuestro**
vuestra casa, your house	**la vuestra**
vuestros gatos, your cats	**los vuestros** } yours
vuestras maletas, your suitcases	**las vuestras**

su edificio { your / his / her / their } building   **el suyo** }

su biblioteca { your / his / her / their } library   **la suya** } yours, his, hers, theirs

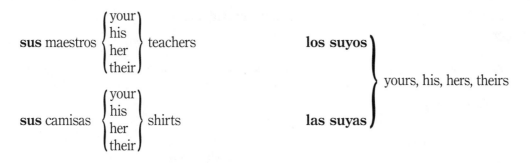

Practice E: Change each expression to a pronoun.

EXAMPLE: mis lecciones   *las mías*

1. su casa   _____   **4.** tu cartera   _____

2. nuestros libros   _____   **5.** vuestras tías   _____

3. sus problemas   _____

Practice F: Write an expression consisting of a possessive adjective and a noun that could be replaced by the given possessive pronoun. Use any suitable noun.

EXAMPLE: los míos   *mis tíos (mis libros, mis maestros, etc.)*

1. las nuestras   _____   **4.** los suyos   _____

2. la suya   _____   **5.** el tuyo   _____

3. el mío   _____

EL SUYO AND ITS SUBSTITUTES

—Aquí está el libro de María. ¿Lo quiere Ud.?   "Here is María's book. Do you want it?"

—No, ya tengo **el suyo.**   "No, I already have ---."

—¿El mío?   "Mine?"

—No, **el de ella.**   "No, *hers.*"

5. Each of the forms **el suyo, la suya, los suyos,** and **las suyas** has several meanings: *yours, his, hers, its,* or *theirs.* For greater clarity, they can be replaced by expressions like the following:

mi libro y **el suyo**	my book and yours, his, hers, theirs
el de Ud(s).	yours
el de él	his
el de ella	hers
el de ellos (ellas)	theirs

nuestras flores y **las suyas**	our flowers and yours, his, hers, theirs
las de Ud(s).	yours
las de él	his
las de ella	hers
las de ellos (ellas)	theirs

6. *Keep in mind:* These forms agree in gender and number with *the person or thing possessed,* not with the possessor.

> *Practice G:* Use a clarifying phrase instead of the possessive pronoun.

EXAMPLE: Yo tengo mi cinta y ___*la de él*___.
                                          (his)

1. Como mi postre y _____.
                                    (hers)

2. Buscamos nuestras cartas y _____.
                                              (yours [Uds.])

3. Me gustan mis juegos y _____.
                                        (his)

4. Quiero tener estos diamantes y _____.
                                                (yours [Ud.])

5. Visitamos tu ciudad y _____.
                                      (theirs)

SER + Possessive Pronoun

El gato es **mío.**	The cat is mine.
Estas revistas son **tuyas.**	These magazines are yours.

7. If a possessive pronoun is the object of the verb **ser,** the article (**el** mío, **las** suyas, etc.) is usually dropped.

> *Practice H:* Complete the Spanish sentences.

EXAMPLE: The skirt is hers.

          La falda ____*es suya*____.

1. This necktie is his.

   Esta corbata _____.

2. These books are mine.

   Estos libros _____.

3. This notebook isn't yours (*familiar sing*).

   Este cuaderno no _____.

4. The chairs are ours.

   Las sillas _____.

5. Here are some pencils; aren't they yours (*formal sing*)?

   Aquí están unos lápices; ¿no _____?

6. "Gentlemen, this car is yours, isn't it?" "No, it is not ours."

   —Señores, este coche _____, ¿verdad?

   —No, no _____.

In 7–10, use a clarifying phrase instead of a form of *suyo.*

EXAMPLES: The skirt is hers.   The books are yours (*sing*)

La falda ___*es de ella*___.   Los libros ___*son de Ud.*___.

7. These caps are not his.

Estas gorras no _____.

8. The house is theirs (*f.*).

La casa _____.

9. This table is yours (*pl.*).

Esta mesa _____.

10. "These magazines are mine; those are yours (*sing*), aren't they?" "No, those are theirs (*m.*)."

—Estas revistas son mías; ésas _____, ¿no?

—No, ésas _____.

Possessive Pronouns Used as Adjectives

Juana es una amiga **mía.**   Juana is a friend *of mine.*

Ellos son vecinos **nuestros.**   They are neighbors *of ours.*

8. A possessive adjective may *follow* the noun it modifies, in which case the adjective is replaced by the pronoun form: **mi** amiga—una amiga **mía; sus** cosas—unas cosas **suyas,** etc. Possessive pronouns used in this way are expressed in English by *of* + a possessive: *of mine, of yours, of hers,* etc.

Practice I: Write in Spanish.

1. three books of hers   _____

2. some friend (*f.*) of ours   _____

3. some pens of his   _____

4. a watch of mine   _____

5. four diamonds of yours (*familiar sing*) _____

▲ EJERCICIOS ▲

A. Write the form of the possessive adjective that corresponds to the subject of the sentence.

EXAMPLE: Yo tengo ___*mis*___ libros.

1. ¿Toca ella _____ discos hoy?   **2.**   No queremos conducir _____ coche.

3. Escribimos a _____ amigos en Puerto Rico.

4. Tú no tienes _____ tarea.

5. Ellos hablan con _____ profesor de ciencia.

6. ¿Tenéis _____ maletas?

7. Hablo con _____ primas por teléfono.

8. ¿Trae Ud. _____ guitarra a la fiesta?

9. Vemos _____ programas favoritos.

10. ¿Escribes a _____ parientes en Venezuela?

B. Each of the following statements is a reply to a question. Write the question, using a possessive adjective.

EXAMPLE: Sí, tengo mis libros. $\begin{cases} \textit{¿Tienes tus libros?} \\ \qquad\text{or} \\ \textit{¿Tiene Ud. sus libros?} \end{cases}$

1. No, no visitamos a nuestros abuelos. _____

2. Sí, voy a buscar mi ropa. _____

3. No, ellos no tienen su dinero. _____

4. No, tú no puedes jugar con tus amigos. _____

5. Sí, él llega con su hermano. _____

C. Complete the sentence with a possessive pronoun, as shown in the example.

EXAMPLE: Tú tienes tu comida y yo tengo ___*la mía*___.

1. Ellos van a su casa y nosotros vamos a _____.

2. Nosotros leemos nuestros periódicos y José lee _____.

3. Ellos juegan con sus amigos y yo juego con _____.

4. Diana va con su familia y Juan va con _____.

5. Ellos van a su escuela y tú vas a _____.

D. Answer with a complete sentence, using a possessive pronoun.

EXAMPLE: ¿Qué abrigo llevas esta noche?   *Llevo el mío.*

1. ¿Qué ropa llevan ellos? _____

2. ¿Qué libros tiene Ud.? _____

3. ¿De qué clase viene él? _____

4. ¿Qué bicicleta usa Felipe? _____

5. ¿En qué cuarto duermes tú? _____

E. Answer with a complete sentence, using the clue in parentheses.

EXAMPLE: ¿De quién es esta caja? (*his*)
           Esta caja es suya.

1. ¿De quiénes son estas camisas? (*mine*)

    _____

2. ¿De quién son estos vestidos? (*hers*)

    _____

3. ¿De quiénes es esa casa? (*ours*)

    _____

4. ¿De quiénes son estos coches? (*theirs*)

    _____

5. ¿De quién son estos libros? (*yours,* familiar sing.)

    _____

F. Your brother José wants to know where everyone's belongings are (including his own). Answer his questions as in the example.

EXAMPLES: ¿Dónde está mi reloj?   (en la mesa)
           El tuyo está en la mesa.

           ¿Dónde están los lápices de Ana?   (en el suelo)
           Los suyos están en el suelo.

1. ¿Dónde están tus cintas?   (en mi cuarto)

    _____

2. ¿Dónde está el periódico de mamá?   (en su mesa)

    _____

3. ¿Dónde está la camisa de papá?   (en su armario)

    _____

4. ¿Dónde están las revistas del profesor?   (en su sala de clase)

    _____

5. ¿Dónde están mis discos compactos?   (en tu sala)

    _____

G. Give the Spanish equivalents.

1. *a.* Our printer and yours (*familiar sing*) are modern. _____

   b. Your printer and ours are old. _____

2. *a.* Where are her relatives and yours (*formal pl.*)? _____

   b. Your relatives and hers are going to the party. _____

3. *a.* My apartment and hers are small. _____

   b. Her apartment and mine are not large. _____

4. *a.* Two friends (*f.*) of his are coming tonight. _____

   b. Some friends (*m.*) of mine are leaving for Spain. _____

5. *a.* Some neighbors (*m.*) of ours are in the country. _____

   b. Some neighbors (*f.*) of yours (*formal sing*) are here. _____

H. *Listening Comprehension.* Your teacher will read aloud ten questions in Spanish. In each case, underline the most appropriate reply.

1. *a.* Es mío.
   b. Son mías.
   c. Son tuyos.

2. *a.* Es nuestra.
   b. Es mía.
   c. Son suyas.

3. *a.* Sí, voy a las mías.
   b. No, voy a la mía.
   c. No, voy a la de él.

4. *a.* No, no tengo la tuya.
   b. Sí, tengo los suyos.
   c. Sí, tengo el tuyo.

5. *a.* Sí, salgo con la suya.
   b. Sí, salgo con la de ella.
   c. Sí, salgo con el suyo.

6. *a.* los de ella
   b. el de ellos
   c. la de él

7. *a.* las tuyas
   b. los tuyos
   c. la suya

8. *a.* los nuestros
   b. la nuestra
   c. el de Ud.

9. *a.* el suyo
   b. los tuyos
   c. la suya

10. *a.* No, es un amigo mío.
    b. Sí, es un amigo nuestro.
    c. Sí, es un amigo mío.

Part 5
Pronouns

24
The Personal A; Direct Object Pronouns LO, LA, LOS, LAS*

Helps and Hints

Observe the following two sentences:

1. Albert sees Helen.
2. Helen sees Albert.

In the first sentence, *Albert* is the subject, since he is performing the action of seeing. *Helen* is the direct object, since she is receiving the action of seeing. In the second sentence, the roles are reversed, where Helen is the subject and Albert is the direct object. In Spanish, a person who is the direct object is preceded by the preposition **a,** which we do not translate into English.

In this chapter, we shall also cover direct object pronouns which refer to people or things. These pronouns precede the conjugated verb, as opposed to English, where they follow the verb. We will deal with the object pronouns *him, her, you, it, them.*

 The Personal A

A	B
REFERRING TO THINGS	REFERRING TO PEOPLE
¿Qué?	¿A quién? ¿A quiénes?
¿Qué ven Uds.?	¿A quién ven Uds.?
What do you see?	Whom do you see?
Vemos la mesa.	Vemos **a** la chica (**a** Juana).
We see the table.	We see the girl (Juana).
Vemos los edificios.	¿A quiénes ven Uds.?
We see the buildings.	Vemos **a** los chicos.
	We see the boys.
	Vemos **a** las chicas (**a** María y Elena).
	We see the girls (María and Elena).

*In Chapters 24–27, object pronouns are used only with verbs in the present tense in order to focus on constructions in which object pronouns precede the verb. Their position in relation to other verb forms is presented in Chapter 28.

175

1. The direct object may be a thing (column *A*) or a person (column *B*). In Spanish, if the direct object refers to persons, it is preceded by **a.** This preposition, called the personal **a,** has no equivalent in English.

2. The personal **a** is usually not used with **tener. (Tengo una hermana.)**

    Practice A: Write the personal **a** in the blank if it is required. (Remember: **a + el = al.**)

    1. ¿Comprendes _____ la palabra?

    2. No veo _____ mi padre.

    3. Vamos a visitar _____ ese país.

    4. ¿Quién conoce _____ el hombre?

    5. Siempre ayudamos _____ nuestra madre.

    6. No oímos _____ la música.

    7. Tiene _____ cuatro hermanos.

    8. Esta noche invitamos _____ María.

    9. No recuerdo _____ las mujeres.

    10. El profesor describe _____ su familia.

■ Direct Object Pronouns

lo, him, it (*m.*)   **los,** them (*m.* or "mixed" genders)
la, her, it (*f.*)   **las,** them (*f.*)

Yo tengo **el libro.**	Yo **lo** tengo.
I have *the book.*	I have *it.*
Vemos **al muchacho.**	**Lo** vemos.
We see *the boy.*	We see *him.*
Usan **la computadora.**	**La** usan.
They use *the computer.*	They use *it.*
¿Oyes a **Rosa?**	¿**La** oyes?
Do you hear *Rosa?*	Do you hear *her?*
¿Leen Uds. **los periódicos?**	¿**Los** leen Uds.?
Do you read *the newspapers?*	Do you read *them?*
Ella no conoce a **mis amigos.**	Ella no **los** conoce.
She does not know *my friends.*	She does not know *them.*
No escribimos **las cartas.**	No **las** escribimos.
We're not writing *the letters.*	We're not writing *them.*
¿No invitas a **las chicas?**	¿No **las** invitas?
Aren't you inviting *the girls?*	Aren't you inviting *them?*

3. The direct object pronouns **lo, la, los, las** may refer to things or persons.

4. The direct object pronouns directly precede the conjugated form of the verb.

_____

lo }
la } *you,* formal sing.   **los** }
                                  las } *you,* plural

No **lo** comprendo, señor. Hable Ud. más despacio, por favor.

I don't understand you, sir. Please speak more slowly.

Ellos dicen que **las** conocen, señoras. ¿Los conocen Uds.?

They say they know you, ladies. Do you know them?

5. As object pronouns meaning *you,* **lo** and **la** are used only when speaking to someone addressed as **usted.** The plural forms, however, are both formal and familiar (except in Spain—see Chapter 25).

¿Dónde están Uds., niños? No **los** veo.

Where are you, children? I don't see you.

6. *Caution:* In English, the pronoun *you* may be either subject ("*you* see Mary") or object ("Mary sees *you*"). As subject, *you* = **usted** ("**Ud.** ve a María"); as direct object, *you* = **lo, la, los,** or **las** ("María **lo** [**la,** etc.] ve").

Practice B: Express in Spanish, using the correct equivalent of *you:* **Ud., Uds., lo, la, los,** or **las.**

1. (you, *f. pl.*)

    a. Do you know them (*m.*)? _____

    b. Do they know you? _____

2. (you, *m. sing*)

    a. She sees you. _____

    b. You see her. _____

3. (you, *f. sing*)

    a. Does she understand you? _____

    b. Do you understand her? _____

4. (you, *m. pl.;* they/them = las profesoras)

    a. They greet you. _____

    b. You listen to them. (Do not translate *to.*) _____

Summary

lo,* you (*m. sing*), him, it (*m.*)   **los,** you (*m. pl.*), them (*m.* or "mixed" genders)
la, you (*f. sing*), her, it (*f.*)   **las,** you (*f. pl.*), them (*f.*)

Practice C: Rewrite the sentence to include the Spanish equivalent of the object pronoun in parentheses.

EXAMPLE: (them, *f.*) ¿No ve ella?   *¿No las ve ella?*

1. (her)   No comprenden bien.   _____

2. (it, *f.*)   ¿Dices tú siempre?   _____

---

*In Spain, the form **le** is used for persons, **lo** for things.

3. (you, *m. sing.*)　　Nosotros vemos claramente.　　_____

4. (them, *f.*)　　Usamos todos los días.　　_____

5. (it, *m.*)　　¿No quiere Ud.?　　_____

6. (you, *f. pl.*)　　No entendemos bien.　　_____

7. (her)　　¿Visitan Uds. mañana?　　_____

8. (it, *m.*)　　Escribimos todas las semanas.　　_____

9. (him)　　¿Oyes tú bien?　　_____

10. (them, *m. & f.*)　　Yo no compro con frecuencia.　　_____

▰▰ Clarifying the Meanings of Pronouns LO, LOS, LA, LAS

7. Since each of the pronouns **lo, los, la,** and **las** may have several meanings, the intended meaning may be clarified or emphasized by adding as follows:

Yo **lo** veo.	I see it.
Yo **lo** veo *a él.*	I see him.
Yo **lo** veo *a Ud.*	I see you.
¿**La** comprende él?	Does he understand it?
¿**La** comprende él *a ella*?	Does he understand her?
¿**La** comprende él *a Ud.*?	Does he understand you (*f.*)?
No **los** oímos.	We don't hear them (*ref. to things.*)
No **los** oímos *a ellos.*	We don't hear them (*ref. to persons*).
No **los** oímos *a Uds.*	We don't hear you.
Las ve.	He sees them (*ref. to things*).
Las ve *a ellas.*	He sees them (*ref. to persons*).
Las ve *a Uds.*	He sees you.

▲ EJERCICIOS ▲

A. Rewrite the sentence, changing the underlined words to object pronouns.

EXAMPLE:　¿Tiene Ud. el diccionario?　　*¿Lo tiene Ud.?*

1. Los alumnos leen la novela.　　_____

2. ¿Dónde compramos las verduras?　　_____

3. No conozco a ese hombre.　　_____

4. Ellos ven a sus primos. _____

5. ¿Necesitas el mapa? _____

6. Mañana recibimos los paquetes. _____

7. Escuchamos a la profesora. _____

8. ¿Quién vende los coches? _____

9. ¿Mira Ud. a Luisa? _____

10. ¿Dónde construyen la escuela? _____

B. Answer your friend's questions in Spanish, using the same object pronoun.

EXAMPLE: Allí está José.   ¿Lo _ves_?
            Sí, _lo veo._   Or: No, _no lo veo._

1. Es una buena computadora. ¿La usas todos los días?

   Sí, _____.

2. Necesito el libro. ¿Lo tienes?

   No, _____.

3. Mi tía vive en el segundo piso. ¿La conoces?

   No, _____.

4. Me gustan estos _blue-jeans._ ¿Los compras en aquella tienda?

   Sí, _____.

5. Este video está roto. ¿Lo reparan Uds. aquí?

   No, _____.

C. Write a question for each statement using a noun, as shown in the examples.

EXAMPLES: Sí, lo vemos.   _¿Ven Uds. el edificio?_

            No, no las compro.   {_¿Compras las cintas?_
                                       {_¿Compra Ud. las cintas?_

            Lo venden allí.   _¿Dónde venden pan?_

            La estudian por la tarde. _¿Cuándo estudian la lección?_

1. La escucho en la sala. _____

2. Sí, los tengo. _____

3. Ellos los practican en el gimnasio. _____

4. Las vende en la esquina. _____

5. La oímos todas las mañanas. _____

D. Write the Spanish equivalents.

1. *a.* Are you visiting the city? _____

   b. Yes, I am visiting it. _____

2. *a.* Is she studying Spanish? _____

   b. No, she isn't studying it. _____

3. *a.* They are reading the novels? _____

   b. Are you (*tú*) reading them too? _____

4. *a.* Who is listening to the teacher (*f.*)? _____

   b. I am listening to her. _____

5. *a.* I don't know you, sir. _____

   b. Does he know you, madam? _____

6. *a.* We understand you well, sir. _____

   b. Do they understand you, gentlemen? _____

7. *a.* I'm inviting my cousin Henry and my friend Anne. _____

   b. I'm inviting them tonight. _____

8. *a.* Are you (*Uds.*) watching television? _____

   b. Yes, we're watching it now. _____

9. *a.* My father is buying that car. _____

   b. Where is he buying it? _____

10. *a.* I hear him well. _____

    b. I don't hear you, Mr. López. _____

E. *Listening Comprehension.* Your teacher will read aloud ten questions in Spanish. After each question is read, circle the letter of the most appropriate reply.

1. *a.* Yo lo conozco a él.
   b. Ramón la conoce.
   c. Eva lo conoce a Ud.

2. *a.* Sí, la escucho a ella.
   b. No, no la escucho.
   c. Sí, lo escucho ahora.

3. *a.* No, no los leemos.
   b. Sí, la leemos siempre.
   c. No, no las leemos ahora.

4. *a.* Los chicos la ven.
   b. Los hombres lo ven.
   c. Mis padres las ven.

5. *a.* Visito a mis abuelos.
   b. Visito la ciudad.
   c. Visito a mi amigo.

6. *a.* Sí, lo traigo.
   b. Sí, los traigo.
   c. No, no las traigo.

7. *a.* Yo lo entiendo.
   b. Juan la entiende.
   c. Carlota los entiende.

8. *a.* Lo compramos en la ciudad.
   b. La compramos en esa tienda.
   c. Las compramos en el centro.

9. *a.* No, no los oigo claramente.
   b. No, no lo oigo bien.
   c. Sí, las oigo perfectamente.

10. *a.* No, no las tomo nunca.
    b. Sí, la tomo todas las noches.
    c. Sí, lo tomo siempre.

Costa Irregular de las Islas Galápagos, Ecuador

25

Indirect Object Pronouns LE and LES; Object Pronouns ME, TE, NOS, OS

Helps and Hints

An indirect object answers the question *to whom* or *for whom*. In the sentence "*I'm sending my father the letter*," we can also say "*I'm sending the letter to my father.*" *Father* is the indirect object and *letter* is the direct object. In the sentence "*I'm sending John the package*," *John* is the indirect object, since we can also say "*I'm sending the package to John.*" In the sentence "*I'm sending John to school*," *John* is the direct object, since he is receiving the action of sending.

Here are some verbs that often take indirect objects:

contar, to tell	**explicar,** to explain	**prestar,** to lend
contestar, to answer	**hablar,** to speak	**prometer,** to promise
dar, to give	**leer,** to read	**servir,** to serve
decir, to tell, to say	**mandar,** to send	**traer,** to bring
escribir, to write	**preguntar,** to ask	**vender,** to sell

 LE and LES

A. **le,** (*to*) *him,* (*to*) *her*
   les, (*to*) *them*

Hablamos **a Enrique (a Marta).***   **Le** hablamos.
We speak to Enrique (to Marta).   We speak to him (her).

¿Quién escribe **a las mujeres (a los hombres)**?*   ¿Quién **les** escribe?
Who writes to the women (to the men)?   Who writes to them?

B. **le,** (*to*) *you,* formal singular
   les, (*to*) *you,* plural

Él **le** trae el periódico, señor (señorita).   {He is bringing you the newspaper, sir (miss).
                                              {He is bringing the newspaper to you, sir (miss).

Les decimos la verdad.   We are telling you the truth.

1. The indirect object answers the question *to whom*? For example, "**le** hablamos" (we speak to him) answers the question "**¿a quién** hablamos?" (*to whom* do we speak?); "**les** trae la carta" (he is bringing them the letter) answers the question "**¿a quiénes** trae la carta?" (*to whom* is he bringing the letter?).

---

*For simplicity, we are not using the redundant use of the object pronoun and the noun. (See §3, below.)

2. Since **le** and **les** have several meanings, the intended meaning may be clarified or emphasized by adding one of the following phrases: **a Ud., a Uds., a él, a ella, a ellos, a ellas.**

—¿No **le** escribe *a Ud.*?	"Doesn't she write to *you*?"
—No, ella **le** escribe *a él.*	"No, she writes to *him*."
Les escriben *a Uds.;* nunca **les** escriben *a ellos.*	They write to *you* (*pl.*); they never write to *them.*

3. As we have seen, **le** and **les** are substituted for phrases of the type **a** + *noun:* **a Marta, a los hombres.** For example, "trae la carta **a Marta**" (he brings Marta the letter) can be replaced by "**le** trae la carta" (he brings her the letter). Often, however, both the phrase and its pronoun substitute are used, rather than one *or* the other:

Yo **le** doy el libro **a Juan.**	I give Juan the book.
¿**Les** presta dinero **a sus hermanos**?	Does she lend money to her brothers?

In this construction—very common in spoken Spanish—**le** or **les** does not affect the meaning of the sentence. Note the similarity between this type of sentence and the use of clarifying phrases:

Yo **le** doy el libro **a él.**	I give him the book.
Yo **le** doy el libro **a Juana.**	I give Juana the book.

4. *Caution:* The English pronouns *you, him, her,* and *them* may be direct or indirect objects, depending upon how they are used:

(direct object)	I see *her* = yo **la** veo
(indirect object)	I write *her* a letter = yo **le** escribo una carta
(direct object)	we see *you* = **los** vemos
(indirect object)	we send *you* the packages = **les** mandamos los paquetes

Practice A: Express in Spanish as shown by the examples in italics.

1. I speak to him.   *Yo le hablo a él.*

   a. I speak to her.   _____

   b. I speak to them.   _____

   c. I speak to you (*sing*).   _____

2. Do they write to you often?   *¿Le escriben a Ud. a menudo?*

   a. Do they write to him often?   _____

   b. Do they write to them (*m.*) often? _____

   c. Do they write to you (*pl.*) often? _____

3. What is she giving you?   *¿Qué le da ella a Ud.?*

   a. What is she giving him?   _____

   b. What is she giving her?   _____

   c. What is she giving her brother?   _____
       (Use noun and pronoun as in §3 above.)

4. We aren't speaking to her.   *No le hablamos a ella.*

   a. We aren't speaking to you. (*pl.*).   _____

   b. We aren't speaking to you. (*sing.*).   _____

   c. We aren't speaking to our friends.   _____
   (Use noun and pronoun.)

5. Juan is lending her money.   *Juan le presta dinero a ella.*

   a. Juan is lending him money.   _____

   b. Juan is lending them money.   _____

   c. Juan is lending you (*sing*) money.   _____

Practice B: Direct and Indirect Object Pronouns. Complete the Spanish sentences with the correct object pronoun, choosing among the following:

direct objects: **lo, la, los, las**   indirect objects: **le, les**

1. you, *f. pl.*

   a. I see you.   Yo _____ veo.

   b. I write to you.   Yo _____ escribo.

2. them, *m.*

   a. We send them a letter.   _____ enviamos una carta.

   b. We invite them to the house. _____ invitamos a la casa.

3. *a.* I show her the card.   _____ muestro la tarjeta.

   b. I meet her in class.   _____ encuentro en la clase.

4. you, *m. sing.*

   a. They don't hear you.   Ellos no _____ oyen.

   b. They tell you the truth.   _____ dicen la verdad.

5. *a.* She brings him a gift.   _____ trae un regalo.

   b. She looks at him.   _____ mira.

ME, TE, NOS, OS

Ellos **me** ven.   Ellos **me** hablan.
They see me.   They speak to me.

¿**Te** oyen ellos?   ¿**Te** escriben ellos?
Do they hear you?   Do they write to you?

No **nos** comprenden.   No **nos** dan dinero.
They don't understand us.   They are not giving us money. (They are not giving money to us.)

Os veo bien.   **Os** presto los libros.
I see you well.   I am lending you the books. (I am lending the books to you.)

5. The pronouns **me, te, nos,** and **os** are both direct and indirect objects.*

6. Os, the object-pronoun form of **vosotros,** is used only in Spain. In Spanish America, the familiar plural as object pronoun is expressed by the forms corresponding to **ustedes,** that is, by **los, las,** or **les.**

Practice C: Express in Spanish as shown by the examples in italics. (In this exercise, "you" = **te** or **os.**)

1. Do they see you (*sing*)?   *¿Te ven?*

    a. Do they see us?   _____

    b. Do they see me?   _____

    c. Do they see you (*pl.*)?   _____

2. He is sending us the CDs.   *Nos manda los discos compactos.*

    a. He's sending you the CDs.   _____

    b. He's sending me the CDs.   _____

    c. He's sending you (*pl.*) the CDs.   _____

3. Isn't she telling you the truth?   *¿No os dice ella la verdad?*

    a. Isn't she telling you (*sing*) the truth?   _____

    b. Isn't she telling us the truth?   _____

    c. Isn't she telling me the truth?   _____

 EJERCICIOS

A. Complete the answers to the questions.

    EXAMPLES: ¿Quién me habla?   *Yo te hablo.*

             ¿Quién nos oye?   {Ella *os oye.*
                               {Ella *los oye a Uds.*

    1. ¿Quiénes nos saludan?   {Los jefes _____.
                                        {Los jefes _____.

    2. ¿Quién te quiere?   Mi novio (novia) _____.

---

*Since each of these pronouns has only one meaning, they never require clarifying phrases like those often used with **le** and **les** (see §2, page 183.) For *emphasis,* however, one of the following phrases may be added: **a mí, a ti, a nosotros(-as), a vosotros(-as):**

Ella **me** llama ***a mí,*** no a ellos.   She is calling *me,* not them.
No **nos** escriben ***a nosotros;*** **te** escriben ***a ti.***   They do not write to *us;* they write to *you.*

3. ¿Quién me llama?   La profesora _____.

4. ¿Quiénes os traen los juguetes?   Los abuelos _____.

5. ¿Quién nos sirve la comida?*   ⎰ El camarero _____.
                                     ⎱ El camarero _____.

B. You and your friend are conversing. Answer his/her questions with a complete sentence in Spanish, using the clue in parentheses.

EXAMPLE: ¿Qué le† das a José? (los billetes)
            Yo le doy los billetes.

1. ¿Qué le prestas a tu amigo Juan? (diez dólares)

    _____

2. ¿De qué me hablas tú? (del examen de español)

    _____

3. ¿Qué les dicen tus padres a tus hermanos? (que la familia va a hacer un viaje)

    _____

4. ¿Qué le escribes a tu abuela? (una carta larga)

    _____

5. ¿Qué nos trae tu tía de Madrid? (unos regalos bonitos)

    _____

6. ¿Qué les sirves a tus amigos en la fiesta? (pasteles y helado)

    _____

7. ¿Qué te cuenta María? (lo que pasa en su casa)

    _____

8. ¿Qué le mandas a tu novia (novio)? (una caja de dulces)

    _____

9. ¿Qué te pregunta tu papá? (lo que hago en la escuela)

    _____

10. ¿Qué les dicen a Uds. tus padres? (que están enojados)

    _____

_____

Hint: In this question, **nos** is an indirect object.
†See §3, page 183.

C. Express in Spanish:

1. *a.* Who is serving us dinner tonight?

    _____

    b. My cousin is serving you (*formal pl.*) dinner.

    _____

2. *a.* Is your friend sending you (*familiar sing*) the stamps?

    _____

    b. No, he is not sending me the stamps.

    _____

3. *a.* What are they telling her?

    _____

    b. They're telling her a lie.

    _____

4. *a.* When are you (*Ud.*) giving them the money?

    _____

    b. I'm giving them the money next week.

    _____

5. *a.* Who is lending you (*familiar sing*) the racket?

    _____

    b. My friend is lending me the racket?

    _____

6. *a.* When does she write to you (*formal sing.*)?

    _____

    b. She writes to me every week.

    _____

7. *a.* What is the teacher reading to us?

    _____

    b. She's reading us *Don Quijote*.

    _____

8. *a.* Are you (*tú*) speaking to *them* on the phone?

    _____

    b. No, I'm speaking to *her*.

    _____

9. *a.* What are you (*vosotros*) asking me?

_____

   b. I'm asking you (*familiar pl.*) how you are.

_____

10. *a.* What are they bringing him later?

_____

   b. They're bringing him some magazines and some newspapers.

_____

D. *Listening Comprehension.* Your teacher will read aloud ten questions in Spanish. After each question is read, circle the letter of the most appropriate answer.

1. *a.* Te doy un regalo.
   b. Le doy un libro a ella.
   c. Nos dan dinero.

2. *a.* Sí, te mandamos los billetes.
   b. Sí, les mandamos los billetes.
   c. No, no le mandamos los billetes.

3. *a.* Les digo la verdad.
   b. Le digo un secreto.
   c. Me dice una mentira.

4. *a.* Sí, te leo un cuento.
   b. No, no les leo nada.
   c. Sí, me lees un cuento.

5. *a.* Nos escribe una carta.
   b. No te escribe nada.
   c. Les escribo una tarjeta postal.

6. *a.* No, no nos escuchan
   b. Sí, los escuchan mucho.
   c. Sí, me escuchan siempre.

7. *a.* Nos pregunta qué tiempo hace.
   b. Le pregunta cómo está.
   c. Me pregunta qué hora es.

8. *a.* Sí, me presta el coche.
   b. Sí, le presto el coche.
   c. No, no le presto el coche a ella.

9. *a.* Les contestan a Uds. por teléfono.
   b. Le contestan con un telegrama.
   c. Me contestan por correo aéreo.

10. *a.* Les paso la sal a ellos.
   b. Nos pasa la sal a nosotros.
   c. Le paso la sal a mi padre.

26
Double Object Pronouns

Helps and Hints

In this chapter you will learn how to use two object pronouns together in one sentence. Just remember the difference between the direct and indirect object. For example, in the sentence "I sent her them," we can also say "I sent them to her," so *her* is the indirect object and *them* is the direct object. Now in the sentence "I sent them them," which *them* is the direct object and which *them* is the indirect object?

Using *ME, TE, NOS, OS* With Direct Object Pronouns

Juan **me** manda **el paquete.**
Juan is sending me the package.

Juan **me lo** manda.
Juan is sending it to me.

¿**Te** muestra ella **la foto**?
Is she showing you the photo?

¿**Te la** muestra ella?
Is she showing it to you?

Nos dan **los libros.**
They are giving us the books.

Nos los dan.
They are giving them to us. (They are giving us them.)

No **os** prestan las **cintas.**
They are not lending you the tapes.

No **os las** prestan.
They are not lending them to you. (... are not lending you them.)

1. When a direct and an indirect object pronoun are used together, the indirect object (usually a person) precedes the direct object (usually a thing).

SOME DOUBLE-OBJECT COMBINATIONS

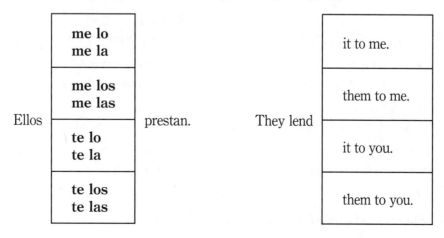

Ellos	me lo / me la	prestan.	They lend	it to me.
	me los / me las			them to me.
	te lo / te la			it to you.
	te los / te las			them to you.

nos lo **nos la**	it to us.
nos los **nos las**	them to us.
os lo **os la**	it to you.
os los **os las**	them to you.

Ellos ... prestan.   They lend ...

Practice A: Repeat each sentence, substituting the indicated expressions.

EXAMPLE: No te los *doy.*

traemos	*No te los traemos.*
prestan	*No te los prestan.*
ofrecen	*No te los ofrecen.*

1. ¿Nos la *escriben*?

    dan _____

    manda él _____

    prometes tú _____

2. ¿Me las *das tú*?

    trae él _____

    venden Uds. _____

    presta Ud. _____

3. Ellos te lo *venden.*

    mandan _____

    traen _____

    escriben _____

LE and *LES* Become *SE* Before a Direct Object Pronoun

¿**Le** traen ellos **el billete**?
Are they bringing you (him, her) the ticket?

Les mostramos **la pintura**.
We are showing you (them) the painting.

No **le** mandan **las cartas**.
They are not sending you (him, her) the letters.

Yo **les** doy **los libros**.
I am giving you (them) the books.

¿**Se lo** traen ellos?
Are they bringing it to you (him, her)?

Se la mostramos.
We are showing it to you (them).

No **se las** mandan.
They are not sending them to you (him, her).

Yo **se los** doy.
I am giving them to you (them).

2. When **le** or **les** is used with **lo, la, los,** or **las,** it changes to **se.**

SOME DOUBLE-OBJECT COMBINATIONS WITH *SE*

Ellos
| se lo |
se la
se los
se las
mandan.

They send
it to	you.
	him.
	her.
	them.
them to	you.
	him.
	her.
	them.

3. Since **se lo, se la,** etc. may have several meanings, the intended meaning can be clarified by adding **a Ud., a Uds., a él, a ella, a ellos,** or **a ellas:**

Se lo mandamos ***a ella.***   We are sending it to *her.*

¿**Se los** prestan ***a Ud.***?   Are they lending them to *you*?

Practice B: Repeat each sentence, substituting the indicated verbs.

EXAMPLE: Se lo *prometo.*

doy	*Se lo doy.*
ofrecen	*Se lo ofrecen.*
contamos	*Se lo contamos.*

1. Se la *decimos.*

digo _____

dan _____

manda _____

3. ¿Se los *presta* Ud. a ellos?

escribe _____

vende _____

da _____

2. Ellos se lo *venden* a él.

escriben _____

explican _____

dan _____

 EJERCICIOS

A. Rewrite the sentence, changing the noun object to a direct object pronoun.

EXAMPLE: Ella me da el dinero.   *Ella me lo da.*

1. Yo te traigo las flores.   _____

2. Ellos nos dicen la verdad.   _____

3. ¿Le manda él los discos compactos a ella? _____

4. No les damos los billetes a Uds. _____

5. ¿Cuándo me prestas diez dólares? _____

6. Juanita les escribe la tarjeta. _____

7. ¿Quién te lee los cuentos? _____

8. ¿Nos vende Ud. la casa? _____

9. Papá os sirve la comida. _____

10. La profesora les explica el concepto a ellos. _____

B. In your answers to the following questions, change the noun objects to object pronouns.

EXAMPLE: ¿Le dan Uds. el dinero al comerciante? [Note the redundant use of the object
        Sí, *se lo damos.* Or: No, *no se lo damos.* pronouns *le* and *les* (see §3, page 183).]

1. ¿Le llevas tú las flores a tu novia?

No, _____.

2. ¿Le escriben los alumnos la carta al alcalde?

Sí, _____.

3. ¿Les dices siempre la verdad a tus padres?

Sí, _____.

4. ¿Le dan Uds. dinero al dependiente?

Sí, _____.

5. ¿Les manda él los sellos a sus amigos?

No, _____.

6. ¿Me explicas el problema?

No, _____.

7. ¿Te vende la bicicleta?

Sí, _____.

8. ¿Le lee el profesor el cuento a Ud.?

Sí, _____.

9. ¿Nos cuentan ellos la anécdota?

No, _____.

10. ¿Les presta él la caja a Uds.?

Sí, _____.

C. Express in Spanish:

1. *a.* They are sending them (*f.*) to us. _____

   b. Are they sending them (*m.*) to us? _____

   c. They are not sending them (*m.*) to us. _____

2. *a.* I am not lending it (*f.*) to you (*familiar sing*). _____

   b. I am not lending her them (*m.*). _____

   c. I am not lending it (*m.*) to them. _____

3. *a.* Are you (*tú*) bringing them (*m.*) to me? _____

   b. Are you bringing them to her? _____

   c. Are you bringing it (*f.*) to us? _____

4. *a.* He's writing it (*f.*) to me. _____

   b. He's writing it to us. _____

   c. He's writing it (*m.*) to her. _____

5. *a.* Are they giving them (*m.*) to you
    (*formal pl.*)? _____

   b. Are they giving them (*f.*) to him? _____

   c. Are they giving them (*f.*) to us? _____

D. *Listening Comprehension.* Your teacher will read aloud ten questions in Spanish. After each question is read, circle the letter of the most appropriate answer.

1. *a.* Sí, te los doy.
   b. Sí, me los das.
   c. Sí, os los doy.

2. *a.* Sí, se lo traigo a Ud.
   b. No, no te lo traemos.
   c. No, no se lo traemos a Uds.

3. *a.* Sí, nos la escribe.
   b. Sí, te la escribe.
   c. Sí, me la escribe.

4. *a.* Sí, se los mandan.
   b. Sí, nos los mandan.
   c. No, no me los mandan.

5. *a.* Sí, me lo muestra.
   b. No, no me la muestra.
   c. No, no te la muestra.

6. *a.* Sí, nos la da.
   b. Sí, se la da a él.
   c. Sí, te la da.

7. *a.* Sí, nos la promete.
   b. Sí, nos las promete.
   c. Sí, nos lo promete.

8. *a.* No, no te la dice.
   b. No, no me la dice.
   c. No, no me lo dice.

9. *a.* Sí, me lo lee.
   b. Sí, te lo lee.
   c. Sí, se lo lee.

10. *a.* Sí, te los presto.
   b. Sí, te lo presto.
   c. No, no se lo presto a ella.

El Mercado de San Blas, Cuzco, Perú

27
Reflexive Pronouns

Helps and Hints

"Mamá, yo me visto ahora.

In this chapter, you will learn that many verbs in Spanish are used with what we call *reflexive pronouns,* or object pronouns that refer back to the subject.

---

me, myself	**nos,** ourselves
te, yourself	**os,** yourselves
se, (*sing.*) yourself, himself, herself, itself; (*pl.*) yourselves, themselves	

1. A reflexive pronoun refers to the same person as the subject of the verb:

   Yo me lavo.　　　*I* wash *myself.*

2. Like all other object pronouns, the reflexive pronoun directly precedes the conjugated verb form.

Reflexive Verbs

vestirse (i), to dress oneself　　　　**enojarse,** to get angry, annoyed

yo	*me*	visto		yo	*me*	enojo

I dress myself,　　　　　　　　　　I get angry
　get dressed, etc.　　　　　　　　　(annoyed), etc.

tú	*te*	vistes		tú	*te*	enojas
Ud.⎫ él ⎬ ella ⎭	*se*	viste		Ud.⎫ él ⎬ ella ⎭	*se*	enoja

nosotros nosotras	*nos*	vestimos	nosotros nosotras	*nos*	enojamos
vosotros vosotras	*os*	vestís	vosotros vosotras	*os*	enojáis
Uds. ellos ellas	*se*	visten	Uds. ellos ellas	*se*	enojan

3. A reflexive verb is a verb that is used most often with a reflexive pronoun (see the list below), but almost any verb that can take a direct object may have a reflexive pronoun as its object:

Ellos **se** preparan para la prueba.   They are preparing (themselves) for the test.

◾◢ Some Common Reflexive Verbs

acordarse (ue) de, to remember
  Me acuerdo de la película.   I remember the film.

acostarse (ue), to go to bed, lie down
  Se acuestan a las once.   They go to bed at eleven o'clock.

alegrarse (de), to be glad (to, of)
  Nos alegramos de verle.   We are glad to see you.

asustarse, to become frightened
  El niño **se asustó** al ver al perro.   The child became frightened on seeing the dog.

bañarse, to bathe (oneself)
  Yo **me baño** todas las mañanas.   I bathe every morning.

callarse, to become silent, stop talking
  Él nunca **se calla.**   He never stops talking.

desayunarse,* to have breakfast
  Nos desayunamos a las ocho.   We have breakfast at eight o'clock.

despertarse (ie), to wake up
  Se despierta cuando suena el despertador.   She wakes up when the alarm clock rings.

dirigirse (a), to direct oneself (to), go (toward)
  Si Uds. **se dirigen** al gerente, obtendrán los   If you go to the manager, you will get the
    informes que necesitan.   information you need.

dormirse (ue), to fall asleep
  Siempre **me duermo** en su clase.   I always fall asleep in his class.

encontrarse (ue), to be (situated), find oneself
  Ahora **se encuentran** en Madrid.   They are now in Madrid.

enfadarse⎫ to get angry
enojarse ⎭
  ¿**Se enfada (Se enoja)** su maestra si no   Does your teacher get angry if you don't do
    hacen sus tareas?   your homework?

*****Desayunarse** is often nonreflexive (**desayunar**).

equivocarse, to be mistaken
El meteorólogo **se equivoca;** no lloverá hoy

The weatherman is mistaken; it will not rain today.

irse
marcharse } to go away, leave
Se fueron (Se marcharon) la semana pasada.

They left last week.

levantarse, to rise, get up ("raise oneself")
¿A qué hora **te levantas?**

At what time do you get up?

llamarse, to be called ("call oneself"), named
¿Cómo **se llama** ese hombre?

What's that man's name?

moverse (ue), to move (oneself)
Se movió a la otra silla.

She moved to the other chair.

pasearse, to take a walk, stroll, ride
Vamos a **pasearnos** por la avenida.
Las muchachas **se pasean** en bicicleta por el parque.

Let's stroll along the avenue.
The girls are riding their bicycles through the park.

peinarse, to comb one's hair
¿Por qué no **te peinas?**

Why don't you comb your hair?

ponerse, to put on (an article of clothing); to become
Me pongo el sombrero.
Se pone enferma.

I put on my hat.
She is becoming ill (getting sick).

quedarse, to stay, remain
Nos quedamos en casa.

We are staying home.

quejarse (de), to complain (about)
Se quejan de la comida.

They're complaining about the food.

quitarse, to remove, take off (clothing)
Me quito el abrigo.

I am taking off my coat.

sentarse (ie), to sit down ("seat oneself")
¿Dónde **te sientas** en la clase de español?

Where do you sit in the Spanish class?

vestirse (i), to get dressed (dress oneself)
Se visten después del desayuno.

They get dressed after breakfast.

4. Note that many reflexive verbs (**irse, quedarse,** etc.) do not have a reflexive equivalent in English.

▮▮ Position of the Reflexive Pronoun in Questions and Negative Clauses

¿**Te quitas** tú los guantes?   Are you taking off your gloves?

Ella **no se marcha** esta tarde.   She isn't leaving this afternoon.

5. In questions and negative clauses, reflexive pronouns have the same position as other object pronouns: *pronoun first, conjugated verb second.* (For their position with verb forms other than those of the present tense, see Chapter 28.)

Practice A: Write the indicated form of the verb in the present tense.

1. yo   _____   _____   _____
                  (peinarse)   (sentarse)   (quejarse)

2. Ud.   _____   _____   _____
                  (encontrarse)   (irse)   (enfadarse)

3. ella   _____   _____   _____
                  (moverse)   (vestirse)   (alegrarse)

4. nosotros   _____   _____   _____
                  (ponerse)   (bañarse)   (acostarse)

5. tú   _____   _____   _____
                  (irse)   (llamarse)   (dirigirse)

Practice B: Change the sentence to a question.

EXAMPLE: José se lava la cara.   *¿Se lava José la cara?*

1. Ellas se peinan ahora.   _____

2. Tú te equivocas siempre.   _____

3. Su padre se despierta temprano todos
     los días.   _____

Practice C: Make the sentence negative.

EXAMPLE: Juan se queda en casa.   *Juan no se queda en casa.*

1. Mi madre se llama Beatriz.   _____

2. Yo me quejo del maestro.   _____

3. Los chicos se levantan tarde.   _____

◼▨ Reflexive Verbs Used With Articles of Clothing and Parts of the Body

Se lavan la cara y **las manos.**	They wash their faces and hands.
Nos ponemos los zapatos y **el sombrero.**	We put on our shoes and hats.

6.   *a.* When the object of a reflexive verb is an article of clothing or a part of the body, the definite article (**el, la, los, las**) is used instead of the possessive adjective (**mi, tu, su,** etc.).

     b. If the subject of the verb is in the plural, the article of clothing or part of the body remains in the singular—unless it normally "comes in two's":

         Ellos **se quitan el sombrero.**   They remove their hats.
         Nos lavamos la cara.   We wash our faces.

     But:

         Nos ponemos los guantes.   We put on our gloves.

Practice D: Complete the Spanish sentences.

1. They are taking off their gloves. Se quitan _____.

2. We are washing our hands. Nos lavamos _____.

3. She is putting on her coat. Ella se pone _____.

4. I am taking off my shoes. Me quito _____.

5. Are you washing your faces? ¿Se lavan Uds. _____?

▲ EJERCICIOS ▲

A. For each statement you make or question you ask, your friend makes a similar statement or asks a similar question. Follow the example.

EXAMPLE: Yo *me baño* todos los días. (peinarse) Yo *me peino* todos los días.

1. Los atletas *se ponen* el uniforme. (quitarse) _____

2. ¿A qué hora *te marchas* mañana? (irse) _____

3. *Se levantan* temprano todos los días. (acostarse) _____

4. *Me despierto* tarde los sábados. (dormirse) _____

5. Mis padres *se enfadan* cuando vuelvo a casa tarde. (enojarse) _____

6. Hoy no *nos desayunamos* en casa. (quedarse) _____

7. ¿Por qué *te asustas*? (callarse) _____

8. Yo *me dirijo* por esa calle. (pasearse) _____

9. ¿*Te alegras* de leer las noticias? (acordarse) _____

10. ¿Dónde *se encuentran* ellas hoy? (sentarse) _____

B. Your uncle is helping you with your Spanish and tests your command of reflexive verbs. Answer him with a complete sentence in Spanish.

1. ¿En qué parte de la casa se desayunan Uds.?

   _____

2. ¿Cuándo te quitas el abrigo?

   _____

3. ¿Se acuerda el profesor (la profesora) de dar muchos exámenes a la clase?

   _____

4. ¿Cómo se llaman tus mejores amigos?

   _____

5. ¿De qué se quejan los alumnos generalmente?

_____

6. ¿Qué te pones cuando hace mucho frío?

_____

7. ¿Dónde se lavan Uds. la cara y las manos?

_____

8. ¿Cuándo se enoja la profesora (el profesor) de español?

_____

9. ¿Con qué te peinas?

_____

10. ¿Cuántas veces por semana (por año) te bañas tú?

_____

C. Write the question that is answered by the given statement.

EXAMPLE: Me lavo con agua y jabón.   _¿Con qué se lava Ud.?_

1. Nos vamos porque estamos cansados.   _____

2. Me acuesto a las once.   _____

3. Nos quedamos aquí tres horas.   _____

4. Me llamo Felipe Rodríguez.   _____

5. Se ponen el sombrero cuando tienen frío.   _____

D. Answer the following questions as shown in the pictures.

1. ¿A qué hora se levanta ella?   **2.** ¿Se ponen el abrigo?

_____   _____

3. ¿Te vas mañana por la mañana?

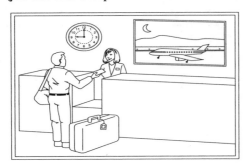

_____

4. ¿Por dónde se pasean?

_____

5. ¿Quiénes se enfadan?

_____

6. ¿Cuándo te acuestas?

_____

7. ¿Se lava ella las manos?

_____

8. ¿Dónde se sientan Uds.?

_____

9. ¿Cómo se llama ese hombre?

_____

10. ¿Qué hacen?

_____

E. *Listening Comprehension.* Your teacher will read aloud ten questions in Spanish. After each question is read, circle the letter of the most appropriate answer.

1. *a.* No, me baño por la noche.
   b. Sí, nos bañamos por la mañana.
   c. Sí, se bañan todos los días.

2. *a.* Sí, me voy a las siete.
   b. No, no se van.
   c. Sí, nos vamos muy temprano.

3. *a.* Sí, te pones los guantes.
   b. No, no me pongo los guantes.
   c. No, nos ponemos los zapatos.

4. *a.* Sí, se acuerda bien de la canción.
   b. Sí, se acuerdan de esa canción.
   c. No, no me acuerdo de la canción.

5. *a.* Te levantas a las ocho.
   b. Nos levantamos a las cinco y media.
   c. Se levantan a las seis.

6. *a.* Me encuentro en la ciudad.
   b. Se encuentran lejos del cine.
   c. Se encuentra cerca de la iglesia.

7. *a.* Me paseo por la plaza.
   b. Nos paseamos por el parque.
   c. Te paseas por la avenida.

8. *a.* Sí, se duerme rápidamente.
   b. Sí, me duermo en diez minutos.
   c. No, no nos dormimos pronto.

9. *a.* Se queda en la calle.
   b. Nos quedamos en la escuela.
   c. Me quedo en casa.

10. *a.* Me quejo de mi profesor de español.
    b. Se queja de sus padres.
    c. Nos quejamos de nuestros amigos.

28
Position of Object Pronouns

Helps and Hints

Object pronouns (direct, indirect, reflexive) are placed according to the type of verb form with which they go. This chapter will deal with the proper placement of the object pronouns. In English, they normally follow any form of the verb, but in Spanish their placement follows certain rules.

      ## In All Tenses

PRESENT:
    Le escribo una carta.

I'm writing him a letter.

PRETERIT:
    Me la vendieron ayer.

They sold it to me yesterday.

IMPERFECT:
    Yo siempre **me** levantaba a las seis.

I always used to get up at six o'clock.

FUTURE:
    Los pondremos en la mesa.

We will put them on the table.

CONDITIONAL:
    ¿**Nos lo** darías tú?

Would you give it to us?

PRESENT PERFECT:
    Lo hemos visto.

We have seen him.

PLUPERFECT:
    ¿Cuándo **se lo** habían enviado ellos?

When had they sent it to you?

PROGRESSIVE TENSES (*see* Chapter 12):
    Estamos esperándo**la.** ⎫
    La estamos esperando. ⎭

We are waiting for her.

1. Object pronouns precede the conjugated form of a verb in any tense.

2. In the compound tenses (the present perfect and pluperfect), object pronouns precede the conjugated form of **haber.**

    Practice A: Insert the object pronouns to form a sentence as shown in the example.

    EXAMPLE: (te lo)   han dado tres veces   *Te lo han dado tres veces.*

    1. (me)   prestarán los libros mañana   _____

    2. (se)   ellos miraron en el espejo   _____

3. (se los) ¿dieron ellos ayer? _____

4. (te) veremos más tarde _____

5. (nos la) tú no habías dicho _____

As Objects of Infinitives

Ellos quieren sentar**se** allí. }
Ellos **se** quieren sentar allí. }   They want to sit there.

Yo no podía hacer**lo.** }
Yo no **lo** podía hacer. }   I could not (was not able to) do it.

Voy a decír**selo.** }
Se lo voy a decir. }   I'm going to tell it to her.

Ellos desearán prestár**melo.** }
Ellos **me lo** desearán prestar. }   They will wish to lend it to me.

3. If a pronoun is the object of an infinitive, it is either attached to the infinitive (quieren sentar**se**) or placed directly before the conjugated verb form that precedes the infinitive (**se** quieren sentar). When double object pronouns are attached to an infinitive, an accent mark is placed on the last vowel of the infinitive (desean prestármelo).

Practice B: Form a sentence in two ways by inserting the object pronouns.

EXAMPLE: (se las) voy a mostrar   _Voy a mostrárselas._
Se las voy a mostrar.

1. (les) no quieren hablar _____

2. (nos) nosotros vamos a levantar _____

3. (me lo) pueden escribir _____

4. (las) van a aprender _____

5. (se lo) ¿deseas mandar? _____

As Objects of Present Participles in the Progressive Tenses

Ella está haciéndo**lo.** }
Ella **lo** está haciendo. }   She is doing it.

Estamos sentándo**nos.** }
Nos estamos sentando. }   We are sitting down.

¿Estabas mandándo**selo?** }
¿**Se lo** estabas mandando? }   Were you sending it to her?

Yo estoy diciéndo**telo.** }
Yo **te lo** estoy diciendo. }   I'm telling it to you.

4. If a pronoun is the object of a present participle, it is either attached to the participle (están esperándo**la**) or placed directly before the form of **estar** that precedes the participle (**la** están esperando). When object pronouns are attached to the participle, an accent mark is placed on the stressed vowel.

> *Practice C:* Form a sentence in two ways by inserting the object pronouns.

> EXAMPLE: (me los)   estaban mandando   *Estaban mandándomelos.*
> *Me los estaban mandando.*

> **1.** (nos)   estamos lavando   _____

> _____

> **2.** (te)   estoy mirando   _____

> _____

> **3.** (se la)   estaba vendiendo   _____

> _____

> **4.** (la)   ellos están aprendiendo _____

> _____

> **5.** (se lo)   ¿estás dando?   _____

> _____

As Objects of Commands

Affirmative	*Negative*
Quédate aquí.	No te quedes aquí.
Remain here.	Don't remain here.
Escríba**me** Ud. una nota.	No **me** escriba Ud. una nota.
Write me a note.	Don't write me a note.
Díga**selo** Uds. ahora.	No **se lo** digan Uds. ahora.
Tell it to her now.	Don't tell it to her now.
Préste**noslos** Ud., por favor.	No **nos los** preste Ud., por favor.
Lend them to us, please.	Don't lend them to us, please.

5. Pronoun objects of an affirmative command are attached to the verb—in which case, an accent mark is placed on the stressed vowel. As objects of a negative command, the pronouns are placed between the word **no** and the verb.

> *Practice D:* Include the indicated object pronouns in the given commands.

> EXAMPLE: (le)   Hable Ud. ___*Háblele Ud.*___ ;   No hable Ud. ___*No le hable Ud.*___

> **1.** (se)   Levante Ud. _____ ;   No levante Ud. _____

> **2.** (me)   Canten Uds. _____ ;   No canten Uds. _____

3. (se las)   Escriba Ud. _____; No escriba Ud. _____

4. (me lo)   Cuenten Uds. _____; No cuenten Uds. _____

5. (se)   Miren Uds. _____; No miren uds. _____

6. (nos la) Diga Ud. _____; No diga Ud. _____

7. (se lo)   Muestre Ud. _____; No muestre Ud. _____

In your answers to items 3, 4, 6, and 7, replace the direct object pronoun with a suitable noun phrase that it could "stand for."

EXAMPLE: Préstesela.   *Préstele la revista.*
           No se la preste.   *No le preste la revista.*

8. _____   _____

9. _____   _____

10. _____   _____

11. _____   _____

◢ EJERCICIOS ◣

A. Form a sentence by inserting the pronouns in parentheses. (In items 1, 7, 9, and 10, form two sentences that differ only in word order.)

EXAMPLES: (lo)   ella vio   *Ella lo vio.*
            (te las)   han prestado   *Te las han prestado.*

1. (me)   no quiere hablar   _____

                                        _____

2. (las)   ¿compraste tú ayer?   _____

3. (le)   no lea Ud. el cuento _____

4. (se)   no miraron en el espejo _____

5. (os)   ¿levantáis vosotros? _____

6. (se)   no vaya Ud.   _____

7. (los)   ¿están Uds. comiendo? _____

                                        _____

8. (lo)   aprendan Uds. ahora   _____

9. (se lo)   estábamos diciendo   _____

                                        _____

10. (me los) ¿pueden mandar?   _____

                                        _____

11. (se las)   digan Uds. más tarde   _____

12. (me la)   no den uds.   _____

13. (os lo)   nosotros hemos dicho   _____

14. (te lo)   ¿contaron ellos?   _____

15. (se los)   ¿quién dijo?   _____

B. Change the sentence from affirmative to negative or vice versa.

EXAMPLES: Déle Ud. el libro.   *No le dé Ud. el libro.*
             No me la escriba.   *Escríbamela.*

1. Dígale la verdad a ella.   _____

2. No me cuente esa historia.   _____

3. Lávense Uds. las manos.   _____

4. No lo haga Ud. ahora.   _____

5. Póngalos en el sofá.   _____

6. No nos los mande Ud.   _____

7. Llévenselo Uds. a él.   _____

8. No se las preste Ud. a ellos.   _____

9. Véndamelo Ud., por favor.   _____

10. No se lo lean Uds. a ella.   _____

C. Repeat the sentence, substituting object pronouns for the underlined words.

EXAMPLES: ¿Ven Uds. el programa?   *¿Lo ven Uds.?*

             Van a mostrar la foto al maestro.   *a. Van a mostrársela.   b. Se la van a mostrar.*

1. ¿Han terminado ellos la tarea?

   _____

2. Empiecen Uds. el trabajo.

   _____

3. Debes estudiar las lecciones.

   a. _____   *b.* _____

4. Estamos mirando la televisión.

   a. _____   *b.* _____

5. ¿Cuándo construyeron esos edificios?

   _____

6. ¿Vas a mandar <u>el mensaje a tus padres</u>?

　　a. _____　　*b.* _____

7. Los niños no dijeron <u>la verdad a su padre</u>.

_____

8. No vendan Uds. <u>el coche a esa señora</u>.

_____

9. ¿Puede Ud. darme <u>cinco dólares</u>?

　　a. _____　　*b.* _____

10. El banco nos prestó <u>el dinero</u>.

_____

D. Express in Spanish.

1. *a.* I saw him last night. _____

　　b. I sent it (*m.*) to him yesterday. _____

2. *a.* Tell her the truth. _____

　　b. Tell it to her. _____

3. They want to speak to him. (Translate in two ways.)

　　(1) _____

　　(2) _____

4. *a.* Don't write to me yet. _____

　　b. Don't write it (*f.*) to me yet. _____

5. I am not bringing you (*Ud.*) the package. (Use the progressive tense and write it two ways.)

　　(1) _____

　　(2) _____

6. I am not bringing it to you. (Use the progressive tense and write it two ways.)

　　(1) _____

　　(2) _____

7. *a.* Pass me the salt and pepper. _____

　　b. Pass them to me. _____

8. *a.* Sit here, please. (Use *Ud.*) _____

　　b. Don't sit there. _____

9. *a.* Put on your hats. (Use *Uds.*) _____

   b. Don't put on your coats. _____

10. We cannot stay here today. (Translate in two ways.)

    (1) _____

    (2) _____

E. *Listening Comprehension.* Your teacher will read aloud ten questions in Spanish. After each question is read, circle the letter of the most appropriate answer.

1. *a.* Sí, lo voy a ver.
   b. Sí, voy a verlos.
   c. No, no la voy a ver.

2. *a.* Se levantaron a las siete y media.
   b. Nos levantamos a las diez.
   c. Me levanté a las ocho y cuarto.

3. *a.* Sí, estoy mirándola.
   b. Sí, lo estoy mirando.
   c. Sí, estoy mirándolas.

4. *a.* No, no la queremos comprar.
   b. No, no queremos comprarlo.
   c. Sí, queremos comprarla.

5. *a.* Sí, las vi ayer.
   b. No, no lo vi.
   c. No, no la vi.

6. *a.* Sí, se los di.
   b. Sí, se lo di.
   c. No, no se la di.

7. *a.* Sí, estamos diciéndoselos.
   b. No, no se la estamos diciendo.
   c. No, no se las estamos diciendo.

8. *a.* Sí, puedo prestárselo.
   b. No, no se los puedo prestar.
   c. No, no puedo prestársela.

9. *a.* No, no puedo mostrárselo.
   b. No, no se la puedo mostrar.
   c. No, no puedo mostrártelos.

10. *a.* Sí, te lo venderé.
    b. Sí, te la venderé.
    c. Sí, se lo venderé a Ud.

29
GUSTAR and Other Verbs Used With Indirect Object Pronouns

Helps and Hints

Since there is no direct translation of "to like" in Spanish, a different construction must be used, as shown in this chapter. There are several other verbs that use a similar construction.

GUSTAR

Me **gusta el disco compacto.**	I like the CD.
Me **gustan los discos compactos.**	I like the CDs.
Me **gusta cantar.**	I like to sing.
Le **gusta la casa.**	{You (*sing*) like / He (She) likes} the house.
¿Le **gustan las casas**?	{Do you like / Does he (she) like} the houses?
Nos **gusta el fútbol.**	We like soccer.
Nos **gustan los deportes.**	We like sports.
Nos **gusta jugar** al tenis.	We like to play tennis.
No les **gusta el programa.**	{You (*pl.*) / They} do not like the program.
¿No les **gustan los programas**?	Don't {you (*pl.*) / they} like the programs?

1. *To like* is expressed in Spanish by using the verb **gustar,** *to please.* Thus, *I like the house* becomes, "The house is pleasing to me": **La casa me gusta.** Note that the subject often *follows* the verb: **Me gusta la casa.**

2. In constructions with the verb **gustar,** the object of the verb "to like" becomes the subject of **gustar.** The subject of "to like" becomes the indirect object of **gustar:**

	SUBJECT	VERB	OBJECT
English	I	like	{the movie / to read
	INDIRECT OBJECT	**VERB** (agrees with subject)	**SUBJECT**
Spanish	**me**	**gusta**	{la película / leer

	SUBJECT	VERB	OBJECT
English	I	like	the tapes
	INDIRECT OBJECT	VERB (agrees with subject)	SUBJECT
Spanish	**me**	**gustan**	las cintas

3. **Gustar** is used in the third person singular (**gusta**) if what is liked is in the singular or expressed by an infinitive. It is used in the third person plual (**gustan**) if what is liked is in the plural.

4. **Gusta** and **gustan** are regularly preceded by an indirect object pronoun, that is, by **me, te, le, nos, os,** or **les.**

5. When **gustar** is used, a statement can be changed to a question without changing the word order:

   Le gusta comer.   He likes to eat.
   ¿Le gusta comer?   Does he like to eat?

   Practice A: Change the verb from singular to plural or vice versa.

   1. Nos gusta el juguete.   _____ los juguetes.

   2. No les gustan los gatos.   _____ el gato.

   3. ¿Te gusta la comida?   ¿_____ las comidas?

   4. No me gustan las revistas.   _____ la revista.

   5. ¿Le gusta estudiar?   ¿_____ las lecciones?

Using GUSTAR When the Subject of "To Like" Is a Noun

   A Robert le gusta la canción.   Robert likes the song.

   ¿A los chicos les gusta correr?   Do the boys like to run?

   A la niña no le gustan los dulces.   The child (*f*) does not like the candy.

6. *a.* When the subject of *to like* is a noun—for example, the name of a person—the equivalent Spanish expression has the form **a** + *person* + **le** or **les** + **gusta(n)** + *the thing liked:*

   A Juan le gustan <u>los zapatos nuevos</u> .
                          (the thing liked)

   b. **The phrase** a + *person* may also *follow* the verb:

   Le gustan **a Juan** los zapatos nuevos.

   c. The thing liked may be expressed by an infinitive:

   A Juan le gusta **trabajar.**

Practice B: In each pair of expressions, the first refers to persons, the second, to what they like. Express this idea in a sentence.

EXAMPLE: Juana, la casa   *A Juana le gusta la casa.*

1. mis amigos, jugar   _____

2. la chica, los discos compactos _____

3. Roberto, el equipo   _____

4. los profesores, la clase   _____

5. el padre, mirar la televisión _____

In items 6–8, the second expression refers to what is *not* liked.

EXAMPLE: Juana, la casa   *A Juana no le gusta la casa.*

6. los alumnos, el examen   _____

7. mis amigos, trabajar   _____

8. Elena, las novelas   _____

In items 9 and 10, form questions.

EXAMPLE: Juana, la casa   *¿A Juana le gusta la casa?*
                              or
                              ¿Le gusta a Juana la casa?

9. el muchacho, estudiar   _____

10. tus amigas, el tenis   _____

◼️▰ Clarifying the Meanings of *LE* and *LES*

Le gusta el perro.	You like the dog.	A **Ud.** le gusta el perro.
	He likes the dog.	A **él** le gusta el perro.
	She likes the dog.	A **ella** le gusta el perro.

¿No **les** gusta?	Don't you (*pl.*) like it?	¿A **Uds.** no les gusta?
	Don't they (*m.*) like it?	¿A **ellos** no les gusta?
	Don't they (*f.*) like it?	¿A **ellas** no les gusta?

7. Since **le** and **les** have several possible meanings, the intended meaning can be clarified by adding one of the following phrases:

| for **le:** | for **les:** |
| **a Ud., a él, a ella** | **a Uds., a ellos, a ellas** |

Practice C: Add the correct phrase to clarify the meaning of the Spanish pronoun.

1. They (*f.*) do not like the work.

_____ no les gusta el trabajo.

2. Do you (*sing*) like to eat?

¿_____ le gusta comer?

3. She likes the flowers.

_____ le gustan las flores.

4. Don't you (*pl.*) like the gift?

¿_____ no les gusta el regalo?

5. He does not like the tapes.

_____ no le gustan las cintas.

The clarifying phrase may either precede or follow the verb. Continue as before:

6. She likes the books.

Le gustan _____ los libros.

7. Doesn't he like to swim?

¿No le gusta _____ nadar?

8. They (*m.*) like the new house.

Les gusta _____ la casa nueva.

Using GUSTAR When "To Like" Has the Object "It" or "Them"

—¿Te gusta mi traje?   "Do you like my suit?"
—Sí, me gusta.   "Yes, I like it."

—¿A él le gustan las corbatas? "Does he like the ties?"
—No, no le gustan.   "No, he does not like them."

8. In Spanish, *I like it* becomes "it pleases me," *she likes them* becomes "they please her," etc. Thus, the object pronouns *it* and *them* would be expressed by *subject* pronouns in Spanish. Since the subject of **gustar** is not expressed if it is a pronoun, no equivalent of *it* or *them* appears in the Spanish translation:

$$\text{we like it} = \underset{\text{(us)}}{nos} \ \underset{\text{(it pleases)}}{gusta}$$

Practice D: Express in Spanish.

1. We do not like it.   _____

2. I do not like them.   _____

3. Do they like it?   _____

4. She does not like them.   _____

5. Don't you (*familiar sing*) like them? _____

GUSTAR In All Tenses

| *Singular* | *Plural* |

PRESENT:

Me **gusta** el programa.   Me **gustan** los programas.
I like the program.   I like the programs.

PRETERIT:

¿No te **gustó** el espectáculo?   ¿No te **gustaron** los espectáculos?
Didn't you like the show?   Didn't you like the shows?

IMPERFECT:

Siempre le **gustaba** el español.   Siempre le **gustaban** sus clases.
He always liked Spanish.   He always liked his classes.

FUTURE:

Le **gustará** el vestido.   No le **gustarán** los zapatos.
She will like the dress.   She will not like the shoes.

CONDITIONAL:

Les **gustaría** salir.   Les **gustarían** estos regalos.
They would like to leave.   They would like these gifts.

PRESENT PERFECT:

Nos **ha gustado** la pieza.   No nos **han gustado** los libros.
We have liked the play.   We have not liked the books.

PLUPERFECT:

Le **había gustado** la cinta.   Le **habían gustado** las cintas.
He had liked the tape.   He had liked the tapes.

9. In all tenses, **gustar** is used only in the third person singular and plural.*

Practice E: Complete the Spanish sentences.

1. They used to like tennis.   _____ el tenis.

2. Has he liked the gifts?   ¿_____ los regalos?

3. She will not like the program.   _____ el programa.

4. Did you (*familiar sing*) like the ice cream?   ¿_____ el helado?

5. We would like to play.   _____ jugar.

6. They had not liked the new house.   _____ la casa nueva.

▰▰ Other Verbs Used Like GUSTAR

faltar, to be lacking (to) [*to need*]
  Nos falta dinero.   We need money. ("Money is lacking to us.")
  Le faltan camisas.   He needs shirts.

importar, to be important (to) [*to care, to matter*]

                                            ⎧ I don't care about the prices.
  No **me importan** los precios.   ⎨ The prices don't matter (are not important)
                                            ⎩   to me.

                                            ⎧ What do you care about television?
  ¿Que **te** importa la televisión?   ⎨ What does television matter to you?

_____

*There are exceptions to this rule, but they are beyond the scope of this book.

interesar, to interest (someone) [*to be interested in*]
   ¿Les interesaba a Uds. la música?

   No **me interesan** las cintas.

Were you interested in the music?
("Did the music interest you?")
I'm not interested in the tapes.
(The tapes do not interest me.)

parecer, to seem [*to think, be of the opinion*]
   Me parece que no vienen.

   —¿Qué **les parecieron** las canciones?
   —**Nos parecieron** muy buenas.

I think (It seems to me) that they are not
   coming.
"What did you think of the songs?"
"We thought they were very good."

quedar, to be left (to someone), to have left
   Nos quedaron diez dólares.
   Les queda una hora.

We had ten dollars left.
They have one hour left.

tocar, to be someone's turn (generally with infinitive)
   A Juanito **le tocará** jugar más tarde.

It will be Juanito's turn to play later.

10. The verbs **faltar, importar, interesar, parecer, quedar,** and **tocar** are used like **gustar;**
   that is, the forms of the third person singular and plural are always preceded by an indirect
   object pronoun (**me, te, le, nos, os,** or **les**):

   A las chicas **les quedó** sólo un billete.   The girls had only one ticket left.

   Practice F: Complete the sentence by changing the verb from the singular to the plural or vice
   versa.

   1. Nos faltaban libros.

      Nos _____ un libro.

   2. No me interesa la pieza.

      No me _____ las piezas.

   3. ¿Qué te parecían los conciertos?

      ¿Qué te _____ el concierto.

   4. ¿No les importa el dinero?

      ¿No les _____ los programas?

   5. ¿Cuántos dólares le quedaban al maestro?

      ¿Cuánto tiempo le _____?

▲ EJERCICIOS ▲

A. Rewrite the sentence, replacing the verb with the corresponding form of the verb in parentheses.

   EXAMPLE: Me quedan tres dólares. (faltar)
                  Me faltan tres dólares.

   1. No nos gusta hacerlo. (importar)   _____

   2. ¿Te tocó escribir en la pizarra? (gustar)   _____

   3. No me importaban esas cosas. (interesar)   _____

   4. ¿Les gustaría salir temprano? (importar)   _____

   5. No me interesarían sus chistes. (gustar)   _____

B. The authors' word processor has gone haywire. Arrange the words to form a sentence.

1. ¿   ellos   les   a   gustaba   cartas   escribir   no   ?

_____

2. parque   los   me   andar   domingos   el   por   gusta

_____

3. ¿   cuaderno   quedan   el   cuántos   te   papeles   en   ?

_____

4. novelas   de   no   interesan   Hemingway   esas   nos

_____

5. ¿   noche   te   ir   una   conmigo   esta   discoteca   a   gustaría   ?

_____

C. Answer your friend's questions with a complete sentence in Spanish.

1. ¿Te gustan las películas extranjeras? _____

_____

2. ¿Te gusta pasar los domingos leyendo o jugando? _____

_____

3. ¿Cuándo les gusta a Uds. ir a la playa? _____

_____

4. ¿Te parece interesante la música clásica? _____

_____

5. ¿Cuánto dinero te queda al fin de la semana? _____

_____

D. Write the question that is answered by the given statement.

EXAMPLE: No, me gusta leer revistas.
        ¿Le gusta leer libros?

1. No, no nos gustaría viajar este verano. _____

2. Sí, me interesan estos videos. _____

3. Les gustaba esuchar la radio. _____

4. No, no le gustan a María. _____

5. Te tocará mañana. _____

E. Two friends are speaking. When one makes a statement, the other one restates it as shown in the example. Be careful of the tense used.

EXAMPLE: Me gustan estos vídeos. (a José)
          A José le gustan también.

1. A Pepita le interesó la cinta. (a mí)   _____

2. Ahora nos toca recitar. (a ellas)   _____

3. Me gustaría ver esa película. (a Pepe)   _____

4. A ellos les queda un minuto para hablar. (a ti)   _____

5. Te importa estudiar más. (a tu hermano)   _____

F. As in the previous exercise, the friend restates the sentence, but this time it is in the negative.

EXAMPLE: No me gustan estos vídeos.
          A José no le gustan tampoco.

1. A Pepita no le interesó la cinta. (a mí)   _____

2. Ahora no nos toca recitar. (a ellas)   _____

3. No me gustaría ver esa película. (a Pepe) _____

4. A ellos no les queda un minuto. (a ti)   _____

5. No te importa estudiar más. (a tu hermano) _____

G. Express in Spanish.

1. *a.* I do not like these programs.   _____

       b. I do not like this program.   _____

2. *a.* Do they like to play baseball?   _____

       b. Does she like to play tennis?   _____

3. *a.* We like those paintings.   _____

       b. My father likes those paintings too.   _____

4. *a.* He needs ("lacks") twenty dollars.   _____

       b. I need fifteen pesos.   _____

5. *a.* It doesn't matter to us. (We don't care.) _____

       b. It did not matter to Mary. (Mary didn't care.) _____

6. *a.* Who likes to see foreign films? (*¿A quién le. . .?*)   _____

       b. Who is interested in Spanish films?   _____

7. *a.* Does he like them a lot?   _____

       b. No, he doesn't like them.   _____

8. *a.* Would she like to go to the movies with me? _____

   b. Would they like to go downtown with us? _____

9. *a.* It's your turn to play now. (Use the familiar sing.) _____

   b. It's not my turn to drive tonight. _____

10. *a.* What do you (*pl.*) think of the show? (Use *parecer*.) _____

    b. We think it's very bad. _____

H. *Listening Comprehension.* Your teacher will read aloud ten questions in Spanish. After each question is read, circle the letter of the most appropriate answer.

1. *a.* Sí, me gustan mucho.
   b. No, no te gustan.
   c. No, no me gusta.

2. *a.* No, no le gustaba.
   b. Sí, le gustan.
   c. No, le gusta jugar al béisbol.

3. *a.* No, prefiero ir a un restaurante.
   b. Sí, nos gustaría mucho.
   c. Sí, le gustaría.

4. *a.* Sí, me interesa mucho.
   b. No, prefieren la televisión.
   c. No, no les interesaba.

5. *a.* Me parecen malas.
   b. Nos parece muy buena.
   c. No me parece interesante.

6. *a.* Nos gustaría quedarnos en casa.
   b. Me gustaría ir a la Florida.
   c. Me ha gustado viajar por España.

7. *a.* Le quedan veinte dólares.
   b. Te quedan diez centavos.
   c. Les queda un peso.

8. *a.* Me tocó anoche.
   b. Nos tocará más tarde.
   c. Me tocará mañana.

9. *a.* No, no le gustan.
   b. No, le gusta salir a la calle.
   c. No, les gusta jugar en la calle.

10. *a.* Les interesan las discotecas.
    b. Le interesa la música *rock*.
    c. Me interesan los deportes.

Criadero de Alpacas, Ecuador

30
Prepositional Pronouns

Helps and Hints

Pronouns that follow prepositions in Spanish are for the most part the same as the subject pronouns, with a few exceptions, as you will see in this chapter.

Prepositions

COMMON ONE-WORD PREPOSITIONS

a, to, at
con, with
de, of, form, about
en, in, on, at (a place)

para, for
por, through, by, for
sin, without
sobre, on, about

COMMON TWO-WORD PREPOSITIONS

acerca de, about, concerning
antes de, before
cerca de, near
delante de, in front of

después de, after
detrás de, behind, in back of
lejos de, far from

Pronouns That Follow Prepositions

El regalo es **para mí.**	The gift is for me.
Hablaban **de ti.**	They were talking about you.
Vamos **con Ud. (Uds.)**	We are going with you.
Estoy **cerca de él.**	I am near him.
Salen **sin ella.**	They are leaving without her.
El edificio está **delante de nosotros(-as).**	The building is in front of us.
El sótano está **debajo de vosotros(-as).**	The cellar is under you.
Estoy **lejos de ellos(-as).**	I am far from them.

1. Prepositional pronouns are the same as the subject pronouns except for **yo**, which becomes **mí**, and **tú**, which becomes **ti.**

2. Note these special forms:

conmigo, with me   **contigo,** with you (*familiar sing*)

Practice A: Write in Spanish.

1. for us   _____

2. near you (*familiar sing.*)   _____

3. in front of me   _____

4. without them (*m.*)   _____

5. after her   _____

6. with me   _____

Spanish Equivalents of "It" and "Them" as Objects of Prepositions

Expressions such as "They are going to it" as a substitute for "They are going to the movies" are generally not expressed in an equivalent way in Spanish and therefore are beyond the scope of this book.

The Pronoun *SÍ*

Juan compró el libro **para sí.**	Juan bought the book for himself.
Ellas hablan **acerca de sí.**	They're talking about themselves.
Llevan su ropa **consigo.**	They're taking their clothes with them.
	(They're taking along their clothes.)
Juana habla **consigo.**	Juana talks to herself.

3. As object of a preposition, **sí** means *yourself, yourselves, himself, herself,* or *themselves.* Note the special form **consigo** (= **con** + **sí**).

> *Practice B:* Underline the expression that completes the sentence correctly.

1. José goes with him.
   José va (con él, consigo).

2. Pancho takes his book with him.
   Pancho trae sus libros (con él, consigo).

3. The books are for her.
   Los libros son (para ella, para sí).

4. The men talk about themselves.
   Los hombres hablan (de ellos, de sí).

5. Are you bringing the candy with you?
   ¿Trae Ud. los dulces (con Ud., consigo)?

6. Are they going with you?
   ¿Van (con Ud., consigo)?

Objects of Verbs and Objects of Prepositions

Les escribo.	I write to them.
Tengo una carta para **ellos.**	I have a letter for them.

4. Do not confuse the kinds of pronouns presented in Chapters 24–28 with the type of pronoun discussed in this chapter. The terms "direct object" and "indirect object" refer to objects of *verbs,* whereas prepositional pronouns are the objects of *prepositions:*

DIRECT OBJECT	INDIRECT OBJECT	OBJECT OF PREPOSITION
yo **la** veo	yo **le** doy el libro	yo voy con **ella**
I see *her*	I give *her* the book	I go with *her*

When a clarifying phrase is added (see §2, page 183), note that **a** is followed by prepositional pronouns: "yo le doy el libro a **Ud.** (a **él**, a **ella**).

Practice C: Underline the phrase or pronoun that completes the sentence correctly.

1. Nosotros (les, a ellos) escribimos.

2. Yo hablo con (la, ella).

3. (Me, mí) dicen cosas interesantes.

4. La silla está detrás de (te, ti, tú).

5. ¿(Lo, a Ud.) ven ellos?

6. Nunca les hablamos a (los, ellos) porque ellos nunca nos hablan a (nos, nosotros).

 **EJERCICIOS**

A. Repeat the sentence orally, substituting a pronoun for the words following the preposition in the underlined expression. (Write the new expression in the blank at the right.)

EXAMPLE: Hablamos con la hermana de Alberto.   *con ella*
            Hablamos con ella.

1. Estos discos compactos son para mi amigo Pedro.   _____

2. Vivo cerca de mis primas.   _____

3. Sin los profesores no sabríamos nada.   _____

4. El profesor está delante de los estudiantes.   _____

5. ¿Qué hay detrás de Juan?   _____

6. Fuimos al cine con Ana y Lola.   _____

7. No quiero ir a una universidad lejos de mis padres.   _____

8. Siempre pensamos en nuestras familias.   _____

9. Entre después de Elena.   _____

10. Hemos traído unos libros para la profesora.   _____

B. Answer with a complete sentence in Spanish. (In **3** and **4,** use the familiar singular in your reply.)

1. ¿Es para Ud. el libro?   Sí, _____

2. ¿Podemos ir al museo contigo?   No, _____

3. ¿Hablas de mí?   Sí, _____

4. ¿Vas al baile sin mí?   Sí, _____

5. ¿Viven ellos lejos de Uds.?   No, _____

C. Give the Spanish equivalents.

1. Who is traveling with you (*familiar sing*) next summer?

_____

2. Without him we can't finish our work.

_____

3. We are not going to the concert without you (*familiar sing*)

_____

4. Do you (*Ud.*) want to go to the tennis match with me?

_____

5. They are buying the food for themselves.

_____

6. Who is in front of you (*familiar sing*)?

_____

7. Nobody is in front of me.

_____

8. Are you talking about us?

_____

9. No, we are talking about them (*f.*).

_____

10. I'm sending the package to him. (Include a clarifying phrase—see §2, page 183.)

D. *Listening Comprehension.* Your teacher will read aloud ten questions in Spanish. After each question is read, circle the letter of the most appropriate answer.

1. *a.* Nadie va contigo.
   b. Carmen va conmigo.
   c. José va con ella.

2. *a.* Hay un árbol detrás de ti.
   b. Hay una mesa detrás de mí.
   c. Hay un edificio detrás de ella.

3. *a.* Nuestros padres hablan acerca de nosotros.
   b. Nosotros hablamos acerca de ti.
   c. Mis amigos hablan acerca de mí.

4. *a.* Alfonso vive cerca de nosotros.
   b. Mi vecino Roberto vive cerca de mí.
   c. La familia López vive cerca de ellos.

5. *a.* No, no es para ti.
   b. Sí, es para Uds.
   c. Sí, es para Ud.

6. *a.* No, no vengo contigo.
   b. No, no vengo con él.
   c. Sí, vengo con ellos.

7. *a.* No, no voy contigo.
   b. No, no voy con él.
   c. Sí, voy con ella.

8. *a.* Traen un pastel consigo.
   b. Traemos los libros con nosotras.
   c. Traigo un cuaderno conmigo.

9. *a.* Felipe entró antes de ti.
   b. Ella entró antes de mí.
   c. Elena entró antes de ella.

10. *a.* José habla conmigo.
    b. Nadie habla con nosotros.
    c. El profesor habla consigo.

31

The Passive SE and the Indefinite SE

The Passive *SE*

¿Qué **se vende** en esa tienda?
What is sold in that store?

Se vende pan.   **Se venden** computadoras.
Bread is sold.   Computers are sold.

¿Qué **se compra** allí?
What is bought there?

Se compra buena comida.   **Se compran** refrescos.
Good food is bought.   Soft drinks are bought.

¿Qué **se ve** en la televisión?
What is seen on television?

Se ve un programa bueno.   **Se ven** muchos programas.
A good program is seen.   Many programs are seen.

1. **Se** + a third-person verb form is often equivalent to a third-person form of *to be* + a past participle: bread *is sold,* the programs *are seen,* the food *was eaten.* In this construction, the pronoun **se** is called the passive **se.** The verb is third person singular if the subject is in the singular, third person plural if the subject is in the plural.*

2. When the passive **se** is used, the sentence may be expressed in English in several ways:

Se venden buenos discos compactos en esa tienda.
$$\left.\begin{array}{l}\text{Good CDs are sold} \\ \text{One sells good CDs} \\ \left.\begin{array}{l}\text{You} \\ \text{They} \\ \text{People}\end{array}\right\} \text{ sell good CDs}\end{array}\right\} \text{ in that store.}$$

---

*In other words, the verb is used reflexively: see Chapter 27. When **se** is passive, note that the subject usually *follows* the verb:

(reflexive **se**) **Los niños** se lavan.   The children wash themselves.
(passive **se**) Se lavan **los platos.**   The dishes are being washed.

Practice A: Complete the answers to each question.

EXAMPLE: ¿Qué se compra en esa tienda?

a. ___*Se compra*___ ropa.

b. ___*Se compran*___ sellos.

1. ¿Qué se aprende en nuestra escuela?

a. _____ español.

b. _____ tres lenguas.

c. _____ matemáticas.

d. _____ biología.

2. ¿Qué se oye en la radio?

a. _____ música.

b. _____ noticias.

c. _____ una sinfonía.

d. _____ los partidos de fútbol.

3. Qué se come en este restaurante?

a. _____ postres buenos.

b. _____ arroz con pollo.

c. _____ biftec.

d. _____ muchas variedades de pescado.

3. The passive **se** is also used when the subject is an infinitive phrase.

No **se permite** <u>fumar en este edificio</u>.
    subject
	Smoking is not permitted in this building.
	    ("To-smoke-in-this building is not permitted.")

Se puede <u>viajar allí en autobús</u>. subject	You (One, People) can travel there by bus.
Se debe <u>ayudar a los pobres</u>. subject	The poor should be helped.

Practice B: Complete the Spanish sentence with an expression containing **se.**

1. One should study in order to learn. (Use the verb **deber.**)

_____ para aprender.

2. Where is smoking forbidden?

¿Dónde _____?

3. You can't read without light.

No _____ sin luz.

The Indefinite *SE*

Se dice que es inteligente.	It is said that he is intelligent.

No **se sabe** mucho acerca de ellos.

$$\left.\begin{array}{l}\text{Not much is known}\\\text{One doesn't know much}\\\left.\begin{array}{l}\text{We}\\\text{People}\end{array}\right\}\text{ don't know much}\end{array}\right\}\text{ about them.}$$

En la sala de recreo **se juega** a las cartas o **se lee.**

$$\left\{\begin{array}{l}\text{In the recreation room,}\\\text{one plays cards or reads.}\\\left.\begin{array}{l}\text{you}\\\text{we}\\\text{they}\\\text{people}\end{array}\right\}\text{ play cards or read.}\\\text{(There is card playing and reading.)}\end{array}\right.$$

No **se come** en mi clase.

$$\left\{\begin{array}{l}\left.\begin{array}{l}\text{One doesn't eat}\\\text{You}\\\text{We}\\\text{They}\\\text{People}\end{array}\right\}\text{ don't eat in my class.}\\\text{(No eating in my class.)}\end{array}\right.$$

4. **Se** is used with the third person singular form of the verb if the verb does not have a definite subject. This construction can be translated in several ways: **se dice** = *it is said, one says, you say, we (they) say, people say.*

   Practice C: Complete the Spanish sentences with expressions containing **se.**

   1. We pay before entering.

      _____ antes de entrar.

   2. How do you say *cine* in English?

      ¿Cómo _____ *cine* en inglés?

   3. You say *movies.*

      _____ *movies.*

   4. What do people do here on Sundays?

      ¿Qué _____ aquí los domingos?

   5. They play tennis or they swim in the pool.

      _____ al tenis o _____ en la piscina.

   6. There is dancing at their party.

      _____ en su fiesta.

Using the Passive *SE*

A. IN VARIOUS TENSES

Singular	*Plural*
PRESENT:	
Se abre la puerta.	**Se abren** las puertas.
The door is opened.	The doors are opened.
PRETERIT:	
Se abrió la puerta.	**Se abrieron** las puertas.
The door was opened.	The doors were opened.
IMPERFECT:	
Se abría la puerta.	**Se abrían** las puertas.
The door was being opened.	The doors were being opened.
FUTURE:	
Se abrirá la puerta.	**Se abrirán** las puertas.
The door will be opened.	The doors will be opened.
CONDITIONAL:	
Se abriría la puerta.	**Se abrirían** las puertas.
The door would be opened.	The doors would be opened.
PRESENT PERFECT:	
Se ha abierto la puerta.	**Se han abierto** las puertas.
The door has been opened.	The doors have been opened.
PLUPERFECT:	
Se había abierto la puerta.	**Se habían abierto** las puertas.
The door had been opened.	The doors had been opened.

B. WITH INFINITIVES AND PRESENT PARTICIPLES

INFINITIVE:

{**Se puede** abrir la puerta.}
{**Puede** abrirse la puerta. }
The door can be opened.

{**Se pueden** abrir las puertas.}
{**Pueden** abrirse las puertas. }
The doors can be opened.

PRESENT PARTICIPLE:

{**Se está abriendo** la puerta.}
{**Está abriéndose** la puerta. }
The door is being opened.

{**Se están abriendo** las puertas.}
{**Están abriéndose** las puertas. }
The doors are being opened.

Practice D: Change the verb form from the singular to the plural or vice versa.

1. Mañana *se verán* buenos programas en la televisión.

   Esta noche _____ un programa especial.

2. Esta tarde *se ha encontrado* dinero en la calle.

   Esta mañana _____ veinte dólares.

3. *Se sabía* la causa del accidente.

_____ muchas cosas acerca de ellos.

4. En la clase de inglés *se leyeron* seis novelas.

En la clase de español _____ una novela el semestre pasado.

5. *Se está lavando* la ropa.

_____ los platos.

6. *Se han vendido* las joyas.

_____ el coche.

Practice E: Change to the indicated tense.

1. Se prohíbe comer en esta clase.

(imperfect)   _____ comer en la clase.

2. No se permitirá fumar allí.

(conditional)   No _____ jugar allí.

3. Se debe ir a la escuela.

(present perfect)   _____ volver a casa.

4. Se necesitaba aprender la lengua.

(present)   _____ estudiar mucho.

5. Se ha podido tomar el autobús.

(future)   _____ tomar el tren.

Using the Indefinite *SE* in Various Tenses

PRESENT:
Se dice, it is said, one says, you say, they say, people say

PRETERIT:
se dijo, it was said, one said, you said, they said, people said

IMPERFECT:
se decía, it was being said, people were saying, etc.

FUTURE:
se dirá, it will be said, people will say, etc.

CONDITIONAL:
se diría, it would be said, people would say, etc.

PRESENT PERFECT:
se ha dicho, it has been said, people have said, etc.

PLUPERFECT:
se había dicho, it had been said, people had been saying, etc.

WITH INFINITIVES AND PRESENT PARTICIPLES:

se puede decir⎫
puede decirse⎬ it can be said, one can say, etc.

se está diciendo⎫
está diciéndose⎬ it is being said, people are saying, etc.

Practice F: Change to the indicated tense.

1. Se decía que eran tontos.

   (present) _____ que son inteligentes.

2. Se sabe que vienen mañana.

   (present perfect) _____ que van al cine.

3. Se jugaba al béisbol en el verano.

   (future) _____ al tenis si hace buen tiempo.

4. ¿Qué se hacía allí?

   (pluperfect) ¿Qué _____ antes?

5. Se está insistiendo en que el informe es falso.

   (imperfect) _____ en que la historia era verdadera.

▲ **EJERCICIOS** ▲

A. Repeat the sentence orally, replacing the underlined verb with the corresponding form of the verb in parentheses. (Write the new verb form in the blank at the right.)

EXAMPLE: Se enseñan cuatro lenguas. (aprender)   *Se aprenden*
           Se aprenden cuatro lenguas.

1. ¿A qué hora se toma café en su casa? (beber)   _____

2. En ese restaurante se sirven buenas comidas. (preparar)   _____

3. ¿A qué hora se abrirá el cine? (cerrar)   _____

4. ¿Dónde se compraron esos zapatos baratos? (vender)   _____

5. ¿En qué estación se esperaba el tren? (tomar)   _____

6. Se visitarán muchas ciudades en el viaje. (ver)   _____

7. Para ir de un piso a otro se baja la escalera. (subir)   _____

8. En nuestra clase se discuten muchas cosas. (decir)   _____

9. ¿Qué se sabía acerca de ese autor? (escribir)   _____

10. En el concierto se escucharon muchas canciones. (oír)   _____

B. Change the verb to the indicated tense.

EXAMPLE: Se ve que son inteligentes.
   (imperfect) *Se veía* que eran inteligentes.

1. Se sabe que es un buen profesor.

   (future)   _____ que es un buen jugador.

2. ¿Qué se dice acerca del Presidente?

   (preterit)   ¿Qué _____ ayer en la clase?

3. Se cree que la guerra es inevitable.

   (imperfect)   _____ que la guerra era horrible.

4. Se prohíbe cruzar la calle con la luz roja.

   (present perfect)   _____ cruzar ese puente.

5. No se paga para entrar en la biblioteca.

   (conditional)   No _____ para entrar en el zoo.

C. A friend of your Spanish teacher from Argentina is visiting your class and asks questions about your school and city. Answer her questions with a complete sentence in Spanish.

1. ¿Cuántas lenguas se enseñan en su escuela?

   _____

2. ¿Se permite fumar en ciertos restaurantes?

   _____

3. ¿A qué hora se abren las puertas de su tienda favorita?

   _____

4. ¿Dónde se puede oír buena música *rock*?

   _____

5. ¿Por dónde se entra en su escuela?

   _____

6. ¿Qué se dice acerca del alcalde de su ciudad?

   _____

7. ¿Qué cosas se observan en una calle típica de su ciudad?

   _____

8. ¿Dónde se puede bailar por la noche?

   _____

9. ¿Dónde se pueden comprar revistas y periódicos extranjeros?

_____

10. ¿Por qué se estudia español en su escuela?

_____

D. Write the question that is answered by the given statement. Choose from the list of starting words or phrases and use each one only once: **dónde, cuántas, qué, a qué hora, con qué.**

EXAMPLE: Se venden computadoras.
            ¿Qué se vende en esa tienda?

1. Se sirven tres comidas al día.   _____

2. Se corta con un cuchillo.   _____

3. Se vieron en la televisión.   _____

4. En mi casa se toma a mediodía.   _____

5. Se bailará, se cantará y se tomarán refrescos. _____

E. Describe what is happening in each picture, starting with "**se.**" The verb to be used is supplied.

EXAMPLE:

(escuchar) Se escucha la música.

1. (hacer) _____

3. (jugar) _____

2. (comer) _____

4. (bailar) _____

5. (leer) _____

8. (pagar) _____

6. (subir) _____

9. (esperar) _____

7. (cruzar) _____

10. (ver) _____

F. *Listening Comprehension.* Your teacher will read aloud ten questions in Spanish. After each question is read, circle the letter of the most appropriate answer.

1. *a.* Se ven pinturas famosas.
   b. Se veían cuadros interesantes.
   c. Se oye música clásica.

2. *a.* Se compraba pan.
   b. Se compran corbatas, camisas y zapatos.
   c. Se compraban trajes, vestidos y sombreros.

3. *a.* Se venden en una librería.
   b. Se vende en una librería.
   c. Se venden en la biblioteca.

4. *a.* Sí, se sabían los verbos.
   b. No, se sabía muy poco.
   c. Sí, la lección se sabía bien.

5. *a.* Se saldrá por la puerta principal.
   b. Se saldría por la la tarde.
   c. Se saldrá a las tres.

6. *a.* Se aprende a hablar, a escribir y a leer.
   b. Se aprende a jugar al tenis.
   c. Se aprende a tomar limonada.

7. *a.* Cuando se está bien.
   b. Cuando se está enfermo.
   c. Cuando se sabe la lección.

8. *a.* Se estudiaron las lecturas.
   b. Se estudiarán los verbos, el vocabulario y la gramática.
   c. Se estudiará biología.

9. *a.* Se permite en ciertos lugares.
   b. Se permite en la sala de clase.
   c. Se permitía en el teatro.

10. *a.* Se miraba para saber qué hora era.
   b. Se mira para dormir.
   c. Se mira para saber la hora.

Part 6
Other Grammar Topics

⋈⋈⋈⋈⋈⋈⋈⋈⋈⋈⋈⋈⋈⋈⋈⋈⋈⋈⋈⋈⋈⋈⋈⋈⋈⋈⋈⋈⋈⋈

32
Using HACE and HACÍA to Express the Passage of Time

Helps and Hints

In this chapter, you will learn how to express sentences like "I have been living here for three years" or "How long had they been playing tennis when it began to rain."

¿Cuánto tiempo hace?

¿**Cuánto tiempo hace** que **vives** aquí?

How long have you been living here? ("How much time does-it-make that you are living here?")

Hace dos años que **vivo** aquí.

I have been living here for two years. ("It makes two years that I am living here.")

1. The sentences above express an action or situation that began in the past and continues into the present. To construct sentences like these, use the following formulas:

   To form a question: ¿**cuánto tiempo hace que** + *present tense*?
   To form a statement: **hace** + *time* + **que** + *present tense*

   Practice A: Complete the Spanish sentences.

   1. How long have they been working there?

      ¿Cuánto tiempo hace que _____ allí?

   2. We have been studying Spanish for three years.

      Hace tres años que _____ español.

3. How long have you been waiting for the report?

   ¿_____ que esperas el informe?

4. Raquel has been reading that novel for two weeks.

   _____ que Raquel lee esa novela.

5. The boys have been playing baseball for several years.

   Hace varios años que los muchachos _____ al béisbol.

6. How long has she been ill?

   ¿Cuánto tiempo hace que ella _____ enferma?

7. I haven't had lunch with them for several days.

   _____ que no tomo el almuerzo con ellos.

¿Cuánto tiempo hacía?

¿Cuánto tiempo hacía que **trabajaban** allí cuando tú los viste?

Hacía cinco meses que **trabajaban** allí cuando los vi.

How long had they been working there when you saw them?

They had been working there for five months when I saw them.

2. The sentences above express an action or situation that had begun in the past and was still going on at some point in the past—usually indicated by an occurrence expressed in the preterit (**. . . cuando los vi**). To construct sentences like these, use the following formulas:

   To form a question: **¿cuánto tiempo hacía que** + *imperfect tense*?
   To form a statement: **hacía** + *time* + **que** + *imperfect tense*

   Practice B: Complete the Spanish sentences.

1. How long had they been living in Puerto Rico when he met them?

   ¿_____ que vivían en Puerto Rico cuando los conoció?

2. They had been living there for about four months.

   Hacía unos cuatro meses que _____ allí.

3. How long had Paul been sleeping when we arrived?

   ¿Cuánto tiempo hacía que Pablo _____ cuando llegamos?

4. Mary had been playing the piano for twenty minutes when the doorbell rang.

   _____ que María tocaba el piano cuando sonó el timbre de la puerta.

5. How long had you known these gentlemen when the robbery occurred?

   ¿_____ que Ud. conocía a estos señores cuando ocurrió el robo?

6. I had known them for six years.

   Hacía seis años que yo los _____.

▲ **EJERCICIOS** ▲

A. Answer the question or write the question that is answered by the given statement.

EXAMPLES: ¿Cuánto tiempo hace que compras discos compactos?
Hace tres años que compro discos compactos.

Hace dos días que estamos aquí.
¿Cuánto tiempo hace que Uds. están aquí?

1. ¿Cuánto tiempo hace que Ud. vive en su casa?

_____

2. Hace una hora que miro la televisión.

_____

3. ¿Cuánto tiempo hace que los Mets están en Nueva York?

_____

4. Hace dos años que asistimos a esta escuela.

_____

5. ¿Cuánto tiempo hace que Ud. estudia español?

_____

6. Hace cuatro horas que Alberto trabaja con la computadora.

_____

B. Answer the question or write the question that is answered by the given statement.

EXAMPLES: ¿Cuánto tiempo hacía que jugabas en ese parque?
Hacía cuatro meses que yo jugaba en ese parque.

Hacía una semana que estaban allí.
¿Cuánto tiempo hacía que estaban allí?

1. ¿Cuánto tiempo hacía que sus amigos jugaban en la calle cuando su madre los llamó?

_____

2. Hacía mucho tiempo que trabajábamos en esa tienda.

_____

3. ¿Cuánto tiempo hacía que Uds. vivían en su casa?

_____

4. Hacía una hora que yo escuchaba la radio cuando entró Teresa.

_____

  5. ¿Cuánto tiempo hacía que ellos estaban en la playa cuando empezó a llover?

  _____

  6. Hacía seis minutos que ella conducía su coche cuando tuvo el accidente.

  _____

C. Express in Spanish.

  1. How long have you (*tú*) had this printer?

  _____

  2. How long had they had that television set?

  _____

  3. We had been dancing for fifteen minutes when they arrived.

  _____

  4. I have been going to that discotheque for five years.

  _____

  5. How long had he been traveling when he met her?

  _____

  6. How long has she been waiting here?

  _____

  7. We have been in this hotel for six days.

  _____

  8. We had been in that store for a half hour.

  _____

  9. How long have you (*Ud.*) been his friend?

  _____

  10. How long had you (*tú*) been his friend when he died?

  _____

SUPPLEMENT

Using *LLEVAR* to Express the Passage of Time

¿Cuánto tiempo **lleva** Ud. aquí?	How long have you been here?
Yo **llevo** dos semanas aquí.	I have been here for two weeks.
¿Cuánto tiempo **llevan** las muchachas **jugando** al tenis?	How long have the girls been playing tennis?
Llevan tres horas **jugando** al tenis.	They have been playing tennis for three hours.

3. The verb **llevar** is often used instead of **estar** before a time interval. If the interval begins in the past and continues into the present, **llevar** is used in the present tense and means *has been* or *have been* (depending on whether its subject is in the singular or the plural): **llevamos dos días aquí,** *we have been here for two days.*

4. The verb **llevar** followed by a present participle is often used to express an action or situation that began in the past and continues into the present. Note the similar meanings:

> **¿Cuánto tiempo llevan ellos durmiendo?**
> **= ¿Cuánto tiempo hace que ellos duermen?**
>
> **Ellos llevan seis horas durmiendo.**
> **= Hace seis horas que ellos duermen.**

▲ EJERCICIOS ▲

D. Replace the sentence with an equivalent sentence using the verb *llevar.*

EXAMPLES: ¿Cuánto tiempo hace que estás aquí?
¿Cuánto tiempo llevas aquí?

Hace tres horas que esperamos.
Llevamos tres horas esperando.

1. ¿Cuánto tiempo hace que Uds. están en Madrid?   _____

2. Hace tres meses que estamos en la ciudad.   _____

3. ¿Cuánto tiempo hace que Ud. trabaja aquí?   _____

4. Hace dos años que estudio español.   _____

5. ¿Cuánto tiempo hace que tocas el piano?   _____

6. Hace seis años que hago este tipo de trabajo.   _____

E. Translate into Spanish, using the verb *llevar.*

1. How long have you (*tú*) been waiting?   _____

2. I have been waiting here for an hour.   _____

3. They have been in that hotel for three days.   _____

4. She has been traveling with us for two weeks.   _____

5. How long have you (*Uds.*) been using these computers?   _____

6. We have been using these computers for three hours.   _____

33
Indefinite Pronouns and Negatives

Helps and Hints

Your English teachers have taught you not to use two negatives together; for example: "I don't have nothing" or "She doesn't see nobody," etc. In this chapter you will see that this is possible in Spanish.

AFFIRMATIVE		NEGATIVE	
Tengo **algo.**	I have something	**Nada** tengo. ⎫	I have nothing.
¿Tienes **algo?**	Do you have anything?	No tengo **nada.** ⎭	I do not have anything.
Todo está listo.	Everything is ready.	**Nada** está listo.	Nothing is ready.
Alguien viene.	Someone (Somebody) is coming.	**Nadie** viene. ⎫	No one (Nobody) is coming.
¿Viene **alguien?**	Is someone (anyone) coming?	No viene **nadie.** ⎭	
Veo a **alguien.**	I see somebody.	A **nadie** veo. ⎫	I see no one (nobody).
		No veo a **nadie** ⎭	I do not see anyone (anybody)

Siempre hay exámenes los viernes.
There are always exams on Friday.

Nunca (Jamás) hay exámenes los jueves.
There are never exams on Thursday.

¿Has visto **jamás** tal película?

Have you ever seen such a movie?

No, **jamás (nunca)** he visto tal película.
⎧No, no he visto **jamás (nunca)** tal película.
⎩No, I have never seen such a movie.

Ella lee mucho.	She reads a lot.	Ella no lee mucho.	She doesn't read a lot.
Yo leo mucho **también.**	I read a lot too (also).	⎧Yo no leo mucho **tampoco.** ⎨Yo **tampoco** leo mucho.	I don't read much either. (Neither do I read much.)

SUMMARY

AFFIRMATIVE	NEGATIVE
algo, something, anything **todo,** everything	**nada,** nothing (not) anything
alguien, someone, somebody, anyone, anybody	**nadie,** no one, nobody, (not) anybody
siempre, always	**nunca**⎫
jamás, ever	**jamás**⎭ never, (not) ever
también, also (too)	**tampoco,** neither, (not) either

1. The personal **a** precedes **alguien** and **nadie** when they are direct objects: veo **a** alguien; **a** nadie veo (no veo **a** nadie).

2. Negative words may precede or follow the verb. If they follow the verb, they are preceded by **no:**

Nada tengo.	*But:* **No** tengo **nada.**
A **nadie** veo.	**No** veo a **nadie.**
Nunca estudian.	**No** estudian **nunca.**

3. The words **jamás** and **nunca** are interchangeable in negative sentences, but only **jamás** can be used if the sentence is affirmative:

Es el edificio más alto que **jamás** he visto.   It is the tallest building that I have ever seen.

Jamás (nunca) he oído tal música. ⎫
No he oído **jamás (nunca)** tal música. ⎭   I have never heard such music.

4. Although the words *anything* and *anybody* are included among the meanings of **algo** and **alguien,** avoid the error of using **algo** or **alguien** in translating negative sentences such as "I did not see anything (anybody)." The word *not* indicates that the negative words **nada** and **nadie** should be used instead.

◢ EJERCICIOS ◣

A. Paco makes a statement and Juana negates it. Play the role of Juana as in the example.

EXAMPLE: Alguien tiene la respuesta.   *a. Nadie tiene la respuesta.*
                                                          b. No tiene nadie la respuesta.

1. Tú siempre dices mentiras.   a. _____
                                                  b. _____

2. Conozco a alguien en ese club.   a. _____
                                                        b. _____

3. Tengo algo para ti.   a. _____
                                        b. _____

4. ¿Han oído Uds. jamás esta canción?   a. _____
   (Reply in the negative.)   b. _____

5. Alguien nos acompaña al baile.   a. _____
                                                        b. _____

6. Mi amigo va al cine también.   a. _____
                                                    b. _____

B. During a conversation with a friend, you ask questions and receive negative answers. Answer negatively in two ways.

EXAMPLE: ¿Han hecho Uds. todo?   *a. No hemos hecho nada.*
                                  b. Nada hemos hecho.

1. ¿Has ido jamás a esa discoteca?

a. _____

b. _____

2. ¿Ves todo en la televisión por la noche?

a. _____

b. _____

3. ¿Te da algo en tu cumpleaños tu profesor(-ora) de español?

a. _____

b. _____

4. ¿Siempre visitas a tus abuelos?

a. _____

b. _____

5. ¿Oyes a alguien en la calle?

a. _____

b. _____

6. Jorge no va al cine esta noche. ¿Vas tú al cine? (use **tampoco**)

a. _____

b. _____

7. ¿Ha visitado tu padre jamás a la directora (al director) de tu escuela?

a. _____

b. _____

8. ¿Tienes algo interesante que decir a tus padres hoy?

a. _____

b. _____

9. ¿Saben Uds. todo acerca de la cultura sudamericana?

a. _____

b. _____

10. ¿Viene alguien contigo a la escuela por la mañana?

a. _____

b. _____

C. Express in Spanish. Write the negative sentences in two ways.

1. Have you anything for me?

_____

2. No, I have nothing for you.

a. _____

b. _____

3. Someone is knocking at the door.

_____

4. Nobody watches television in our house.

a. _____

b. _____

5. Do you (*Uds.*) ever to go the museum?

_____

6. No, we never go.

a. _____

b. _____

7. Does she know anyone there?   _____

8. No, she does not know anybody.   *a.* _____

                                      b. _____

9. Say something to the class.   _____

10. She isn't saying anything to her parents. *a.* _____

                                      b. _____

Corrida de Toros, España

34
POR and PARA

Helps and Hints
Expressing "for" presents some difficulty in Spanish for the speaker of English. This chapter will clarify whether to use "por" or "para" and will also show other meanings for "por" and "para."

Some Uses of POR

A. *for* (see page 241)

B. *by*

El libro fue escrito **por** un famoso autor.   The book was written by a famous author.

C. *through*

Siempre andamos **por** el parque.   We always walk through the park.

D. *along*

Muchos coches iban **por** la carretera.   Many cars were going along the highway.

E. *because of*

Nos quedamos en casa **por** la lluvia.   We stayed home because of the rain.

F. *in* or *at* = *during*

Visitaban a sus amigos...   They used to visit their friends...
  ... **por** la mañana.   ... in the morning.
  ... **por** la tarde.   ... in the afternoon.
  ... **por** la noche.   ... in the evening, at night.

Some Uses of PARA

A. *for* (see page 241)

B. *by* (= "at the latest")

Terminaré el trabajo **para** las ocho.   I'll finish the work by eight o'clock.

Dijeron que llegarían **para** el viernes.   They said that they would arrive by Friday.

C. *to* = *in order to* (+ an infinitive)

Para hacer eso, necesitas mucho dinero.   To do that, you need a lot of money.

Estudiamos **para sacar** buenas notas.   We study to (in order to) get good marks.

Practice A: POR or PARA? Complete the sentence with the correct preposition.

1. _____ llegar temprano, hay que tomar el tren.

2. Muchos autobuses pasaban _____ la avenida.

3. La lección fue explicada _____ el profesor.

4. Uds. tienen que terminar la tarea _____ el jueves.

5. Yo siempre llego temprano _____ satisfacer a mis padres.

6. _____ la nieve las escuelas estaban cerradas.

7. ¿Qué vas a hacer el sábado _____ la noche?

Using POR and PARA to Express the Different Meanings of "For"

POR

A. *in exchange for*

Mi madre pagó quince mil dólares **por** el coche.

My mother paid fifteen thousand dollars for the car.

B. *for the sake of*

Mi padre hace todo **por** la familia.

My father does everything for the family.

C. *for the period of* (+ time interval)

Se quedaron allí **por** tres días.

They stayed there for three days.

D. *in search of, to get*

Mi amigo vino **por** el disco compacto.

My friend came for (= came to get) the CD.

Vamos **por** una hamburguesa.

Let's go for ("get") a hamburger.

La enfermera mandó **por** el médico.

The nurse sent for the doctor.

PARA

A. *meant or intended for*

Esta cinta es **para** ti.

This tape is for you.

B. *bound for* (+ destination)

Mañana partimos **para** Puerto Rico.

Tomorrow we leave for Puerto Rico.

Practice B: POR or PARA? Complete the sentence with the correct preposition.

1. El verano próximo saldrán _____ España.

2. Anoche estudié _____ tres horas.

3. Estas revistas son _____ Ud.

4. Las aspirinas son buenas _____ la fiebre y los dolores de cabeza.

5. Hay que pagar cien dólares _____ el abrigo.

6. Nuestros profesores siempre hacen todo lo posible _____ sus alumnos.

7. Este autobús sale _____ la ciudad en cinco minutos.

8. Iremos al restaurante _____ un sándwich y una bebida.

9. ¿Cuánto pagaron Uds. _____ ese televisor en colores?

10. Tengo un regalo _____ mi tío.

◢ EJERCICIOS ◣

A. POR or PARA? Complete the sentence with the correct preposition.

1. _____ comer bien iremos a ese restaruante.

2. ¿_____ cuántos días estuvieron ellos en Buenos Aires?

3. Tienen que terminar el proyecto _____ el quince de enero.

4. Voy al banco _____ mi dinero.

5. ¿Quiere Ud. aceptar este cheque _____ cincuenta dólares?

6. _____ la temperatura baja tenemos que llevar abrigo y sombrero.

7. ¿A qué hora sales _____ la escuela esta mañana?

8. Mis padres dicen que la musica *rock* es mala _____ los oídos.

9. Mandamos la carta _____ avión.

10. ¿Qué hacen Uds. _____ ganar tanto dinero?

B. Answer with a complete sentence in Spanish.

1. ¿Por dónde le gusta a Ud. caminar los domingos?

_____

2. ¿Por cuánto tiempo tocó la orquesta?

_____

3. ¿Para quién es el libro de español?

_____

4. ¿Para qué usamos el ascensor?

_____

5. ¿Adónde va Ud. por libros?

_____

6. ¿Cuánto dinero se paga generalmente por una buena bicicleta?

_____

7. ¿Vive Ud. para comer o come Ud. para vivir?

_____

8. ¿Qué modo de transporte tomamos para ir de los Ángeles a Nueva York en cinco horas?

_____

9. ¿Qué hace Ud. por sus amigos?

_____

10. ¿Conduce su padre el coche por la acera?

_____

C. Express in Spanish.

1. These packages are for them.　　_____

2. Last night I studied for four hours.　_____

3. Let's go there for a good meal.　_____

4. You need (One needs) to get a ticket to see
    the movie.　　　　　　　　　　_____

5. When are you (*tú*) leaving for the country?　_____

6. Don't walk through the garden.　_____

7. How much did you (*Ud.*) pay for the CD?　_____

8. We stayed home because of the bad weather.　_____

9. These eyeglasses are not good for the eyes.　_____

10. Finish the job by three o'clock.　_____

Part 7

Reviewing Vocabulary and Idioms in Context

Passages and Dialogues on School Life, Popular Pastimes, etc.;
Practice in Composition

⋈⋈⋈⋈⋈⋈⋈⋈⋈⋈⋈⋈⋈⋈⋈⋈⋈⋈⋈⋈⋈

35
Llegando a la escuela

Before reading the passages and dialogues of Chapters 35–40, study the introductory vocabulary and idioms in each of the chapters.

VOCABULARY

adentro, inside
afuera, outside
ausente, absent
casi, almost
charlar, to chat

el **destino,** destination
la **esquina,** (street) corner
llevar, to take
la **sala (de clase),** classroom

IDIOMS

a eso de, about (with time of day)
al lado de, next to
a propósito, by the way
a tiempo, on time
en medio de, in the middle of

en punto, sharp, on the dot (with time of day)
frente a, opposite
por eso, therefore, for that reason
por completo, completely

asistir a, to attend

bajar de, to get off or out of (a vehicle)

despedirse de, to say good-bye to

encontrarse, to be situated

encontrarse con, to meet (with)

hay que + *inf.,* one must, it is necessary

pasar un rato, to spend a while

se me olvidó, I forgot

subir a, to get into (a vehicle)

tener prisa, to be in a hurry

tratar de + *inf.,* to try to

A. Me llamo Lola. Mi escuela se encuentra en medio de la ciudad al lado de una iglesia y frente a un parque. Todas las mañanas trato de llegar a la escuela a tiempo, y por eso me despido de mi familia a eso de las siete y media. Espero el autobús que me lleva a la escuela. El autobús casi siempre llega a mi esquina a las ocho menos veinte. Subo al autobús y me encuentro con mis amigos que asisten a la misma escuela. Me gusta charlar con ellos acerca de nuestras clases y nuestros profesores. A las ocho en punto llego a mi destino y bajo del autobús.

Circle the letter of the correct answer.

1. La escuela está

  a. cerca de un parque
  b. detrás de una iglesia
  c. en el campo

2. Lola sale de casa

  a. después de mediodía
  b. a las ocho y veinte
  c. antes de las ocho

3. ¿Quiénes están en el autobús?

  a. Lola y unos compañeros suyos
  b. muy pocas personas
  c. los profesores y los estudiantes

4. ¿De qué hablan los chicos?

  a. del cine
  b. de cosas de la escuela
  c. del autobús

5. ¿Adónde llega Lola a las ocho?

  a. a la escuela
  b. al autobús
  c. a la esquina

B. This paragraph is a continuation of the passage in **A,** but several words have been left out. Write the missing words, choosing them from among the words that appear below the blanks.

Hay que _____ veinte minutos para _____ a la
　　　　　(volar / caminar / dormir)　　　　　　　　　　　　(llegar / salir / amar)

escuela. No tengo _____ porque las clases no _____
　　　　　　　　　(helado / prisa / razón)　　　　　　　　　(empiezan / terminan / interesan)

hasta las ocho y media. _____ de entrar en la escuela paso un
　　　　　　　　　　　　(Cerca / Lejos / Antes)

_____ afuera charlando. Por fin tengo _____ entrar.
　(día / rato / desayuno)　　　　　　　　　　　　　　　　　(de / a / que)

Otro día escolar va a _____. ¿Qué me espera _____?
　　　　　　　　　(comenzar / leer / mirar)　　　　　　　　　(ayer / adentro / semana)

C. *Diálogo:* Pepe y Lola están charlando en el autobús.

PEPE: Estoy alegre cuando un profesor está ausente.

LOLA: ¿Por qué, chico?

PEPE: Porque no tenemos que hacer nada.

LOLA: Es verdad. Y podemos hacer mucho ruido y echar aviones de papel de un lado de la sala al otro.

PEPE: A propósito, ¿has escrito tu composición para la clase de inglés?

LOLA: ¡Ay, Dios mío! Se me olvidó por completo.

PEPE: ¿Qué vas a hacer?

LOLA: Aceptaré el cero muy valientemente.

PEPE: Ahora llegamos. Vamos a bajar.

LOLA: Allí están Ramón y Rita. Vamos a caminar con ellos.

Circle the letter of the correct answer.

1. ¿Cuándo está contento el chico?

   a. cuando se queda en casa
   b. cuando tiene muchas cosas que hacer
   c. cuando un profesor no está presente

2. ¿Qué hacen los alumnos durante la ausencia del profesor?

   a. Hacen cosas ridículas.
   b. Leen y escriben composiciones.
   c. Comen y beben.

3. ¿Qué ha olvidado la chica?

   a. su sándwich
   b. hacer una tarea para una de sus clases
   c. algo en el autobús

4. ¿Qué va a recibir Lola?

   a. un cero
   b. una composición
   c. un avión de papel

5. ¿Qué van a hacer Pepe y Lola después de bajar del autobús?

   a. volver a casa
   b. escribir una composición
   c. ir a la escuela con unos amigos

D. Complete the following dialogue, using expressions such as:

el **club,** club

debiera (+ *inf.*), ought to

el **director**
la **directora** } principal

el **equipo,** team

estar de acuerdo, to agree

pasar, to spend (time)

el **semestre,** (school) term

severo, -a, strict

PEPE: No me gusta esta escuela. Los profesores son muy severos.

LOLA: (Tell him you agree, and the principal is even (aun) stricter.)

   1. _____

PEPE: Todos mis profesores asignan muchas horas de trabajo.

LOLA: (Tell him you spend three hours every night doing homework [*haciendo mis tareas*].)

   2. _____

PEPE: No hay suficientes actividades después de las clases.

LOLA: (Tell him the school ought to have more clubs and teams.)

3. _____

PEPE: Sólo hay un equipo de básquetbol.

LOLA: (Tell him the school ought to have a baseball and football team too.)

4. _____

E. *Temas*

1. On the lines below, write a composition in Spanish about getting to school every morning. Include the following ideas: (*a*) You are always in a hurry in the morning and try to arrive at school on time. (*b*) You say good-bye to your parents after having breakfast. (*c*) You wait for the bus on the corner opposite your house. (*d*) You chat with your friends on the bus and talk about yesterday's activities. (*e*) After getting off the bus, you spend a short time (a while) outside the school.

Llegando a la escuela

_____

_____

_____

_____

_____

_____

_____

2. Vary the above composition by telling how you got to school yesterday. Start with the Spanish equivalent of a statement such as "Yesterday morning I was in a hurry because I wanted to get to school on time." You might want to review the preterit and imperfect tenses before writing your composition.

_____

_____

_____

_____

_____

_____

_____

36
El esquí

VOCABULARY

la **alfombra,** rug, carpet
la **carretera,** road, highway
cercano, -a, nearby
el **chófer,** driver
criticar, to criticize
demasiado, too much
el **esquí,** skiing
esquiar (yo esquío), to ski
los **esquíes,** skis

ir a esquiar, to go skiing
la **manera** } way, manner
el **modo** }
el **patinaje sobre hielo,** ice skating
patinar, to skate
la **pista de patinaje,** skating rink
la **pista de salto (de esquí),** ski run
próximo, -a, next
el **salto de esquí,** ski jump

IDIOMS

dentro de, inside of, within
de prisa, fast
encima de, on top of

aprovecharse de, to take advantage of
estar listo(-a), to be ready
gozar de,* to enjoy
pensar en, to think of

para el desayuno, for breakfast
por ahora, for now

ponerse en camino, to start out
tener cuidado, to be careful
tener muchas (tantas) ganas de + *inf.,* to
  be eager to

---

*Do not use this expression if the thing enjoyed is a form or source of entertainment (a play, film, book, concert, etc.); use
  gustar instead:

  Me gustó la novela.   I enjoyed the novel.
But:
  Yo **gozaba de** la vida de campo.   I enjoyed life in the country.

248

A. Hola, soy Pepe. A veces tenemos un largo fin de semana que dura tres o cuatro días. Hay que aprovecharse de estas ocasiones para gozar de la vida sin pensar en la escuela. El próximo lunes será el Día de los Presidentes. Como estamos en invierno, hay que pensar en deportes como el patinaje sobre hielo y el esquí. Hay una pista de patinaje no muy lejos de nuestra casa. Para ir a esquiar, en cambio, tenemos que viajar dos o tres horas en coche. La pista de salto más cercana queda a unos ciento sesenta kilómetros (100 miles) de la ciudad. Pues, como tenemos tres días de libertad, ¿por qué no ir a esquiar?

Circle the letter of the correct answer.

1. Al narrador le gusta
   a. divertirse
   b. pensar en la escuela
   c. quedarse en casa

2. Pepe quiere ir
   a. a Wáshington
   b. a esquiar
   c. a patinar sobre hielo

3. ¿Cómo puede ir a esquiar el narrador?
   a. en automóvil
   b. en tren
   c. a pie

4. ¿Dónde está situada la pista de salto?
   a. a cierta distancia de la ciudad
   b. cerca de Wáshington
   c. dentro de la ciudad

B. Complete the paragraph by writing the missing words, choosing them from among the words that appear below the blanks.

Según mis padres, el salto de esquí es muy _____, pero esto no me impide
(peligroso / pintura / correr)

(*stops*). Hay que divertirse de vez en _____. Mi padre ha prometido llevarnos
(día / cuando / tarde)

en su _____. A él le gusta esquiar _____. Aquí están
(alfombra / mesa / coche)   (también / ayer / dinero)

nuestros planes:

El día de nuestra excursión _____ levantaremos a las cinco en punto de la
(me / te / nos)

mañana y saldremos de casa a las seis porque queremos _____ a la pista a eso
(llegar / comer / salir)

de las ocho. _____ tan temprano porque el esquí es un _____
(Partimos / Cenamos / Cantamos)   (cine / deporte / diversión)

muy popular y queremos evitar la muchedumbre (*crowd*). Creo que pasaremos un buen

_____ si no hay accidentes. Por eso hay que tener mucho _____.
(mañana / rato / fin)   (cuidado / dinero / pronto)

¡Hasta el fin de semana!

C. *Diálogo:* Padre e hijo se preparan para un día de esquí.

PADRE: Levántate, Pepe. Tenemos que salir de casa muy temprano. La pista está muy lejos.

HIJO: Sí, papá, ya me desperté hace poco. Estaré listo en quince minutos.

PADRE: Pero antes de salir, tenemos que tomar el desayuno. ¿Qué vas a tomar: huevos, jugo, café?

HIJO: Quiero sólo un vaso de jugo de naranja. Estoy muy (*too*) nervioso para comer.

PADRE: Está bien. Podremos tomar algo al llegar a la pista.

HIJO: Estoy listo, papá. Vámonos. Ya puse los esquíes encima del coche.

PADRE: ¡Perfecto! Pero no hay que tener prisa. Quiero evitar un accidente en el camino.

HIJO: Si me dejas conducir el coche, no tendremos ningún accidente.

PADRE: Ya veremos. Primero vamos a ponernos en camino. Por ahora conduciré yo.

HIJO: ¡Qué lástima! Qué manera de empezar un fin de semana largo.

Circle the letter of the correct answer.

1. ¿Quiénes van a esquiar?
   a. dos chicos
   b. tres membros de una familia
   c. un chico con su padre

2. Tienen que levantarse temprano para
   a. no llegar tarde a la pista
   b. tomar el desayuno
   c. encontrarse con sus amigos

3. ¿Qué va a tomar el hijo para el desayuno?
   a. café y huevos
   b. nada
   c. jugo de naranja

4. Puede ocurrir un accidente si uno
   a. come demasiado antes de salir
   b. va de prisa
   c. conduce con cuidado

5. ¿Qué quiere hacer el hijo?
   a. conducir el automóvil
   b. tener un accidente
   c. comer mientras viaja

D. Complete the following dialogue, putting yourself in your father's place.

HIJO: Papá, ya has conducido por una hora. ¿No estás cansado? ¿Puedo conducir ahora?

PADRE: (Tell him you know he wants to drive but you're not tired.)

1. _____

HIJO: ¿Cuándo me vas a dar la oportunidad de conducir?

PADRE: (Tell him you'll let him drive soon.)

2. _____

HIJO: Papá, estás conduciendo muy de prisa. Cuidado con los otros coches en el camino.

PADRE: (Tell him you are a good driver and that he should not criticize you.)

3. _____

HIJO: No te critico, papá. Sé que eres un buen chófer. Mira: la carretera está llena de coches esta mañana.

PADRE: (Tell him they're all going skiing too.)

4. _____

HIJO: Estoy tan impaciente. ¿Cuándo llegamos?

PADRE: (Tell him that you will arrive within a quarter of an hour [*un cuarto de hora*].)

5. _____

E. *Temas*

1. On the lines below, write a composition about a ski trip you intend to take. Include the following ideas: (*a*) You are eager to go skiing this weekend. (*b*) There is a ski run not too far from your city or town. (*c*) You generally take advantage of long weekends to enjoy life. (*d*) You will start out very early in the morning. (*e*) For breakfast you will have ("take") only one or two things because you're too (*muy*) nervous to eat.

_____

_____

_____

_____

_____

_____

2. Write about your drive to the ski run. Include the following ideas: (*a*) Your father or mother drove too fast. (*b*) You wanted to drive, but your father (or mother) was afraid. (*c*) The roads were filled with cars that morning. (*d*) During the ride (*el paseo*) you thought of your arrival at the ski run. (*e*) You promised your father (or mother) to be careful on the ski jumps. You may write this in the form of a letter to a friend. The salutation may be "Querido Juan (Querida Paca). You may end the letter as follows:

Con cariño
Abrazos
Saludos a la familia
    María (Alberto)

_____

_____

_____

_____

_____

_____

37
Preparativos para un viaje a Puerto Rico

Before reading the passages and dialogues of this chapter, study the following vocabulary and idioms.

VOCABULARY

además, besides

arreglar, to arrange, fix

la **confianza,** confidence

el **equipo de escafandra,** diving equipment

extranjero, -a, foreign

inolvidable, unforgettable

ligero, -a, light (in weight)

la **maleta,** suitcase

el **paisaje,** landscape, countryside

partir, to leave, depart

recorrer, to tour, go through

la **reservación** reservation

seguro, -a, sure (used with **estar**)

el **sitio** ⎫
el **lugar** ⎭ place

la **suerte,** luck

el **traje de baño,** bathing suit, swimsuit

tratar, to treat

las **vacaciones de Navidad,** Christmas vacation

valer, to be worth

ya, already

IDIOMS

fuera de, outside of

hacer la maleta, to pack the suitcase

no hacer caso a, to ignore, not to pay attention to (a person)

pensar + *inf.,* to intend to

tener muchas ganas de + *inf.,* to be eager to

la mayor parte de, most of

quisiera ⎫
me gustaría ⎭ I would like

sacar fotos, to take pictures

tener celos (de), to be jealous (of)

A. Me llamo Rosa. Durante mis vacaciones de Navidad mis padres piensan hacer un viaje a Puerto Rico. Van a llevar a toda la familia. Como éste es mi primer viaje fuera de los Estados Unidos, tengo muchas ganas de ir. El profesor de español dice que será una experiencia muy buena y educativa. Ahora tendré la oportunidad de practicar el español que he aprendido en la escuela. Partimos en avión el veinticuatro de diciembre. Mis amigos tienen celos. Todos dicen que les gustaría ir conmigo.

Circle the letter of the correct answer.

1. La familia va a Puerto Rico
   a. en diciembre
   b. durante la primavera
   c. por un fin de semana

2. Hasta ahora, ¿cuántos viajes a otros países ha hecho Rosa?
   a. dos
   b. tres
   c. ninguno

3. El profesor de español dice que
   a. no se debe visitar Puerto Rico
   b. él ha visitado Puerto Rico muchas veces
   c. Rosa podrá aprender algo en su viaje

4. ¿Quiénes irán a Puerto Rico?
   a. todos los miembros de la familia
   b. sólo el padre
   c. los padres de Rosa

5. Rosa
   a. va a estudiar español en Puerto Rico
   b. habla español ya
   c. invita a sus amigos a ir con ella

B. Complete the paragraph by writing the missing words, choosing them from among the words that appear below the blanks.

Voy a hacer mi _____ la noche anterior al viaje. Como siempre hace
          (maleta / coche / avión)

_____ en Puerto Rico, necesito llevar _____ ligera de
   (frío / calor / tiempo)   (guante / zapato / ropa)

verano. Y no debo _____ mi traje de baño y el equipo de escafandra. También
               (olvidar / comer / volar)

voy a llevar mi cámara fotográfica para sacar muchas _____ . Dicen que en
                                              (veces / fotos / bicicletas)

Puerto Rico hay mucho que ver y que _____ de San Juan hay un paisaje muy
                                  (a eso / fuera / dentro)

bonito. Podremos visitar algunos _____ de interés, además de pasar tiempo en
                              (lugares / casas / libros)

la _____ tomando el sol y _____ en el mar. Yo creo que
   (escuela / playa / sitio)   (escribiendo / trayendo / nadando)

este _____ será inolvidable para mí.
   (viaje / océano / excursión)

C. *Diálogo:* Rosa charla con su profesor de español.

PROFESOR: ¡Rosa, qué suerte tienes! Un viaje a un país hispano vale mucho.

ROSA: Ud. ha dicho siempre que es importante viajar por países extranjeros.

PROFESOR: Ahora vas a utilizar el español hablando con los habitantes del país.

ROSA: ¿Cree Ud. que podré conversar con ellos?

PROFESOR: Eres una estudiante muy aplicada. No tendrás ninguna dificultad con la lengua. Además, los puertorriqueños son muy amables y te ayudarán.

ROSA: Gracias, señor Aguador. Ud. me ha dado mucha confianza.

PROFESOR: ¿Cuándo parten Uds.?

ROSA: El día 24 de diciembre. Mi papá ha hecho ya las reservaciones en los hoteles.

PROFESOR: ¿Y dónde van a quedarse?

ROSA: La mayor parte del tiempo en San Juan. Pero por unos días vamos a recorrer la isla.

Circle the letter of the correct answer.

1. ¿Qué piensa el profesor de los planes de Rosa?
  a. Le gustan.
  b. Cree que es una mala idea.
  c. Quiere ir con ella.

2. ¿Qué va a hacer Rosa en Puerto Rico?
  a. Visitará a una amiga suya.
  b. Irá a la playa todos los días.
  c. Conversará con los puertorriqueños.

3. Los puertorriqueños
  a. tratarán bien a Rosa
  b. no le harán caso a Rosa
  c. llevaran a Rosa a sus casas

4. ¿Quién ha arreglado el viaje?
  a. el señor Aguador
  b. el padre de Rosa
  c. una amiga puertorriqueña de Rosa

5. ¿Qué verá Rosa en Puerto Rico?
  a. solamente la ciudad de San Juan
  b. unas playas bonitas
  c. varias partes de la isla

D. Complete the following dialogue.

PANCHO: Me dicen que vas a Puerto Rico. Quisiera ir contigo. ¿Quiénes van?

DIEGO: (Tell him the whole family is going.)

  1. _____

PANCHO: ¿Por cuántos días van a estar allí?

DIEGO: (Tell him you will be there for ten days, the whole Christmas vacation.)

  2. _____

PANCHO: ¿Y qué van a hacer allí en la Isla del Encanto?

DIEGO: (Tell him you will see San Juan, go swimming, and use your diving outfit.)

  3. _____

PANCHO: ¿Piensan visitar otros sitios?

DIEGO: (Tell him you intend to go around the island to see the beautiful landscape.)

  4. _____

PANCHO: ¿Vas a hablar español con los puertorriqueños?

DIEGO: (Tell him your teacher is sure you will be able to converse in Spanish with the people there.)

  5. _____

E. *Temas*

1. On the lines below, write about a trip you intend to take to a Spanish-speaking country. Include answers to the following questions: (*a*) Who is arranging the trip? (*b*) When are you going? With whom? Where? (*c*) What will you take along with you? (*d*) What do you intend to do there most of the time? (*e*) Will you be able to converse with the inhabitants?

_____

_____

_____

_____

_____

_____

_____

2. Rewrite the above composition in the past tense, telling about a trip that you took. If you wish, you may write this as a letter to a relative.

Here are some salutations: Queridos abuelos
                             Querida tía Elena

Here are some endings: Besos y abrazos
                         Saludos al tío Carlos

_____

_____

_____

_____

_____

_____

_____

38
Una fiesta

Before reading the passages and dialogues of this chapter, study the following vocabulary and idioms.

VOCABULARY

adivinar, to guess

el **bizcocho,** cake

la **costumbre,** custom

la **empanada de carne,** meat pie

la **gaseosa,** (carbonated) soda

el **sótano,** basement

IDIOMS

algo de comer (beber), something to eat (to drink)

a medianoche, at midnight

a pie, on foot

de nada, you're welcome

de ninguna manera
de ningún modo } in no way

hacer un viaje, to take a trip

el año pasado, last year

él mismo, he himself

el primero
la primera } **en** + *inf.,* the first (one) to

todo el mundo, everybody

quedar, to be (situated); **¿Dónde queda su casa?** Where is your house?

A. Hola. Soy Diego. Me gustan las fiestas. Este fin de semana habrá una fiesta en casa de María. Ella vive en una casa muy grande que tiene un sótano amplio (spacious) para fiestas. Ella ha invitado a treinta personas. Cada persona tiene que traer algo de comer o de beber. Yo traeré una empanada de carne que mi mamá va a preparar. Ella aprendió a preparar las empanadas cuando hizo un viaje a la Argentina el año pasado. Creo que son deliciosas. Todo el mundo va a llevar *blue jeans,* el uniforme de los jóvenes de hoy día. Nadie se viste de etiqueta (dresses up) en las fiestas.

Circle the letter of the correct answer.

1. ¿Dónde tendrá lugar la fiesta?

   a. en casa del narrador
   b. en la escuela
   c. en casa de una amiga del narrador

2. ¿Cuántas personas irán a la fiesta?

   a. más de veinte
   b. muy pocas
   c. menos de quince

3. ¿Quién va a traer una empanada?

   a. la madre del narrador
   b. el narrador
   c. María

4. ¿Por qué llevan todos *blue jeans*?

   a. Es la costumbre.
   b. Los padres insisten.
   c. Los jóvenes son pobres.

5. ¿Quién visito la Argentina?

   a. Paco
   b. María
   c. la madre del narrador

B. *Diálogo*

DIEGO: Hola, María, parece que soy el primero en llegar a la fiesta.

MARÍA: De ninguna manera. Ya han llegado ocho personas. ¿Qué has traído?

DIEGO: Te traje una empanada preparada por mi mamá.

MARÍA: ¡Ay! Me encantan las empanadas. Muchas gracias.

DIEGO: ¿Qué han traído los demás?

MARÍA: Roberto trajo un bizcocho de chocolate y Ana trajo una botella grande de gaseosa. ¿Y sabes lo que trajo José?

DIEGO: No puedo adivinar. Dime.

MARÍA: Un rosbif que él mismo preparó.

DIEGO: Dios mío. No sabía que José sabía preparar rosbif. Tengo que probarlo.

MARÍA: Veremos si es tan delicioso como tu empanada. Ahora, vamos a bailar. Comeremos más tarde.

Circle the letter of the correct answer.

1. ¿Cuántas personas ya han venido a la fiesta?

   a. nueve   *b.* ocho   *c.* sólo una

2. ¿Quién dice que le gustan las empanadas?

   a. nadie   *b.* Diego   *c.* María

3. ¿Quién trajo el rosbif?

   a. María   *b.* José   *c.* la madre de Diego

4. ¿Qué le sorprende a Diego?

   a. Él es el primero en llegar.
   b. Roberto y Ana trajeron refrescos también.
   c. José sabe preparar rosbif.

5. ¿Cuándo van a comer?

   a. antes de bailar
   b. después de bailar
   c. al comienzo de la fiesta

C. Complete the following dialogue, using expressions such as:

tener mucho gusto en + *inf.*, to be very glad to

estar aburrido, -a, to be bored

simpático, -a, nice, likeable

estar de acuerdo, to agree

probar, to taste, try

sobre todo, especially

no hacer caso a, to ignore (someone)

DIEGO: Hola, Rosa, ¿quieres bailar conmigo?

ROSA: (Tell him you would be very glad to dance with him.)

1. _____

DIEGO: ¿Te gusta la fiesta?

ROSA: (Tell him you don't like it because you are bored.)

2. _____

DIEGO: ¿Aburrida? Pero, ¿por qué?

ROSA: (Tell him some of the guests [*algunos invitados*] are not nice.)

3. _____

DIEGO: ¿Por qué dices eso?

ROSA: (Tell him they ignore you. They only talk to [*con*] their school friends.)

4. _____

DIEGO: Hay tales personas en todas las fiestas. Pero yo estoy aquí, y yo soy muy simpático, ¿verdad?

ROSA: (Agree with him, and tell him that he dances well, too.)

5. _____

DIEGO: Gracias. Mi hermana menor me enseñó a bailar. A ella le encanta bailar.

ROSA: (Tell him that his younger sister is a good teacher. Now you would like to try some of the refreshments.)

6. _____

_____

D. *Temas*

1. On the lines below, write about a party you attended. Include the following information: (*a*) where and when the party took place; (*b*) how you got there; (*c*) who the guests were—describe some of them; (*d*) what activities you took part in; (*e*) what you had to eat and drink.

_____

_____

_____

_____

_____

_____

_____

2. Write about a trip you will have to take to attend a party. Include answers to the following questions: (*a*) In what city or country will the party take place? (*b*) How will you get there? (*c*) What gift will you bring to the host (*el anfitrión*) or the hostess (*la anfitriona*)? (*d*) How many people will attend the party? (*e*) Where will you stay? (at the home of the host or hostess, in a hotel, etc.) You may wish to review the future tense before writing your composition.

_____

_____

_____

_____

_____

_____

_____

39
Aprendiendo a conducir (manejar)

ESTUDIANTE CONDUCTOR

Before reading the passages and dialogues of this chapter, study the following vocabulary and idioms.

VOCABULARY

andar, to go; **el coche anda,** the car is going

así, (in) this way

conducir } to drive
manejar }

el **espejo retrovisor,** rear-view mirror

el **freno,** brake

la **lección de conducción (de manejo),** driving lesson

libremente, freely

moverse, to move

pasearse, to ride

pegar, to hit, strike

el **permiso** } **de conducir,** driver's license
la **licencia** }

recordar, to remind

soltar, to loosen, set free

la **ventanilla,** window (in a vehicle)

IDIOMS

hoy día, nowadays

lo más pronto posible, as soon as possible

lo mejor, the best

abrocharse el cinturón de seguridad, to fasten one's seat belt

acercarse a, to approach

alegrarse de + *inf.,* to be glad to

hacer arrancar el motor, to start the engine

negarse a + *inf.,* to refuse to

ponerse en marcha, to start out, "get going"

salir bien en } **un examen,** to pass a test
aprobar (ue) }

salir mal en } **un examen,** to fail a test
no aprobar }

A. Soy Luisa. Me acerco a la edad de conducir un coche. Como todos los jóvenes de hoy día, tengo muchas ganas de aprender a manejar. Es muy divertido y también es importante saber conducir. El señor Ruiz, uno de los profesores de nuestra escuela, da lecciones de conducción después de las clases. Él lleva a cuatro estudiantes en el coche. Cada uno tiene su turno de media hora. Todos tratamos de hacer lo mejor que podemos porque para nosotros es muy importante obtener la licencia de conducir lo más pronto posible. Mientras nos paseamos, hablamos de nuestras experiencias en la escuela, pero no podemos hablar muy libremente porque el señor Ruiz está escuchando.

Circle the letter of the correct answer.

1. ¿Qué desean hacer los jóvenes?

   a. dar lecciones de conducción a sus profesores

   b. aprender a manejar un coche

   c. divertirse todos los días

2. Es muy importante para los estudiantes

   a. conseguir su licencia

   b. llevar a sus amigos en coche

   c. salir mal en los exámenes

3. ¿Qué hacen los estudiantes en el coche?

   a. Se quedan silenciosos.

   b. Hablan acerca del señor Ruiz.

   c. Discuten sus actividades en la escuela.

4. ¿Qué hace el señor Ruiz mientras los estudiantes conducen?

   a. Oye sus conversaciones.

   b. Lee un libro.

   c. Habla con ellos.

5. ¿Cuánto tiempo maneja cada joven?

   a. más de una hora

   b. treinta minutos

   c. un cuarto de hora

B. Complete the paragraph by writing the missing words, choosing them from among the words that appear below the blanks.

Los inspectores son muy severos con los _____ y muchas veces uno sale
(profesores / jóvenes / padres)

_____ en el examen de conducción. Por eso hay que _____
(mal / coche / paseo)   (llevar / comer / practicar)

mucho. Mi padre me deja manejar su coche los domingos por una hora. Pero él me critica

demasiado. Todos los _____ son así, ¿verdad? Mamá se niega a
(amigos / padres / años)

_____ en coche conmigo porque tiene mucho _____. Así
(pasearse / beber / poder)   (paciencia / dinero / miedo)

son todas las madres, ¿verdad? El Sr. Ruiz tiene mucha _____, y cuando
(escuela / paciencia / carácter)

cometo un error, me _____ con mucha calma, explicándome lo que debo hacer.
(pega / corrige / grita)

Estoy _____ de que saldré bien en mi _____.
(segura / bien / cansado)   (conducir / examen / profesor)

C. *Diálogo*

   SR. RUIZ: Luisa, ¿estás lista para la lección hoy?

   LUISA: Claro. Siempre estoy lista. Me encanta manejar un coche.

   SR. RUIZ: Primero tienes que abrocharte el cinturón de seguridad.

LUISA: Yo nunca olvido este detalle, señor. No es necesario recordarme.

SR. RUIZ: Me alegro mucho de oír esto. Y ahora, ¿qué haces?

LUISA: Muy fácil. Hay que hacer arrancar el motor. Luego hay que mirar en el espejo retrovisor y luego por la ventanilla para ver si vienen otros coches.

SR. RUIZ: ¡Perfecto! Parece que sabes exactamente lo que se debe hacer. Entonces, vamos a ponernos en marcha.

LUISA: ¿Qué pasa? El coche no se mueve.

SR. RUIZ: ¿Has soltado el freno de emergencia?

LUISA: ¡Ay, Dios mío! Ahora sé por qué el coche no anda.

Circle the letter of the correct answer.

1. ¿Quién es el Sr. Ruiz?

  a. el profesor de manejo
  b. el padre de Luisa
  c. un profesor de español

2. ¿Qué le gusta a Luisa?

  a. insultar al señor Ruiz
  b. estudiar sus lecciones
  c. conducir un automóvil

3. ¿Cuándo es necesario abrocharse el cinturón de seguridad?

  a. después de hacer arrancar el motor
  b. antes de subir al coche
  c. antes de ponerse en marcha

4. ¿Por qué se debe mirar por la ventanilla?

  a. para abrocharse el cinturón de seguridad
  b. para ver si se acercan otros automóviles
  c. para ver si viene un policía

5. ¿Por qué no se mueve el coche?

  a. Luisa no ha soltado el freno de emergencia.
  b. No hay gasolina en el tanque.
  c. El profesor no le permite a Luisa manejar.

D. Complete the following dialogue, using expressions such as:

ahora mismo, right now
aprobar el examen, to pass the exam
así, (in) this way, so, thus
  ciego, -a, blind

la confianza, confidence
parar, to stop
pierde cuidado, don't worry

PADRE: Vamos a ver lo que has aprendido. Llévame a la estación de gasolina. Tenemos que llenar el tanque.

HIJA: (Tell him you have learned a lot and that you will take him there right now.)

  1. _____

PADRE: ¡Cuidado! Hay una señal de *Stop* a unos pocos metros. ¿No la ves?

HIJA: (Tell him of course you see the sign and that you are going to stop.)

  2. _____

PADRE: ¡Ay, Dios mío! Hay luz roja. ¿No vas a parar?

HIJA: (Tell him not to worry; you are not blind.)

  3. _____

PADRE: No sé si vas a salir bien en el examen de manejo. Tú manejas con poco cuidado.

HIJA: (Tell him that he should have more confidence in you, that you are a good driver.)

4. _____

PADRE: Tengo que decir la verdad: estoy muy nervioso.

HIJA: (Tell him that all fathers are like that [*así*].)

5. _____

E. *Temas*

1. On the lines below, write about your desire to learn to drive. Include the following ideas: (*a*) You would like to learn; tell why. (*b*) Your mother or father refuses to teach you; tell why. (*c*) A driving school (*auto-escuela*) is best for you; tell why. (*d*) You intend to practice a lot; tell when. (*e*) You want to start your lessons as soon as possible.

_____

_____

_____

_____

_____

_____

_____

2. Write about a driving lesson. Include the following information: (*a*) who is teaching you and where; (*b*) how good your teacher is (describe him or her); (*c*) what was said in a conversation with your teacher; (*d*) an error you made during the lesson; (*e*) you hope to pass the test the first time. You may also write this in the form of a letter to a parent who is away on a business trip.

Suggested salutations: Querido papá
Querida mamá
Hola, mamá (papá)

Suggested endings: Espero verte pronto
Hasta muy pronto
Abrazos de tu hijo (hija) que te quiere mucho

_____

_____

_____

_____

_____

_____

_____

40
El centro comercial

Before reading the passages and dialogues of this chapter, study the following vocabulary and idioms.

VOCABULARY

atraer, to attract

el **barco,** boat

el **centro comercial,** shopping mall, business district

la **computadora,** computer

deber, should, have to, to be supposed to; **debo hablar,** I should speak

la **heladería,** ice-cream shop

la **impresora,** printer

llevar, to take; to wear

meter, to put in(to), insert

la **moneda,** coin

la **ranura,** (coin) slot

el **sonido,** sound

tanto, -a, so much

la **tienda de informática,** computer-related store

tras, after, behind

IDIOMS

al + *inf.,* upon . . . -ing

de acuerdo, agreed, OK

de ningún modo, no way

de veras, really

en vez de, instead of

lo mismo, the same

mientras tanto, meanwhile

por fin, finally

por medio de, by means of

o sea, or rather

por lo menos, at least

A. Me llamo Pedro. La escuela no ocupa toda mi vida. Soy un chico activo. Al salir de la escuela, después de mi última clase, pienso en lo que voy a hacer el resto del día. No hago siempre lo mismo. Por ejemplo, hoy tengo que volver directamente a casa porque mi mamá quiere llevarme a comprar ropa. Al llegar a casa, saludo a mi mamá, quien me dice que el coche está averiado (broken down) y que papá tuvo que llevarlo a la estación de servicio por medio de un camión-grúa (tow-truck). Por eso tenemos que tomar el autobús en vez del coche.

El centro comercial contiene tiendas de todos tipos: restaurantes, heladerías, tiendas de ropa, de música, de deportes, de informática, etc. Me gustan más las galerías de juegos electrónicos. Allí uno puede entrar en otro mundo por algunos minutos. A mí me interesan más los juegos de tiro (shooting games). Puedo pasar mucho tiempo metiendo moneda tras moneda en la ranura para destruir barcos, aviones y otros objetos móviles (moving). Las luces y los sonidos electrónicos son muy emocionantes (exciting). Los juegos de billar romano (pinball) también me atraen, y trato de ganar un gran número de puntos. Pero hoy recuerdo que no he venido aquí para pasar tiempo con los juegos electrónicos. Hay que comprar ropa. Mamá insiste.

Circle the letter of the correct answer.

1. Madre e hijo van al centro comercial
   a. en coche
   b. en autobús
   c. en un camión-grúa

2. ¿Dónde está el coche?
   a. en el garaje de la casa
   b. en el centro
   c. en la estación de servicio

3. En el centro comercial no se puede
   a. ir a la escuela
   b. comer
   c. comprar impresoras

4. ¿Qué prefiere Pedro?
   a. las tiendas de ropa
   b. el billar romano
   c. los juegos de tiro

5. Los dos van el centro comercial para
   a. comprar ropa
   b. jugar con los juegos electrónicos
   c. pasar tiempo

B. *Diálogo*

MADRE: Ahora, Pedro, estamos en el *mall*. Te doy un cuarto de hora para los juegos electrónicos.

HIJO: Pero, mamá, me gustan tanto los juegos electrónicos. Quiero quedarme por lo menos media hora.

MADRE: Pues, vamos a llegar a un acuerdo (reach an agreement). Veinte minutos, pero no más. ¿Entiendes?

HIJO: De acuerdo. Vamos a encontrarnos delante de la tienda llamada "Ropa de Moda" en veinte minutos.

MADRE: Mientras tanto, yo iré a buscar un regalo para la tía Paquita, que va a celebrar su cumpleaños el domingo.

HIJO: Hasta entonces, mamá.

Circle the letter of the correct answer.

1. Pedro y su madre están en
   a. una tienda de ropa
   b. una fiesta de cumpleaños
   c. un centro comercial

2. El chico quiere divertirse por
   a. treinta minutos
   b. un cuarto de hora
   c. veinte minutos

3. ¿Quién va a recibir un regalo?
   a. la madre
   b. la hermana de la madre
   c. el chico

4. ¿Qué harán los dos después de veinte minutos?
   a. Comerán en un restaurante.
   b. Comprarán ropa.
   c. Irán a casa.

5. ¿Dónde van a encontrarse Pedro y su madre?

    a. en la galería de juegos electrónicos
    b. en casa de la tía Paquita
    c. cerca de una tienda

C. Complete the following dialogue.

MADRE: Hijo, llegaste tarde. ¿Qué hacías?

HIJO: (Tell her you were in the electronic-games gallery.)

    1. _____

MADRE: Sé que te gustan esos juegos, pero tenemos que comprarte una camisa, un par de pantalones y zapatos. Vamos a entrar en la tienda, por fin.

HIJO: (Ask her what you and she will buy first.)

    2. _____

MADRE: Primero veremos las camisas. ¿Cuál prefieres?

HIJO: (Tell her you prefer the red one [*la roja*] with horizontal stripes, because it's pretty.)

    3. _____

    _____

MADRE: De ningún modo. Las camisas con rayas horizontales son muy feas. Yo prefiero esta blanca y verde.

HIJO: (Tell her you really want the red one.)

    4. _____

MADRE: Muy bien, si insistes, aunque de veras no me gusta.

HIJO: (Thank her but tell her you should wear what [*lo que*] you like.)

    5. _____

D. *Temas*

  1. On the lines below, write about a visit to a shopping mall. Include answers to the following questions: (*a*) Why do you go to a shopping mall? (*b*) Where is the shopping mall that is nearest to your home? (*c*) How large is the mall? (number of stores, restaurants, etc.) (*d*) What do you like to do most when you are there? (*e*) How often do you go to the mall? (*dos veces al día, una vez por semana,* etc.)

_____

_____

_____

_____

_____

_____

2. Write about a shopping trip that you will take. Include the following information: (*a*) why you are going, and with whom; (*b*) how long you will stay there; (*c*) how you will get there; (*d*) how you feel about a particular store or restaurant—describe it in detail; (*e*) how much money you think you will spend and where you will get it. (to spend = *gastar*)

_____

_____

_____

_____

_____

_____

_____

Tenerife, las Islas Canarias, España

Part 8
El mundo de habla española

41
El mundo hispánico

El mundo de habla española

Al usar la palabra «hispano(-a)» o «hispánico(-a)», nos referimos a todas las personas que hablan español o a cualquier cosa típica del mundo de habla española. La palabra «español(-la)», en cambio, se refiere solamente a las personas y la cultura de España. Un *hispano* puede ser de México, Cuba, la Argentina o España, pero sólo un habitante de España puede ser *español*. Un plato hispano como enchiladas con guacamole no es un ejemplo de «comida española» sino de comida mexicana.

1. Un español es de _____. Todos los que hablan español son _____.

El mundo hispánico se compone de España y los diecinueve países de habla española del Hemisferio Occidental (Western). Como parte de España incluimos su provincia de las Islas Baleares en el Mar Mediterráneo al este de la Península Ibérica, dos provincias de las Islas Canarias en el Océano Atlántico al oeste de Marruecos (Morocco) en África, y los dos enclaves (territorios pequeños) de Ceuta y Melilla, en la costa mediterránea de Marruecos. La población hispana del mundo es de unos 390.000.000 habitantes. El español es la lengua materna (native) de unos 25.000.000 de norteamericanos.

2. _____ naciones del mundo son hispánicas.

Hispanomérica (la América Española)

Los países de Hispanomérica se pueden dividir en los siguientes grupos:

A. México

B. Centroamérica (la América Central). Las repúblicas hispánicas de la América Central son:

1. *Guatemala*   3. *Nicaragua*   5. *Costa Rica*
2. *Honduras*   4. *El Salvador*   6. *Panamá*

(No se incluye *Belice* en esta lista porque su lengua oficial es el inglés, pero muchos de sus habitantes hablan español también.)

C. Las Antillas (las islas del Caribe). Los países hispanos de este grupo son:

1. *Puerto Rico,* un Estado Libre Asociado a los Estados Unidos
2. *Cuba*
3. *La República Dominicana,* que comparte (shares) con Haití la isla llamada *Hispaniola* o *La Española.* Como la lengua oficial de Haití es el francés, Haití no es parte del mundo hispánico.

3. Haití no es un país hispano porque allí no se habla _____.

D. Sudamérica (La América del Sur). Los países hispánicos de Sudamérica son:

1. *Venezuela*   4. *Perú*   7. *(la) Argentina*
2. *Colombia*   5. *Chile*   8. *Uruguay*
3. *Ecuador*   6. *Bolivia*   9. *Paraguay*

Estos países se difieren el uno del otro en unos aspectos importantes, pero todos tienen una lengua en común y muchas semejanzas (similarities) culturales que reflejan la misma herencia (heritage) española.

4. En _____ naciones de Sudamérica se habla _____.

Unos aspectos de la civilización hispánica

1. LA LENGUA ESPAÑOLA

La lengua española tiene sus variaciones. Cada país hispano tiene sus diferencias con respecto al idioma. Por ejemplo, hay diferencias en la pronunciación. En España, la mayoría de los españoles pronuncian la letra *z* y la *c* en *ce* y *ci* (a*c*era, *ci*nco) como la *th* en la palabra inglesa *think*. La letra *j* tiene un sonido mucho más fuerte en España que la *j* de Hispanomérica. Los argentinos (y otros hispanoamericanos) pronuncian la *ll* y la *y* como la *s* en la palabra inglesa «pleasure». En Hispanoamérica y la España meridional (southern), muchas personas no pronuncian ni la *s* final ni la *s* que precede a una consonante. Tampoco pronuncian la *d* de la terminación *-ado* o *-ido*. Por ejemplo, *los mismos estados* se pronuncia «lo' mi'mo e'tao». A pesar de estas variaciones en la pronunciación, los hispanos de los diferentes países generalmente se entienden (understand one another) sin dificultad.

5. Hay diferencias en la _____ del español en los _____ donde se habla.

Tambíen hay diferencias en el vocabulario. Una *patata* en España es una *papa* en la América Española. Una naranja es una naranja para todos los hispanos menos los puertorriqueños, quienes la llaman una *china*. El autobús u ómnibus se llama una *guagua* en Cuba, Puerto Rico y las Islas Canarias. La misma palabra, *guagua,* quiere decir *bebé* (baby) en Chile. En México, la palabra *camión* (truck) también se usa como sinónimo de *autobús*.

Como ya saben ustedes, para la mayor parte de España el plural de *tú* es *vosotros(-as),* mientras que los hispanoamericanos usan *ustedes* como plural de *tú* así como (as well as) *usted.*

6. Los _____ no usan la palabra *vosotros.*

2. NOMBRES Y APELLIDOS

Muchos hispanos llevan los nombres de santos: *Pedro, José, Juan, María, Teresa,* etc. Generalmente celebran el día de su santo en vez de su cumpleaños. En general, los hispanos tienen más de un apellido. Por ejemplo, en el nombre *Ramón López Rodríguez,* López es el apellido del padre de Ramón, y Rodríguez es el apellido de soltera (maiden name) de su madre. Otro ejemplo: María Rodríguez Molina se casa con Pedro Vargas Vélez. Ahora ella se llama María Rodríguez de Vargas porque es la esposa *de* Vargas. La podemos llamar «señora de Vargas» o simplemente «señora Vargas». Carmen, la hija de Pedro y María, se llama Carmen Vargas Rodríguez—el apellido del padre seguido del (followed by the) apellido de la madre. La podemos llamar «señorita Vargas».

7. El apellido del padre de Felipe Santos González es _____.

8. Juan García Meléndez se casa con Ana Benítez Rivera. Ahora Ana se llama Ana
_____ de _____.

3. LOS DEPORTES

Lo que los hispanos llaman **el fútbol** es nuestro «soccer». Este deporte es muy popular en todo el mundo hispano. No debemos confundirlo con el juego norteamericano de «football».

9. El football se juega en los _____; el *fútbol* se juega allí también, pero lo
llamamos _____.

Por más de dos siglos **la corrida de toros** ha sido el deporte más popular de España y de algunos países hispanoamericanos. Hoy día, sin embargo, el fútbol ha llegado a ser más popular que la corrida de toros. Durante la temporada (season) de las corridas, la corrida tiene lugar los domingos a eso de las cinco de la tarde. En algunas ocasiones especiales, las corridas pueden tener lugar otros días de la semana.

10. Se puede ver una corrida de toros los _____.

11. La _____ ya no es tan popular en los países hispanos.

El jai alai, un deporte parecido al «handball», tuvo su origen en el País Vasco de España (Basque Country). Se juega en una cancha (court) llamada un *frontón.* Es un juego rapidísimo y exige (requires) mucha destreza (skill).

12. El jai alai se jugaba originalmente en _____.

El béisbol (baseball) es un deporte muy popular en Puerto Rico, Cuba, la República Dominicana, México y Venezuela. Varios jugadores de estos países han venido a los Estados Unidos para formar parte de los equipos norteamericanos de béisbol.

13. Hay jugadores de béisbol hispanos que son miembros de _____.

4. LA SIESTA

Por muchos siglos los pueblos (peoples) de habla española han observado en la tarde un largo período de descanso llamado *la siesta.* Esta costumbre tiene un motivo práctico: en España y otros países hispanos es muy difícil trabajar durante las primeras horas de la tarde porque hace mucho calor. Por eso, muchas tiendas y oficinas se cierran desde la una o la una y media hasta las cuatro o las cuatro y media de la tarde. Durante estas horas muchos vuelven a casa para tomar el almuerzo, que es generalmente una comida fuerte (heavy meal). Por lo común, descansan o duermen después de comer. En los últimos años, la costumbre de *tomar* (o *echar*) *una siesta* ha disminuido en muchas ciudades hispanas. Hoy día muchas tiendas se quedan abiertas durante las horas de la siesta.

14. En los pueblos hispanos se toma una _____ durante la _____

porque hace _____.

5. LAS COMIDAS

En los países de habla española las comidas se pueden describir así:

El desayuno, que se toma por la mañana, consiste en una taza de café o chocolate con un panecillo o bollo (bun). El café hispano es mucho más fuerte que el café norteamericano, y a menudo se toma con una gran cantidad de leche hervida (boiled) con azúcar.

15. Los hispanos toman el café con _____.

El almuerzo. En algunos países el almuerzo es un segundo desayuno y se toma a eso de las nueve y media o las diez. En otros países corresponde más a un «lunch» norteamericano, y se toma entre la una y media y las tres, es decir, inmediatamente antes de la siesta. En algunos lugares el almuerzo se llama **la comida** y normalmente consiste en varios platos.

16. En algunos sitios _____ es sinónimo de *almuerzo.*

La merienda (snack) se toma al final de la siesta y consiste en varias cosas como café, chocolate, panecillos y bollos. Muchas veces se toma un **aperitivo,** que puede ser cualquier (any) bebida alcohólica.

17. Al terminar la siesta, los hispanos toman _____.

La cena, que se toma muy tarde—entre las diez y las once de la noche—es por lo general una comida ligera.

6. LAS FIESTAS PATRONALES

En el mundo hispánico, cada país, ciudad y pueblo tiene al menos un santo patrón, quien ha sido adoptado como su protector. Por ejemplo, una santa patrona de Perú es Santa Rosa de Lima; el santo patrón de Madrid es San Isidro; el santo patrón de Puerto Rico es San Juan Bautista. Las fiestas patronales anuales son celebraciones que tienen lugar en honor del santo patrón. Estas festividades, que pueden durar una semana, incluyen fuegos artificiales (fireworks), desfiles (parades), y la venta de cosas de comer y beber en unas casetas provisionales (temporary stalls) construidas para la ocasión. Tiovivos (merry-go-rounds) y various juegos añaden al ambiente festivo.

18. Las fiestas patronales pueden consistir en _____

y _____.

Un aspecto notable de la fiesta patronal de Pamplona, una ciudad del nordeste de España, es la embestida (charge) de los toros bravos (wild bulls) por las calles de la ciudad. La celebración de San Fermín, santo patrón de Pamplona, empieza el 7 de julio y dura ocho días. Todos los días a las siete de la mañana explota un cohete (a rocket explodes) que anuncia que las puertas del corral están abiertas. Entonces los toros se escapan a la calle. Los toros corren por las calles hasta la plaza de toros. Muchas personas atrevidas (daring) corren con los toros, tratando de evitar sus cuernos (horns). Algunas de estas personas quedan heridas (get hurt). Después de este suceso (event) hay varias actividades, incluyendo una corrida de toros, que duran todo el día. El festival de Pamplona es una de la fiestas más emocionantes (exciting) que ocurren por todo el mundo hispano.

19. La celebración de _____ tiene lugar en Pamplona el

    _____ de _____ y dura _____.

7. LAS ESCUELAS

   Los niños de los países hispanos generalmente empiezan su enseñanza (education) en una **escuela primaria** o **escuela elemental,** donde se quedan por seis años. Luego pasan a una escuela secundaria llamada un **instituto,** un **liceo** o un **colegio**—el nombre de la escuela secundaria depende del país. Los niños asisten a esta escuela por cinco o seis años. Al graduarse, reciben un diploma llamado **el bachillerato,** y luego van a la **universidad.** No se debe confundir un *colegio* con el «college» de los Estados Unidos. El colegio es un tipo de «private high school». «College» en español es *universidad.* En los países hispanos, el día escolar es por lo general más largo que el nuestro, y los estudiantes hispanos estudian más asignaturas por semestre que los estudiantes norteamericanos. Los muchachos y las muchachas suelen ir (generally go) a escuelas separadas.

20. Los institutos y colegios son _____.

21. El día escolar hispano dura más _____ que el día escolar de los Estados Unidos.

22. Los muchachos y las muchachas normalmente no van a la misma _____.

8. LOS DÍAS DE FIESTA

   La **Navidad** (Christmas), la **Pascua de Resurrección** (Easter) y el **Día de la Raza** (Columbus Day), también llamado el **Día de la Hispanidad,** se celebran en todos los países de habla española. El Día de la Raza es el día en que todos los pueblos (peoples) hispanos celebran el descubrimiento de América por Cristóbal Colón.

23. _____ descubrió América.

   Hasta hoy día los niños hispanos solían recibir (were accustomed to receiving) regalos el seis de enero en vez del día de Navidad. El 6 de enero, llamado el **Día de los Reyes Magos,** se celebra el día en que los Reyes Magos (the Three Wise Men) trajeron regalos al niño Jesús. Sin embargo, en algunos sitios de la América española se ha adoptado la costumbre de repartir (distribute) los regalos en la Navidad, como en los Estados Unidos.

24. En algunas partes de Hispanomérica los niños reciben _____ el _____

    de _____. En otras partes los reciben el _____ de _____,

    como nosotros.

Cada país hispano tiene su propio día de fiesta para conmemorar su descubrimiento o su independencia de España. Por ejemplo, Puerto Rico celebra su descubrimiento el 19 de noviembre. El Día de la Independencia de México es el 16 de septiembre.

25. El 19 de noviembre es un día de fiesta en _____.

9. El mercado

El mercado en España y en los países hispanoamericanos es un lugar vivo y pintoresco. Muchos pueblos y aldeas tienen mercados al aire libre (outdoors) que se montan (are assembled) una vez por semana. Cada pueblo tiene su propio día de mercado. En los numerosos puestos (booths) y quioscos (stands), se vende toda clase de mercancías (merchandise): alimentos (food) y bebidas, ropa, recuerdos (souvenirs), juguetes, etc. El cliente muchas veces no acepta el primer precio que se pide y suele regatear (generally bargains) con el vendedor para rebajar (lower) el precio.

26. Una variedad de cosas se vende en _____.

Todos los pueblos tienen por lo menos un mercado situado dentro de un edificio. Este mercado generalmente queda abierto todos los días excepto los domingos. Aquí también se vende todo, incluso comestibles (groceries). El ama de casa (housewife) pasa de puesto en puesto, comparando los precios. Como muchas casas de los pueblos pequeños carecen de (lack) refrigeración adecuada, la típica ama de casa va al mercado todas las mañanas para comprar comida fresca.

27. Los mercados interiores se cierran los _____.

28. La mujer hispana generalmente va al mercado cada _____ para

comprar sólo los alimentos que necesita para el mismo _____.

▲ EJERCICIOS ▲

A. *Cierto o falso.* Write *cierto* if the statement is true. If it is false, replace the words in capital letters with words that would make the statement true. (Write the correct words in the blanks.)

1. Después de terminar sus estudios en LA UNIVERSIDAD, los estudiantes hispanos reciben su bachillerato. _____

2. El 16 de SEPTIEMBRE es un día de fiesta en México. _____

3. En los mercados de los países hispanos, los VENDEDORES buscan precios bajos. _____

4. EL INSTITUTO es la primera escuela a que asisten los niños hispanos. _____

5. El día de SAN JUAN se celebra en Puerto Rico. _____

6. EL DÍA DE LA HISPANIDAD se celebra el 25 de diciembre. _____

7. "Orange juice" generalmente se llama jugo de NARANJA en Puerto Rico. _____

8. En Haití se habla FRANCÉS. _____

9. El desayuno se toma por LA NOCHE. _____

10. Varias tiendas se cierran durante las horas de LA SIESTA. _____

11. EL FRONTÓN es un deporte popular que se parece al _handball._ _____

12. Los españoles toman LA CENA por la noche. _____

13. El béisbol es un deporte muy popular en FRANCIA. _____

14. El Salvador es una nación DEL CARIBE. _____

15. En Pamplona, una ciudad de ESPAÑA, hay una gran celebración en julio. _____

B. To the left of each expression in column I, write the letter of the related expression that appears in column II.

I	II
_____ **1.** aperitivo	_a._ almuerzo
_____ **2.** Honduras	_b._ Pamplona
_____ **3.** Hispaniola	_c._ autobús
_____ **4.** fútbol	_d._ soccer
_____ **5.** guagua	_e._ Sudamérica
_____ **6.** López	_f._ liceo
_____ **7.** los Reyes Magos	_g._ café
_____ **8.** San Fermín	_h._ Centroamérica
_____ **9.** Bolivia	_i._ merienda
_____ **10.** leche hervida	_j._ apellido
	_k._ isla del Caribe
	_l._ patata
	_m._ el 6 de enero

42
Influencias hispánicas en los Estados Unidos

Al mirar un mapa de los Estados Unidos, podemos ver muchas señales de la influencia de España en nuestro país. Por todo el Sudoeste hay lugares que tienen nombres españoles: por ejemplo, los estados de Texas, Colorado y Nuevo México; las ciudades de Los Angeles, San Francisco, Sacramento, Santa Fe y El Paso; el Parque Nacional de Mesa Verde; el Río Grande; el Valle de San Joaquín.

1. Muchos lugares del Sudoeste de los Estados Unidos tienen _____ españoles.

Otros indicios (signs) de la influencia hispana se encuentran en nuestra lengua. En las películas del «Wild West» se usan muchas expresiones de origen hispano: «lasso» (*lazo*), «lariat» (*la reata*), «vamoos» (*vamos*), «hoosegow» (*juzgado*), «sierra», «mesa», «rodeo», «sombrero».

■■▀ España y México en los Estados Unidos: Una breve historia

España y México han hecho un papel (role) muy importante en la historia norteamericana. Después que Cristóbal Colón descubrió el Nuevo Mundo en 1492, vinieron muchos exploradores y conquistadores. En abril de 1513 Juan **Ponce de León** llegó a la embocadura (mouth) de un río que se encuentra cerca del sitio actual (present) de Jacksonville, Florida, y tomó posesión de toda la península, pensando que era una isla. La llamó *la Florida* a causa de sus muchas flores bonitas («florida» quiere decir *flowery*), y también porque la descubrió durante la temporada de la Pascua Florida (Easter).

2. _____ descubrió la Florida.

En 1519 Hernán **Cortés,** con unos 550 soldados, llegó al Golfo de México cerca de la actual ciudad de Veracruz. Después de dos años y medio de guerras intermitentes, Cortés subyugó (subdued) a los indios aztecas, mató a su rey, Moctezuma, y capturó su capital, Tenochtitlán (el sitio de la actual ciudad de México). Después de esta victoria, los españoles conquistaron poco a poco todo México. El territorio de esta conquista incluía la mayor parte del Sudoeste norteamericano, que permaneció una parte íntegra de México hasta la Guerra Mexicana (1846–48).

3. Cortés conquistó a los _____. Moctezuma fue el _____ de los

_____.

En el año 1528, Álvar Núñez **Cabeza de Vaca** comandó una fuerza expedicionaria que se puso en camino en la Bahía de Tampa, Florida, y navegó por la costa de la península. Al llegar los españoles a la embocadura del río Misisipí, una tormenta violenta llevó el barco hasta la Isla de Galveston, cerca de la costa de Texas.

4. Cabeza de Vaca y sus hombres empezaron su viaje en _____.

Después de cruzar a tierra firme (mainland), Cabeza de Vaca y otros tres sobrevivientes (survivors) caminaron centenares (hundreds) de kilómetros a través de Texas, hasta que llegaron a San Miguel de

Culiacán, un sitio en lo que hoy es el estado de Sinaloa, México. Durante esta expedición por México, Cabeza de Vaca fue capturado por los indios Sioux, y vivió un tiempo entre ellos, sirviendo de su hechicero (witch doctor).

5. _____ fue una vez el hechicero de los indios Sioux.

En 1539, Hernando **de Soto,** gobernador de Cuba, viajó a la Florida y las Carolinas. Después, volvió (he turned) hacie el oeste y descubrió el río Misisipí. En México, Francisco Vázquez **de Coronado,** conquistador, dirigió, una expedición hacia el norte en busca de las fabulosas (fabled) ciudades de Cíbola. Muchos creían que estas siete "ciudades de oro" se encontraban en la región que hoy se llama Nuevo México. Coronado nunca logró encontrar estas ciudades legendarias, pero en cambio (instead) su expedición descubrió el Gran Cañón.

6. El río Misisipí fue descubierto por _____.

7. _____ descubrió el Gran Cañón.

Hay que mencionar a otros dos conquistadores importantes, aunque ellos no hicieron un papel en la historia de los Estados Unidos: Vasco Núñez de **Balboa,** que descubrió el Océano Pacífico a orillas de Panamá, y Francisco **Pizarro,** conquistador de Perú.

Cuando California formaba parte del imperio español, se fundaron misiones allí con el propósito (purpose) de convertir a los indios al cristianismo. Esta tarea fue asignada a los misioneros franciscanos, cuyo (whose) jefe era el Padre Junípero **Serra.** Entre 1769 y 1823, los misioneros españoles construyeron 21 misiones a lo largo del *Camino Real* (the King's Highway), el cual (which) se extendía de San Diego a San Francisco. En 1824 México ganó su independencia de España—un suceso que abrió un capítulo nuevo en la historia del Sudoeste de los Estados Unidos.

8. Los _____ trataron de convertir a los indios al cristianismo.

9. El Camino Real va desde _____ hasta _____.

◼ Comunidades hispanas en los Estados Unidos

1. El sudoeste

La mayor parte de los residentes hispanos de California, Texas y otros estados del Sudoeste son descendientes de los colonizadores españoles que habían vivido en esas regiones cuando todavía eran partes de México. A estos residentes hay que añadir los miles de mexicanos que han estado cruzando nuestra frontera meridional (southern) desde el principio del siglo 20. Muchos de ellos se establecieron permanentemente en California y otros estados.

10. Los _____ forman parte de la población de California.

2. La Florida

Después de la Revolución Cubana de 1959, muchos cubanos que no deseaban vivir bajo un gobierno comunista buscaron refugio en los Estados Unidos. Unos 500.000 de ellos se establecieron en la región de Miami, Florida. La mayor parte de estos refugiados eran graduados de una escuela secundaria o de la universidad, quienes habían tenido negocios o habían sido personas profesionales (médicos, abogados, etc.) antes de salir de Cuba. Aunque tenían que empezar la vida de nuevo (again) al llegar a la Florida, muchos de ellos lograron establecer nuevas empresas (businesses) o recomenzaron sus carreras (careers) anteriores. Hoy día la *colonia* cubana en Miami es una de las comunidades hispanas más prósperas de los Estados Unidos.

11. Muchos cubanos que vinieron a los Estados Unidos viven ahora en _____.

3. LA CIUDAD DE NUEVA YORK

Los neoyorquinos (New Yorkers) de habla española vienen de todas partes del mundo hispánico, pero gran parte de ellos son de la isla de Puerto Rico.

12. Muchos de los hispanos de Nueva York son de _____.

Los puertorriqueños comenzaron a venir al continente cuando los Estados Unidos ganaron posesión de la isla de Puerto Rico en 1898, a fines de la Guerra Hispanoamericana. Gran número de ellos han podido entrar en el país porque, como ciudadanos (citizens) de los Estados Unidos, no están sujetos (subject) a las cuotas de inmigración.

13. Los puertorriqueños son _____ de los Estados Unidos.

La entrada del mayor número de puertorriqueños ocurrió entre 1945 y 1951. La mayoría de ellos se establecieron en Nueva York porque tenían amigos y parientes en esa ciudad, la cual (which) también ofrecía una gran variedad de oportunidades de empleo.

14. Había muchas oportunidades de empleo para los _____ en

_____.

Muchos puertorriqueños que llegaron a Nueva York en las décadas de 1940 y 1950 han llegado a ser americanos asimilados, y ahora viven en todas partes de la ciudad. Algunos de sus hijos hablan muy poco español. Muchos borinqueños,* sin embargo, continúan hablando español entre sí (among themselves).

15. Los puertorriqueños se llaman también _____.

4. OTROS GRUPOS HISPÁNICOS

Como hemos visto, muchos de los hispanos que viven en los Estados Unidos son de origen mexicano, cubano o puertorriqueño. Pero hay también un gran número de inmigrantes que vinieron de España, la República Dominicana y los países de Centroamérica y Sudamérica. Como todos los demás inmigrantes de cualquier nacionalidad, estas personas han venido a nuestro país por las mismas razones básicas: para escaparse de una pobreza irremediable (hopeless) o de la opresión política, para hacerse una vida mejor y para obtener un porvenir mejor para sus hijos.

16. Los inmigrantes hispanos vienen a los Estados Unidos para _____

_____.

---

*Los puertorriqueños se llaman también *borinqueños* o *boricuas,* los nombres indios de los antiguos habitantes de la isla.

◤ EJERCICIOS ◥

A. *Cierto o falso.* If the statement is true, write *cierto.* If it is false, replace the words in capital letters with words that would make the statement true. (Write the correct words in the blank.)

1. La palabra inglesa «lariat» es de origen FRANCÉS. _____

2. Coronado ENCONTRÓ las «siete ciudades de Cíbola». _____

3. La ciudad de VERACRUZ está en el Golfo de México. _____

4. JUNÍPERO SERRA fue el jefe de los misioneros franciscanos. _____

5. Los puertorriqueños vinieron a NUEVA YORK en busca de trabajo. _____

6. Ponce de León descubrió MÉXICO. _____

7. Muchos CUBANOS se establecieron en Nueva York en 1959. _____

8. Cortés conquistó a los AZTECAS. _____

9. En el NORDESTE de los Estados Unidos hay mucha influencia hispana. _____

10. MOCTEZUMA fue el rey de los aztecas. _____

11. Sacramento es un nombre ESPAÑOL. _____

12. La revolución PUERTORRIQUEÑA tuvo lugar en 1959. _____

13. Hay una colonia cubana en MIAMI. _____

14. Balboa descubrió el Océano ATLÁNTICO. _____

15. Cabeza de Vaca hizo una expedición por COLORADO. _____

B. To the left of each expression in column I, write the letter of the related expression that appears in column II.

I	II
_____ 1. Pizarro	*a.* de San Francisco a San Diego
_____ 2. Texas	*b.* San Miguel de Culiacán
	c. Nuevo Mundo
_____ 3. el Gran Cañón	*d.* Perú
_____ 4. Colorado	*e.* el río Misisipí
	f. puertorriqueños
_____ 5. Cristóbal Colón	*g.* estado norteamericano
_____ 6. hoosegow	*h.* Pancho Gonzales
	i. 1898
_____ 7. borinqueños	*j.* Coronado
_____ 8. Guerra Hispanoamericana	*k.* 1846
	l. juzgado
_____ 9. Camino Real	*m.* Balboa
_____ 10. Hernando de Soto	*n.* estado del Sudoeste

43

Quiz on Hispanic Culture

For those of you who are knowledgeable about Hispanic culture and civilization or who would like to do some research, here are fifty incomplete statements for you to complete. You may use whatever references are available to you, and those include encyclopedias, almanacs, dictionaries, atlases, and, of course, the Internet (or perhaps your textbook). Your Spanish teacher may wish to grant extra credit to those who complete a specified number of questions.

(*Note:* Each dash may represent one or more words.)

¡Buena suerte!

1. The Iberian Peninsula refers to the countries of _____ and _____.

2. The famous Caves of _____ are located in northern Spain, near the town of _____.

3. The capital of Spain is _____.

4. A very active seaport on the Mediterranean coast of Spain is _____.

5. The famous Guggenheim Museum in New York has a branch in the Spanish city of _____.

6. The famous Prado Museum is in the Spanish city of _____.

7. The Río Grande, which is part of the border between the United States and Mexico, is known as the _____ in Mexico.

8. The famous Volcano of _____, in Mexico, was not known until 1943, when it erupted in a _____.

9. The famous central square of Mexico City is called _____.

10. The famous Pyramids of _____ are about 30 miles from Mexico City.

11. The silver city of Mexico is _____.

12. Many tourists visit the seaside resort of _____ on the southern Pacific coast of Mexico.

13. The Mayan ruins of Chichén-Itzá are located on the _____ Peninsula of Mexico.

14. The smallest Central American republic is _____.

15. The largest Central American republic is _____.

16. Haiti and the _____ share the Island of _____ in the _____ Sea.

17. The capital of Cuba is _____.

18. The taínos were the original inhabitants of the Island of _____.

19. *Estado Libre Asociado* refers to _____.

20. The famous Liberator of South America, _____, was born in Venezuela.

21. Bogotá is the capital of _____.

22. The famous Inca ruins of the lost city of Machu Picchu are in _____.

23. The highest capital in the world is _____, which is in _____.

24. The famous Lake _____ is in Peru and Bolivia.

25. The Statue called Cristo de los Andes is between the two countries of _____ and _____.

26. The highest mountain peak in the Western Hemisphere is _____, and is in _____.

27. The Teatro Colón, the renowned opera house, is located in the city of _____.

28. Montevideo is the capital of _____.

29. *Los porteños* are natives of the city of _____ in _____.

30. The walled city of Spain is _____.

31. The famous Roman aqueduct is in the city of _____, Spain.

32. The ancient capital of the Incas of Peru is _____.

33. In the Pacific Ocean to the west of Ecuador are the _____ Islands, known for their famous enormous _____.

34. The famous waterfalls of _____ are located on the border between Brazil and Argentina.

35. About 2300 miles west of the coast of Chile is the island called _____, which contains many stone statues called _____, erected on pedestals called _____.

36. The famous _____, a monastery, palace and mausoleum built by King _____, at a distance of about 25 miles from Madrid, is a great tourist attraction.

37. _____, the famous national hero of Spain in the Middle Ages, is buried in _____.

38. Luis Muñoz Marín was the first governor of _____ to be elected by the people.

39. The language of the Incas was called _____.

40. The vast flatland to the west and south of Buenos Aires, Argentina, is called

_____.

41. The two countries of South America that have no seacoast are _____ and

_____.

42. El Canal de la Mona separates _____ from _____.

43. The famous novel *Don Quijote de la Mancha* was written by _____.

44. The well-known statue of a bear and a tree, called _____, is situated in a

popular square of Madrid called _____.

45. The mountains that separate Spain from France are called _____.

46. _____ is the largest of the Balearic Islands.

47. The body of water that separates Spain from Africa is the _____.

48. The Moors (los moros), who invaded the Iberian Peninsula, and who came from

_____, remained for approximately _____ years, and

were finally expelled in the year _____ a.d.

49. Many of the conquerors and explorers of Spain came from the region called

_____.

50. The Spanish dessert that resembles caramel custard is called _____.

«Casco Viejo», la parte antigua de la Ciudad de Panamá

Part 9
Additional Practice in Reading and Listening

>‹›‹<

44
Reading Practice

I

En España los hombres pasan mucho tiempo charlando con sus amigos en los cafés y casinos. Estos cafés y casinos no sólo son importantes como centros de la vida social; allí se hacen también transacciones comerciales y pactos políticos. Muchas veces los hombres se quedan en los cafés y casinos hasta muy tarde por la noche. Por lo general, los españoles se acuestan mucho más tarde que los norteamericanos: en cualquier ciudad española, es muy común ver a los niños pequeños pasearse con sus padres o jugar en los parques a las once de la noche.

Fill in each blank with a word or words that best complete the sentence.

1. Hay casinos y _____ en _____.

2. Los cafés y casinos son lugares para _____.

3. Los norteamericanos generalmente se acuestan más _____ que los españoles.

4. Por la noche muchas veces hay _____ que _____ en los parques y

   _____ con sus _____.

II

No se debe hacer un viaje a Madrid sin visitar el Parque Zoológico (el Zoo) y el Parque de Atracciones. Los dos están situados en una área cubierta de árboles llamada la *Casa de Campo*. El Zoo es moderno y está bien organizado: tiene pequeños terrenos (plots of land) y lagos para los animales y flechas (arrows) que indican el circuito principal (main route). Así los que visitan el Zoo no pueden perder ninguna exhibición.

En el Parque de Atracciones hay toda clase de diversiones, juegos, tiovivos (merry-go-rounds), montañas rusas (roller-coasters), y muchos lugares donde comer y tomar refrescos. Una vía de cable (elevated cableway), llamada el *teleférico,* viaja encima del Parque de Atracciones y también sale del parque para dar una vista aérea muy impresionante de la ciudad.

Fill in each blank with a word or words that best complete(s) the sentence.

1. El Zoo y el Parque de Atracciones están en la ciudad de _____, y están en una

sección de la ciudad llamada _____.

2. Los animales del Zoo viven en _____.

3. Los que visitan el Zoo no pueden perderse si siguen los _____.

4. Los tiovivos y _____ se encuentran en _____.

5. Se puede ver la ciudad desde _____.

III

México tiene muchos volcanes. Los más famosos, *Ixtaccíhuatl* (pronounced "iss-tak-SEE-watl") y *Popocatépetl,* ahora son inactivos. No están lejos de la capital, pero para verlos hay que viajar al pueblo de Amecameca. Desde este pueblo, se pueden ver en un día claro. Cuando se pueden ver, cada volcán parece estar cerce del otro. Los nombres de estos dos volcanes aparecen en una leyenda azteca muy conocida, que es una historia muy triste. Ixtaccíhuatl es una princesa que espera a su amante (lover)

Popocatépetl, que va a volver de la guerra. Cuando él vuelve, después de muchos años, descubre que su novia ha muerto durante su ausencia (absence). Afligido por el dolor (grief-stricken), le construye una tumba enorme y decide quedarse para siempre a su lado.

Fill in each blank with a word or words that best complete(s) the sentence.

1. Popocatépetl está cerca del volcán llamado _____.

2. Los dos volcanes están _____ de la Ciudad de México.

3. Hay una _____ acerca de los dos volcanes.

4. _____ y _____ son amantes.

5. Popocatépetl está muy _____ cuando ve que su _____ está muerta.

IV

Ricky, un chico norteamericano de Nueva York, estudió español por cuatro años, pero, como no estudiaba mucho, aprendió muy poco. Le gustaba más divertirse. Un verano sus padres decidieron hacer un viaje por España y se llevaron a Ricky con ellos. Le gustaba mucho el país y se divertía mucho, pero no podía conversar con los españoles. Observaba que toda la gente, hasta los chicos de tres o cuatro años, hablaban español, y esto le sorprendía mucho. Cuando volvió a casa, le dijo a uno de sus amigos: —¡Qué inteligentes son los españoles! Todos saben hablar español, una lengua tan difícil.

Each statement based on the story is either true or false. If the statement is true, write "cierto." If it is false, write "falso." If your teacher so directs, you may rewrite the false sentences to make them correct.

1. Ricky sabía hablar español muy bien. _____

2. Ricky y sus padres fueron a España. _____

3. Ricky pasó un buen rato durante el verano. _____

4. Los españoles hablaban español con Ricky. _____

5. El amigo de Ricky creía que el español era muy difícil. _____

V

Hola, soy Pedro. Como estamos en verano y hace mucho calor, pienso ir a la playa. No tengo otra cosa que hacer y me gustaría ir esta mañana. El problema es que la playa está a unos doce kilómetros de mi casa. Se me ocurre una idea: mi amiga Catalina tiene su licencia de conducir y muchas veces usa el coche de sus padres. ¿Por qué no llamarla por teléfono? También voy a llamar a mi amiga Dorotea; ella siempre me pregunta: «Oye, Pedro, ¿por qué no vamos a la playa algún día? Me gustaría usar mi nueva escafandra (scuba-diving equipment)». Y recuerdo ahora que debo invitar a Vicente también. Él acaba de comprar su equipo de esquí acuático (water-skiing equipment) y quiere probarlo cuanto antes. Los cuatro somos muy buenos amigos. Pasaremos un día muy divertido—¡si no llueve! Según la radio, hará mucho sol y calor en todo el día. Pues, a la playa, entonces. ¡Ay! Hay un problema. Tengo que pedirles permiso a mis padres para ir, y los dos están trabajando ahora. ¿Qué hago?

Each statement based on the story is either true or false. If the statement is true, write "cierto." If it is false, write "falso." If your teacher so directs, you may rewrite the false sentences to make them correct.

1. El narrador del cuento se llama Vicente.   _____

2. Los chicos están de vacaciones.   _____

3. Pedro quiere usar el coche de sus padres para ir a la playa. _____

4. Parece que a Dorotea le gusta ir a la playa.   _____

5. En la playa Pedro va a usar su escafandra.   _____

6. Tres chicos y una chica van a la playa juntos.   _____

7. La radio dice que hará buen tiempo hoy.   _____

8. Pedro ya tiene permiso de sus padres para ir a la playa.   _____

VI

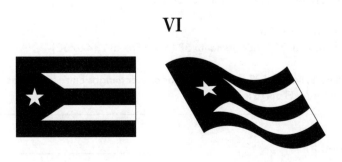

Puerto Rico fue descubierto por Cristóbal Colón el 19 de noviembre de 1493. Entre los habitantes originales de la isla estaban los *taínos,* quienes llamaban su isla *Boriquén* ("Tierra del noble señor"). Más tarde los colonizadores españoles cambiaron el nombre a *Borinquen.* En 1509 Ponce de León empezó a colonizar la isla, y fue nombrado el primer gobernador.

Puerto Rico siguió siendo una colonia española hasta 1898, cuando fue cedido (ceded) a los Estados Unidos al final de la Guerra Hispanoamericana. Por un decreto (act) del Congreso en 1917, los puertorriqueños se hicieron (became) ciudadanos de los Estados Unidos. En 1952 Puerto Rico se hizo autónomo (self-governing) asumiendo el título de *Estado Libre Asociado* (Commonwealth) *de Puerto Rico.* Aunque está asociado a los Estados Unidos, Puerto Rico tiene su propia constitución y su gobernador es elegido por el pueblo (people).

Fill in each blank with a word or words that best complete(s) the sentence.

1. _____ descubrió Puerto Rico en _____.

2. Originalmente los _____ vivían en Puerto Rico y le dieron a la isla el nombre de

   _____.

3. Ponce de León fue el _____ de Puerto Rico.

4. Los puertorriqueños son _____ de los Estados Unidos.

5. Los puertorriqueños eligen (elect) a su _____.

VII

Read the following advertisement and answer the questions based on it.

¿Quiere Ud. ganar un poco de dinero trabajando unas horas durante la semana? Buscamos un/una joven entre 15 y 17 años de edad para cuidar a un perro muy cariñoso. Tres días por semana, entre las 6 y las 9 de la noche. Sólo tiene que darle de comer y pasearlo por quince minutos. Buena paga.

Escriba una carta incluyendo sus aptitudes, con dos referencias, preferiblemente de dos profesores/profesoras o del director/de la directora de su escuela. Dirija su carta a :

los señores Ramírez
Calle Ancha, 326, apartamento 5B (o por Fax al 234-6752)

Si quiere, llame al 234-6740 los sábados y domingos entre las 2 y las 5 de la tarde. El perro le espera.

1. What is this position for?   _____

2. What are the age requirements?   _____

3. How many hours a week does the job call for? _____

4. What are the specific duties called for? _____

5. In what three ways may the applicant get in touch with the prospective employer? _____

VIII

Examine the following I.D. card and answer the questions based on it.

CARNET DE IDENTIDAD
COLEGIO REGIONAL DE LA PAZ

NOMBRE: Roberto Larra Rodriguez
DIRECCIÓN: Calle Alejandro 547, La Paz
TELÉFONO: 653-47-92
FECHA DE NACIMIENTO: 19-III-51
SEXO: M   **ESTADO CIVIL:** soltero
OJOS: azules   **PELO:** castaño
ESTATURA: 1,81 metros   **PESO:** 75 kilos
CIUDADANÍA: boliviano
LUGAR DE NACIMIENTO: Sucre, Bolivia
CATEGORÍA: profesor

1. Where does Mr. Larra work? (Be careful with the meaning of *colegio*.) _____.

2. What is his full birth date? (Remember that outside of the U.S. the order of dates is: day-month-year) _____.

3. In what city and country was he born? _____.

4. Is he working in the above city? _____. How do you know? _____.

5. What is his mother's family name? _____.

6. What are his height and weight? (Use your knowledge of the metric system, or look up the formulas.) _____, _____.

7. What do you think "estado civil" means? _____. Is he married? _____.

   How do you know? _____.

IX

Answer the questions based on the following advertisement.

**HOTEL PRESIDENTE
RESERVACIONES**

AVENIDA SAN CARLOS, 125
Teléfonos: 4356798 4356702 Fax: 4356704
Correo electrónico: hotelpres@bienvenida.com

150 Habitaciones individuales y dobles recién
modernizadas con teléfonos equipados para
correo electrónico, internet y fax

Restaurante abierto 24 horas

Servicio a habitación a todas horas

Bar-Discoteca

Salas para reuniones comerciales y familiares

Galería comercial con todo tipo de tiendas

Garaje con 60 estacionamientos

Salón de juegos para niños

Precios rebajados los fines de semana

Póngase en contacto con nosotros. Le esperamos.

1. In what three ways may one contact this hotel for reservations? _____,

   _____, _____.

2. Would a client be able to use his/her laptop computer? _____. How would he/she

   know? _____.

3. Where could a guest find some diversion in this hotel? _____.

4. What days would be the best for someone who wishes to save money on his/her room?

   _____.

5. What types of meetings may be held here? _____.

6. Would a guest have to leave the room to look for food? _____. How do you know?

   _____.

7. Are children welcome? _____. How do you know? (Name two ways)

   _____, _____.

X

Un señor muy rico, pero muy tacaño (stingy), que vivía solo en un apartamento lujoso (luxurious), llamaba por teléfono todos los días al mismo restaurante para pedir algo de comer. Y todos los días el mismo muchacho le entregaba su comida, pero de mala gana (unwillingly), porque el señor rico nunca le daba una propina (tip). Un día el chico tocó el timbre. Y cuando el señor preguntó quién era, el chico le contestó: «Su comida, señor. Diez dólares, por favor», sin decir otra cosa. Cuando el señor abrió la puerta, el muchacho le dio la comida, el señor le pagó lo que debía y el chico iba a salir sin decir palabra. El señor quedó muy ofendido y decidió darle al chico una lección de cortesía.

—Oiga, joven,—dijo el señor. —Quiero darle una lección de cortesía. Siéntese aquí en esta silla. Ud. estará en mi lugar.

El señor fue a la puerta y entró otra vez con la bolsa (bag) de comida, y le dijo al joven:

—Buenas tardes, señor. Aquí le traigo su comida y espero que le guste.

—Oh, muchas gracias, señor.—le contestó el joven.— Ud. es muy amable. Aquí tiene Ud. el dinero por la comida y dos dólares de propina.

El señor rico se rió mucho, y en pago de la lección que había aprendido, le devolvió todo el dinero al chico y le dio cinco dólares más de propina.

Based on the above passage, choose the statement or phrase that best answers each question.

1. El señor rico no le daba una propina al muchacho porque

   a. no tenía dinero.   *c.* el chico era descortés.
   b. era tacaño.   *d.* el chico también era rico.

2. ¿Quién le traía la comida al señor?

   a. un muchacho joven   *c.* la esposa del señor
   b. el dueño del restaurante   *d.* el hijo del dueño del restaurante

3. ¿Por qué quedó ofendido el señor?

   a. La comida no era buena.   *c.* El chico no dijo nada al salir.
   b. El muchacho lo insultó.   *d.* El chico comió la comida.

4. ¿Qué quiso hacer el señor?

   a. enseñarle algo al chico   *c.* llamar al dueño del restaurante
   b. salir de su apartamento   *d.* echar al muchacho de su casa

5. Al fin, ¿qué recibió el muchacho del señor?

   a. diecisiete dólares   *c.* las gracias
   b. sólo una propina   *d.* quince dólares

XI

Hola, Me llamo Isabel, pero mis amigos me llaman Belita. Tengo quince años. Soy una estudiante diligente los días de escuela, pero durante los fines de semana me gusta divertirme. En nuestra ciudad hay mucho que hacer. Los sábados y domingos hago mis tareas por la mañana. Así el resto del día queda para las diversiones. Muchas veces me paseo en bicicleta. Pasé el sábado pasado del siguiente modo:

Me levanté a las nueve. Hice mis tareas hasta las once. Llamé por teléfono a mi amiga Lola para preguntarle qué quería hacer. Como hacía mal tiempo, decidimos ir al cine para ver una película sobre la vida de una mujer policía. Al salir del cine, fuimos a tomar un refresco. Por la noche tuve que quedarme en casa para cuidar a mi hermano menor, Carlos. Él tiene diez años y tiene miedo de quedarse en casa solo. Soy una buena hermana, ¿verdad?

Mis padres tenían que asistir a una reunión muy importante con unos amigos. Después de la cena, miramos la televisión por una hora y luego jugamos una partida de ajedrez (game of chess). Mi hermano ganó la partida y yo quedé muy desilusionada (disappointed). A las nueve mi hermanito fue a su cuarto para trabajar con su computadora antes de acostarse. Y yo llamé otra vez por teléfono a Lola para discutir nuestros planes para el próximo fin de semana.

Based on the above passage, choose the statement or phrase that best answers each question.

1. Los sábados y domingos por la tarde a Belita le gusta

    a. pasar buenos ratos con sus amigas.   *c.* ayudar a sus padres.

    b. quedarse en casa.   *d.* preparar la cena.

2. ¿Por qué llamó Belita a su amiga Lola?

    a. para hablar de sus amigos   *c.* para divertirse

    b. para discutir sus planes   *d.* para darle información

3. Después de ver la película, las dos chicas

    a. fueron a casa.   *c.* tomaron algo de beber.

    b. hablaron con una mujer policía.   *d.* llamaron a otra amiga.

4. El hermano de Belita

    a. tiene menos años que ella.   *c.* prefiere quedarse en casa solo.

    b. va al cine con las chicas.   *d.* no sabe jugar al ajedrez.

5. ¿Qué hizo Carlos a las nueve?

    a. miró la televisión con Belita   *c.* se acostó

    b. llamó a sus padres   *d.* trabajó en su cuarto

XII

Queridos padres:

Llegamos a Lima muy tarde por la noche. A primera vista, la ciudad inspiraba mucho: las luces de los antiguos edificios coloniales en las calles llenas de gente, los edificios modernos, y especialmente nuestro hotel, un edificio lujoso situado en el centro de la ciudad, al lado de la Plaza de San Martín. Dormimos muy bien, cansados del vuelo de tantas horas. Por la mañana estábamos libres para pasear por la ciudad y comprar recuerdos en las varias tiendas turísticas. Por la tarde nuestro guía nos llevó por varias partes de la ciudad. Situada cerca del Palacio Presidencial, está la magnífica Catedral, donde están enterrados los restos de Pizarro, el conquistador de Perú. Después de visitar la Catedral, fuimos en autobús a otra sección de la ciudad para visitar el famoso Museo del Oro, que contiene una magnífica colección de objetos de oro que datan de la época de los incas y de las civilizaciones preincaicas. Nuestra cena en un restaurante típico era deliciosa y todos conversamos acerca de nuestras impresiones de la ciudad. Mañana por la mañana volamos a Cuzco, desde donde les escribiré otra vez. Un abrazo (hug), y saludos (regards) de todos mis compañeros de la escuela. El profesor Martínez también manda sus saludos y dice que estoy en buenas manos y que Uds. no deben preocuparse.

Su hija que los quiere mucho.

Julia

Each statement based on the story is either true or false. If the statement is true, write "cierto." If it is false, write "falso." If your teacher so directs, you may rewrite the false sentences to make them correct.

1. Julia estaba sola.   _____

2. La ciudad de Lima le causó una buena impresión a Julia.   _____

3. A Julia le gustó su hotel.   _____

4. El grupo fue a Lima en tren.   _____

5. El guía encontró al grupo por la mañana.   _____

6. El hotel estaba dentro de la Plaza de San Martín.   _____

7. Pizarro está enterrado en el Palacio del Presidente.   _____

8. El Museo del Oro está muy cerca de la Catedral.   _____

9. Esa noche comieron bien.   _____

10. El grupo consiste en varios estudiantes con su profesor. _____

XIII

Queridos padres:

Después de un vuelo muy corto, llegamos al aeropuerto de Cuzco. Como estábamos a una altura de más de 11.000 pies sobre el nivel del mar, teníamos que descansar un rato antes de empezar nuestra visita a Cuzco. Yo estaba un poco mareada y no quería sufrir un ataque de «soroche», la enfermedad causada por la altitud. Después de dormir un rato, decidimos explorar la ciudad de los incas, esta vez sin guía. El recepcionista del hotel nos dio un plano de la ciudad y nos indicó algunos sitios de interés. Lo primero que encontramos fue un mercado al aire libre muy grande. Aquí me compré un suéter (o "chompa", como los llaman aquí) muy vistoso (flashy) pero recio (thick) porque en Cuzco hace mucho frío, especialmente por la noche. Luego empezamos a explorar la ciudad. Por todas partes se ven las ruinas de los incas. Pasamos una buena parte del día paseando por Cuzco y observando a la gente. Por todas las calles hay indias que venden distintas mercancías. Parece que nunca duermen porque se encuentran en las calles día y noche. Y todas llevan la pollera (hoopskirt) típica y el bombín (bowler hat). Y nunca se acepta el primer precio que piden, sino que hay que regatear (haggle) un poco. Es la costumbre aquí.

Pasado mañana vamos a Machu Picchu y tengo muchas ganas de ver esa famosa ciudad perdida de los incas.

Con cariño y muchos abrazos, y saludos a toda la familia.

Julia

Based on the above passage, choose the statement or phrase that best answers each question.

1. ¿Cómo llegaron a su destino?

   a. en avión   *b.* en tren   *c.* en coche   *d.* a caballo

2. ¿Por qué tenían que descansar?

   a. Estaban enfermos.   *c.* Podían enfermarse.
   b. Habían viajado mucho tiempo.   *d.* Cuzco era peligroso.

3. ¿Cómo iban a ver la ciudad?

   a. con la ayuda de un guía   *b.* solos   *c.* en coche   *d.* en taxi

4. ¿Por qué compró Julia un suéter?

   a. No quería tener frío.   *c.* Le gustaba comprar cosas.
   b. Era para su madre.   *d.* Deseaba explorar la ciudad.

5. ¿Qué piensa hacer Julia?

   a. regatear siempre con las indias   *c.* comprarse un bombín y una pollera
   b. vender mercancías por las calles   *d.* viajar a otro lugar

XIV

Queridos padres:

El viaje en tren desde Cuzco a Machu Picchu fue muy interesante y pintoresco. Tuvimos que levantarnos muy temprano para recorrer los 112 kilómetros (o sea 70 millas). Durante el viaje vimos muchos grandes contrastes panorámicos. Por fin llegamos al pie de una montaña donde había muchas personas esperando su turno para tomar uno de los microbuses que los llevarían a la cumbre de la montaña. Afortunadamente teníamos una reservación en el único hotel. Si no, ¡hubiéramos tenido que dormir al aire libre! ¡Y hace mucho frío aquí por la noche! Seguimos subiendo la montaña sin ver nada hasta que doblamos una curva y . . . ¿qué vimos? La vista espectacular de Machu Picchu. Todo el mundo la llama «la ciudad perdida de los incas», pero yo la llamo «la ciudad encontrada». Hay varias teorías acerca de Machu Picchu. Algunos dicen que fue una fortaleza (fortress) construida por los incas para protegerse contra sus enemigos. Otros creen que fue un santuario (sanctuary) de un grupo de mujeres escogidas (chosen) por el Dios Sol. Otros creen que, y esto puede ser lo más probable, que fue el refugio final del último rey inca y de su comitiva (retinue) al huir (on fleeing) de los españoles hacia la seguridad (safety) de la selva (jungle). Después de depositar nuestras maletas en las habitaciones del hotel, nos dirigimos en seguida hasta el sitio de las ruinas. ¡Ah! Es hora de cenar y luego nos reunimos en el gran salón para discutir nuestras actividades del día. Mañana les escribiré otra vez y les daré más detalles.

Mil abrazos de su hija que los quiere mucho y echa de menos (misses) a toda la familia.

Julia

Each statement based on the story is either true or false. If the statement is true, write "cierto." If it is false, write "falso." If your teacher so directs, you may rewrite the false sentences to make them correct.

1. Julia viajó de Machu Picchu a Cuzco en tren.   _____

2. El grupo hizo el viaje por la noche.   _____

3. Muchas personas querían subir a Machu Picchu.   _____

4. Julia y sus amigos iban a dormir al aire libre esa noche.   _____

5. Al subir en el microbús, la primera cosa que vieron
   fueron las ruinas de Machu Picchu.   _____

6. Nadie está seguro del origen de Machu Picchu.   _____

7. El grupo dejó su equipaje entre las ruinas.   _____

8. Julia iba a hablar de su visita a las ruinas en su
   habitación   _____

9. Julia les mandará la próxima carta a sus padres al
   día siguiente.   _____

10. Durante su viaje, Julia pensaba en su familia.   _____

XV

Queridos padres:

Ahora estoy muy cansada porque pasé casi todo el día explorando las ruinas de Machu Picchu. Hay tanto que ver que se podría pasar una semana aquí sin verlo todo. Caminábamos por las ruinas, viendo las casas, los santuarios y las terrazas de los incas. Se cree que los incas construían estas terrazas para cultivar sus productos agrícolas (farm produce). Luego subimos al pico (mountain peak) de Huayna Picchu desde donde se podía gozar de una vista espectacular de todo Machu Picchu. Después de bajar del pico, entramos al Templo del Sol. Este templo contiene el Reloj del Sol, que está en buen estado (condition). Me parece que los incas eran excelentes astrónomos y matemáticos. Saqué muchas fotos para no olvidar las maravillas de este lugar. Pasamos el resto del día subiendo y bajando las numerosas escaleras de piedra que se encuentran por todas partes. Por fin decidimos regresar al hotel para descansar un rato. Ahora tengo tiempo para escribirles a Uds. No se puede visitar Perú sin ir a Machu Picchu. Ha sido una gran aventura. Dentro de dos días nuestras vacaciones van a terminar y volvemos a casa.

Saludos y abrazos a todos, y hasta muy pronto.

Julia

Each statement based on the story is either true or false. If the statement is true, write "cierto." If it is false, write "falso." If your teacher so directs, you may rewrite the false sentences to make them correct.

1. Julia exploró Machu Picchu sólo por la tarde.   _____

2. Julia y sus amigos construyeron las terrazas.   _____

3. El grupo podía ver Machu Picchu desde el pico de
   Huayna Picchu.   _____

4. El Reloj del Sol está en el Templo del Sol. _____

5. Huayna Picchu sacó muchas fotos del grupo. _____

6. Hay muchas escaleras de piedra en Machu Picchu. _____

7. El grupo descansó en el hotel. _____

8. Julia les escribe a sus padres desde el Templo del Sol. _____

9. Después de visitar Machu Picchu, Julia va a regresar a casa. _____

XVI

Cierto día el famoso músico, Roberto Méndez, entró en una tienda de música para buscar un disco compacto raro. Como no pudo encontrar lo que buscaba, le preguntó a un dependiente si lo tenía.

—Ud. tiene suerte, señor. Es el último que tenemos.

—¿Cuánto vale el disco compacto?—le preguntó el señor Méndez al dependiente.

—Treinta dólares—le contestó.

—Es muy caro. ¿No me lo puede vender por menos?

—No es posible, señor. Es el último que tenemos. Y, además, en esta tienda no se puede regatear (haggle).

—Pues, ¿puedo hablar con el gerente (manager)?

—Está muy ocupado, pero ahora mismo voy a llamarlo.

Dentro de dos minutos apareció el gerente y le dijo al músico:

—Buenas tardes, caballero. ¿En qué puedo servirle?

—¿Cuánto vale este disco compacto?—le preguntó el músico al gerente.

—Treinta y cinco dólares, señor.

—Pero, ¿cómo es posible? Su dependiente me ha pedido sólo treinta dólares hace dos minutos.

—Y yo le pido treinta y cinco dólares.

El señor Méndez no dijo nada y así pasaron cinco minutos. Luego le preguntó al gerente:

—Bien, ¿cuál es su último precio?

—Cuarenta dólares—le contestó el gerente.

—¡Pero hace unos minutos usted me pidió treinta y cinco dólares!—dijo furiosamente el músico.

—Es verdad, señor. Pero, mire Ud. cuánto tiempo he perdido hablando con Ud. Soy un hombre muy ocupado y mi tiempo vale mucho. Ud. puede tener el disco compacto por cincuenta dólares.

—¿Cómo?—gritó el músico.—El primer precio fue treinta dólares. Y ahora Ud. me pide cincuenta. No lo comprendo.

—Pues,—le contestó el gerente,—es verdad que el libro cuesta treinta dólares. Pero Ud. tiene que darse cuenta de que el tiempo que he pasado con Ud. vale veinte dólares. Por eso le cobro (I'm asking you for) cincuenta dólares.

¿Y qué hizo el pobre hombre? Necesitaba el disco compacto porque contenía ciertas canciones muy antiguas y raras. Pagó el precio y salió de la tienda jurando no regatear nunca más.

Based on the above passage, choose the statement or phrase that best answers each question.

1. ¿Para qué entró el señor Méndez en la tienda?
   - *a.* para vender discos compactos
   - *b.* para comprar algo
   - *c.* para hablar con el gerente
   - *d.* para buscar a un amigo

2. ¿Por qué habló el señor Méndez con el dependiente?
   - *a.* Necesitaba su ayuda.
   - *b.* Era su amigo.
   - *c.* Quería hablar con alguien.
   - *d.* Deseaba darle un regalo.

3. El dependiente llamó al gerente porque
   - *a.* su esposa estaba allí.
   - *b.* quería cerrar la tienda.
   - *c.* era un buen hombre.
   - *d.* el músico quería hablar con él.

4. ¿Qué no comprendió el músico?
   - *a.* por qué el gerente pedía varios precios
   - *b.* la música de la tienda
   - *c.* las palabras del dependiente
   - *d.* por qué el gerente salió a hablar con él

5. El señor Méndez se dio cuenta de que
   - *a.* no hay discos compactos raros.
   - *b.* los gerentes son simpáticos.
   - *c.* es mejor aceptar el primer precio que piden.
   - *d.* los dependientes saben muy poco.

XVII

Don Octavio Buscapenas sufría de una enfermedad bastante común: estaba aburrido de la vida. No podía interesarse en nada. Por eso fue a ver a una psicóloga (psychologist). Ella le dijo que debía buscar actividades interesantes y estimulantes. Al salir del consultorio de la psicóloga, don Octavio pensaba en los consejos que ella le había dado. Como primera actividad, decidió ir al teatro para ver una pieza que trataba de un crimen misterioso. Siempre le habían gustado los cuentos policíacos. Cuando salió del teatro, ya era casi medianoche. Como no tenía sueño, decidió volver a casa a pie en vez de esperar el autobús. A esas horas el autobús tardaba mucho en llegar. También quería estar solo un rato para pensar en la pieza que acababa de ver. Al pasar por una calle desierta, se fijó en un objeto que se hallaba en el suelo. Se acercó al objeto y vio una forma grande. Era el cuerpo de un hombre bien vestido. ¡Un cadáver! Don Octavio no reconoció la cara del muerto. Al principio quiso llamar a la policía desde una cabina telefónica que se encontraba muy cerca del sitio. Pero de repente se acordó de los consejos de la psicóloga: «buscar actividades interesantes y estimulantes». Don Octavio iba a hacer el papel de detective.

1. ¿Qué se sabe de don Octavio?
   - *a.* Estaba aburrido.
   - *b.* No le gustaban los psicólogos.
   - *c.* Nunca seguía los consejos de nadie.
   - *d.* Estaba enfermo.

2. ¿Por qué fue al teatro don Octavio?
   - *a.* Quería ver una pieza emocionante.
   - *b.* Le gustaba mucho el teatro.
   - *c.* Allí se podía encontrar con amigos.
   - *d.* No quería seguir los consejos de la psicóloga.

3. ¿Por qué no quiso don Octavio esperar el autobús?
   - *a.* No le gustaban los transportes públicos.
   - *b.* Los autobuses venían con poca frecuencia.
   - *c.* Prefería tomar un taxi.
   - *d.* Hacía buen tiempo.

4. ¿Qué vio don Octavio en la calle?

    a. un animal feroz

    b. un abrigo viejo

    c. el cuerpo de una persona sin vida

    d. una moneda de mucho valor

5. ¿Por qué no llamó don Octavio a la policía?

    a. Él mismo deseaba solucionar el crimen.

    b. Tenía miedo de la policía.

    c. La policía no venía tan tarde por la noche.

    d. No había teléfono cerca del lugar del crimen.

XVIII

Una vez llegó a nuestro pueblo un hombre que tenía fama de interpretar sueños y de ser especialista en cosas del otro mundo. Nadie sabía de dónde había venido. Sus horas de consulta eran desde la una hasta las cuatro de la mañana, todos los días, incluso los sábados y domingos. A pesar de las horas extrañas, su oficina siempre estaba llena de gente. Una noche llegó a su oficina un campesino que había tenido un sueño muy extraño. Había soñado que llovía mucho, pero en vez de lluvia, caían unos palos (sticks) muy grandes. El intérprete le dijo al campesino que su sueño era muy fácil de interpretar. El sueño quería decir que el campesino iba a recibir una paliza (beating). El campesino salió de la oficina riéndose de esta tonta interpretación. Dos noches después, el campesino andaba hacia su casa por la noche. Antes de llegar a la puerta, un hombre que llevaba una máscara le dio una paliza muy grande. No se sabía quién había sido el asaltante ni de dónde había venido. Pero los más inteligentes del pueblo sospechaban que el criminal había sido el intérprete de sueños, quien quería cumplir con su profecía.

1. De dónde era el especialista en sueños?

    a. de un pueblo lejano

    b. del mismo pueblo

    c. No se sabía.

    d. de una ciudad extranjera

2. ¿Cuándo recibía el intérprete a sus clientes?

    a. después de la medianoche

    b. por la tarde

    c. una vez por semana

    d. sólo los sábados y domingos

3. ¿Por qué vino el campesino a ver al intérprete?

    a. Le faltaba agua.

    b. Quería obtener la interpretación de un sueño.

    c. Tenía ganas de darle unos golpes.

    d. No podía tolerar la lluvia.

4. ¿Qué pensaba el campesino de la interpretación de su sueño?

    a. Pensaba que era correcta.

    b. Él mismo podía interpretarlo mejor.

    c. No la comprendió

    d. No la creyó.

5. ¿De quién sospechaban algunos?

    a. de nadie

    b. de un hombre del pueblo

    c. del intérprete del sueño

    d. de uno de los amigos del campesino

XIX

El Sr. Oviedo era profesor de español. Un día anunció a la clase que cada uno de sus alumnos iba a adquirir un amigo hispánico por correspondencia.

—Tengo un amigo, Raúl Ortega, que vive en Santiago, Chile. El Sr. Ortega enseña inglés en un colegio de esa ciudad. Uds. les escribirán en español a sus alumnos, y en su clase ellos les escribirán a Uds. en inglés.

Este proyecto les gustó mucho a los alumnos del Sr. Oviedo. Ricardo preguntó al profesor cuándo iban a empezar. El profesor le contestó:

—Hoy mismo. Aquí tengo los nombres y las direcciones de todos los alumnos de mi amigo chileno. Jóvenes, cada uno de Uds. ya tiene un amigo chileno. Ahora Uds. van a poner en práctica el español que han aprendido en esta clase. ¿Hay preguntas?

—Sí —dijo Lupe—, ¿cómo se empieza la carta?

—Se empieza así: «Querido Juan» o «Querida María» —respondió el Sr. Oviedo.

—¿Y cómo se termina?

—Sólo hay que decir «sinceramente» o «su amiga». Y ahora, vamos a empezar.

1. ¿Qué harán los estudiantes del Sr. Oviedo?

    a. Les escribirán a unos estudiantes en otro país.

    b. Harán un viaje a Santiago.

    c. Visitarán al Sr. Ortega.

    d. Vivirán en Chile por un mes.

2. ¿Quién era el Sr. Ortega?

    a. un amigo de Ricardo

    b. un profesor de español

    c. un profesor de inglés

    d. un pariente del Sr. Oviedo

3. ¿Qué pensaban los estudiantes de la idea del Sr. Oviedo?

    a. Creían que era tonta.

    b. Pensaban que sería mejor viajar a Chile.

    c. No les gustaba.

    d. Les interesaba.

4. ¿Qué tenía el Sr. Oviedo?

   a. cartas de Chile

   b. toda la información necesaria

   c. sólo los nombres de algunos niños chilenos

   d. algunos amigos chilenos

5. ¿Qué deseaba saber una estudiante?

   a. cómo debía comenzar y terminar la carta

   b. cómo eran los chicos chilenos

   c. cómo se llamaba el profesor chileno

   d. por qué tenían que escribir cartas

XX

Antonio Temelotodo era un hombre que tenía miedo de todo en la vida: las caídas, los coches, los autobuses, los trenes y, sobre todo, las enfermedades. Él siempre pensaba que iba a ponerse enfermo. Por eso tomaba muchas precauciones. Una vez estaba tan enfermo que su médico le aconsejó tomar unas vacaciones en el campo. Antonio discutía con su esposa cuál sería el mejor lugar en que pasar sus vacaciones.

—Si vamos al norte —dijo él— hará mucho frío, y muchas veces nieva. Si vamos al sur, hará mucho calor. Y además, he leído en el periódico que allí hay una gran epidemia de fiebre tifoidea.

Por fin decidieron ir a un pueblo pequeño en la parte oeste del país. Antonio estaba bastante seguro de que allí no habría ni enfermedades ni personas enfermas.

Cuando llegaron al hotel, se instalaron en un cuarto muy pequeño pero cómodo. En seguida Antonio notó un olor muy fuerte a desinfectante. Llamó al director del hotel para preguntarle quién se había quedado antes en esa habitación. El director contestó que el cuarto había estado desocupado desde hacía mucho tiempo. Sin embargo Antonio insistió en cambiar de habitación. En la próxima habitación había el mismo olor. Después de cambiar de cuarto cinco veces, Antonio decidió ir a otro hotel. Allí pasó lo mismo: siempre el mismo olor. Por fin decidió volver a casa en el próximo tren. Por desgracia, había el olor conocido en su compartimiento del tren. Antonio pensó que todo el mundo estaba enfermo a causa de una gran epidemia.

Al llegar a casa, antonio empezó a deshacer su maleta, de donde se escapó un fuerte olor. Allí estaba la causa de todo. Fue el olor del medicamento que él había traído. La botella se había roto y el líquido, con su fuerte olor, se había difundido (spread) por toda la maleta.

—Aquí tienes tu epidemia de fiebre tifoidea—le dijo su esposa.

1. ¿Qué creía Antonio Temelotodo?

   a. Siempre estaría enfermo.

   b. Los médicos no podían curar nada.

   c. No era necesario tomar precauciones.

   d. La vida valía poco.

2. ¿Qué consejos le dio el médico a Antonio?

    a. Era necesario consultar a otro médico.   *c.* Tenía que evitar los autobuses.

    b. No debía viajar en tren.   *d.* Debía salir de la ciudad.

3. ¿Qué problema discutió Antonio con su esposa?

    a. No le gustaba el campo.   *c.* No quería seguir los consejos del doctor.

    b. No sabía dónde pasar sus vacaciones.   *d.* Había epidemias por todo el país.

4. ¿Qué encontró Antonio en todas las habitaciones de los hoteles?

    a. Había un olor muy fuerte.   *c.* Nadie había limpiado las habitaciones.

    b. Las habitaciones eran muy pequeñas.   *d.* Había insectos debajo de la cama.

5. ¿Cuál fue la causa de los problemas de Antonio?

    a. una epidemia verdadera   *c.* algo que encontró en su maleta

    b. algo que hizo el dueño del primer hotel   *d.* su mujer obstinada

XXI

    Muy lejos de la Tierra, en otro sistema solar, había un planeta muy semejante al nuestro. Los habitantes del planeta lo llamaban Xplz. Los xplzeros eran seres humanos como nosotros, pero más avanzados intelectualmente. Por ejemplo, algunos de sus científicos no tenían más de diez años.

    En uno de los observatorios astronómicos del planeta trabajaba un joven científico llamado Ndnk. Tenía sólo dieciséis años. Un día, Ndnk miraba por su supertelescopio a cierta región de la galaxia. De repente observó, a muchos millares de millones de kilómetros de distancia, un pequeño planeta casi idéntico al suyo. Parecía tener los mismos mares, los mismos continentes, etc. Aquel planeta que acababa de descubrir era . . . ¡la Tierra!

    El astrónomo dirigió su telescopio a una región del planeta donde era domingo por la tarde. Luego fijó el telescopio en un banco de un parque donde estaba sentada una señorita muy hermosa. En seguida el joven se enamoró de la dama y empezó a calcular cuánto tiempo necesitaría para viajar a la Tierra. Discutió su problema con otro astrónomo más viejo y más sabio que él. Su amigo le explicó que la mujer probablemente ya no existía, o, si existía todavía, debía de ser muy vieja.

    —Ndnk, debes tener en cuenta la enorme distancia que hay entre su planeta y el nuestro.

    El joven astrónomo se dio cuenta de que la luz que le llevaba la imagen de la señorita a través del espacio habría (would have) tardado muchos años en llegar a la lente de su telescopio. El pobre Ndnk se puso tan triste que no volvió a su telescopio y trató de olvidar a la linda muchacha. ¡Qué solitaria es la vida de un astrónomo!

1. ¿Cómo son los habitantes de Xplz?

    a. Son más inteligentes que nosotros.   *c.* No asisten a la escuela.

    b. Son más viejos que nosotros.   *d.* Todos son científicos.

2. Sabemos que nosotros podríamos vivir en Xplz porque el planeta está

    a. cerca de la Tierra.   *c.* en otro sistema solar.

    b. habitado por seres humanos.   *d.* sin mares y continentes.

3. ¿Qué hacía el joven astrónomo?

    a. Estaba viajando a otro planeta.   *c.* Iba a la iglesia a oír misa.

    b. Ayudaba a otro astrónomo en el   *d.* Estaba observando otro planeta.
        observatorio.

4. ¿Por qué quería Ndnk ir a la Tierra?

    a. Quería visitar a un amigo.   *c.* Deseaba conocer a una muchacha que vivía allí.

    b. Tenía familia allí.   *d.* Pensaba vivir allí.

5. ¿Por qué estaba triste el joven?

    a. Se dio cuenta de que sería imposible   *c.* Los telescopios no servían para nada.
        satisfacer su deseo.   *d.* Su amigo no le decía la verdad.

    b. La muchacha no lo quería.

XXII

Una noche dos amigos estaban charlando en un café y se sentían muy alegres. Los amigos se llamaban Quique y Paquito. En tono de burla (jest). Paquito le dijo a Quique:

—Tú sabes mucho acerca de las matemáticas.

El pobre Quique, que apenas sabía sumar dos y dos sin usar los dedos, movió la cabeza afirmativamente. Un hombre que estaba sentado al lado de los dos amigos oyó esta conversación, y pronto les dio la noticia a sus amigos. Dentro de una semana todo el pueblo hablaba del gran talento de Quique. Todos los que lo encontraban en la calle lo saludaban con mucho respeto. Su país lo mandó a un Congreso Internacional para dar un discurso. Su discurso tuvo mucho éxito porque nadie entendía lo que decía. Habló en español, lengua que nadie hablaba en el Congreso. Todo el mundo le hacía preguntas acerca de su vida privada, sus intereses, sus platos favoritos, qué programas de televisión prefería, etc. Pero nadie se atrevía a hacerle preguntas sobre las matemáticas, porque creían que sus respuestas serían muy complejas y difíciles de comprender. Se decía que Quique tenía en su casa una computadora misteriosa, pero a nadie le era permitido verla. Quique llegó a ser una de las personas más famosas de su época.

Por desgracia, después de un fuerte ataque al corazón. Quique murió. Toda la nación lloró su muerte. Una comisión de matemáticos decidió inspeccionar el cuarto donde guardaba su computadora. Al entrar, descubrieron un cuarto tan vacío como la cabeza de su dueño. No había ni computadora, ni papeles, ni cuadernos. Algunas personas creían que Quique había sido un embustero (faker). Otros creían que toda su sabiduría (wisdom), que estaba en su cabeza, murió con él.

1. ¿Qué hacían los dos amigos?
   a. Estaban conversando en una taberna.
   b. Estaban andando por el centro del pueblo.
   c. Hablaban de sus familias.
   d. Estaban cenando.

2. ¿Cómo llegaron todos a saber del talento de Quique?
   a. Quique se lo anunció a todo el mundo por radio.
   b. Se anunció en la televisión.
   c. Se leyó en un periódico.
   d. Alguien escuchaba la conversación de los dos.

3. ¿Por qué aceptaron el discurso de Quique?
   a. Quique habló muy bien.
   b. Nadie lo comprendió.
   c. Todos sabían las matemáticas.
   d. Sus amigos le aplaudieron mucho.

4. ¿Por qué continuaba Quique con su reputación?
   a. Nadie podía disputar su talento.
   b. Él sabía mucho sobre las matemáticas.
   c. Sus discursos eran interesantes.
   d. Los matemáticos decían que él era un gran hombre.

5. ¿Qué encontraron en la habitación de Quique?
   a. nada
   b. muchas obras de matemáticas
   c. libros complicados
   d. papeles importantes

In each of the following four passages, there are five blank spaces numbered 1 to 5. Each blank represents a word that will complete the meaning of the sentence. At the end of the selection, there are four possible completions. Only one of the completions makes sense according to the reading selection. After reading the selection carefully for its general meaning, choose the completion that makes sense.

XXIII

La Puerta del Sol, la plaza muy popular de Madrid, está más _____ a la hora de la
1.

merienda. Se dice que todas las carreteras de España empiezan aquí. Lo más _____ de
2.

esta plaza es una escultura compuesta de dos objetos: un oso y un árbol llamado el *madroño* (strawberry

tree or arbutus). El oso y el árbol aparecen en el escudo de armas (coat of arms) de Madrid. Por las calles

de la Puerta del Sol se ven muchos bares parecidos a los "snackbars" de los Estados Unidos. En Madrid

y en otras _____ españolas, estos bares sirven toda clase de refrescos ligeros. Algo muy
3.

popular es el *chocolate con churros*. El chocolate es una _____ muy espesa (thick) de
4.

chocolate caliente que se _____ con churros (cylindrical-shaped fritters) que se parecen
5.

a los "donuts" norteamericanos.

1. ocupada, cansada, enferma, escrita   4. bebida, banda, fecha, loma

2. verde, listo, interesante, lleno   5. habla, escribe, manda, toma

3. tierras, ciudades, aguas, familias

XXIV

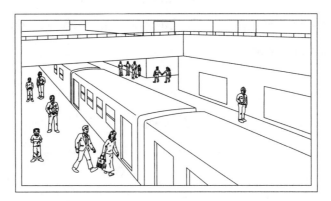

En 1969 se abrió el *Sistema de Transporte Colectivo,* el metro (subway) de la Ciudad de México. De

35 kilómetros (22 miles) de largo, es una _____ extraordinaria de ingeniería. Para
1.

_____ el metro, era necesario vencer (overcome) grandes _____, porque
2.   3.

la ciudad está construida sobre un lago antiguo y también está situada en una zona de terremotos (earth-

quakes) activos. Los vagones (cars) de los _____ tienen ruedas de caucho (rubber
4.

wheels), y por eso los _____ gozan de un viaje cómodo y sin ruido.
5.

1. casa, obra, tierra, ola

2. construir, destruir, aprender, cerrar

3. mares, océanos, techos, dificultades

4. hombres, trenes, datos, salones

5. pasajeros, climas, derechos, frenos

XXV

La República Dominicana comparte (shares) con Haití la isla llamada **La Española,** o **Hispaniola.**
La _____ oficial de Haití es el francés. La República Dominicana está en la parte orien-
1.
tal (eastern) de La Española y _____ dos tercios (thirds) de la isla. Sus productos princi-
2.
pales son el azúcar, el café y el tabaco. Los dominicanos ganaron su independencia de España en 1865.
Muchos historiadores creen que Cristóbal Colón está _____ en la antigua catedral de la
3.
ciudad. La **Universidad de Santo Tomás,** en Santo Domingo, la capital del país, es una de las uni-
versidades más antiguas del Nuevo _____. El nombre popular del país es *Quisqueya*
4.
("madre de todas las tierras"), el _____ nombre nativo de Hispaniola.
5.

1. casa, lengua, comida, zona

2. encuentra, ocupa, desea, manda

3. contento, sentado, lleno, enterrado

4. Mundo, País, Lado, Pastor

5. buen, antiguo, pequeño, todo

XXVI

Buenos aires, capital de la Argentina, se encuentra a orillas del Río de la Plata. Es el centro comercial y puerto principal del _____. Buenos Aires es llamada «el cerebro» de la Argentina
1.

por sus numerosas bibliotecas, museos e instituciones científicas. También rivaliza con la Ciudad de

México como el _____ cultural de Hispanomérica, sobre todo en los campos de la música,
                              2.

del teatro, de la literatura, de la _____ de libros y de la industria cinematográfica
                                            3.

(movie). El elegante **Teatro Colón** es un magnífico teatro de ópera en que los más famosos cantantes

del mundo han _____ representaciones (performances). Los habitantes de Buenos Aires
                        4.

se llaman _porteños_ ("habitantes del puerto"). La **Avenida Nueve de Julio** tiene fama de ser la calle

más ancha del mundo. Debajo de esta calle hay un garaje con sitios para mil _____. Un
                                                                                        5.

impresionante obelisco se halla a un extremo de la avenida.

1. rato, país, foro, lado   **4.** devuelto, hecho, comido, sido

2. centro, país, favor, amigo   **5.** coches, consejos, fuegos, ovejas

3. calle, costa, universidad, publicación

45
Listening Practice

To the teacher: The passages pertaining to this exercise will be found in the Answer-Key booklet.

To the student: The three groups of passages that follow are arranged in order of difficulty and length. In each part your teacher will read aloud some short passages in Spanish. Each passage will be read twice. After the second reading, the teacher will pause briefly, then read aloud the question (below) that refers to the passage. Circle the letter of the correct answer.

Group One: In this part the questions and possible answers are in English.

1. Where are these people?

    a. in a garage   *c.* at a street crossing
    b. in a park

2. Who is calling Mr. Méndez?

    a. his son's teacher
    b. his daughter's friend
    c. his wife's employer

3. What is confusing this person?

    a. the fact that a store is not open
    b. that his watch is showing the wrong time
    c. why he can't use a public phone

4. What is this person's request?

    a. to talk with someone
    b. to visit a friend
    c. to invite someone to dinner

5. Where does this scene take place?

    a. in a park   *c.* in a library
    b. in a bookstore

6. Why are these people's plans upset?

    a. Their house is undergoing repairs.
    b. The park is closed.
    c. The weather is bad.

7. Why is this person hysterical?

    a. A child is sick.
    b. There is no hot water.
    c. Part of the house is flooded.

8. Who is talking here?

    a. a traffic officer   *c.* a truck driver
    b. a close relative

9. Why can't this person go to the party?

    a. He expects a visit from some relatives.
    b. He has too much work to do.
    c. His car broke down.

10. What is this person doing?

    a. trying to read a book
    b. watching a T.V. program
    c. surfing the T.V. channels

11. Whom is this person complaining about?

    a. her friend
    b. her teacher
    c. a radio announcer

12. What do these people have to do?

    a. catch a plane
    b. go shopping
    c. get to a concert

13. What is this person's problem?

    a. The weather is cold.
    b. She feels sick.
    c. She doesn't like the movie.

14. Why does this person wish to stop?

    a. He is hungry.
    b. He likes the restaurant.
    c. He's tired of driving.

15. Where does this scene take place?

    a. in a bakery
    b. in a music store
    c. in a pharmacy

Group Two: In the following passages, the questions and possible answers are in Spanish.

1. ¿De qué se habla?

   a. de una fiesta
   b. de una familia
   c. del tiempo
   d. de una cita

2. ¿Qué consejos se dan aquí?

   a. Es necesario viajar en seguida.
   b. No hay que esperar la luna nueva.
   c. La luna nueva no trae nada importante.
   d. No se debe viajar hasta cierto tiempo.

3. ¿Para quiénes es la clínica?

   a. para los que no pueden ver bien
   b. para los que están gravemente enfermos
   c. para los que sufren de enfermedades de
      los dientes
   d. sólo para los pacientes ricos

4. ¿Dónde tiene lugar esta escena?

   a. en una casa
   b. en una escuela
   c. en un cine
   d. en un restaurante

5. ¿Cuándo ocurre esta escena?

   a. a medianoche
   b. temprano por la mañana
   c. por la tarde
   d. el sábado por la noche

6. ¿Por qué tiene que levantarse Juana?

   a. Ella tiene que ir a la escuela.
   b. Su familia va a hacer un viaje.
   c. Ella va a reunirse con unas amigas.
   d. El desayuno está listo.

7. ¿Para qué quiere Eduardo ir al centro?

   a. Quiere ver una película nueva.
   b. Tiene cita con una amiga.
   c. Desea comprar ropa.
   d. Va a reunirse con su mamá.

8. ¿Qué ocurre?

   a. Alguien aprende a conducir un
      automóvil.
   b. Dos personas hablan acerca de un film.
   c. Hubo un accidente entre dos coches.
   d. Unas amigas andan por el parque.

9. ¿Dónde tiene lugar esta escena?

   a. en un hotel
   b. en un teatro
   c. en un café
   d. en una escuela

10. ¿Quién habla?

    a. un padre de familia
    b. un guía turístico
    c. un profesor de música
    d. un anunciador de radio

11. ¿Con quién fue Manuelito al zoo?

    a. con su padre
    b. con su amigo
    c. con su madre
    d. con su primo

12. ¿Dónde están las Pirámides?

    a. en la Ciudad de México
    b. no muy lejos de la Ciudad de México
    c. fuera del país
    d. en la costa del norte

13. ¿Quién habla aquí?

    a. un profesor a su clase
    b. un vendedor de libros a unos clientes
    c. un estudiante a su profesor
    d. un estudiante a otro estudiante

14. ¿Qué nos indica esta observación?

    a. Alguien tiene que ir al hospital.
    b. No hace mucho calor.
    c. Un chico no se siente bien.
    d. Quique ha tenido un accidente grave.

15. ¿Dónde están estas personas?

    a. en un teatro
    b. en una estación de gasolina
    c. en un hospital
    d. en una fiesta

Group Three: In the following passages the questions and possible answers are in English.

1. Why can't Rosa go out with her friends?

   a. She has to babysit.
   b. The weather is bad.
   c. Her mother is ill.
   d. Her friends are all busy.

2. How may Beatriz be useful?

   a. by explaining Francisco's problem to their teacher
   b. by lending her friend something
   c. by coming to Francisco's house to fix his computer
   d. by writing a composition for him

3. What is the problem?

   a. Someone is sick.
   b. A car is in need of repair.
   c. There's no water in the house.
   d. Nobody wants to repair a defect.

4. Where does this scene take place?

   a. in a park
   b. in a movie theater
   c. in a driving school
   d. in a bank

5. Why can't Pablo go to the beach early?

   a. He has something to do in the morning.
   b. He doesn't like the beach early in the day.
   c. He doesn't feel well.
   d. His friend needs him to do her a favor.

6. Where does this take place?

   a. on a train
   b. aboard a plane
   c. on a ship
   d. in a tour bus

7. Why is this young lady writing this letter?

   a. She wants to enroll in a computer course.
   b. She needs travel information.
   c. She's looking for summer work.
   d. She wants to learn Spanish during the summer.

8. What is the family expecting?

   a. the arrival of some relatives
   b. a visit from some friends
   c. a package from Florida
   d. a letter from aunt Sara

9. What is the lady asking for?

   a. theater tickets
   b. directions to a place
   c. Victoria Street
   d. the nearest restaurant

10. Why were many people forming a group?

    a. They were looking at some men on bicycles.
    b. They were listening to the music of several young men.
    c. They wanted to see a car accident.
    d. They were looking at some interesting animals.

11. Where is this advertisement from?

    a. a famous restaurant
    b. a savings bank
    c. a travel agency
    d. a telephone company

12. Why was Ana López famous?

    a. She died at a very young age.
    b. She had been a celebrated actress.
    c. She had given money to the poor.
    d. She had been a Hollywood favorite.

13. Why did Francisco's father have to stay at home?

    a. He had a lot of work to complete.
    b. He preferred not to go the hospital.
    c. He didn't like leaving the house.
    d. He had to recover from an illness.

14. Why didn't the firefighters have a problem?

    a. It was a false alarm.
    b. The audience helped put out the fire.
    c. They arrived in less than a half hour.
    d. No one was in the theater when they arrived.

15. What seems to be in need of change?

    a. the present President
    b. the way the president is elected
    c. the popular vote
    d. voters' rights

Appendixes

I. Cardinal Numbers

0 TO 99

0	cero	21	veintiuno (veinte y uno)
1	uno, un, una	22	veintidós (veinte y dos)
2	dos	23	veintitrés (veinte y tres)
3	tres	24	veinticuatro (veinte y cuatro)
4	cuatro	25	veinticinco (veinte y cinco)
5	cinco	26	veintiséis (veinte y seis)
6	seis	27	veintisiete (veinte y siete)
7	siete	28	veintiocho (veinte y ocho)
8	ocho	29	veintinueve (veinte y nueve)
9	nueve	30	treinta
10	diez	31	treinta y uno
11	once	40	cuarenta
12	doce	42	cuarenta y dos
13	trece	50	cincuenta
14	catorce	53	cincuenta y tres
15	quince	60	sesenta
16	dieciséis (diez y seis)	67	sesenta y siete
17	diecisiete (diez y siete)	70	setenta
18	dieciocho (diez y ocho)	80	ochenta
19	diecinueve (diez y nueve)	90	noventa
20	veinte	99	noventa y nueve

100 TO 1000

100	ciento, cien	400	cuatrocientos(-as)
104	ciento cuatro	500	quinientos(-as)
185	ciento ochenta y cinco	600	seiscientos(-as)
200	doscientos(-as)	700	setecientos(-as)
217	doscientos(-as) diecisiete	800	ochocientos(-as)
300	trescientos(-as)	900	novecientos(-as)
308	trescientos(-as) ocho	1000	mil

1,001 TO 100,000,000

1001	mil uno	*31.578	treinta y un mil quinientos setenta y ocho
1006	mil seis		
1022	mil veintidós	501.010	quinientos un mil diez
1174	mil ciento setenta y cuatro	713.102	setecientos trece mil ciento dos
1508	mil quinientos ocho	1.000.000	un millón
1776	mil setecientos setenta y seis	2.000.000	dos millones
1945	mil novecientos cuarenta y cinco	35.046.007	treinta y cinco millones cuarenta y seis mil siete
2000	dos mil		
7001	siete mil uno	100.000.000	cien millones
8012	ocho mil doce		

*Spanish notation uses a period instead of a comma to indicate thousands. The comma is used to set off decimal fractions: for example, 5.16 ("five point sixteen") = 5,16 ("cinco coma dieciséis").

UN, UNO, UNA

¿Tienes **un** libro?	Do you have a book?
Sí, tengo **uno.**	Yes, I have one.
¿Cuántas monedas tienes?	How many coins do you have?
Tengo **una** moneda. (Tengo **una.**)	I have *one* coin. (I have *one.*)
¿Cuántos hombres hay aquí?	How many men are there here?
Hay **veintiún** hombres.	There are twenty-one men.
Hay **veintiuno.**	There are twenty-one.
¿Cuántos billetes tienes?	How many tickets do you have?
Tengo cincuenta y **un** billetes.	I have fifty-one tickets.
Tengo cincuenta y **uno.**	I have fifty-one.

1. **Uno** becomes **un** before a masculine noun. The form **uno** is used if the masculine noun is not expressed.

CIEN, CIENTO

Tenemos **ciento un** dólares.	We have 101 dollars.
Tenemos **ciento** ochenta y **un** dólares.	We have 181 dollars.

But:

Tenemos **cien** dólares.	We have a hundred dollars.
Tenemos **cien.**	We have a hundred.

2. **Ciento** becomes **cien** before a noun or when used alone.

DOSCIENTOS(-AS), TRESCIENTOS(-AS), ETC.

doscient**os** chicos	quinient**os** trece **hombres**
doscient**as** chicas	quinient**as** trece **mujeres**

ochocient**os** cuarenta y un **edificios**
ochocient**as** cuarenta y una **casas**

3. In **doscientos, trescientos,** etc., the ending **-os** becomes **-as** before a feminine noun—even when it is separated from the feminine noun by another number-word.

NUMBERS EXPRESSED WITH Y

4. The conjunction **y** is used only between the digits of two-digit numbers (where the second digit is not zero), that is, in the numbers from 16 to 19, from 21 to 29, from 31 to 39, etc:

cuarenta **y** tres   forty-three

NUMBERS 16 TO 19 AND 21 TO 29

5. These numbers may be written either as one word or as three words although the single word is now more common; for example, 24 = **veinticuatro** or **veinte y cuatro.** All other two-digit numbers must be written as three words; for example, 63 = **sesenta y tres.**

MILLÓN, MILLONES

6. These words are used with **de** when followed by the noun they modify:

> a million dollars = un millón **de** dólares
> five million inhabitants = cinco millones **de** habitantes

 ## II. Ordinal Numbers

primero (primer), primera, first (see page 000)	**sexto, sexta,** sixth
segundo, segunda, second	**séptimo, séptima,** seventh
tercero (tercer), tercera, third (see page 000)	**octavo, octava,** eighth
cuarto, cuarta, fourth	**noveno, novena,** ninth
quinto, quinta, fifth	**décimo, décima,** tenth

1. The ordinal numbers are adjectives and agree in gender and number with the noun they modify. They may either precede or follow the noun:

> la **segunda** lección *or* la lección **segunda**
> los **primeros** capítulos *or* los capítulos **primeros**

2. The ordinal numbers are not ordinarily used beyond the tenth:

la lección **once**	the eleventh lesson
el siglo **veinte**	the twentieth century

III. Days of the Week

el **lunes,** Monday	el **viernes,** Friday
el **martes,** Tuesday	el **sábado,** Saturday
el **miércoles,** Wednesday	el **domingo,** Sunday
el **jueves,** Thursday	

1. The Spanish names for the days of the week generally begin with small (lower-case) letters.

2. The article **el** means *on:*

Te veré **el** lunes.	I'll see you on Monday.

3. *On* is expressed as **los** when the days of the week are used in the plural:

No vamos a la escuela **los** domingos.	We don't go to school on Sundays.
Los viernes vamos al cine.	On Fridays we go to the movies.

Caution: In English, the singular form of the day is often used with plural meaning. Before translating into Spanish, decide whether the singular or the plural is meant:

We are going downtown on Tuesday.	Vamos al centro **el** martes.

But:

We go downtown on Tuesday.	Vamos al centro **los** martes.
(= on Tuesdays, every Tuesday).	

IV. Months of the Year

enero, January
febrero, February
marzo, March
abril, April
mayo, May
junio, June

julio, July
agosto, August
septiembre, September
octubre, October
noviembre, November
diciembre, December

The Spanish names for the months are not capitalized.

V. Expressing Dates

¿Cuál es la fecha de hoy?	What is today's date?
Hoy es **el primero de mayo.**	Today is May 1.
Es **el dos de abril.**	It is April 2.
Es **el catorce de octubre.**	It is October 14.
Vamos **el ocho de junio.**	We are going on June 8.
Ayer fue viernes, **el veinte de julio de dos mil uno.**	Yesterday was Friday, July 20, 2001.

1. Except for **el primero,** the cardinal numbers (**dos, tres, cuatro,** etc.) are used in dates.

2. The preposition **de** is used to separate the month from the number, for example, November 21 = el veintiuno **de** noviembre.

3. *On* is expressed in Spanish by **el;** for example, *on* January 1 = **el** primero de enero.

4. In Spanish, the year is expressed in thousands and hundreds; for example, 1921 = **mil novecientos veintiuno** (literally "one thousand nine hundred twenty-one").

VI. Telling Time

¿Qué hora es?	What time is it?
Es la una.	It is one o'clock.
Son las dos.	It is two o'clock.
Son las tres y cuarto (y quince).	It is 3:15.
Son las siete y media (y treinta).	It is 7:30.
Son las ocho y diez.	It is 8:10.
Son las diez menos cuarto.	It is 9:45 (a quarter to ten).
Son las tres menos veinte.	It is 2:40 (twenty minutes to three).
Es mediodía.	It is noon.
Es medianoche.	It is midnight.
Son las nueve y media de la mañana.	It is 9:30 A.M.
Es la una y cuarto de la tarde.	It is 1:15 P.M.
Son las diez menos cinco de la noche.	It is 9:55 P.M.
¿A qué hora empieza la clase?	At what time does the class begin?
La clase empieza **a las once menos diez de la mañana.**	The class begins at ten minutes to eleven in the morning (at 10:50 A.M.)

| Salimos de la escuela **a las tres de la tarde.** | We leave school at three o'clock in the afternoon (at 3:00 P.M.) |

1. To tell time in Spanish, start with **son las** and add the number of the hour. The exception is one o'clock: **Es la una.**

2. To express a quarter past the hour, add **y cuarto** to the hour. To express half past the hour, add **y media** to the hour.

3. To express time past the hour (but not beyond the half hour), add **y** and the number of minutes.

4. To express time after the half hour, start with the *next* hour and subtract the number of minutes from that hour. "It is 4:50" is the same as "It is ten minutes to five": **Son las cinco menos diez.** *

5. To indicate A.M., we add **de la mañana.**

6. To express P.M., we add **de la tarde** between 12:01 P.M. (one minute after 12 noon) and nightfall. From nightfall to midnight, we add **de la noche.**

7. In Spanish-speaking countries, it is actual darkness that determines whether the afternoon has ended. Thus, if it is still light, we express 7:45 P.M. as "las ocho menos cuarto **de la tarde.**"

8. Do not confuse **son las tres** with **a las tres.** The expression **son las tres** means "*it is* 3 o'clock," whereas **a las tres** means "*at* 3 o'clock."

OTHER TIME EXPRESSIONS

Es la una **en punto.**	It is one o'clock *sharp.*
Venga Ud. **a tiempo.**	Come *on time.*
Llegaron **a eso de** las ocho.	They arrived *at about* 8 o'clock.
Es tarde.	It is late.
Se hace tarde.	It is getting late.
No es temprano.	It is not early.
Jugamos **por la tarde (por la noche, por la mañana).**	We play *in the afternoon (in the evening, in the morning).*

9. The expressions **por la mañana, por la tarde,** and **por la noche** refer to parts of the day and are not used after expressions of clock time (see §5 and §6 above).

VII. Special Uses of *Tener, Hacer,* and *Haber*

A. *TENER*

The verb **tener** means *to have,* but it is translated as *to be* in several idiomatic expressions:

¿Cuántos años **tiene** ella?	How old is she?
Ella **tiene** quince años.	She is 15 years old.
Tengo (mucho) calor.	I am (very) warm.
¿**Tiene** Ud. sueño?	Are you sleepy?
Tenemos miedo de salir.	We're afraid to go out.

---

*It is also correct to express clock-time in the same way as we often do in English: *it is 4:50* = **son las cuatro y cincuenta.**

SOME COMMON IDIOMS WITH **tener**

tener . . . años	to be . . . years old
tener (mucho) calor	to be (very) warm
tener (mucho) cuidado	to be (very) careful
tener (mucho) éxito	to be (very) successful
tener (mucho) frío	to be (very) cold
tener (mucho) gusto en + *inf.*	to be (very) glad to
tener (mucha) hambre	to be (very) hungry
tener (mucho) miedo a	to be (very) afraid of (someone)
tener (mucho) miedo de + *inf.*	to be (very) afraid to
tener (mucha) prisa	to be in a (great) hurry
tener razón	to be right
no tener razón	to be wrong
tener (mucha) sed	to be (very) thirsty
tener (mucho) sueño	to be (very) sleepy

B. *HACER*

Hacer in weather expressions is used only in the third person singular:

Hoy **hace** frío.	Today it is cold.
Ayer **hizo** calor.	Yesterday it was warm.
Mañana **hará** mucho sol.	Tomorrow it will be very sunny.

OTHER WEATHER EXPRESSIONS

¿Qué tiempo hace?	How is the weather?
Hace buen tiempo.	The weather is good.
Hace mal tiempo.	The weather is bad.
Hace (mucho) calor.	It is (very) warm.
Hace (mucho) fresco.	It is (very) cool.
Hace (mucho) frío.	It is (very) cold.
Hace (mucho) sol.	It is (very) sunny.
Hace (mucho) viento.	It is (very) windy.

C. *HABER*

Haber has the special form **hay,** *there is, there are.* When used in other tenses, this idiom is expressed by the forms of **haber** in the third person singular—even when the subject is in the plural:

Hay mucho trabajo hoy.	*There is* a lot of work today.
¿Hay cuadros en el cuarto?	*Are there* pictures in the room?
No **había** nada que hacer.	*There was* nothing to do.
Había veinte personas allí.	*There were* 20 people there.
¿Hubo refrescos en el baile?	*Were there* refreshments at the dance?
No **hubo** dinero.	*There was* no money.
Habrá una reunión mañana.	*There will be* a meeting tomorrow.
¿Habrá muchas cosas que hacer?	*Will there be* many things to do?
Ella contestó que **habría** treinta personas en la fiesta.	She answered that *there would be* 30 people at the party.

Ha habido una tormenta.	*There has been* a storm.
Ha habido cuatro tormentas.	*There have been* four storms.
Había habido un robo.	*There had been* a robbery.
Había habido muchos problemas.	*There had been* many problems.

▰▰▰ VIII. The *Nosotros* Commands ("Let's")

Bailemos.	Let's dance.
Comamos.	Let's eat.
Pidamos café.	Let's order coffee.
Durmamos hasta la una.	Let's sleep until one o'clock.
Vengamos temprano.	Let's come early.

1. The **nosotros** form of command is obtained from the **nosotros** form of the present subjunctive (see pages 105–106).

2. A **nosotros** command can also be expressed in the form **vamos a** + *infinitive.* This expression cannot be used in negative commands:

Vamos a poner la radio.	Let's turn on the radio.
But:	
No pongamos la radio.	Let's *not* turn on the radio.
Vamos a salir.	Let's leave.
But:	
No salgamos.	Let's *not* leave.

3. In spoken Spanish, *let's go* is expressed as **vamos** or **vámonos** rather than **vayamos,** which is used in negative constructions:

Vamos (Vámonos) ahora.	Let's go now.
But:	
No vayamos ahora.	Let's *not* go now.

NOSOTROS COMMANDS USED WITH OBJECT PRONOUNS

Visitemos a las muchachas.	Let's visit the girls.
Visitémos**las.** ⎫ Vamos a visitar**las.** ⎭	Let's visit them.
No **las** visitemos.	Let's *not* visit them.

4. *a.* Object pronouns are attached to the verb in the affirmative command but placed between **no** and the verb in a negative command. When an object pronoun is attached to the verb, an accent mark is placed on the vowel preceding the **-mos** endings.*

  b. If the expression **vamos a** + *infinitive* is used, the object pronouns are attached to the infinitive.

---

*When **se lo (la, los, las)** is attached, only one **s** is used.

  Escribámoselo. Let's write it to him (her, them).

5. The rules governing the position of object pronouns also apply to the reflexive pronoun **nos.** When **nos** is attached to the command form, the **s** in the ending **-mos** is dropped:

Nos sentamos.	We sit (are sitting) down.
Sentémonos. **Vamos a sentarnos.** }	Let's sit down.
No nos sentemos.	Let's not sit down.
Vámonos.	Let's go (leave).
No nos vayamos.	Let's not go (leave).

 ## IX. The *Vosotros* Commands

Vosotros(-as) is the plural of **tú,** which is used in familiar address. **Vosotros(-as)** and its verb forms are used only in Spain. In the rest of the Hispanic world, the plural of **tú** is **ustedes.**

The **vosotros** forms of command are obtained as follows:

Affirmative: Change the **-r** ending of the infinitive to **-d.** This rule applies to *all* verbs without exception:

-AR Verbs	-ER Verbs	-IR Verbs
empeza**r**	volve**r**	sali**r**
empeza**d**, begin	volve**d**, return	sali**d**, leave

Negative: Use the **vosotros** form of the present subjunctive (see pages 105–106):

no empecéis, don't begin	**no volváis,** don't return	**no salgáis,** don't leave

Reminder; If an *-IR* verb has a stem-change in the preterit (see page 48), the same stem-change will occur in the **vosotros** form of the subjunctive. Examples: pedir—no p**i**dáis; dormir—no d**u**rmáis.

FORMING *VOSOTROS* COMMANDS WITH REFLEXIVE VERBS

Affirmative: Drop the **-d** of the affirmative command form before attaching the reflexive pronoun **os.** For *-IR* verbs, add an accent mark to the **i** preceding the dropped **-d:**

-AR Verbs	-ER Verbs	-IR Verbs
senta**d**	pone**d**	conduci**d**
senta**os,**	pone**os** los guantes,	conduc**íos** bien,
sit down	put on your gloves	behave yourselves

Exception: **idos,** leave, go away.

Negative: Insert the reflexive pronoun between **no** and the subjunctive verb form:

no os sentéis, don't sit down	**no os pongáis** los guantes, don't put on your gloves	**no os conduzcáis** mal, don't behave badly

Note the stem-changes in the negative command forms of **divertirse** and **dormirse:** no os div**i**rtáis, no os d**u**rmáis.

USING OBJECT PRONOUNS WITH *VOSOTROS* COMMANDS

Habladle.	Speak to her (him).	No le habléis.	Don't speak to him (her).
Bebedlo.	Drink it.	No lo bebáis.	Don't drink it.
Escribidme.	Write to me.	No me escribáis.	Don't write to me.
Mandádnoslos.	Send them to us.	No nos los mandéis.	Don't send them to us.
Vendédselo.	Sell it to them (her, him).	No se lo vendáis.	Don't sell it to them (her, him)
Decídmela.	Tell it to me.	No me la digáis.	Don't tell it to me.

Object pronouns used with **vosotros** commands take the same position as the pronoun objects of the other command forms: the pronoun is attached to the verb in the affirmative command, but precedes the verb in the negative command. Note the written accent on the **a, e** or **i** before the **d** when *two* pronouns are attached.

Verb Charts

 I. REGULAR VERBS

INFINITIVE	ayudar	aprender	vivir
PRESENT PARTICIPLE	ayudando	aprendiendo	viviendo
PRESENT	ayudo	aprendo	vivo
	ayudas	aprendes	vives
	ayuda	aprende	vive
	ayudamos	aprendemos	vivimos
	ayudáis	aprendéis	vivís
	ayudan	aprenden	viven
IMPERFECT	ayudaba	aprendía	vivía
	ayudabas	aprendías	vivías
	ayudaba	aprendía	vivía
	ayudábamos	aprendíamos	vivíamos
	ayudabais	aprendíais	vivíais
	ayudaban	aprendían	vivían
PRETERIT	ayudé	aprendí	viví
	ayudaste	aprendiste	viviste
	ayudó	aprendió	vivío
	ayudamos	aprendimos	vivimos
	ayudasteis	aprendisteis	vivisteis
	ayudaron	aprendieron	vivieron
FUTURE	ayudaré	aprenderé	viviré
	ayudarás	aprenderás	vivirás
	ayudará	aprenderá	vivirá
	ayudaremos	aprenderemos	viviremos
	ayudaréis	aprenderéis	viviréis
	ayudarán	aprenderán	vivirán
CONDITIONAL	ayudaría	aprendería	viviría
	ayudarías	aprenderías	vivirías
	ayudaría	aprendería	viviría
	ayudaríamos	aprenderíamos	viviríamos
	ayudaríais	aprenderíais	viviríais
	ayudarían	aprenderían	vivirían

PRESENT PERFECT	he ayudado	he aprendido	he vivido
	has ayudado	has aprendido	has vivido
	ha ayudado	ha aprendido	ha vivido
	hemos ayudado	hemos aprendido	hemos vivido
	habéis ayudado	habéis aprendido	habéis vivido
	han ayudado	han aprendido	han vivido
PLUPERFECT	había ayudado	había aprendido	había vivido
	habías ayudado	habías aprendido	habías vivido
	había ayudado	había aprendido	había vivido
	habíamos ayudado	habíamos aprendido	habíamos vivido
	habíais ayudado	habíais aprendido	habíais vivido
	habían ayudado	habían aprendido	habían vivido
PRESENT SUBJUNCTIVE	ayude	aprenda	viva
	ayudes	aprendas	vivas
	ayude	aprenda	viva
	ayudemos	aprendamos	vivamos
	ayudéis	aprendáis	viváis
	ayuden	aprendan	vivan
IMPERFECT SUBJUNCTIVE (Since the **-se** form is not used in this book, we have not included it here.)	ayudara	aprendiera	viviera
	ayudaras	aprendieras	vivieras
	ayudara	aprendiera	viviera
	ayudáramos	aprendiéramos	viviéramos
	ayudarais	aprendierais	vivierais
	ayudaran	aprendieran	vivieran
FORMAL COMMANDS	(no) ayude Ud.	(no) aprenda Ud.	(no) viva Ud.
	(no) ayuden Uds.	(no) aprendan Uds.	(no) vivan Uds.
FAMILIAR COMMANDS	ayuda tú	come tú	vive tú
	no ayudes tú	no comas tú	no vivas tú
	ayudad vosotros	comed vosotros	vivid vosotros
	no ayudéis vosotros	no comáis vosotros	no viváis vosotros

▪◢ II. VERBS WITH IRREGULAR FORMS

NOTES: 1. Except for the forms needed to complete a conjugation, only the irregular forms are displayed in this section, and are in **bold** print. For the regular forms, please refer to the previous section on Regular Verbs.

2. The stem-changing verbs and verbs with spelling changes are in separate sections to follow.

3. The formal commands and the negative **tú** commands are the same as the corresponding forms of the present subjunctive.

4. The following key is used:

a. present participle	*e.* preterit	*h.* present subjunctive
b. past participle	*f.* future	*i.* imperfect subjunctive (-ra form)
c. present indicative	*g.* conditional	*j.* affirmative familiar command
d. imperfect indicative		

1. **Andar**   *e.* **anduve, anduviste, anduvo, anduvimos, anduvisteis, anduvieron**

   i. **anduviera, anduvieras, anduviera, anduviéramos, anduvierais, anduvieran**

2. **Caber**   *c.* **quepo,** cabes, cabe, cabemos, cabéis, caben

   e. **cupe, cupiste, cupo, cupimos, cupisteis, cupieron**

   f. **cabré, cabrás, cabrá, cabremos, cabréis, cabrán**

   g. **cabría, cabrías, cabría, cabríamos, cabríais, cabrían**

   h. **quepa, quepas, quepa, quepamos, quepáis, quepan**

   i. **cupiera, cupieras, cupiera, cupiéramos, cupierais, cupieran**

3. **Caer**   *a.* **cayendo**

   b. **caído**

   c. **caigo,** caes, cae, caemos, caéis, caen

   e. caí, **caíste, cayó, caímos, caísteis, cayeron**

   h. **caiga, caigas, caiga, caigamos, caigáis, caigan**

   i. **cayera, cayeras, cayera, cayéramos, cayerais, cayeran**

4. **Creer**   *a.* **creyendo**

   b. **creído**

   e. creí, **creíste, creyó, creímos, creísteis, creyeron**

   i. **creyera, creyeras, creyera, creyéramos, creyerais, creyeran**

5. **Dar**   *c.* **doy,** das, da, damos, **dais,** dan

   e. **di, diste, dio, dimos, disteis, dieron**

   h. **dé,** des, **dé,** demos, **deis,** den

   i. **diera, dieras, diera, diéramos, dierais, dieran**

6. **Decir**   *a.* **diciendo**

   b. **dicho**

   c. **digo, dices, dice,** decimos, decís, **dicen**

   e. **dije, dijiste, dijo, dijimos, dijisteis, dijeron**

   f. **diré, dirás, dirá, diremos, diréis, dirán**

   g. **diría, dirías, diría, diríamos, diríais, dirían**

   h. **diga, digas, diga, digamos, digáis, digan**

i. dijera, dijeras, dijera, dijéramos, dijerais, dijeran

j. di

7. Estar

c. estoy, estás, está, estamos, estáis, **están**

e. estuve, estuviste, estuvo, estuvimos, estuvisteis, estuvieron

h. esté, estés, esté, estemos, estéis, **estén**

i. estuviera, estuvieras, estuviera, estuviéramos, estuvierais, estuvieran

j. está

8. Haber
(helping verb used to form the perfect tenses)

c. he, has, ha hemos, habéis, **han**

e. hube, hubiste, hubo, hubimos, hubisteis, hubieron

f. habré, habrás, harbá, habremos, habréis, habrán

g. habría, habrías, habría, habríamos, habríais, habrían

h. haya, hayas, haya, hayamos, hayáis, hayan

i. hubiera, hubieras, hubiera, hubiéramos, hubierais, hubieran

9. Hacer

b. hecho

c. **hago,** haces, hace, hacemos, hacéis, hacen

e. hice, hiciste, hizo, hicimos, hicisteis, hicieron

f. haré, harás, hará, haremos, haréis, harán

g. haría, harías, haría, haríamos, harías, harían

h. haga, hagas, haga, hagamos, hagáis, hagan

i. hiciera, hicieras, hiciera, hiciéramos, hicierais, hicieran

j. haz

10. Ir

a. yendo

c. voy, vas, va, vamos, vais, van

d. iba, ibas, iba, íbamos, ibais, iban

e. fui, fuiste, fue, fuimos, fuisteis, fueron

h. vaya, vayas, vaya, vayamos, vayáis, vayan

i. fuera, fueras, fuera, fuéramos, fuerais, fueran

j. ve

11. Oír

a. oyendo

b. oído

c. oigo, oyes, oye, oímos, oís, oyen

e. oí, oíste, oyó, oímos, oísteis, oyeron

f. oiré, oirás, oirá, oiremos, oiréis, oirán

g. oiría, oirías, oiría, oiríamos, oiríais, oriían

h. oiga, oigas, oiga, oigamos, oigáis, oigan

i oyera, oyeras, oyera, oyéramos, oyerais, oyeran

j. oye

12. **Poder**   *a.* **pudiendo**

                c. **puedo, puedes, puede,** podemos, podéis, **pueden**

                e. **pude, pudiste, pudo, pudimos, pudisteis, pudieron**

                f. **podré, podrás, podrá, podremos, podréis, podrán**

                g. **podría, podrías, podría, podríamos, podríais, podrían**

                h. **pueda, puedas, pueda,** podamos, podáis, **puedan**

                i. **pudiera, pudieras, pudiera, pudiéramos, pudierais, pudieran**

                j. (There is no command form for **poder**)

13. **Poner**   *b.* **puesto**

                c. **pongo,** pones, pone, ponemos, ponéis, ponen

                e. **puse, pusiste, puso, pusimos, pusisteis, pusieron**

                f. **pondré, pondrás, pondrá, pondremos, pondréis, pondrán**

                g. **pondría, pondrías, pondría, pondríamos, pondríais, pondrían**

                h. **ponga, pongas, ponga, pongamos, pongáis, pongan**

                i. **pusiera, pusieras, pusiera, pusiéramos, pusierais, pusieran**

                j. **pon**

14. **Querer**   *c.* **quiero, quieres, quiere,** queremos, queréis, **quieren**

                e. **quise, quisiste, quiso, quisimos, quisisteis, quisieron**

                f. **querré, querrás, querrá, querremos, querréis, querrán**

                g. **querría, querrías, querría, querríamos, querríais, querrían**

                h. **quiera, quieras, quiera,** queramos, queráis, **quieran**

                i. **quisiera, quisieras, quisiera, quisiéramos, quisierais, quisieran**

                j. **quiere**

15. **Saber**   *c.* **sé,** sabes, sabe, sabemos, sabéis, saben

                e. **supe, supiste, supo, supimos, supisteis, supieron**

                f. **sabré, sabrás, sabrá, sabremos, sabréis, sabrán**

                g. **sabría, sabrías, sabría, sabríamos, sabríais, sabrían**

                h. **sepa, sepas, sepa, sepamos, sepáis, sepan**

                i. **supiera, supieras, supiera, supiéramos, supierais, supieran**

16. **Salir**   *c.* **salgo,** sales, sale, salimos, salís, salen

                f. **saldré, saldrás, saldrá, saldremos, saldréis, saldrán**

                g. **saldría, saldrías, saldría, saldríamos, saldríais, saldrían**

                h. **salga, salgas, salga, salgamos, salgáis, salgan**

                j. **sal**

17. **Ser**   *c.* **soy, eres, es, somos, sois, son**

                e. **fui, fuiste, fue, fuimos, fuisteis, fueron**

                d. **era, eras, era, éramos, erais, eran**

                h. **sea, seas, sea, seamos, seáis, sean**

                i. **fuera, fueras, fuera, fuéramos, fuerais, fueran**

                j. **sé**

18. Tener *c.* **tengo, tienes, tiene,** tenemos, tenéis, **tienen**

    e. **tuve, tuviste, tuvo, tuvimos, tuvisteis, tuvieron**

    f. **tendré, tendrás, tendrá, tendremos, tendréis, tendrán**

    g. **tendría, tendrías, tendría, tendríamos, tendríais, tendrían**

    h. **tenga, tengas, tenga, tengamos, tengáis, tengan**

    i. **tuviera, tuvieras, tuviera, tuviéramos, tuvierais, tuvieran**

    j. **ten**

19. Traer *a.* **trayendo**

    b. **traído**

    c. **traigo,** traes, trae, traemos, traéis, traen

    e. **traje, trajiste, trajo, trajimos, trajisteis, trajeron**

    h. **traiga, traigas, traiga, traigamos, traigáis, traigan**

    i. **trajera, trajeras, trajera, trajéramos, trajerais, trajeran**

20. Valer *c.* **valgo,** vales, vale, valemos, valéis, valen

    f. **valdré, valdrás, valdrá, valdremos, valdréis, valdrán**

    g. **valdría, valdrías, valdría, valdríamos, valdríais, valdrían**

    h. **valga, valgas, valga, valgamos, valgáis, valgan**

21. Venir *a.* **viniendo**

    c. **vengo, vienes, viene,** venimos, venís, **vienen**

    e. **vine, viniste, vino, vinimos, vinisteis, vinieron**

    f. **vendré, vendrás, vendrá, vendremos, vendréis, vendrán**

    g. **vendría, vendrías, vendría, vendríamos, vendríais, vendrían**

    h. **venga, vengas, venga, vengamos, vengáis, vengan**

    i. **viniera, vinieras, viniera, viniéramos, vinierais, vivieran**

    j. **ven**

22. Ver *b.* **visto**

    c. **veo,** ves, ve, vemos, **veis,** ven

    d. **veía, veías, veía, veíamos, veíais, veían**

    h. **vea, veas, vea, veamos, veáis, vean**

▰▰ III. STEM-CHANGING VERBS

Stem-changing verbs are divided into three groups. In this section, one model is given for each type of verb. Remember that these verbs are conjugated as regular verbs, except for changes in the stem vowel (the vowel that immediately precedes the infinitive ending). Commonly used verbs that are conjugated similarly are listed at the end.

Group 1: -ar and -er verbs in which the stem vowel changes from **o** to **ue,** and **e** to **ie,** as shown in the models. Changes occur only in the present indicative, present subjunctive, formal, and familiar commands. The stem vowels are in **bold** print in the models.

Models

	pres. ind.	pres. subj.	formal command	familiar command
Recordar	recuerdo	recuerde	(no) recuerde (Ud.)	recuerda (tú)
	recuerdas	recuerdes	(no) recuerden (Uds.)	no recuerdes (tú)
	recuerda	recuerde		
	recordamos	recordemos		
	recordáis	recordéis		
	recuerdan	recuerden		
Volver	vuelvo	vuelva	(no) vuelva (Ud.)	vuelve (tú)
	vuelves	vuelvas	(no) vuelvan (Uds.)	no vuelvas (tú)
	vuelve	vuelva		
	volvemos	volvamos		
	volvéis	volváis		
	vuelven	vuelvan		
Pensar	pienso	piense	(no) piense (Ud.)	piensa (tú)
	piensas	pienses	(no) piensen (Uds.)	no pienses (tú)
	piensa	piense		
	pensamos	pensemos		
	pensáis	penséis		
	piensan	piensen		
Entender	entiendo	entienda	(no) entienda (Ud.)	entiende (tú)
	entiendes	entiendas	(no) entiendan (Uds.)	no entiendas (tú)
	entiende	entienda		
	entendemos	entendamos		
	entendéis	entendáis		
	entienden	entiendan		

Group 2: *a.* **-ir** verbs with stem vowel **e.** The stem vowel changes to **ie** and sometimes **i,** as shown in the models. Changes occur in the present indicative, present subjunctive, preterit, present participle, imperfect subjunctive, and commands.

        b. The stem vowel of **dormir** and **morir** changes from **o** to **ue** and sometimes **u,** as shown in the model. (The changes are in the same forms as *a* above.)

Models

	pres. ind.	pres. subj.	preterit	imp. subj.	commands
Mentir	miento	mienta	mentí	mintiera	(no) mienta (Ud.)
	mientes	mientas	mentiste	mintieras	(no) mientan (Uds.)
	miente	mienta	mintió	mintiera	miente (tú)
	mentimos	mintamos	mentimos	mintiéramos	no mientas (tú)
	mentís	mintáis	mentisteis	mintierais	no mintáis vosotros
	mienten	mientan	mintieron	mintieran	[*pres. part.:* mintiendo]

	pres. ind.	pres. subj.	preterit	imp. subj.	commands
Dormir	duermo	duerma	dormí	durmiera	(no) duerma (Ud.)
	duermes	duermas	dormiste	durmieras	(no) duerman (Uds.)
	duerme	duerma	durmió	durmiera	duerme (tú)
	dormimos	durmamos	dormimos	durmiéramos	no duermas (tú)
	dormís	durmáis	dormisteis	durmierais	no durmáis (vosotros)
	duermen	duerman	durmieron	durmieran	[*pres. part.:* durmiendo]

Group 3: -**ir** verbs with stem vowel **e,** which changes to **i** only as shown in the model. The stem changes occur in the same forms that are specified for Group 2 above.

Models

	pres. ind.	pres. subj.	preterit	imp. subj.	commands
Repetir	repito	repita	repetí	repitiera	(no) repita (Ud.)
	repites	repitas	repetiste	repitieras	(no) repitan (Uds.)
	repite	repita	repitió	repitera	repite (tú)
	repetimos	repitamos	repetimos	repitiéramos	no repitas (tú)
	repetís	repitáis	repetisteis	repitierais	no repitáis (vosotros)
	repiten	repitan	repitieron	repitieran	[*pres. part.:* repitiendo]

Note the forms of **reír** and **sonreír:**

(son)río	**(son)ría**	**(son)reí**	**(son)riera**	(no) **(son)ría** (Ud.)
(son)ríes	**(son)rías**	**(son)reíste**	**(son)rieras**	(no) **(son)rían** (Uds.)
(son)ríe	**(son)ría**	**(son)rió**	**(son)riera**	**(son)ríe** (tú)
(son)reímos	**(son)riamos**	**(son)reímos**	**(son)riéramos**	no **(son)rías** (tú)
(son)reís	**(son)riáis**	**(son)reísteis**	**(son)rierais**	no **(son)riáis** (vosotros)
(son)ríen	**(son)rían**	**(son)rieron**	**(son)rieran**	[*pres. part.:* **(son)riendo**]

COMMON STEM-CHANGING VERBS

Starred verbs also have spelling changes (See next section). **Llover** and **nevar** occur only in the third person singular. **Costar** generally occurs in the third person singular or plural.

Group 1

o to ue		e to ie	
-AR	**-ER**	**-AR**	**-ER**
acostarse	devolver	cerrar	defender
almorzar*	llover	comenzar*	encender
contar	morder	confesar	entender
costar	mover(se)	despertar(se)	perder
encontrar	oler (huelo)	empezar*	
jugar* (**u** to **ue**)	resolver	nevar	
mostrar	soler	pensar	
recordar	volver	sentarse	
sonar			
soñar			
volar			

Group 2

e to ie and e to i   o to ue and o to u

convertir	dormir(se)
divertirse	morir(se)
mentir	
preferir	
sentir(se)	

Group 3

e to i

conseguir*	repetir
despedirse	seguir*
impedir	servir
pedir	sonreír
reír(se)	vestir(se)

IV. VERBS WITH SPELLING CHANGES

In most of these verbs, the spelling changes affect the consonant immediately preceding the **-ar, -er,** or **-ir** infinitive ending.

GROUP A: VERBS WITH INFINITIVES THAT END IN **-car, -gar, -zar**

The following changes occur in the first person singular of the preterit, in all forms of the present subjunctive, in the formal commands, and in the negative familiar commands.

-car changes **c** to **qu** before **e**

-gar changes **g** to **gu** before **e**

-zar changes **z** to **c** before **e**

Common **-car** verbs: **acercarse, atacar, buscar, explicar, sacar, tocar**

Spelling changes in **sacar:**

preterit	pres. subj.	formal commands
saqué	**saque**	(no) **saque** (Ud.)
sacaste	**saques**	(no **saquen** (Uds.)
sacó	**saque**	
sacamos	**saque**	*negative familiar commands*
sacasteis	**saquemos**	**no saques** (tú)
sacaron	**saquen**	**no saquéis** (vosotros)

Common **-gar** verbs: **castigar, entregar, jugar (ue), llegar, pagar**

Spelling changes in **pagar:**

preterit	pres. subj.	formal commands
pagué	**pague**	(no) **pague** (Ud.)
pagaste	**pagues**	(no) **paguen** (Uds.)
pagó	**pague**	
pagamos	**paguemos**	*negative familiar commands*
pagasteis	**paguéis**	**no pagues** (tú)
pagaron	**paguen**	**no paguéis** (vosotros)

Common **-zar** verbs: **abrazar, almorzar (ue), comenzar (ie), cruzar, empezar (ie), gozar**

Spelling changes in **cruzar:**

	preterit	pres. subj.	formal commands
	crucé	**cruce**	(no) **cruce** (Ud.)
	cruzaste	**cruces**	(no) **crucen** (Uds.)
	cruzó	**cruce**	
	cruzamos	**crucemos**	negative familiar commands
	cruzasteis	**crucéis**	**no cruces** (tú)
	cruzaron	**crucen**	**no crucéis** (vosotros)

Note the formal commands and negative familiar **tú** commands of the verbs that are stem-changing as well as spelling-changing:

jugar:	(no) **juegue(n)** (Ud.) (Uds.)	**no juegues** (tú)
almorzar:	(no) **almuerce(n)** (Ud.) (Uds.)	**no almuerces** (tú)
empezar:	(no) **empiece(n)** (Ud.) (Uds.)	**no empieces** (tú)

Remember that in the present subjunctive of the above verbs, the forms for nosotros and vosotros do not change their stem vowels. (juguemos, juguéis; almorcemos, almorcéis; empecemos, empecéis.)

GROUP B: VERBS WITH INFINITIVES THAT END IN **-ger, -gir, -guir**

The following changes occur in the first person singular of the present indicative, in all forms of the present subjunctive, in the formal commands, and in the negative familiar commands.

-**ger** changes **g** to **j** before **o** and **a**

-**gir** changes **g** to **j** before **o** and **a**

-**guir** changes **gu** to **g** before **o** and **a**

Common **-ger** verbs: **coger, escoger, proteger, recoger**

Spelling changes in **recoger:**

	pres. ind.	pres. subj.	formal commands
	recojo	**recoja**	(no) **recoja** (Ud.)
	recoges	**recojas**	(no) **recojan** (Uds.)
	recoge	**recoja**	
	recogemos	**recojamos**	negative familiar commands
	recogéis	**recojáis**	**no recojas** (tú)
	recogen	**recojan**	**no recojáis** (vosotros)

Common **-gir** verbs: **corregir (i), dirigir**

Spelling changes in **dirigir:**

	pres. ind.	pres. subj.	formal commands
	dirijo	**dirija**	(no) **dirija(n)** (Ud.) (Uds.)
	diriges	**dirijas**	negative familiar commands
	dirige	**dirija**	**no dirijas** (tú)
	dirigimos	**dirijamos**	**no dirijáis** (vosotros)
	dirigís	**dirijáis**	
	dirigen	**dirijan**	

Note the irregular forms of **corregir,** which is also stem-changing: yo **corrijo, corrija, corrijas,** etc., **corrija(n)** (Ud.) (Uds.), **no corrijas** tú, **no corrijáis** vosotros.

Common **-guir** verbs: **conseguir (i), seguir (i)**

Spelling changes in **conseguir:**	*pres. ind.*	*pres. subj.*	*formal commands*
	consigo	**consiga**	(no) **consiga(n)** (Ud.) (Uds.)
	consigues	**consigas**	*negative familiar commands*
	consigue	**consiga**	**no consigas** (tú)
	conseguimos	**consigamos**	**no consigáis** (vosotros)
	conseguís	**consigáis**	
	consiguen	**consigan**	

GROUP C: VERBS WITH INFINITIVES THAT END IN -ecer, -ocer, -ucir

In these verbs, **c** changes to **zc** in the first person singular of the present indicative, in all forms of the present subjunctive and the formal commands, and the negative familiar commands.

Common verbs in this group:

> **agradecer, aparecer, conocer, desaparecer, merecer, nacer, obedecer, ofrecer, parecer, permanecer, reconocer, conducir, producir, reducir, traducir**

Spelling changes in **merecer** and **traducir:**

pres. ind.		*pres. subj.*		*formal commands*
merezco	**traduzco**	**merezca**	**traduzca**	(no) **merezca** (Ud.) (Uds.)
				(no) **traduzca** (Ud.) (Uds.)
mereces	traduces	**merezcas**	**traduzcas**	
merece	traduce	**merezca**	**traduzca**	*negative familiar commands*
merecemos	traducimos	**merezcamos**	**traduzcamos**	
merecéis	traducís	**merezcáis**	**traduzcáis**	**no merezcas** (tú)
				no traduzcas (tú)
merecen	traducen	**merezcan**	**traduzcan**	**no merezcáis** (vosotros)
				no traduzcáis (vosotros)

Note that the preterit forms of the verbs ending in **-ducir** are irregular (See Chapter 7: Irregular preterits.) Therefore, the imperfect subjunctive would follow the pattern of the preterit forms.

pret:	**traduje**	**tradujiste**	**tradujo**	**tradujimos**	**tradujisteis**	**tradujeron**
imp. subj:	**tradujera**	**tradujeras**	**tradujera**	**tradujéramos**	**tradujerais**	**tradujeran**

Note: The verb **vencer** has a consonant before the **-cer** ending and is therefore conjugated as follows:

pres. ind.:	**venzo**	vences	vence	vencemos	vencéis	vencen
pres. subj.:	**venza**	**venzas**	**venza**	**venzamos**	**venzáis**	**venzan**
commands:	(no) **venza(n)** (Ud.) (Uds.)			**no venzas** (tú)		**no venzáis** (vosotros)

GROUP D: SOME VERBS WITH INFINITIVES THAT END IN **-iar** and **-uar**

In verbs of this group, the **i** in **-iar** and the **u** in **-uar** take an accent mark in the present indicative and present subjunctive, except for the **nosotros** and **vosotros** forms. These accent marks also occur in the formal commands and the affirmative and the negative familiar **tú** commands.

Common **-iar** verbs in this group: **enviar, guiar, fiar, esquiar**

Common **-uar** verbs in this group: **continuar, graduarse**

Spelling changes in this group for **enviar** and **continuar:**

pres. ind.		pres. subj.		formal commands
envío	**continúo**	**envíe**	**continúe**	(no) **envíe(n)** (Ud.) (Uds.)
envías	**continúas**	**envíes**	**continúes**	(no) **continúe(n)** (Ud.) (Uds.)
envía	**continúa**	**envíe**	**continúe**	
enviamos	continuamos	enviemos	continuemos	*familiar commands*
enviáis	continuáis	enviéis	continuéis	**envía** (tú) **no envíes** (tú)
envían	**continúan**	**envíen**	**continúen**	**continúa** (tú) **no continúes** (tú)

Note that several verbs that end in **-iar** do not follow the pattern of **enviar**; for example, **anunciar, cambiar, copiar, estudiar, pronunciar,** (yo **cambio, copie** (Ud.), **no estudies** (tú), etc.)

GROUP E: VERBS WITH INFINITIVES THAT END IN **-uir** (BUT NOT **-guir**)

In verbs of this group, the **i** in **-uir** changes to **y** in the following cases: (*a*) the present indicative, except for the **nosotros** and **vosotros** forms; (*b*) all forms of the present subjunctive; (*c*) the formal commands; (*d*) the affirmative and negative **tú** commands; (*e*) the third person singular and plural of the preterit; (*f*) all forms of the imperfect subjunctive; and (*g*) the present participle.

Common verbs in this group: **concluir, construir, contribuir, destruir, distribuir, huir**

Spelling changes in **construir:**

pres. ind.	pres. subj.	formal commands	tú commands
construyo	**construya**	(no) **construya(n)** (Ud.) (Uds.)	**construye** (tú)
construyes	**construyas**		**no construyas** (tú)
construye	**construya**		
construimos	**construyamos**	*pres. part.*	
construís	**construyáis**	**construyendo**	
construyen	**construyan**		

preterit	imp. subj.
construí	**construyera**
construiste	**construyeras**
construyó	**construyera**
construimos	**construyéramos**
construisteis	**construyerais**
construyeron	**construyeran**

Spanish-English Vocabulary

NOTES: 1. Verbs marked with an asterisk (*) have irregular forms that appear in Section II of the Verb charts (Pages 319–323). The number in parentheses indicated the verb's position in the list. For example, *decir (6) shows that decir is verb #6. A number following an unstarred verb indicates that the verb is conjugated like the starred verb with that number; for example, proponer (13).

2. Verbs with spelling changes are followed by a letter in parentheses referring to Section IV of the Verb Charts (Pages 326–329). For example, dirigir (B) indicates that dirigir undergoes spelling changes shown in Group B of Section IV, Page 327.

3. Also indicated in parentheses are stem-vowel changes. For example, divertir (ie, i) shows that the stem vowel e changes to ie and sometimes i (See Section III, Pages 323–326, of the Verb Charts).

4. Nouns that have both a masculine and a feminine form are displayed in the same style as adjectives. For example, director, -ra represents the forms director, m, and directora, f. Similarly, médico, -a indicates that a woman doctor is una médica.

5. Since the letters ch and ll are no longer considered single letters, they are not placed in the vocabulary as such.

a, to, at
abajo, below
abierto, -a, open
abogado, -a, lawyer
abrazar (A), to embrace
abrigo, m, coat
abril, m, April
abrir (pp abierto), to open
abrochar, to button, fasten; abrochar el cinturón de seguridad, to fasten the safety (seat) belt
absorto, -a, absorbed
abuelo, -a, m grandfather, f grandmother; los abuelos, grandparents
aburrido, -a, bored, boring
aburrimiento, m, boredom
aburrir, to bore
acabar de + inf., to have just
aceptar, to accept
acera, f, sidewalk
acerca de, about, concerning
acercarse (A) a, to approach
acompañar, to accompany
acondicionador de aire, air conditioner
aconsejar, to advise
acordarse (ue) de, to remember
acostado, -a, lying down
acostarse (ue), to lie down, go to bed
actual, present (time); actualmente, at present

acuerdo, m, agreement; estar de acuerdo, to agree; ponerse a un acuerdo, to come to an agreement
adecuado, -a, adequate
además (de), besides, in addition (to)
adentro, inside
adivinar, to guess
¿adónde?, (to) where?
adquirir (ie, i), to acquire
aéreo, -a, air, overhead
afortunadamente, fortunately
afuera, outside
agradable, pleasant
agradecer (C), to thank
agrícola, agricultural
agruparse, to group, cluster
agua (el), f, water
aguantar, to stand, endure, tolerate
águila (el), f, eagle
ahora, now; ahora mismo, right now
ahorrar, to save (money)
ahorros, m pl, savings
aire, m, air; al aire libre, outdoors; aire acondicionado, air conditioning
ají, m, chili
ala (el), f, wing; brim (of a hat)
alcalde, m, mayor
aldea, f, village
alegrarse de + inf., to be glad to

alegre, happy, merry
alemán, alemana, German
Alemania, Germany
algo, something, anything; somewhat
algodón, m, cotton
alguien, someone, anyone
alguno, -a (algún), some; pl a few; algunas veces, sometimes
alimento, m, food
aliviar, to relieve, alleviate
allá, allí, there
almacén, m, department store
almendra, f, almond
almirante, m, admiral
almorzar (ue) (A), to eat lunch
almuerzo, m, lunch
alrededor de, around
altavoz (pl altavoces), m, loudspeaker
alto, -a, tall, high; lo alto, the top
altura, f, height, altitude
alumno, -a, pupil, student
amable, kind, nice (= obliging)
amar, to love
amarillo, -a, yellow
ambiente, m, atmosphere, ambience, surroundings
amenazar (A), to threaten
amigo, -a, friend
amistad, f, friendship
amor, m, love
ancho, -a, wide

*andar (1), to walk, go
anillo, *m,* ring
anoche, last night
anterior, previous;
    anteriormente, formerly
antes (de), before
antiguo, -a, old, ancient, former
anunciador, -ra, announcer
anunciar, to announce
anuncio, *m,* announcement,
    advertisement
añadir, to add
año, *m,* year
apagar (A), to put out, extinguish,
    turn off
aparato, *m,* apparatus, (radio or
    TV) set
aparecer (C), to appear
apellido, *m,* family name,
    surname; **apellido de soltera,**
    maiden name
apenas, hardly, scarcely
aperitivo, *m,* apéritif, *a wine or*
    liquor taken customarily before
    a meal
aplicado, -a, studious
aprender, to learn
aprobar (ue) un examen, to
    pass a test
aprovecharse de, to take
    advantage of
aptitudes, *f. pl.,* qualifications
aquel, aquella, aquello, that;
    aquél, aquélla, that one; the
    former; **aquellos, -as,** those
aquí, here
árbol, *m,* tree
arena, *f,* sand
arrancar (A): **hacer arrancar**
    el motor, to start the engine
arreglar, to arrange; to fix,
    repair
arroz, *m,* rice
artículo, *m,* article
asaltante, *m,* attacker
ascensor, *m,* elevator
así, so, thus, (in) this way; **así**
    que, as soon as
asignar, to assign
asignatura, *f,* (school) subject
asistir, a, to attend
asociado, -a, associated
asombrado, -a, astonished
aspecto, *m,* aspect, appearance
asustarse, to become frightened
atacar (A), to attack

atención, *f:* **prestar atención,**
    to pay attention
atento, -a, attentive
atleta, *m & f,* athlete
atraer (19), to attract
atreverse a + *inf.,* to dare to
atún, *m,* tuna fish
aunque, although
ausencia, *f,* absence
ausente, absent
autobús, *m,* bus
automóvil, *m,* automobile
autor, -ra, author
avanzado, -a, advanced
avenida, *f,* avenue
avión, *m,* airplane
ayer, yesterday
ayudar, to help
azúcar, *m,* sugar
azul, blue

bachillerato, *m, diploma received*
    upon graduation from a
    secondary school
bahía, *f,* bay
bailar, to dance
baile, *m,* dance
bajar, to go down(stairs); to get
    off, out of (a train or vehicle)
bajo, under, below; **bajo, -a,** low,
    short
balneario, *m,* beach resort
banco, *m,* bank; bench
bañarse, to bathe, take a bath
baño, *m,* bath; **cuarto de baño,**
    bathroom
barato, -a, cheap
barco, *m,* boat, ship
barrio, *m,* neighborhood
basílica, *f,* large church
¡basta! that's enough!
bastante, enough, quite
bate, *m,* (baseball) bat
beber, to drink
bebida, *f,* drink, beverage
Belita, *nickname for Isabel*
belleza, *f,* beauty
bello, -a, beautiful
besar, to kiss
biblioteca, *f,* library
bicicleta, *f,* bicycle
bien, well
biftec, *m,* steak
bilingüe, bilingual
billete, *m,* ticket
bizcocho, *m,* cake, biscuit

blanco, -a, white
blusa, *f,* blouse
bollo, *m,* bun
bolsillo, *m,* pocket
bombero, -ra, firefighter
bondad, *f,* kindness
bonito, -a, pretty
borracho, -a, drunk; drunkard
bosque, *m,* woods
botella, *f,* bottle
bracero, -ra, farm worker, day
    laborer
brazo, *m,* arm
breve, brief, short
brillar, to shine
broncearse, to get a suntan
bueno, -a (buen), good
busca: en busca de, in search of
buscar (A), to seek, look for

*caber (2), to fit
cabeza, *f,* head
cabina telefónica, *f,* telephone
    booth
cada, each, every
cadáver, *m,* corpse
*caer(se) (3), to fall
café, *m,* coffee; cafe
caja, *f,* box
cajero, -a, cashier
caída, *f,* fall
caliente, warm, hot
callarse, to become silent, stop
    talking
calle, *f,* street
calor, *m,* heat; **hace calor,** it
    is warm; **tener calor,** to be
    (= feel) warm
caluroso, -a, warm, cordial
cama, *f,* bed
camarero, -a, *m* waiter, *f*
    waitress
cambiar (de), to change
cambio, *m,* change; **en cambio,**
    on the other hand
caminar, to walk, go
camino, *m,* road, way; **ponerse**
    en camino, to start out
camisa, *f,* shirt
campeonato, *m,* championship
campesino, -a, farmer, peasant
campo, *m,* country; field
canal, *m,* (television) channel
canción, *f,* song
cansado, -a, tired
cantante, *m & f,* singer

cantar, to sing
cantidad, *f,* quantity, amount
canto, *m,* singing, song
capítulo, *m,* chapter
cara, *f,* face
cariño, *m,* love, affection
cariñoso, -a, affectionate
Carlos, Charles
carne, *f,* meat; **carne de vaca,** beef
caro, -a, expensive
carrera, *f,* career; race (= running)
carretera, *f,* highway, road
carta, *f,* letter
cartaginés, -esa, Carthaginian
cartera, *f,* wallet
casa, *f,* house; **en casa,** at home; **ir (volver) a casa,** to go (return) home
casarse (con), to get married (to)
casi, almost, nearly
casino, *m,* clubhouse, casino
caso, *m,* case; **no hacer caso a,** to ignore, pay no attention to (someone)
castaño, -a, brown (hair, eyes)
castellano, -a, Castilian
castigar (A), to punish
castillo, *m,* castle
catalán, -ana, Catalonian
Cataluña, *f,* Catalonia
catorce, fourteen
causa, *f,* cause; **a causa de,** because of
celebrar, to celebrate
célebre, famous
cena, *f,* supper
cenar, to have supper
centro, *m,* center; downtown; **en el centro,** downtown; **ir al centro,** to go downtown; **centro comercial,** business district; shopping mall
Centroamérica, *f,* Central America
cerca (de), near
cercano, -a, nearby
cerebro, *m,* brain
cereza, *f,* cherry
cero, *m,* zero
cerrado, -a, closed
cerrar (ie), to close
cerveza, *f,* beer
cesar (de) + *inf,* to stop (doing something)

cesta, *f,* basket
chaqueta, *f,* jacket
charlar, to chat
cheque, *m,* check
chico, -a, child, *m* boy, *f* girl
chiste, *m,* joke
cielo, *m,* sky
cien, ciento, one hundred
ciencia, *f,* science
científico, -a, scientific; (*noun*) scientist
cierto, -a, certain; true
cigarrillo, *m,* cigarette
cinco, five
cincuenta, fifty
cine, *m,* movies, movie theater; **ir al cine,** to go to the movies
cinta, *f,* tape
cinturón, *m,* belt; **cinturón de seguridad,** safety belt, seat belt
cita, *f,* date, appointment
ciudad, *f,* city
ciudadano, -a, citizen
claro, -a, clear, light; **¡claro!** of course!
clase, *f,* class; kind, type
clásico, -a, classical
cliente, *m & f,* customer, client
clima, *m,* climate
cocina, *f,* kitchen
cocinar, to cook
cocinero, -a, cook
coche, *m,* car, automobile
coger (B), to take, catch, grab
colegio, *m,* secondary school
colina, *f,* hill
colocar (A), to place, put, set
colonizador, -ra, colonist
comedor, *m,* dining room
comenzar (ie) (A), to begin
comer, to eat
comerciante, *m & f,* merchant
comestibles, *m pl,* groceries
cometer, to commit
comida, *f,* food; meal; dinner; *midday meal in some countries*
comisionado, -a, commissioner
como, as, like; **¿cómo?** how?
cómodo, -a, comfortable
compañero, -a, companion; **compañero(-a) de clase,** classmate
compañía, *f,* company
comparar, to compare
compartir, to share

complejo, -a, complex
completo: por completo, completely
componerse (13) **de,** to be composed of
compositor, *m,* composer
compra, *f,* purchase; **hacer (ir de) compras,** to go shopping
comprar, to buy
comprender, to understand
computadora, *f,* computer
común, common; **por lo común,** generally
comunidad, *f,* community
con, with
concierto, *m,* concert
concluir (E), to conclude
concurso, *m,* contest
conducir (C), to drive; **licencia de conducir,** driver's license
confesar (ie), to confess
confundir, to confuse
conmigo, with me
conocer (C), to know (persons or places)
conocido, -a, well known
conocimiento, *m,* knowledge
conquista, *f,* conquest
conquistador, *m,* conqueror
conquistar, to conquer
conseguir (i) (B), to get, obtain
consejo, *m,* advice
consistir en, to consist of
construido, -a, constructed, built
construir (E), to build, construct
consultorio, *m,* (doctor's or lawyer's) office
contar (ue), to count; to tell, relate, narrate
contener (18), to contain
contento, -a, happy, glad
contestar, to answer
contigo, with you
continuar (D), to continue
contra, against
contrario: al contrario, on the contrary
conversar, to converse
copa, *f,* goblet, wine glass
corazón, *m,* heart
corbata, *f,* necktie
cordillera, *f,* mountain range
corregir (i) (B), to correct
correo, *m,* mail; **correo aéreo,** air mail
correr, to run

correspondencia: amigo(-a) por correspondencia, "pen pal," a friend acquired by correspondence

corrida de toros, bullfight

cortar, to cut

cortejar, to court

cortés, courteous, polite

cortina, *f,* curtain

corto, -a, short

cosa, *f,* thing; **cosa de,** about (with numbers)

costa, *f,* coast

costar (ue), to cost

costumbre, *f,* custom

***creer** (4),** to believe

criado, -a, servant, maid

crimen (*pl* **crímenes**), *m,* crime

cristianismo, *m,* Christianity

crucigrama, *m,* crossword puzzle

cruzar (A), to cross

cuaderno, *m,* notebook

cual: el (la) cual, los (las) cuales, which, who

cualquier, any

cuando, when; **¿cuándo?** when?

¿cuánto, -a? how much?; **¿cuántos, -as?** how many?; **cuanto antes,** as soon as possible; **unos cuantos (unas cuantas),** some, a few

cuarenta, forty

cuarto, *m,* room; quarter; **cuarto de baño,** bathroom; **a las dos y cuarto,** at a quarter past two (o'clock)

cuatro, four

cubano, -a, Cuban

cubrir (*pp* **cubierto**), to cover

cuchillo, *m,* knife

cuenta, *f,* bill, check; **darse cuenta de,** to realize; **tener en cuenta,** to bear in mind

cuento, *m,* story; **cuento policíaco,** detective story

cuero, *m,* leather

cuerpo, *m,* body

cueva, *f,* cave

cuidado, *m,* care; **con cuidado,** carefully; **tener cuidado,** to be careful

cuidar, to take care of

cumbre, *f,* top, summit

cumpleaños, *m,* birthday

cumplir con, to fulfill

cuyo, -a, whose

dama, *f,* lady

***dar** (5),** to give; **dar un paseo,** to take a walk (ride)

de, of, from, in: **de joven,** as a young man (woman); **de repente,** suddenly

debajo (de), under, underneath, below

deber + *inf.,* should, to have to, be supposed to; **debes venir a las dos,** you should (are supposed to) come at two o'clock; **deber de** + *inf.,* must (= probably); **ella debe de estar en casa,** she must be (is probably) at home

débil, weak

***decir** (6),** to say, tell; **es decir,** that is (to say)

dedo, *m,* finger

defender (ie), to defend

dejar, to leave; to let, allow; **dejar de** + *inf.,* to stop (doing something)

delante de, in front of

delgado, -a, thin, slender

demás: los (las) demás, the others, the rest (of them)

demasiado, -a, too much; *pl* too many; *adv.* too

dentro de, inside (of)

dependiente, -a, sales clerk, shop assistant

deporte, *m,* sport

derecho, -a, right; **a la derecha,** at (to) the right; **todo derecho,** straight ahead

desarrollar(se), to develop

desarrollo, *m,* development

desayunar(se), to have breakfast

desayuno, *m,* breakfast

descansar, to rest

descanso, *m,* rest

desconocido, -a, unknown

describir (*pp* **descrito**), to describe

descubrimiento, *m,* discovery

descubrir (*pp* **descubierto**), to discover

desde, from, since

desear, to wish, want

desgracia: por desgracia, unfortunately

deshacer (9), to undo; **deshacer la maleta,** to unpack

desierto, *m,* desert

desocupado, -a, unoccupied

despacio, slowly

despedirse (i) de, to say good-bye to

despegar (A), (*aircraft*) to take off

despertarse (ie), to wake up

después, afterward; **después (de) que,** after

destino, *m,* destination

destreza, *f,* skill

destruir (E), to destroy

detalle, *m,* detail

detenerse (18), to stop

detrás (de), behind, in back (of)

devolver (ue), to return, give back

día, *m,* day; **al día,** a day, per day; **día de fiesta,** holiday; **todos los días,** every day

diamante, *m,* diamond

diario, -a, daily

dibujo, *m,* drawing; **dibujo animado,** movie cartoon

dictadura, *f,* dictatorship

Diego, James

diente, *m,* tooth

diez, ten

diferirse (ie, i) de, to differ (be different) from

difícil, hard, difficult

dificultad, *f,* difficulty

dime, tell me

dinero, *m,* money

dios, *m,* god; idol

dirección, *f,* address

director, -ra, (school) principal; manager

dirigir (B), to direct

disco, *m,* phonograph record; **disco compacto,** *m,* CD

discoteca, *f,* discotheque, *a small nightclub for dancing*

discurso, *m,* speech

discutir, to discuss

disminuir (E), to diminish, decrease

disputa, *f,* argument

distinto, -a, distinct, different

diversos, -as, various

divertido, -a, amusing, enjoyable, fun

divertir (ie, i), to amuse, entertain; **divertirse,** to enjoy oneself, have a good time

dividir, to divide

doblar, to turn (a corner); **doble Ud. a la izquierda,** turn to the left

doce, twelve

dólar, *m,* dollar

dolor, *m,* pain; grief; **dolor de cabeza,** headache

domingo, *m,* Sunday

donde, where; **¿dónde?** where?; **¿adónde?** (to) where?

dormido, -a, asleep

dormir (ue, u), to sleep; **dormirse,** to fall asleep

Dorotea, Dorothy

dudar, to doubt

dudoso, -a, doubtful

dueño, -a, owner

dulce, sweet; *m* piece of candy; *pl* candy

durante, during

durar, to last

duro, -a, hard

echar, to throw

edad, *f,* age

edificio, *m,* building

ejemplo, *m,* example; **por ejemplo,** for example

ejercicio, *m,* exercise

ejército, *m,* army

elegir (i) (B), to elect

Elena, Helen

embargo: sin embargo, nevertheless, however

emocionante, exciting

empanada, *f,* (meat) pie, patty

empezar (ie) (A), to begin

empleado, -a, employee, clerk

empresa, *f,* enterprise

en, in, on, at; **en seguida,** at once, immediately

enamorarse (de), to fall in love (with)

encantador, -ra, charming

encantar, to enchant, charm; **me encanta manejar,** I love to drive

encender (ie), to light, turn on

encerrar (ie), to enclose, lock up, shut in

encima (de), above, on top of

encontrar (ue), to find; to meet; **encontrarse con,** to meet

enero, *m,* January

enfadado, -a, angry

enfadarse, to get angry

enfermedad, *f,* sickness, illness

enfermo, -a, sick, ill

enfrente de, in front of; **de enfrente,** opposite

enojado, -a, angry, annoyed

Enrique, Henry

ensalada, *f,* salad

enseñanza, *f,* teaching, education

enseñar, to teach

entender (ie), to understand

entero, a, entire, whole

enterrado, -a, buried

entonces, then

entrada, *f,* entry, entrance

entrar (en), to enter

entre, between, among

entregar (A), to deliver, hand over

enviar (D), to send

envolver (ue), to wrap

época, *f,* epoch, (historical) period

equipo, *m,* team; equipment

equivocarse (A), to be mistaken

erigir (B), to erect

escalera, *f,* staircase, stairs

escaparate, *m,* store window

escaparse, to escape

escena, *f,* scene; stage

escoger (B), to choose

escolar, *(adj.)* school; **libro escolar,** schoolbook

escribir (*pp* escrito), to write

escritorio, *m,* desk

escuchar, to listen (to)

escuela, *f,* school; **escuela primaria,** elementary school; **escuela intermedia,** intermediate school; **escuela secundaria,** secondary school

escultor, -ra, sculptor

escultura, *f,* sculpture

ese, -a, that; **esos, -as,** those; **eso,** that; **a eso de,** at about (with clock-time); **por eso,** for that reason, therefore

espacio, *m,* space

espectador, -ra, spectator

espejo, *m,* mirror; **espejo retrovisor,** rear-view mirror

esperar, to wait (for); to hope; to expect

esposa, *f,* wife

esquiar (D), to ski

esquina, *f,* street corner

establecerse (C), to settle (in a city or country)

estación, *f,* season; station

estadio, *m,* stadium

estado, *m,* state

Estados Unidos, *m pl,* United States

estante, *m,* bookshelf

*estar (7), to be; **está bien,** (it's) all right

estatua, *f,* statue

este, *m,* east

este, -a, this; **estos, -as,** these; **éste, -a, éstos, -as,** the latter

estereofónico, -a, stereophonic

estrecho, -a, narrow; **Estrecho de Magallanes,** Strait of Magellan

estrella, *f,* star; **estrella del cine,** movie star

estudiante, *m & f,* student

estudiar, to study

estudio, *m,* study

estúpido, -a, stupid

europeo, -a, European

evitar, to avoid

examen (*pl* exámenes), *m,* examination, test

excursión, *f,* outing, (pleasure) trip

éxito, *m,* success; **tener éxito,** to be successful

explicar (A), to explain

explorador, -ra, explorer

extranjero, -a, foreign

extraño, -a, strange

extremo, *m,* end

fábrica, *f,* factory

fácil, easy

falda, *f,* skirt

falta, *f,* mistake, error

faltar, to be lacking; **me falta dinero,** I lack (need) money

fama, *f,* fame; reputation; **tiene fama de ser,** (he, she, it) is reputed (said) to be

favor, *m,* favor; **haga Ud. el favor de + *inf,*** please; **por favor,** please

febrero, *m,* February

fecha, *f,* date

Felipe, Philip

feliz (*pl* felices), happy

fenicio, -a, Phoenician

feo, -a, ugly

feroz (*pl* feroces), fierce

ferrocarril, *m,* railroad

fiebre, *f,* fever

fieltro, *m,* felt
fiesta, *f,* party; holiday; **fiesta patronal,** feast of the patron saint
fijarse en, to notice
fin, *m,* end; **a fines de,** at (toward) the end of; **fin de semana,** weekend; **poner fin a,** to put an end to; **por fin,** finally
final: al final de, at the end of
flaco, -a, skinny
flirtear, to flirt
flor, *f,* flower
flotar, to float
fluir (E), to flow
fomentar, to foster, encourage, promote
foro, *m,* forum
fortaleza, *f,* fortress
foto, *f,* photo; **sacar fotos,** to take pictures (snapshots)
francés, francesa, French
Francisca, Frances (girl's name)
Francisco, Frank (boy's name)
frase, *f,* phrase, sentence
frecuencia: con frecuencia, frequently
freno, *m,* brake
frente a, opposite
fresco, -a, cool; fresh; **hace fresco,** it is cool (weather)
frío, -a, cold; **hace frío,** it is cold (weather); **tener frío,** to be (= feel) cold
frito, -a, fried
frontera, *f,* frontier, border
frontón, *m,* jai-alai court
fuego, *m,* fire
fuera (de), outside
fuerte, strong
fuerza, *f,* force, strength
fui, fuiste, fue, etc., *forms of the preterit tense of* **ser** *and* **ir**
fumar, to smoke
fundar, to found, establish
fútbol, *m,* soccer
gana, *f,* desire; **tener ganas de +** *inf.,* to feel like; **tener muchas ganas de +** *inf.,* to be eager to
ganar, to win; to earn
garaje, *m,* garage
gaseosa, *f,* carbonated soda
gastar, to spend (money)
gato, -a, cat
general: por lo general, generally

gente, *f,* people
gobernador, -ra, governor
gobierno, *m,* government
godo, -a, Gothic; (*noun*) Goth
golpe, *m,* blow, stroke, hit; **dar un golpe,** to hit
golpear, to hit, strike
gorra, *f,* cap
gozar (A) de, to enjoy
grabadora, *f,* tape recorder
grabar (en cinta), to record (on tape)
gracias, thanks, thank you
grado, *m,* degree, grade
graduarse (D), to be graduated
gramática, *f,* grammar
gran, great
grande, big, large; (*preceding a noun in the plural*) great: **los grandes jefes,** the great leaders
grave, serious
griego, -a, Greek
gritar, to shout
grupo, *m,* group
guante, *m,* glove
guapo, -a, handsome, beautiful
guardar, to keep; **guardar cama,** to stay in bed
guerra, *f,* war; **guerra mundial,** world war
guiar (D), to guide; to drive
Guillermo, William
gustar, to please; **me gusta(n),** I like it (them)

*haber (8), to have (*aux, verb*): **haber hablado (tomado,** etc.**)** to have spoken (taken, etc.)
había, there was, there were
habitación, *f,* room
habitante, *m & f,* inhabitant
habitar, to inhabit
habla (el), *f,* speech; **de habla española,** Spanish-speaking
hablar, to speak, talk
habrá, there will be
*hacer (9), to do, make; **hace poco,** a short while ago; **hace un año,** a year ago; **hace buen tiempo,** the weather is nice; **hace calor,** it is warm (see VII-B); **hacer un papel,** to play a role; **hacerse,** to become
hacia, towards

hallarse, to be (situated), to find oneself
hambre, *f,* hunger; **tener hambre,** to be hungry
hasta, until; up to; even; **hasta que +** *verb,* until
hay, there is, there are; **hay que +** *inf.,* one must, it is necessary to; **no hay de qué,** you're welcome, don't mention it
helado, *m,* ice cream
henequén, *m,* hemp
herencia, *f,* inheritance, heritage
herir (ie, i), to injure, hurt, wound
hermano, *m,* brother; **hermana,** *f,* sister; **hermanos,** *m pl,* brother(s) and sister(s)
hermoso, -a, beautiful, handsome
hervido, -a, boiled
hielo, *m,* ice
hijo, *m,* son; **hija,** *f,* daughter; **hijos,** *m pl,* children (= sons and daughters)
hispánico, -a, Hispanic (= Spanish-speaking)
hispano, -a, Hispanic; (*noun*) person whose native language is Spanish
historia, *f,* story; history
hoja, *f,* leaf; sheet of paper
hombre, *m,* man
hombro, *m,* shoulder
honra, *f,* honor
honrar, to honor
hora, *f,* hour, time; **¿a qué hora?** at what time?
hoy, today; **hoy día,** nowadays; **hoy mismo,** this very day
hueso, *m,* bone
huevo, *m,* egg

ibérico, -a, } Iberian (la Península Ibérica, Spain and Portugal mainland)
ibero, -a }
idioma, *m,* language
iglesia, *f,* church
imagen (*pl* **imágenes),** *f,* image, picture
imperio, *m,* empire
importar, to be important; to matter; **no me importa,** I don't care (it doesn't matter to me)
impresionante, impressive
impresora, *f,* printer

incendio, *m,* fire
incesantemente, incessantly, continuously
incluir (E)**,** to include
incluso, including
influjo, *m,* influx
informe, *m,* report; piece of information
ingeniería, *f,* engineering
Inglaterra, *f,* England
inglés, inglesa, English
iniciar, to initiate, begin
inmediatemente, immediately
inolvidable, unforgettable
insistir (en), to insist (on)
interés, *m,* interest
interesante, interesting
interesarse en, to be interested in
interminable, endless
intérprete, *m & f,* interpreter
invierno, *m,* winter(time)
invitado, -a, guest
invitar, to invite
***ir** (10)**,** to go; **ir a** + *inf.,* to be going to; **voy a hablar,** I'm going to speak; **irse,** to go away, leave
isla, *f,* island
izquierdo, -a, left; **a la izquierda,** at (to) the left

jabón, *m,* soap
jamás, ever, never
jamón, *m,* ham
jardín, *m,* garden
jefe, *m* ⎫
jefa, *f* ⎭ leader, boss, head
Jorge, George
José, Joseph
joven (*pl* **jóvenes**)**,** young; **de joven,** as a young man (woman)
joya, *f,* jewel
Juan, John; **Juana,** Joan
juego, *m,* game
jueves, *m,* Thursday
juez, *m,* judge
jugador, -ra, player
jugar (ue) (A)**,** to play; **jugar al béisbol,** to play baseball; **jugar a las cartas,** to play cards
jugo, *m,* juice
juguete, *m,* toy
julio, *m,* July
junto a, next to

juntos, -as, together
juntar, to join
jurar, to swear
juzgar (A)**,** to judge

kilo, *m,* kilogram (about 2.2 lb.)
kilómetro, *m,* kilometer (about 5/8 mile)

lado, *m,* side; **al lado de,** next to
ladrón, -ona, thief
lago, *m,* lake
lana, *f,* wool
lápiz (*pl* **lápices**)**,** *m,* pencil
largo, -a, long; **a lo largo de,** along
lástima, *f,* pity; **es lástima,** it's a pity
lavar(se), to wash (oneself)
lección, *f,* lesson
leche, *f,* milk
lectura, *f,* reading, reading selection
leer (4)**,** to read
lejano, -a, distant, far-away
lejos (de), far (from)
lengua, *f,* language, tongue
león (*pl* **leones**)**,** *m,* lion
levantarse, to rise, get up
leyenda, *f,* legend
libertad, *f,* liberty, freedom
libre, free
librería, *f,* bookstore
libro, *m,* book
licencia de conducir, driver's license
ligero, -a, light (in weight)
limpiar, to clean
limpio, -a, clean
lindo, -a, pretty
línea, *f,* line
listo, -a, ready
litoral, *m,* coast, shore
llamado, -a, called, named
llamar, to call; **llamarse,** to be called, named; **llamar por teléfono,** to call up
llanura, *f,* plain
llave, *f,* key
llegada, *f,* arrival
llegar (A)**,** to arrive; **llegar a ser,** to become
llenar, to fill
lleno, -a, full
llevar, to wear; to carry; to take (someone somewhere); **llevarse**

bien con, to get along (well) with (someone)
llorar, to weep, grieve
llover (ue), to rain
lluvia, *f,* rain
lobo, *m,* wolf
loco, -a, crazy; **volver loco(-a) a,** to drive (someone) crazy
lograr + *inf.,* to succeed in
Lola, *nickname for Dolores*
lo que, what, that which
lucha, *f,* struggle, fight
luchar, to struggle, fight
luego, then; **hasta luego,** so long, see you later
lugar, *m,* place; **tener lugar,** to take place
lujo, *m,* luxury
luna, *f,* moon
lunes, *m,* Monday
Luisa, Louise
luz (*pl* **luces**)**,** *f,* light

madera, *f,* wood; **de madera,** wooden
madre, *f,* mother; **madre patria,** mother country
maestro, -a, teacher (*elementary school*)
magnífico, -a, magnificent; **¡Magnífico!** Great! "Super!"
maíz, *m,* corn
mal, badly
maleta, *f,* suitcase
malo, -a (mal), bad
mamá, *f,* mother, mama
mandar, to send; to order
mando, *m,* command, control
manejar, to drive
manera, *f,* way, manner
mano, *f,* hand
mantequilla, *f,* butter
manzana, *f,* apple
mañana, tomorrow; *f* morning; **de la mañana,** in the morning, A.M.; **por la mañana,** in (= during) the morning
mapa, *m,* map
máquina, *f,* machine; **escribir a máquina,** to typewrite
maquinaria, *f,* machinery
mar, *m,* sea
Mar Cantábrico, Bay of Biscay
marcharse, to leave, go away
María, Mary
marido, *m,* husband

mariscos, *m pl,* shellfish, seafood

marzo, *m,* March

más, more, most

máscara, *f,* mask

matar, to kill

matemático, *m,* mathematician

matrimonio, *m,* marriage, married couple

maya, Mayan (Indian)

mayor, older, oldest; greater, greatest; **la mayor parte (de),** most (of)

mayoría, *f,* majority

mecánico, *m,* mechanic

medianoche, *f,* midnight

médico, -a, physician, doctor

medio, -a, half; **a las dos y media,** at half past two (o'clock); **media hora,** half an hour; **por medio de,** by means of

mediodía, *m,* noon

medir (i), to measure

mejor, better, best

mejorar, to improve

melocotón, *m,* peach

menor, younger, youngest

menos, less, fewer; except; **por lo menos,** at least

mensaje, *m,* message

mentir (ie, i), to lie

mentira, *f,* lie

menudo: a menudo, often

mercado, *m,* market

merecer (C), to deserve

meridional, southern

merienda, *f,* afternoon snack

mes, *m,* month

mesa, *f,* table; **a la mesa,** at the table

meseta, *f,* plateau

mestizo, -a, of mixed Indian and Caucasian origin

meter, to put in(to), insert

metro, *m,* subway; meter (= 3.3 feet)

mezcla, *f,* mixture

miedo, *m,* fear; **tener miedo,** to be afraid

miembro, *m & f,* member

mientras, while; **mientras tanto,** meanwhile

miércoles, *m,* Wednesday

milla, *f,* mile

millares, *m pl,* thousands

millón (*pl* **millones**), million

mío, -a, -os, -as, mine, of mine

mirar, to look at; **mirar la televisión,** to watch TV

misa, *f,* mass (*in church*)

misionero, a, missionary

mismo, -a, same; **lo mismo,** the same (thing)

mitad, *f,* half

moda, *f,* style, fashion

modo, *m,* way, means

mojarse, to get wet

molestar, to bother, disturb

moneda, *f,* coin

montaña, *f,* mountain

montañoso, -a, mountainous

montar a caballo, to ride a horse

monte, *m,* mount, mountain

morder (ue), to bite

morir (ue, u) (*pp* **muerto**), to die

moro, -a, Moorish; (*noun*) Moor

mostrar (ue), to show

motocicleta, *f,* motorcycle

moverse (ue), to move

muchedumbre, *f,* crowd

muchísimo, -a, very much, *pl* very many

mucho, -a, much, a great deal of; **muchos, -as,** many

muerte, *f,* death

muerto, -a, dead

mujer, *f,* woman

mundo, *m,* world; **todo el mundo,** everyone, everybody

muralla, *f,* wall

museo, *m,* museum

música, *f,* music

músico, -a, musician

muy, very; too

nacer (C), to be born

nacimiento, *m,* birth

nación, *f,* nation

nada, nothing, (not) anything; **de nada,** you're welcome

nadador, -ra, swimmer

nadar, to swim

nadie, no one, nobody, (not) anybody

naranja, *f,* orange

narrador, -ra, narrator

navegar (A), to sail

Navidad, *f,* Christmas

necesario, -a, necessary

necesitar, to need

negar (ie) (A), to deny; **negarse a** + *inf.,* to refuse to

negocio, *m,* business; **hombre de negocios,** businessman

negro, -a, black

nevar (ie), to snow

nevera, *f,* refrigerator

ni . . . ni, neither . . . nor; **ni siquiera,** not even

nieto, -a, *m* grandson, *f* granddaughter; grandchild

nieve, *f,* snow

nilón, *m,* nylon

ninguno, -a (ningún), none, no, (not) any

niño, -a, *m* boy, *f* girl; child; *pl* children

nivel, *m,* level; **nivel del mar,** sea level; **nivel de vida,** standard of living

noche, *f,* night, evening; **buenas noches,** good evening, good night; **esta noche,** tonight; **por la noche,** in the evening, at night; **de la noche,** in the evening, P.M.

nombrar, to name, appoint

nombre, *m,* name

nordeste, *m,* northeast

noroeste, *m,* northwest

norte, *m,* north

norteamericano, -a, American

nos, us, ourselves

nota, *f,* note; grade, mark (in school); **sacar buenas (malas) notas,** to get good (bad) marks

noticia, *f,* news item; *pl* news

noticiario, *m,* news broadcast

novela, *f,* novel

noveno, -a, ninth

novio, -a, sweetheart, fiancé(e)

nube, *f,* cloud

nuestro, -a, our

nueve, nine

nuevo, -a, new

número, *m,* number

nunca, never, (not) ever

o, or; **o sea,** or rather

obedecer (C), to obey

obra, *f,* work; **obra maestra,** masterpiece

obrero, -a, worker

obtener (18), to obtain

occidental, western

ochenta, eighty

ocho, eight

ocupado, -a, busy, occupied

ocupar, to occupy

ocuparse de, to be concerned
with, deal with, take care of (a
matter)

ocurrir, to occur

odiar, to hate

oeste, *m,* west

oficina, *f,* office

ofrecer (C), to offer

oído, *m,* hearing; (inner) ear

*oír (11), to hear

ojo, *m,* eye

oler (huelo, etc.), to smell

olor, *m,* smell, odor

olvidar ⎱
olvidarse de ⎰ to forget

once, eleven

orilla, *f,* bank (of a river); a
orillas de, on the banks of

oro, *m,* gold; de oro, golden

orquesta, *f,* orchestra

oscuro, -a, dark

oso, *m,* bear

otoño, *m,* autumn, fall

otro, -a, other, another

Pablo, Paul

Paca, *nickname for Francisca
(Frances)*

Paco, *see* Pancho

padre, *m,* father; *pl* parents

paella, *f, yellow rice with chicken,
seafood, and vegetables*

pagar (A), to pay (for)

país, *m,* country, nation

paisaje, *m,* landscape,
countryside

pájaro, *m,* bird

palabra, *f,* word

palacio, *m,* palace

palo, *m,* stick

pan, *m,* bread

Pancho, Frank (*nickname for
Francisco*)

panecillo, *m,* roll

pantalones, *m pl,* pants

papa, *f,* potato (Spanish America)

papel, *m,* paper; hacer un
papel, to play a role

paquete, *m,* package

Paquita, *diminutive of Paca*

par, *m,* pair

para, for; in order to

paraguas, *m,* umbrella

parar, to stop

parecer (C), to seem; parecerse
a, to resemble, look like

parecido, -a, similar, alike

pared, *f,* wall

pariente, *m & f,* relative

parque, *m,* park; parque
zoológico, zoo

parte, *f,* part; por todas partes,
everywhere

partido, *m,* game, match

partir, to leave, depart

pasado, -a, past, last; el año
pasado, last year

pasar, to pass, go; to spend (time);
to happen; pasar un buen
rato, to have a good time; ¿qué
te pasa? what's the matter
with you?

pasear(se), to take a walk (ride),
pasear un perro, to walk a
dog

paseo, *m,* walk, stroll, ride; dar
un paseo, to take a walk (ride)

paso, *m,* footstep

pastel, *m,* pie, pastry

patata, *f,* potato (Spain)

patín, *m,* skate

patinaje, *m,* skating

patinar, to skate

patria, *f,* (native) country,
fatherland; madre patria,
mother country

pavo, *m,* turkey

paz, *f,* peace

pedazo, *m,* piece; hacer
pedazos, to tear or smash to
pieces

pedir (i), to ask (for), to order (in
a restaurant)

Pedro, Peter

pegar (A), to hit, strike

peinar, to comb

película, *f,* film, movie

peligroso, -a, dangerous

pelo, *m,* hair

pelota, *f,* ball

pena, *f,* effort, trouble; valer la
pena, to be worthwhile

pensar (ie), to think; pensar +
inf., to intend to; pensar en, to
think of

peor, worse, worst

Pepe, Joe (*nickname for José*)

pequeño, -a, small, little

perder (ie), to lose; to miss;
perderse, to get lost

perfectamente, perfectly

periódico, *m,* newspaper

periodista, *m & f,* journalist

perla, *f,* pearl

permanecer (C), to stay, remain

permitir, to permit, allow

pero, but

perro, -a, dog

persona, *f,* person; *pl* people

personaje, *m,* character (in a
play, story, or novel)

pesado, -a, heavy

pesar: a pesar de, in spite of

pescado, *m,* fish (*ready to be
cooked and eaten*)

pez, *m,* fish (*alive and still in the
water*)

pico, *m,* (mountain) peak

pie, *m,* foot; de pie, standing; ir
a pie, to walk (*instead of ride*);
ponerse en pie, to stand up

piedra, *f,* stone

piel, *f,* fur, hide

pieza, *f,* room; (theater) play

pintor, -ra, painter

pintoresco, -a, picturesque

pintura, *f,* painting, picture

Pirineos, *m pl,* Pyrenees

piscina, *f,* pool

piso, *m,* floor; apartment

pista, *f,* skating rink; ski run

pizarra, *f,* chalkboard

planear, to plan

plata, *f,* silver

plato, *m,* dish, plate

playa, *f,* beach

plaza, *f,* square; plaza mayor,
main square; plaza de toros,
bullring

población, *f,* population

poblado, -a, populated

pobre, poor

pobreza, *f,* poverty

poco, *adv.,* little; poco, -a, little
(*in quantity*); pocos, -as, few;
hace poco, a short while ago;
poco a poco, little by little

*poder (12), to be able, can, could

policía, *m,* policeman; *f* police;
mujer policía, policewoman

pollo, *m,* chicken

*poner (13), to put; to turn on (the
radio, TV, etc.); poner la
mesa, to set the table;

ponerse, to put on (a garment);
to become; **ponerse en
camino,** to start out, **ponerse
en marcha,** to get moving

por, through, by, for, in, along; **por
eso,** for that reason, therefore;
por favor, please; **por fin,**
finally; **por supuesto,** of
course

¿por qué? why?

porque, because

porvenir, *m,* future

postre, *m,* dessert

practicar (A), to practice

precio, *m,* price

preferir (ie, i), to prefer

pregunta, *f,* question; **hacer una
pregunta,** to ask a question

preguntar, to ask

premio, *m,* prize, reward

preocuparse (por), to worry
(about)

preparar, to prepare

preparativos, *m pl,* preparations

prestar, to lend; **prestar
atención,** to pay attention

pretolteca, before the Toltec
period (see **tolteca**)

primario, -a, primary; **escuela
primaria,** elementary school

primavera, *f,* spring(time)

primero, -a (primer), first

primo, -a, cousin

principio, *m,* beginning; **al
principio,** at first

prisa: de prisa, fast; **darse
prisa,** to hurry; **tener prisa,**
to be in a hurry

privado, -a, private

probar (ue), to try, test, taste

problema, *m,* problem

profesor, -ra, teacher

programa, *m,* program; **ver un
programa,** to watch a program

prohibir, to prohibit, forbid

prometer, to promise

pronto, soon; **de pronto,**
suddenly; **lo más pronto
posible,** as soon as possible

pronunciar, to pronounce

propio, -a, own

proponer (13), to propose

propósito, *m,* purpose; **a
propósito,** by the way,
incidentally

proteger (B), to protect

Provincias Vascongadas,
Basque Country

próximo, -a, next; **la semana
próxima,** next week

proyecto, *m,* project

prueba, *f,* test, proof

pueblo, *m,* town; people

puente, *m,* bridge

puerta, *f,* door

puerto, *m,* port

puertorriqueño, -a, Puerto
Rican

pues, well, then, well then

puesto, *m,* booth, stand; position
(= job)

pulsera, *f,* bracelet

punto, *m,* point; **en punto** (with
clock time), sharp, exactly

que, who, that, which; than;
¿qué? what?

quedarse, to stay, remain

quejarse, to complain

querer (14), to want, wish; to love;
querer decir, to mean; **¿qué
quiere decir esa palabra?**
what does that word mean?

querido, -a, dear

queso, *m,* cheese

¿quién, -es?, who?; **¿a quién, -
es?** (to) whom?; **¿de quién, -
es?** whose?

químico, -a, chemical

quince, fifteen

quinientos, -as, five hundred

quinto, -a, fifth

quitarse, to remove, take off
(clothes)

Ramón, Raymond

rápido, -a, fast, rapid

raqueta, *f,* (tennis) racket

raro, -a, rare

rato, *m,* while; **pasar un buen
rato,** to have a good time

razón, *f,* reason; **tener razón,** to
be right; **no tener razón,** to be
wrong

recibir, to receive

recientemente, recently

recoger (B), to pick up

reconocer (C), to recognize

recordar (ue), to remember; to
remind

recorrer, to tour, go through (*a
city, country, region*)

referirse (ie, i) a, to refer to

reflejar, to reflect

refresco, *m,* soft drink; *pl*
refreshments

refrigerador, *m,* refrigerator

refugiado, -a, refugee

regalar, to give as a gift

regalo, *m,* gift, present

regla, *f,* rule; ruler (= straight-
edge)

regresar, to return, come (go) back

reina, *f,* queen

reír, (río, etc. see p. 19, etc.), to
laugh; **reírse de,** to laugh at,
make fun of

reloj, *m,* watch, clock

rendirse (i), to surrender, give up

repente: de repente, suddenly

repetir (i), to repeat

representación, *f,* show,
performance

reserva, *f,* reservation

resolver (ue), to resolve, solve; to
settle (an issue)

responder, to answer, reply

respuesta, *f,* answer, response

resultar, to result (in), turn out (to
be)

retreta, *f,* outdoor band concert

retrovisor: espejo retrovisor,
rearview mirror

reunión, *f,* meeting

reunirse (me reúno, etc.), to
meet, get together

revista, *f,* magazine

rey, *m,* king; *pl* king and queen,
rulers

rico, -a, rich

rincón, *m,* corner (of a room)

riqueza, *f,* wealth; *pl* riches

río, *m,* river

robar, to steal, rob

robo, *m,* theft, robbery

rojo, -a, red

romper (*pp* **roto**), to break; to
tear (up)

ropa, *f,* clothing, clothes

rosbif, *m,* roast beef

roto, -a, broken; torn

rubio, -a, blond

ruido, *m,* noise

ruta, *f,* route

sábado, *m,* Saturday

*saber (15), to know; **saber +
inf.,** to know how; **¿sabe Ud.**

nadar? do you know how to swim?; *preterit;* found out, learned

sacar (A), to take out, extract; **sacar fotos,** to take pictures (with a camera); **sacar buenas (malas) notas,** to get good (bad) marks (grades)

sal, *f,* salt

sala, *f,* living room; **sala de clase,** classroom

***salir** (16) **de,** to leave, come (go) out; **salir bien (mal) en un examen,** to pass (fail) a test

salón, *m,* meeting room; **salón de actos,** auditorium

salto, *m,* jump

salud, *f,* health

saludar, to greet

sangre, *f,* blood

santo, -a (san), saint; **San Juan Bautista,** St. John the Baptist

santo patrón (santa patrona), patron saint

santuario, *m,* sanctuary, shrine

satisfacer (9), to satisfy

sé I know; be (familiar command)

seco, -a, dry

secundario, -a, secondary

sed, *f,* thirst; **tener sed,** to be thirsty

seda, *f,* silk

seguida: en seguida, at once, immediately

seguir (i) (B), to follow; to continue, keep on; **sigue hablando,** he continues (keeps on) talking; **seguir un curso,** to take a course

según, according to

segundo, -a, second

seguro, -a, sure

seis, six

sello, *m,* postage stamp

semana, *f,* week; **por semana,** a week: **dos veces por semana,** twice a week

semejante, similar

semestre, *m,* (school) term, semester

sentado, -a, seated, sitting

sentarse (ie), to sit down

sentir (ie, i), to be sorry, regret; **sentirse,** to feel (sick, well, etc.)

señal, *f,* sign, signal

señor, gentleman, sir, Mr.

señora, lady, Mrs.; **señorita,** young lady, Miss

separar, to separate

***ser** (17), to be; (*noun*) *m,* being

serio, -a, serious

servir (i), to serve; **servir de,** to serve as

sesenta, sixty

setenta, seventy

severo, -a, strict

si, if

sí, yes

sí: para sí, to himself (herself, etc.)

siempre, always; **para siempre,** forever

sierra, *f,* mountain range

siesta, *f, traditional afternoon rest period observed in some Hispanic countries;* **echar una siesta,** to take a nap

siete, seven

siglo, *m,* century

significar (A), to mean

siguiente, following

silla, *f,* chair

sillón, *m,* armchair

simpático, -a, nice, likeable

sin, without; **sin embargo,** however, nevertheless

sino, but (*after a negative phrase*); **no solamente . . . sino también,** not only . . . but also

siquiera: ni siquiera, not even

sitio, *m,* place

situado, -a, situated, located

sobre, on. on top of, over; about (= concerning); **sobre todo,** especially

sobrino, -a, *m* nephew, *f* niece

sol, *m,* sun; **tomar el sol,** to sunbathe, lie in the sun

solamente, only

soldado, *m & f,* soldier

solicitar, to apply (for)

sólo = solamente

solo, -a, alone

soltar (ue), to loosen, release; **soltar el freno,** to release the brake

soltera, *f,* unmarried woman; **soltero,** *m,* bachelor

sombrero, *m,* hat

sonar (ue), to ring, sound

sonido, *m,* sound

sonreír (*see also* **reír**), to smile

soñar (ue), to dream; **soñar con,** to dream of

sopa, *f,* soup

sorprender, to surprise

sospechar, to suspect

sótano, *m,* basement, cellar

subir, to climb, rise, go up; to get into (a vehicle); **subir la escalera,** to go upstairs; **subir al coche,** to get into the car

suceso, *m,* event

sucio, -a, dirty

Sudamérica, *f,* South America

sudeste, *m,* southeast

sudoeste, *m,* southwest

suelo, *m,* ground; floor

sueño, *m,* sleep; dream; **tener sueño,** to be sleepy

suerte, *f,* luck; **tener suerte,** to be lucky

suéter, *m,* sweater

sufrir, to suffer

suizo, -a, Swiss

sumamente, very, exceedingly

sumar, to add

supermercado, *m,* supermarket

supuesto: por supuesto, of course

sur, *m,* south

suyo, -a, -os, -as, yours, his, hers, theirs

taberna, *f,* tavern

tal, such

también, also, too

tambor, *m,* drum

tampoco, neither, (not) either

tan, so, as

tanto, -a, so much, as much; **tantos, -as,** so many, as many

tardar en + *inf.,* to take (time); **tardé 5 horas en llegar allí,** it took me 5 hours to get there

tarde, late; **más tarde,** later; *f* afternoon; **de la tarde,** in the afternoon, P.M.; **por la tarde,** in (= during) the afternoon

tarea, *f,* task, homework; *pl* homework assignments

tarjeta, *f,* card

taza, *f,* cup

teatro, *m,* theater

techo, *m,* ceiling; roof

teléfono, *m,* telephone

televisión: mirar la televisión, to watch television

televisor, *m,* television set; **televisor en colores,** color TV set

tema, *m,* theme, topic, composition

temer, to fear

temporada, *f,* season

temprano, -a, early

***tener (18),** to have; **tener que +** *inf.,* to have to; **tener . . . años,** to be . . . years old; **tener lugar,** to take place; **tener prisa,** to be in a hurry; *see also* Appendix VII

tenis, *m,* tennis

tercero, -a (tercer), third

terminación, *f,* ending

terminar, to end, finish

terremoto, *m,* earthquake

terreno, *m,* land, ground, plot, terrain

tertulia, *f,* party, social gathering

tesoro, *m,* treasure

tiempo, *m,* time; weather; **a tiempo,** on time; **mucho tiempo,** a long time; **¿cuánto tiempo?** how long?; **hace buen tiempo,** the weather is nice; *see also* Appendix VII

tienda, *f,* store

tierra, *f,* land, earth; **la Tierra,** the Earth

tigre, *m,* tiger

timbre, *m,* bell

tío, -a, *m* uncle, *f* aunt

típico, -a, typical

tipo, *m,* type

título, *m,* title; degree, diploma

tocar (A), to play (an instrument); to touch; to ring (a bell)

todavía, still, yet

todo, -a, all, every; **toda la mañana,** all morning; **todas las semanas,** every week; **todos,** everybody

tolteca, *m & f,* Toltec; *(adj.) pertaining to the civilization of the Toltecs, which flourished in Mexico from A.D. 900–1200*

tomar, to take; to have (food or drink)

tonto, -a, silly, foolish, stupid

tormenta, *f,* storm

toro, *m,* bull

torre, *f,* tower

trabajador, -ra, industrious, hardworking; *(noun)* worker

trabajar, to work

trabajo, *m,* work; **trabajo escolar,** schoolwork

traducir (C), to translate

***traer (19),** to bring

traje, *m,* suit, dress; **traje de baño,** swimsuit

tranquilo, -a, calm, peaceful, quiet

tratar, to treat; **tratar de,** to deal with, be about: **el cuento trata de la vida militar,** the story deals with (is about) army life; **tratar de +** *inf.,* to try to

través: a través de, across, through

trece, thirteen

treinta, thirty

tren, *m,* train

tres, three

tribu, *f,* tribe

trigo, *m,* wheat

triste, sad

tristeza, *f,* sadness

tu, tus, your *(fam. sing.)*

tú, you *(fam. sing.)*

tumba, *f,* tomb

tuyo, -a, -os, -as, yours

último, -a, last

un, uno, una, a, an, one: **a la una,** at one o'clock; **unos, -as,** some, a few

único, -a, only

universidad, *f,* university, college

usar, to use

útil, useful

uva, *f,* grape

va, vas, vamos, vais, van, *forms of the present tense of* **ir**

vacaciones, *f pl,* vacation; **de vacaciones,** on vacation

vacío, -a, empty

***valer (20),** to cost, be worth; **más vale +** *inf.,* it is better to; **valer la pena,** to be worthwhile

valiente, brave

valle, *m,* valley

valor, *m,* value; bravery

vaquero, *m,* cowboy

varios, -as, several, various

vasco, -a, Basque

vascuence, *m,* the Basque language

vaso, *m,* (drinking) glass

véase, see *(referring to a page or chapter)*; **véase la página 45,** see page 45

vecindario, *m,* neighborhood

vecino, -a, neighbor

vegetal, *adj. & m,* vegetable

veinte, twenty

vencer (C), to conquer

vendedor, -ra, seller, vendor

vender, to sell

Venecia, Venice

***venir (21),** to come

venta, *f,* sale

ventana, *f,* window; **ventanilla,** *f,* car or train window

***ver (22),** to see, to watch (a program or a performance)

verano, *m,* summer(time)

verdad, *f,* truth; **es verdad,** it is true, that's right; **¿verdad? (¿no es verdad?)** right? isn't it so? isn't she? don't they? aren't you? etc.

verdadero, -a, true, real

verde, green

verduras, *f pl,* vegetables

vestido, *m,* dress

vestir (i), to dress; **vestirse,** to dress oneself, get dressed

vez (*pl* **veces),** *f,* time; **a veces,** at times; **de vez en cuando,** from time to time; **otra vez,** again; **una vez,** once; **dos veces,** twice; **muchas veces,** often; **en vez de,** instead of

viajar, to travel

viaje, *m,* trip, voyage; **hacer un viaje,** to take a trip

vida, *f,* life

viejo, -a, old; *(noun) m* old man, *f* old woman

viento, *m,* wind; **hace viento,** it's windy

viernes, *m,* Friday

vino, *m,* wine

visitar, to visit

vista, *f,* view, sight; **hasta la vista,** see you again

vivir, to live

vivo, -a, alive; lively
volar (ue), to fly
volcán (*pl* **volcanes),** *m,* volcano
volver (ue) (*pp* **vuelto),** to return, come (go) back; **volver a** + *inf.,* to . . . again; **volver loco(-a) a,** to drive (someone) crazy

voy, I am going (see **ir**)
voz (*pl* **voces),** *f,* voice; **en voz baja,** in a low (soft) voice; **en voz alta,** aloud

y, and
ya, already; **ya no,** no longer, not . . . anymore

yate, *m,* yacht

zapato, *m,* shoe
Zona Templada del Norte, North Temperate Zone
Zona Tórrida, Torrid Zone

English–Spanish Vocabulary

Concerning the Spanish verbs marked with an asterisk (*) and the indications in parentheses: see the first three Notes on Page 331.

able: to be able, *poder (12)

about, (*concerning*) acerca de, sobre; (*approximately*) alrededor de, cosa de, unos, -as

activity, la actividad

actress, la actriz

advantage: to take advantage of, aprovecharse de

affection, el cariño

affectionate, cariñoso, -a

afraid: to be afraid, *tener miedo

after, después (de); **afterward,** después, luego

afternoon, la tarde; **in the afternoon,** por la tarde; (*with clock time*) de la tarde; **yesterday afternoon,** ayer por la tarde

again, otra vez, volver a + *inf;* **he is speaking again,** vuelve a hablar

ago: a year ago, hace un año

agree, *estar de acuerdo

airplane, el avión

all, todo, -a, todos, -as; **all day,** todo el día

along, por, lo largo de

already, ya

also, también

always, siempre

A.M., de la mañana

angry: to get angry, enfadarse, enojarse

Anne, Ana

another, otro, -a

answer, la respuesta; contestar, responder

anybody (*see* **anyone**)

anyone, alguien, nadie; **did you see anyone?** ¿viste a alguien?; **I did not see anyone,** no vi a nadie (a nadie vi)

anything, algo, nada; **did you see anything?** ¿viste algo?; **I did not see anything,** no vi nada, nada vi

apartment, el apartamento; **apartment house,** la casa de apartamentos

apple, la manzana

April, abril

Argentina, la Argentina

around, alrededor (de)

arrange, arreglar

arrival, la llegada

arrive, llegar (A)

Arthur, Arturo

article, el artículo

ask, preguntar; **to ask for** (= *request*), pedir (i)

at, a, (*with place*) en

athlete, el (la) atleta

attend, asistir a

attention, la atención

attentive, atento, -a

aunt, la tía

author, el autor, la autora

automobile, el automóvil

ax, el hacha, *f*

bad, malo, -a (mal)

badly, mal

band, la banda

bank, el banco

baseball, el béisbol

basement, el sótano

be, *estar (7), *ser (17)

beach, la playa

beautiful, hermoso, -a, bello, -a

because, porque; **because of,** a causa de

bed, la cama; **to go to bed,** acostarse (ue)

beer, la cerveza

before, antes (de)

begin, comenzar (ie) (A), empezar (ie) (A)

believe, *creer (4)

best, el (la) mejor, los (las) mejores; **to like best,** gustarle más (a uno): **the sports I like best**

are . . . , los deportes que me gustan más son . . .

better, mejor, mejores

bicycle, la bicicleta

big, grande, grandes

bill, la cuenta

birthday, el cumpleaños

blind, ciego, -a

blouse, la blusa

blue, azul

book, el libro

bookstore, la librería

bored: to be bored, *estar aburrido, -a

bottle, la botella

box, la caja

boy, el muchacho, el chico; **boys and girls,** los muchachos, los chicos

bracelet, la pulsera

break, romper (*pp* roto)

breakfast, el desayuno; **to have breakfast,** tomar el desayuno, desayunar(se)

bridge, el puente

bring, *traer (19)

brother, el hermano

building, el edificio

bus, el autobús; (*in Cuba & Puerto Rico*) la guagua

businessman, el comerciante

buy, comprar

cafe, el café

cafeteria, la cafetería

call, llamar

can (= *be able*), *poder (12)

cap, la gorra

car, el coche, el carro

card, la tarjeta

care, el cuidado

careful, cuidadoso, -a; **to be careful,** *tener cuidado

CD, el disco compacto

center, el centro

chair, la silla

Charles, Carlos

chat, charlar
cheap, barato, -a
child, el niño, la niña
chocolate, el chocolate
Christmas, la Navidad;
   Christmas vacation, las
   vacaciones de Navidad
church, la iglesia
city, la ciudad
class, la clase
classroom, la sala de clase
climate, el clima
close, cerrar (ie)
closed, cerrado, -a
clothes, clothing, la ropa
club, el club
coat, el abrigo
coffee, el café
cold, frío, -a, (*noun*) el frío; **to be
   cold,** (*persons*) *tener frío,
   (*things*) *estar frío, -a, (*weather*)
   *hacer frío; **I am very cold,**
   tengo mucho frío; **the soup is
   very cold,** la sopa está muy
   fría; **it's very cold today,** hoy
   hace mucho frío
comb, el peine; peinarse
come, *venir (21); **to come in,**
   entrar (en)
comfortable, cómodo, -a
complain, quejarse
computer, la computadora
concert, el concierto
construct, construir (E)
continue, continuar (D), seguir (i)
   (B); **he continues to work
   (keeps on working),**
   continúa (sigue) trabajando
converse, conversar
cook, el cocinero, la cocinera;
   cocinar
corner, el rincón; (*street corner*) la
   esquina
could, (past tense of **can**) *use the
   preterit or the imperfect of
   *poder (see page 60); (conditional
   form of **can**) *use the conditional
   form of *poder;* **I could not
   see them yesterday,** no *pude*
   verlos ayer; **in those days I
   could walk to school,** en
   aquellos tiempos yo *podía* ir a la
   escuela a pie; **I could leave
   now but I don't want to,** yo
   podría salir ahora pero no quiero

country, (*nation*) el país; (*opposite
   of the city*) el campo
course, el curso; **of course,**
   claro, por supuesto
courteous, cortés
courtesy, la cortesía
cousin, el primo, la prima
cover, cubrir (*pp* cubierto)
criticize, criticar (A)
crossword puzzle, el crucigrama
cup, la taza

dance, el baile; bailar
dangerous, peligroso, -a
dark, oscuro, -a
day, el día; **all day,** todo el día;
   every day, todos los días
decide, decidir
delicious, sabroso, -a, delicioso, -a
dentist, el (la) dentista
department store, el almacén
describe, describir (*pp* descrito)
dessert, el postre
diamond, el diamante
die, morir (ue, u) (*pp* muerto) (7)
difficult, difícil
dinner, la comida, la cena
dish, el plato
divide, dividir
do, *hacer (9)
doctor, el médico, la médica; el
   doctor, la doctora
dollar, el dólar
door, la puerta
Dorothy, Dorotea
doubt, dudar
doubtful, dudoso, -a
downtown: to go downtown,
   *ir al centro
drama, el drama
dream, soñar (ue); **to dream of,**
   soñar con
drink, la bebida; beber; tomar; **do
   you drink coffee or tea?**
   ¿toma Ud. café o té?
drive, conducir (C), manejar
driver, el conductor, la conductora
dry, seco, -a
during, durante

eager: to be eager to, *tener
   muchas ganas de + *inf.*
early, temprano, -a
earn, ganar
ease, la facilidad

east, el este
easy, fácil
eat, comer; **to eat lunch,** tomar
   el almuerzo
education, la educación
elevator, el ascensor
employee, el empleado, la
   empleada
engineer, el ingeniero, la
   ingeniera
English, inglés, inglesa;
   (*language*) el inglés
enjoy, gustar, gozar (A) de; **I
   enjoyed the movie,** me gustó
   la película; **to enjoy life,** gozar
   de la vida; **to enjoy oneself,**
   divertirse (ie, i)
enjoyable, divertido, -a
enough, bastante, suficiente
enter, entrar (en)
error, el error
evening, la noche; **in the
   evening,** por la noche; (*with
   clock time*) de la noche; **good
   evening,** buenas noches; **this
   evening,** esta noche
ever, jamás
every, cada, todos los, todas las
examination, el examen (*pl*
   exámenes)
exciting, emocionante
expensive, caro, -a
explain, explicar (A)
extremely, . . . -ísimo, . . . -ísima;
   extremely high, altísimo, -a
eye, el ojo
eyeglasses, las gafas, los
   anteojos

face, la cara
fail a test, salir mal en un
   examen, no aprobar (ue) un
   examen
fair, la feria
fall, *caer(se) (3); **fall asleep,**
   dormirse (ue, u)
family, la familia
famous, célebre, famoso, -a
far (from), lejos (de)
fast, (*adj.*) rápido, -a; (*adv.*)
   rápidamente, de prisa
father, el padre
favor, el favor
feel, sentirse (ie, i); **I don't feel
   well,** no me siento bien

few, pocos, -as; **fewer,** menos: **fewer than** 15, menos de 15

fifteen, quince

filled, lleno, -a; **to be filled with,** *estar lleno(-a) de

film, la película

finally, por fin, al fin

finish, terminar

first, primero, -a (primer); **the first time,** la primera vez

fish, (*in its natural habitat*) el pez; (*caught and ready to be eaten*), el pescado

fit, *caber (2)

five, cinco

Florida, la Florida

flower, la flor

follow, seguir (i) (B)

food, el alimento, la comida

for, para, por (*see ch. 34*)

forbid, prohibir

foreign, extranjero, -a

forget, olvidar, olvidarse de

Francis, Francisco

Frank, Francisco; Pancho, Paco

French, francés, francesa; (*language*) el francés

Frenchman, el francés

friend, el amigo, la amiga

from, de

front: in front of, delante de

gallery, la galería

garden, el jardín

general, general; **generally,** generalmente, por lo general

gentleman, el caballero, el señor

German, alemán, alemana; (*language*) el alemán

get, obtener (18), conseguir (i) (B); **to get along with (someone),** llevarse bien con; **to get angry,** enfadarse, enojarse; **to get dressed,** vestirse (i); **to get off, out of (a vehicle),** bajar (de); **to get together,** reunirse; **to get to school,** llegar a la escuela; **to get up,** levantarse

gift, el regalo

girl, la muchacha, la chica

give, *dar (5)

glad: to be glad to, alegrarse de + *inf.*

glass (*for water*), el vaso

glove, el guante

go, *ir (10); **to go away,** *irse, marcharse; **to go out,** *salir (16) (de); **to go up,** subir

going: to be going to, ir a + *inf.*

gone (*pp* of **go**), ido

good, bueno, -a (buen)

good-by, adiós; **to say good-by to,** despedirse (i) de

grandmother, la abuela

grandparents, los abuelos

great, gran *or* grandes + *noun;* a **great actress,** una gran actriz; **the great artists,** los grandes artistas

greet, saludar

group, el grupo

guest, el invitado, la invitada

guitar, la guitarra

hair, el pelo

half, medio, -a; **half hour,** media hora; **at half past two,** a las dos y media

hamburger, la hamburguesa

hand, la mano

handkerchief, el pañuelo

handsome, hermoso, -a, guapo, -a

happy, contento, -a, feliz; **to be happy,** *estar contento, -a, *ser feliz

hat, el sombrero

have, *tener (18); (*a meal or beverage*) tomar; **to have a good time,** divertirse (ie, i), pasar un buen rato; **to have to,** (*obligation*) deber + *inf.,* (*necessity*) tener que + *inf.*

hear, *oír (11)

heat, el calor

Helen, Elena

help, la ayuda; ayudar

Henry, Enrique

her, (*direct object*) la, (*indirect object*) le, (*object of prep.*) ella; (*possessive adj.*) su, -s, de ella

here, aquí

hers, el suyo, la suya, los suyos, las suyas; **this book is hers,** este libro es suyo (. . . es de ella)

high school, la escuela superior, el colegio

him, (*direct object*) lo, (*in Spain*) le; (*indirect object*) le; (*object of prep.*) él

his, (*adj.*) su, -s, de él; (*pron.*) el suyo, la suya, los suyos, las suyas, de él; **this box is his,** esta caja es suya (. . . es de él)

home: at home, en casa; **to go (return) home,** *ir (regresar) a casa; **to leave home,** *salir de casa

hope, esperar

horizontal, horizontal

hot = very warm (*see* **warm**)

hotel, el hotel

hour, la hora

house, la casa; **apartment house,** la casa de apartamentos

how? ¿cómo?; **how many?** ¿cuántos, -as; **how much?** ¿cuánto, -a?

hundred: one hundred, cien, ciento

hungry: to be (very) hungry, *tener (mucha) hambre

hurry: to be in a hurry, *tener prisa

husband, el marido, el esposo

I, yo; **I like,** me gusta(n)

ice cream, el helado

idea, la idea

ignore (= *to snub or show no interest in someone*), no *hacer caso a

important, importante

impossible, imposible

inhabitant, el (la) habitante

innocence, la inocencia

innocent, inocente

insist, insistir (en)

instead of, en vez de

intelligence, la inteligencia

intelligent, inteligente

intend, pensar (ie) + *inf.*

interested: to be interested in, interesarse en

interesting, interesante

invite, invitar

iron, el hierro

island, la isla

it, *as subject, usually not expressed;* (*direct object*) lo, la; (*indirect object*) le; (*object of prep.*) él, ella; **I like it,** me gusta

job, el empleo, el puesto; (*task*) el trabajo

John, Juan

Joseph, José

just: to have just, acabar de + *inf.;* **I have just arrived,** acabo de llegar; **I had just arrived,** acababa de llegar

king, el rey; **king and queen,** los reyes

kitchen, la cocina

knife, el cuchillo

knock (at the door), llamar (a la puerta)

know, (*facts*) *saber (15); (*persons and places*) conocer (C)

laboratory, el laboratorio

lady, la dama, la señora; **young lady** (*unmarried*), la señorita

landscape, el paisaje

language, la lengua, el idioma

large, grande

last, último, -a; **last month,** el mes pasado; **last night,** anoche

late, tarde

later, más tarde; **see you later,** hasta luego

lawyer, el abogado, la abogada

lazy, perezoso, -a

learn, aprender

least, menos; **at least,** por lo menos

leather, el cuero

leave, *salir (16) (de), partir, *irse (10); **to leave for (a place),** salir para

lend, prestar

less, menos

lesson, la lección (*pl* lecciones); **the Spanish lesson,** la lección de español

let (= *allow*), dejar; **I let him drive,** le dejo conducir

letter, la carta

let us (let's), vamos a + *inf,* or use *present subjunctive, 1st pers. plural;* **let's eat,** vamos a comer, comamos; **let's leave,** vamos a salir, salgamos; **let's not . . .** *use present subjunctive, 1st pers. plural;* **let's not go there,** no vayamos allí

lie, la mentira; mentir (ie, i)

light, la luz (*pl* luces); claro, -a

like (be pleasing), gustar; **I like,** me gusta(n)

listen (to), escuchar

little, (*in size*) pequeño, -a; (*in quantity*) poco, -a

live, vivir

living room, la sala

long, largo, -a; **a long time,** mucho tiempo

look at, mirar; **look for,** buscar (A)

lose, perder (ie)

lot: a lot (of), mucho, -a

Louis, Luis

Louise, Luisa

luck, la suerte

lunch, el almuerzo; **to eat (have) lunch,** almorzar (ue) (A), tomar el almuerzo

madam, señora

magazine, la revista

magnificent, magnífico, -a

make, *hacer (9)

mall (=shopping center), el centro comercial

man, el hombre

many, muchos, -as

map, el mapa

March, marzo

marry, casarse (con)

Mary, María

match (game), el partido

matter: it doesn't matter, no importa

meal, la comida

meat, la carne

medicine, la medicina

meet, encontrar (ue), encontrarse con; (*to get together*) reunirse; (*to make the acquaintance of*) conocer (C)

meeting, la reunión

Mexico City, la ciudad de México

midnight, la medianoche

milk, la leche

mine, el mío, la mía, los míos, las mías; **she is a friend of mine,** es una amiga mía; **these books are mine,** estos libros son míos

minute, el minuto

mischievous, travieso, -a

miss, (la) señorita

mister, (el) señor

modern, moderno, -a

moment, el momento; **at this moment,** en este momento

money, el dinero

month, el mes

more, más

morning, la mañana; **in the morning,** por la mañana; (*with clock time*) de la mañana; **good morning,** buenos días; **tomorrow morning,** mañana por la mañana

most of, la mayoría de, la mayor parte de

motorcycle, la motocicleta

movie, la película

movies: to go to the movies, ir *al cine

much, mucho, -a; **very much,** muchísimo

museum, el museo

music, la música

must, (*obligation*) deber + *inf,* (*necessity*) *tener que + *inf,* (*probability*) deber de + *inf.*

mustard, la mostaza

my, mi, -s

name, el nombre; **to be named,** llamarse

narrow, estrecho, -a

near, cerca (de); **nearest,** más cercano, -a (a)

necessary, necesario, -a

necklace, el collar

necktie, la corbata

need, necesitar; (= *to lack*) faltarle a uno; **I need (lack) pencils,** me faltan lápices

neighbor, el vecino, la vecina

neighborhood, el vecindario, el barrio

nervous, nervioso, -a; **to be too nervous to (do something),** *estar muy nervioso(-a) para

never, nunca, jamás

new, nuevo, -a

news, las noticias; (*news item*) la noticia

newspaper, el periódico

next, próximo, -a

nice, (*likeable*) simpático, -a; (*kind, obliging*) amable; (*weather*) bueno (buen tiempo)

night, la noche; **at night,** por la noche

no = not any, ninguno, -a (ningún)

nobody, nadie

noise, el ruido
noon, el mediodía; **at noon,** a mediodía
north, el norte
notebook, el cuaderno
nothing, nada
novel, la novela
now, ahora; **right now,** ahora mismo
nylon, el nilón

o'clock: at seven o'clock, a las siete; **it is one o'clock,** es la una
old, viejo, -a; (= *ancient*) antiguo, -a; **how old is she?** ¿cuántos años tiene ella?; **I am 15 years old,** tengo 15 años; **the oldest,** el (la) mayor, los (las) mayores
on, en; **on Thursday,** el jueves; **on Fridays,** los viernes; **on July 4,** el cuatro de julio; **on . . . -ing,** al + *inf.:* **on arriving,** al llegar
once, una vez; **at once,** en seguida
open, abrir (*pp* abierto)
opposite, enfrente de
order, la orden; (*from a menu*) pedir (i); **in order to,** para + *inf.*
other, otro, -a
our, nuestro, -a
ours, el nuestro, la nuestra, los nuestros, las nuestras; **these chairs are ours,** estas sillas son nuestras
outside, afuera, fuera de

package, el paquete
page, la página
painting, la pintura
paper, el papel; (*newspaper*) el periódico
parents, los padres
park, el parque
party, la fiesta
pass, pasar; **to pass a test,** *salir bien en un examen, aprobar (ue) un examen
past: half past six, las seis y media
patience, la paciencia
patient, paciente
patio, el patio
pay, pagar (A); **I paid for the book,** pagué el libro; **I paid**

ten dollars for the book, pagué diez dólares por el libro; **to pay attention,** prestar atención; **to pay a visit,** *hacer una visita
pearl, la perla
pen, la pluma, el bolígrafo
pencil, el lápiz (*pl* lápices)
people, (*as a group*) la gente; (*as individuals*) las personas; (= *nation or race*) el pueblo; **the people are waiting for the train,** la gente espera el tren; **many people are learning Spanish,** muchas personas aprenden español; **the Mexican people,** el pueblo mexicano
pepper, la pimienta
perfect, perfecto, -a
perfection, la perfección
person, la persona
Peter, Pedro
Philip, Felipe
phone, el teléfono; **to speak on the phone,** hablar por teléfono
photo, la foto; **photograph,** la fotografía
pie, el pastel
pity, la lástima; **it is a pity,** es lástima
place, el lugar, el sitio; **to take place,** *tener lugar
play, (*theater*) la pieza, la comedia; jugar (ue) (A); (*a musical instrument*) tocar (A); **to play a role,** *hacer un papel
player, el jugador, la jugadora
please, por favor, haga el favor de + *inf.;* **please sit down,** siéntese, por favor, haga el favor de sentarse
P.M., de la tarde, de la noche; **at 4 P.M.,** a las cuatro de la tarde; **it is 11 P.M.,** son las once de la noche
pool, la piscina
poor, pobre
popcorn, las palomitas de maíz
popular, popular
port, el puerto
possible, posible; **as soon as possible,** lo más pronto posible
postcard, la tarjeta postal
potato, (*Spain*) la patata, (*Spanish America*) la papa

practice, practicar (A)
prefer, preferir (ie, i)
prepare, preparar
president, el presidente, la presidenta
pretty, bonito, -a
printer, la impresora
problem, el problema
program, el programa
promise, prometer
put, *poner (13); **to put on** (*the radio, TV*), poner, (*clothes*) ponerse

quarter: a quarter past two, las dos y cuarto
queen, la reina
question, la pregunta; **to ask a question,** *hacer una pregunta

race (= *running competition*), la carrera; competir (i) en una carrera
racket, la raqueta
radio, la radio; (*radio set*) el radio
rain, la lluvia; llover (ue)
raincoat, el impermeable
read, leer (4)
ready: to be ready, *estar listo, -a
receive, recibir
recently, recientemente
record, el disco
red, rojo, -a
refreshments, los refrescos
refuse, negarse (ie) (A) a + *inf.;* **he refuses to leave,** se niega a salir
relative, el (la) pariente
religious, religioso, -a
remain, quedarse, permanecer (C)
repeat, repetir (i)
rest, descansar
restaurant, el restaurante
return, (*go back*), regresar, volver (ue) (*pp* vuelto); (*give back*) devolver (ue) (*pp* devuelto)
rich, rico, -a
ride: to go for a ride (in a car), dar *un paseo (en coche)
right, el derecho; (*opposite of left*) derecho, -a; **on the right (side),** a la derecha; **to be right,** *tener razón; **right now,** ahora mismo
ring, el anillo; **diamond ring,** el anillo de diamantes; sonar (ue);

the bell (phone) rang, sonó el timbre (teléfono)

road, el camino, la carretera

Robert, Roberto

rock music, música *rock*

role: to play a role, *hacer un papel

room, el cuarto, la habitación; **to be room** (= *space*) **for,** *caber (2); **there was no room for me in the car,** no cupe en el coche

route, la ruta

rug, la alfombra

run, correr

sad, triste

sadness, la tristeza

saint, el santo, la santa; **Saint Francis,** San Francisco; **Saint Joseph,** San José

salad, la ensalada

salt, la sal

same, mismo, -a

sand, la arena

Saturday, sábado; **on Saturday,** el sábado

say, *decir (6); **to say good-bye to,** despedirse (i) de

school, la escuela; **to school,** a la escuela; **in (at) school,** en la escuela

scientist, el (la) científico, -a

sea, el mar

seated, sentado, -a

see, *ver (22)

seem, parecer (C)

sell, vender

send, mandar, enviar (D)

serve, servir (i)

set: television set, el televisor; **to set the table,** *poner la mesa

several, varios, -as

shelf, el estante

shirt, la camisa

shoe, el zapato

shopping: to go shopping, *ir de compras

shopping center (mall), el centro comercial

should, deber + *inf;* **I should study,** debo estudiar

show, el espectáculo, la función; mostrar (ue)

sick, enfermo, -a

sign, la señal

since (= *because*), puesto que

sing, cantar

singer, el (la) cantante

sir, señor

sister, la hermana

sit, (*to be seated*) *estar sentado, -a; (*to sit down*) sentarse (ie)

situated, situado, -a

six, seis

skate, el patín; patinar

ski, el esquí; esquiar (D); **ski run,** la pista de salto; **to go skiing,** *ir a esquiar

skirt, la falda

sky, el cielo

sleep, dormir (ue, u)

sleepy: to be (very) sleepy, *tener (mucho) sueño

slow, lento, -a; **slowly,** despacio, lentamente

small, pequeño, -a

smart, inteligente

smile, sonreír (conj. like *reír*)

snow, la nieve; nevar (ie)

soccer, el fútbol

sock, (*footwear*) el calcetín (*pl* calcetines)

soda, la gaseosa

sofa, el sofá

soldier, el (la) soldado

solution, la solución

some, alguno, -a (algún); (= *a few*) unos, -as, algunos, -as

somebody, someone, alguien

something, algo

so much, tanto, -a; **so many,** tantos, -as

soon, pronto; **as soon as,** así que; **as soon as possible,** lo más pronto posible

sorry: to be sorry, sentir (ie, i); **I'm sorry,** lo siento

south, el sur

Spain, España

Spanish, español, -la; (*language*) el español

speak, hablar

speech, el discurso

spend, (*time*) pasar, (*money*) gastar

sport, el deporte

stairs, la escalera

stamp, el sello

standing, de pie; **I am standing,** estoy de pie

start out, *ponerse en camino

stay, quedarse

steel, el acero

stereophonic, estereofónico, -a

Steven, Esteban

stop: to stop . . . -ing, cesar de + *inf;* **he stopped running,** cesó de correr; (*to halt*) parar; **the bus stops at the corner,** el autobús para en la esquina

store, la tienda

story, el cuento, la historia

strawberry, la fresa

street, la calle; **along (through) the street,** por la calle

stripe, la raya

strong, fuerte

student, el (la) estudiante

studious, aplicado, -a

study, estudiar

summer, el verano

sunbathe, tomar el sol

Sunday, domingo; **on Sunday,** el domingo

supermarket, el supermercado

sure: to be sure, *estar seguro, -a

Susan, Susana

sweater, el suéter

sweet, dulce

swim, nadar

swimming: to go swimming, *ir a nadar

table, la mesa

take, tomar; (*to take someone or something somewhere*) llevar; **to take a ride,** *dar un paseo (en coche, en bicicleta, etc.); **to take a sunbath,** tomar un baño de sol; **to take a trip,** *hacer un viaje; **to take a walk,** *dar un paseo; **to take off (clothes),** quitarse; **to take part in,** tomar parte en

talk, hablar

tall, alto, -a

tape, la cinta; **to tape** (= *record on tape*) grabar en cinta

tape recorder, la grabadora

taste, el sabor

tea, el té

teach, enseñar

teacher, (*elementary school*) el maestro, la maestra; (*high school and university*) el profesor, la profesora; **Spanish teacher** (= *teacher of Spanish*) el (la) profesor(-ra) de español

team, el equipo

telephone, el teléfono; (*verb*) telefonear, llamar por teléfono

televisión, la televisión; **television set,** el televisor

tell, *decir (6); (= *to narrate*) contar (ue)

ten, diez

tennis, el tenis; **tennis match,** el partido de tenis

test, el examen (*pl* exámenes), la prueba

than, que, de; **she is taller than I,** ella es más alta que yo; **there were more than 50 guests,** había más de 50 invitados

thank, *dar las gracias a

that, (*conj.*) que; (*dem. adj.*) ese, esa, aquel, aquella; **that one,** ése, -a, aquél, -la; **what is that?** ¿qué es eso (aquello)?

theater, el teatro

their, su(-s), de ellos(-as); **theirs,** el suyo, la suya, los suyos, las suyas; **this box is theirs,** esta caja es suya (... es de ellos, -as)

them, (*direct object*) los, las; (*indirect object*) les; (*object of prep.*) ellos, -as

then, (*afterward*) después, luego; (*at that time*) entonces

there, allí, allá

there is, there are, hay (*see* Appendix VII-C)

these, (*adj.*) estos, -as; (*pron.*) éstos, -as

they, ellos, ellas; **they like it,** les gusta

thing, la cosa

think, pensar (ie); **to think of,** pensar en

third, tercero, -a (tercer)

thirsty: to be (very) thirsty, *tener (mucha) sed

this, este, -a; **this one,** éste, -a; **what is this?** ¿qué es esto?

those, (*adj.*) esos, -as, aquellos, -as; (*pron.*) ésos, -as, aquéllos, -as

through, por

ticket, el billete, (*Spanish America*) el boleto; **to get a ticket (to a performance),** sacar una entrada

tie = necktie, la corbata

time, el tiempo, la hora, la vez; **a long time,** mucho tiempo; **at what time?** ¿a qué hora?; **on time,** a tiempo; **four times,** cuatro veces

tired: to be tired, *estar cansado, -a

to, a; (= *in order to*) para + *inf.*

today, hoy

together, juntos, -as

tomorrow, mañana; **tomorrow morning,** mañana por la mañana

tonight, esta noche

train, el tren

travel, viajar

trip, el viaje; **to take a trip,** *hacer un viaje

truck, el camión

truth, la verdad

try, tratar de + *inf.;* (*to taste*) probar (ue)

turn off (a light, etc.), apagar (A)

twenty, veinte

type, el tipo

umbrella, el paraguas (*pl* los paraguas)

uncle, el tío

understand, comprender, entender (ie)

university, la universidad

us, nos; (*object of prep.*) nosotros, -as

use, usar

used to, *use the imperfect tense:* **I used to swim well,** yo nadaba bien

value, el valor

verb, el verbo

very, muy; **very much,** muchísimo; *expressed by* mucho, -a *in idioms with* hacer *and* tener; *see Appendix VII*

videocassette, el video (vídeo)

visit, la visita; visitar; **to pay a visit,** *hacer una visita

voice, la voz (*pl* voces)

wait (for), esperar

waiter, el camarero, el mozo

waitress, la camarera

wake up, despertar(se) (ie)

walk, *andar, caminar; (*instead of ride*) *ir a pie; **to take a walk,** pasearse, *dar un paseo

want, desear, *querer (14)

warm tibio, -a (*not very hot*); **to be warm,** (*weather*) *hacer calor, (*persons*) *tener calor, (*things*) *estar caliente; **it is very warm today,** hoy hace mucho calor; **we are (= feel) very warm,** tenemos mucho calor; **the soup is very warm,** la sopa está muy caliente

wash: to wash oneself, get washed, lavarse

watch, (*wristwatch*) el reloj; **to watch TV,** mirar la televisión; **to watch a program (film, etc.),** ver un programa (una película, etc.); **to watch a baseball game,** mirar un partido de béisbol

water, el agua (*f*)

we, nosotros, nosotras

weak, débil

wear, llevar

weather, el tiempo (*see VII-B*)

week, la semana

weekend, el fin de semana

welcome: you're welcome, de nada, no hay de qué

well, bien

what? ¿qué?

when? ¿cuándo?

where? ¿dónde?

while, mientras; el rato

white, blanco, -a

who? ¿quién, -es?

whole, todo, -a; **the whole day,** todo el día

whom? ¿a quién, -es?

why? ¿por qué?; (*for what reason?*) ¿para qué?

wide, ancho, -a

wife, la esposa

William, Guillermo

win, ganar

window, la ventana; (*in car, train, etc.*) la ventanilla

wine, el vino

winter, el invierno

wish, desear, querer (14)

with, con; **with me,** conmigo; **with you,** contigo, con Ud. (Uds.), con vosotros, -as

within, dentro (de)
without, sin
wood, la madera; **wooden,** de madera
wool, la lana; **woolen,** de lana
word, la palabra
work, el trabajo; trabajar
worry, preocuparse (de); **don't worry,** no tenga(n) cuidado, pierda(n) cuidado
worse, worst, peor
worth: to be worth, valer (20), **it is worthless (not worth anything),** no vale nada

would like: I would like to go, me gustaría ir
write, escribir (*pp* escrito)

year, el año
yesterday, ayer; **yesterday afternoon,** ayer por la tarde
yet, todavía
you, (*subject*) tú, Ud., Uds., vosotros, -as; (*direct object*) te, lo(-s), la(-s), os; (*indirect object*) te, le(-s), os; (*object of prep.*) ti, Ud., Uds., vosotros, -as

young, joven (*pl* jóvenes); **young man (woman),** el (la) joven; **younger,** menor; **the youngest,** el (la) menor, los (las) menores
your, tu(-s), su(-s), de Ud., de Uds., vuestro, -a
yours, el tuyo, la tuya, etc.; el suyo, la suya, etc.; el vuestro, la vuestra, etc.; **these things are yours,** estas cosas con tuyas (suyas, vuestras, . . . son de Ud., de Uds.)